# TRANSNATIONAL JAPAN IN THE
# GLOBAL ENVIRONMENTAL MOVEMENT

# TRANSNATIONAL JAPAN IN THE GLOBAL ENVIRONMENTAL MOVEMENT

Simon Avenell

University of Hawai'i Press
Honolulu

22  21  20  19  18  17          6  5  4  3  2  1

**Library of Congress Cataloging-in-Publication Data**

Names: Avenell, Simon Andrew, author.
Title: Transnational Japan in the global environmental movement /
Simon Avenell.
Description: Honolulu : University of Hawai'i Press, [2017] | Includes
bibliographical references and index.
Identifiers: LCCN 2016044857 | ISBN 9780824867133 (cloth ; alk. paper)
Subjects: LCSH: Green movement—Japan—History. |
Environmentalism—Japan—History. | Environmental protection—
Japan—History.
Classification: LCC GE199.J3 A84 2017 | DDC 363.700952—dc23
LC record available at https://lccn.loc.gov/2016044857

# Contents

# Acknowledgments

First and foremost, I would like to thank my family for their support as I worked on this book. The initial idea was hatched during our time in Singapore and fully developed after our move to Australia. Leaving friends, familiar surroundings, and much-loved schools was not an easy thing to do, and I have been repeatedly impressed by my two sons' capacity to embrace their new lives in a foreign country without complaint and with such vigor and accomplishment. The greatest credit for this must go to my wife who has kept things running smoothly and has been the light at the center of our lives as we moved across borders.

Much of the primary source documentation used in this study is housed at the Kyōsei Shakai Kenkyū Sentā at Rikkyō University in Tokyo. I thank Murano Izumi and all of the staff at the center for generously granting me access to all of this material as well as to endless hours monopolizing the office scanner. My visits to the center also resulted in numerous fortuitous encounters with scholars working on Japanese social movements that greatly enriched my understanding of the field. Most of all, the late Michiba Chikanobu generously shared his views, encyclopedic knowledge, and pathbreaking research on countless movements. Through Michiba-san's work I have come to appreciate just how transnationally active Japanese activists have been throughout the postwar period, especially in Asia.

I have benefited greatly from support and friendships at two institutions: the National University of Singapore (NUS) and the Australian National University (ANU). At NUS, Thang Leng-Leng and Hendrik Meyer-Ohle made it possible for me to begin the research that ultimately led to this book. During my years at NUS, Tim Amos was a trusted confidant who graciously served as a sounding board for my ideas. At the ANU I have been supported and intellectually enriched by many colleagues including Tomoko Akami, Shiro Armstrong, Jenny Corbett, Carol Hayes, Li Narangoa, Tessa Morris-Suzuki, and Veronica Taylor. I am particularly grateful to Tessa Morris-Suzuki for welcoming me into her various research initiatives. Her work on daily life and survival politics has been truly enlightening for me and directly shaped the arguments in this book.

I sincerely thank Stephanie Chun for her interest in the project and wholehearted support throughout the publishing process. Deepest gratitude also to production editor Kristen Bettcher and to Susan Campbell for her careful and thoughtful copyediting of the text. I thank the reviewers for their constructive comments and suggestions, which I have tried to incorporate as much as possible.

Special mention also to the Australian Research Council, which sponsored this project with a generous grant under the *Future Fellowship* scheme. This funding made it possible for me to conduct multiple research trips to Japan and collect a massive amount of data and interview material. Thanks also to the Japan Foundation that supported an initial exploratory research trip to Japan in the latter half of 2012.

# Abbreviations

ACFOD   Asian Cultural Forum on Development
AEIC    Antipollution Export Information Center
CASA    Citizens' Alliance for Saving Earth and Atmosphere
CBO     Community-based organization
CFCs    Chlorofluorocarbons
CNIC    Citizens Nuclear Information Center
COP3    Third Session of the Conference of the Parties to the United
        Nations Framework Convention on Climate Change
ECOSOC  United Nations Economic and Social Council
ENEA    European Nuclear Energy Agency
ENGO    Environmental nongovernmental organization
EPA     Economic Planning Agency
ESCAP   United Nations Economic and Social Commission for Asia
        and the Pacific
ESS     Economic and Scientific Section
FA      Fisheries Agency (of Japan)
FoE     Friends of the Earth
FDI     Foreign direct investment
GNP     Gross national product
G7      Group of Seven
IAEA    International Atomic Energy Agency
ILP     Independent Lectures on Pollution (Kōgai Jishu Kōza)
ISSC    International Social Science Council
JACSES  Japan Center for a Sustainable Environment and Society
JAEC    Japan Atomic Energy Commission
JATAN   Japan Tropical Forest Action Network
JCG     Japan Coast Guard
JCP     Japan Communist Party
EAJ     Environment Agency of Japan
JFBA    Japan Federation of Bar Associations
JMA     Japan Meteorological Agency
JRA     Japan Radioisotope Association

| | |
|---|---|
| JSDF | Japanese Self-Defense Forces |
| JSP | Japan Socialist Party |
| JVC | Japan International Volunteer Center |
| KEPCO | Kansai Electric Power Company |
| LDC | London Dumping Convention (The Convention on the Prevention of Marine Pollution by Dumping of Wastes and Other Matter) |
| LDP | Liberal Democratic Party |
| MAFF | Ministry of Agriculture, Forestry and Fisheries |
| MOFA | Ministry of Foreign Affairs |
| MSH | Maison des Sciences de l'Homme |
| MHW | Ministry of Health and Welfare |
| MIT | Massachusetts Institute of Technology |
| MITI | Ministry of International Trade and Industry |
| MOFA | Ministry of Foreign Affairs |
| NASA | National Aeronautics and Space Administration |
| NFPC | Nuclear-Free Pacific Conference |
| NGO | Nongovernmental organization |
| NHK | Nippon Hōsō Kyōkai |
| NIB | National Indian Brotherhood |
| ODA | Official development assistance |
| OECD | Organisation for Economic Co-operation and Development |
| PARC | Pacific Asia Resource Center |
| PICL | Pacific Islands Conference of Leaders |
| PrepCom | Preparatory Committee (for UNCED) |
| RCP | Research Committee on Pollution |
| SCAP | Supreme Commander of the Allied Powers |
| STA | Science and Technology Agency |
| TACS | Thai-Asahi Caustic Soda Company |
| TEPCO | Tokyo Electric Power Company Limited |
| TVA | Tennessee Valley Authority |
| UN | United Nations |
| UNCED | United Nations Conference on Environment and Development (1992) |
| UNCHE | United Nations Conference on the Human Environment (1972) |
| UNEP | United Nations Environment Program |

UNFCCC   United Nations Framework Convention on Climate Change
USSR         Union of Soviet Socialist Republics
WCED       World Commission on Environment and Development
WEIM        World Environment Investigative Mission
WHO         World Health Organization
WWF         World Wide Fund for Nature
YWCA       Young Women's Christian Association

# Introduction

## Japan and the Global Environmental Movement

I've often said that the problems of pollution in Japan, though regarded as a trifling matter by some, portend the destiny of the whole world.

Ui Jun, 1975[1]

In a document prepared for the United Nations Conference on the Human Environment (UNCHE) in 1972, the activist-engineer Ui Jun declared that Japan probably had "the worst environmental pollution problems of any country in the world."[2] Rejecting triumphalist rhetoric about Japan's economic "miracle," Ui described instead an archipelago disfigured by "pollution department stores" with all measure of ground, water, and atmospheric contaminants.[3] Richard Curtis and Dave Fisher of the *New York Times* could only agree. In a 1971 article for the newspaper, the journalists included smog-choked Tokyo in their list of the "seven pollution wonders of the world," and they irreverently advised travelers to pack a "gasmask."[4] Echoing this sentiment, at the first Earth Day in the United States in 1970 and at UNCHE in 1972 environmental activists marched with placards demanding "No More Tokyos!" and "No More Minamatas." For the influential biologist and environmental advocate Paul Ehrlich, Japan was akin to the coal miner's canary of old: just as the tiny bird had alerted miners to potentially fatal gases, the situation in Japan presaged for humanity an impending global crisis born of industrial pollution and overpopulation.[5] Even William D. Ruckelshaus, head of the newly established Environmental Protection Agency in the United States, found the Japanese case expedient. In arguing for the merits of the Clean Air Act of 1970, Ruckelshaus invoked frightening images

1

of Tokyo, with its "world-class smog" and traffic policemen shielded by pollution-filtering facemasks.[6] Meanwhile, on the other side of the globe, engineers designing a state-of-the-art petrochemical facility in Finland carefully scrutinized Japan's infamous Yokkaichi petrochemical complex, site of asphyxiating air pollution that had caused nearby residents to literally cough themselves to death.[7]

Indeed, Japan's ascent as a polluters' paradise and the struggles of its pollution victims propelled the country to the very forefront of a historic global environmental awakening in the 1960s. Japanese industrial pollution, its victims, and the country's environmental activists became influential components of what Ursula Heise has called the environmental imagination of the global: a moment when the entire planet arguably became "graspable as one's own backyard."[8] Metaphors such as "Spaceship Earth" and the hauntingly beautiful images of Earth from the Lunar Orbiter satellites and the Apollo missions of the 1960s and 1970s encapsulated this sense of a solitary planet with a finite stock of resources and a fragile biosphere. The famous *Apollo 8* "Earthrise" image, of the planet appearing from behind the moon, and the later "Blue Marble" photograph taken from *Apollo 17* helped shape a growing sentiment that the environmental issues of one region could no longer be ignored as the problems of those "over there."

One only need consider the simultaneity of environmental events worldwide to appreciate how Japan became part of a genuinely global-historical moment. In the United States in 1962, marine biologist Rachel Carson shocked the nation with her best seller *Silent Spring* on pesticides and environmental poisons (translated into Japanese in 1964). Only two years later, in 1964, economist Miyamoto Ken'ichi and engineer Shōji Hikaru provoked similar outrage in Japan with their book *Osorubeki Kōgai* (Fearsome pollution), which documented chronic industrial contamination throughout the archipelago. Antipollution and environmental conservation movements proliferated worldwide at this time, not only in the rich "North" but also in developing nations of the global South, as in India where the Chipko or "tree-hugging" movement began in the early 1970s and in Kenya where Wangari Maathai established her famous Green Belt Movement in 1977. Influential international environmental nongovernmental organizations (ENGOs) such as Friends of the Earth (FoE) (1969) and Greenpeace (1971) also formed during this period, and mass media reportage increased dramatically, fueled by numerous high-profile pollution disasters such as Minamata disease in Japan in the late 1950s; the *Torrey Canyon* oil tanker spill off the coast of Cornwall, England, in 1967; and the Union Oil Company platform explosion off the Santa Barbara coast in 1969. Governments were also drawn into the environmental maelstrom as they groped to address mounting public concern about pollution. In 1970 the British government established the world's first cabinet-level Environment Department, followed shortly thereafter by establishment of the Environmental Protection Agency in the United States in 1970, the Environment Agency of Japan (EAJ), and Ministère de l'Environnement in France in 1971.[9] And, at the international level, the convening of UNCHE (the United Nations Conference on the Human Environment) in 1972 broke ground not only as the first UN conference dedicated to a single issue—namely, the environment—but also as a formative networking opportunity for NGOs, including Japanese victims' groups, which traveled to Sweden to participate.

It was against this backdrop of worldwide environmental awakening that Ui Jun could speak of the global-historical significance of his country's pollution situation. As he argued in the 1970s, people elsewhere cared about Japan's polluted archipelago because they could see in it the fate of their own countries. Moreover, they were genuinely interested in the movements of ordinary Japanese citizens, which were battling environmental contamination and human poisoning of a form, scale, and intensity never before experienced by humanity. For Ui's colleague Miyamoto Ken'ichi, Japan had become a "laboratory for pollution" without precedent in world history, with its toxic mixture of "new pollution" born of recent breakneck economic development and "old pollution" carried over from the first phases of heavy industrialization in the nineteenth and early twentieth centuries.[10] As the historian Julia Adeney Thomas has more recently observed, Japan has been less a "peculiarity" than "a participant in the global problematic."[11] "Demographically and in other ways," Thomas suggests, Japan "provides a laboratory for thinking about the global future in relation to the national past."[12] The disaster at the Fukushima Daiichi Nuclear Power Plant after an earthquake and tsunami in 2011 and the resultant worldwide debate about the safety of nuclear power attests to the ongoing relevance of particular national experiences like those in Japan for debates concerning our global future.

## Japan's Environmental Injustice Paradigm and the Role of Rooted Cosmopolitans

In this book I use the national history—or, more correctly, the many local histories—of pollution and protest in postwar Japan as a springboard to investigate an untold transnational history of Japanese environmental activism. I argue that the seminal encounter with industrial pollution—encapsulated in what I call Japan's "environmental injustice paradigm"—has been a critical and ongoing source of motivation for Japanese environmental activism not only within but also, importantly, beyond the archipelago. The agonizing experience of industrial pollution victims in local communities throughout the archipelago inspired some Japanese activists to look abroad, and it profoundly shaped the messages they sent to the world—even when interest shifted from localized pollution to the global environment in the late 1980s. For many Japanese activists who became involved transnationally, industrial pollution victims represented living proof of an unbreakable chain linking political and economic power, environmental degradation, and the violation of basic human rights. On a personal level, the encounter with shocking environmental injustices served as a powerful motivation to act. As scientists, activists, and victims from the world's most polluted nation, individuals such as Ui Jun felt an intense responsibility to ensure that such human injury and injustice did not occur elsewhere.

Although this environmental injustice paradigm underwent important modifications in the process of transnational involvement, throughout the book I show how it provided a coherent vocabulary and concrete vision for groups engaged in a diversity of transnational initiatives over many decades. In essence it was a decidedly anthropocentric and localistic vision of environmentalism that focused attention on the grassroots victims of environmental contamination and degradation, such as industrial pollution disease sufferers and, later, the marginalized people of developing nations. The paradigm pointed to the responsibility of conscientious and knowledgeable individuals to offer support for these local victims and to resist the forces of industrial modernity and capitalist expansion that wreaked havoc on marginalized communities. Although this vision was sensitive to the class implications of environmental injustice, it recognized that class alone was insufficient to explain such injustice or to fashion an effective grassroots response. As the Japanese experience revealed, the victims of pollution did not always fit easily into orthodox class categories, nor did the allies and enemies of protest movements. Moreover, born as it was in the context of local suffering in the face of all-encompassing ideologies of economic growth and the national interest in postwar Japan, the paradigm incorporated a degree of skepticism toward collectivist global discourses like "Spaceship Earth" or "our common future" because experience in Japan taught that such ideas tended to obscure

*resistance*
*common imagings*

instances of local injustice, marginalization, and discrimination as much as they expressed any sense of comradery or common predicament. Coming as it did at a moment of heightened attention to both the environment and human rights worldwide in the 1970s, this focus on the local and injustice propelled Japanese environmental advocates and victims to the very center of debates about the environment and development, the "limits to growth," and the objectives of environmentalism in a world of extreme inequity.[13]

There is a vigorous debate among theorists in globalization studies over the positioning and significance of the local in a global age. Some, such as the eco-critic Ursula Heise, subscribe to a resolutely cosmopolitan and globalist agenda that privileges an enlightened "sense of planet" over a blinkered "sense of place." Heise is skeptical about the value of local knowledge in the environmental movement, arguing that while a "sense of place" might be useful "for environmentally oriented arguments," it "becomes a visionary dead end if it is understood as a founding ideological principle or a principal didactic means of guiding individuals and communities back to nature."[14] Heise points to the "ambivalent ethical and political consequences that might follow from encouraging attachments to place," and she criticizes proponents of the local, such as deep ecology founder Arne Naess, who assume the spontaneity and naturalness of "sociocultural, ethical, and affective allegiances" at the local level while disregarding the possibility of meaningful attachments at larger scales.[15] Instead of "focusing on the recuperation of a sense of place," argues Heise, "environmentalism needs to foster an understanding of how a wide variety of both natural and cultural places and processes are connected and shape each other around the world, and how human impact affects and changes this connectedness."[16]

At the other end of the spectrum are thinkers like Arif Dirlik, who see the local as a necessary counterweight to the hegemony of globalism. Dirlik argues that, precisely because of the entanglement of "contemporary place consciousness" within globalization, "places offer a counter-paradigm for grasping contemporary realities," and "an alternative vision that focuses not on the off-ground operations of global capital . . . but on the concrete conditions of everyday life."[17] From a slightly different perspective, Sheila Jasanoff and Marybeth Long Martello have questioned the "wholesale adoption of shared environmental ontologies among the nations of the earth."[18] They point to the centrality of the local in environmental activism, which has derived "emotional force" from attachments to "particular places, landscapes, livelihoods, and to an ethic of communal living that can sustain stable, long-term regimes for the protection of shared resources."[19] They criticize social science for not adequately incorporating "the resurgence of local epistemologies and their associated politics in the context of globalization," and they call for a conceptualization of the local beyond the epitome of everything "prescientific, traditional, doomed to erasure, and hence not requiring rigorous analysis." Jasanoff and Martello note how the local has been reconstituted and made "richer" through policymaking for the environment and development. No longer is the local constrained to "spatial or cultural particularity," but it becomes also a signifier for "particular communities, histories, institutions, and even expert bodies." The "modern local," Jasanoff and Martello argue, is distinguished not by parochialism but by the way it produces "situated knowledge" that creates "communal affiliations" built on "knowing the world in particular ways."[20] Here they borrow from the globalization scholar Roland Robertson, who famously proposed the notion of "glocalization" in an attempt to highlight the entanglement of the local in translocal, supra-local, and global processes.[21] The local is certainly being reconstituted through globalization, but it retains import as a situated perspective. As the feminist scholar Donna Haraway has astutely put it, "The only way to find a larger vision is to be somewhere in particular."[22]

The local is at the center of the transnational history I recount in this book. For the Japanese activists and groups I explore herein, the local—whether understood as national or subnational space(s)—was a key source of inspiration and by no means a visionary dead end when it came to engaging with global environmental problems. In the 1960s and 1970s, for instance, pioneering advocates for local pollution victims such as Ui Jun and the physician Harada Masazumi undertook overseas investigative tours, which offered the domestic movement an invaluable comparative perspective on the dynamics of Japanese pollution—how it differed from and how it resembled pollution elsewhere. These early transnational environmental advocates used such opportunities to communicate the tragic story of Japanese industrial pollution and injustice to the world. In turn, their knowledge informed and invigorated environmental struggles worldwide, as in Canada where indigenous communities battled mercury contamination in the 1970s, and at UNCHE in 1972 where the Japanese experience became a leitmotif for environmental decay under advanced capitalism. In the 1970s and 1980s Japanese environmental activists extended their reach throughout Asia and the Pacific, protesting the relocation of polluting industries to other East Asian nations and governmental plans to dump radioactive waste in the Pacific Ocean. Articulating their critique, activists pointed to the Japanese pollution experience, arguing that corporations and the government had a moral obligation to not replicate these injustices elsewhere. With the emergence of global-scale environmental issues such as climate change in the late 1980s, Japanese activists modified their message of environmental injustice again: rich countries that were primarily responsible for global-scale environmental problems had no right to demand environmental compliance from developing nations without guarantees of substantive material compensation for centuries of imperialism and exploitation.

What this history reveals, then, is a Japanese environmental movement deeply enmeshed in the contemporary global movement yet driven by a profound sense of responsibility born of very local experiences with environmental injustice. In other words, this is not a history in which "parochial" or "narrow" local sentiments and perspectives finally matured into a "superior" cosmopolitan mentality. On the contrary, it is a history in which transnational involvement became a conduit through which the local could be relativized, understood, and repositioned within regional and global imaginaries without losing its centrality as a site of struggle and identity.

Scholarship to date has masterfully recounted this tortuous, often-tragic, and occasionally redemptive local experience in Japan.[23] It began around the mid-1950s, when numerous cases of toxic industrial contamination and urban pollution emerged. In regional communities methyl mercury, cadmium, and other chemical pollutants contaminated local ecosystems and poisoned human bodies, while in cities like Tokyo children collapsed in school playgrounds from photochemical smog pollution. In response, people in isolated villages, regional cities, and crowded metropolises mobilized in protracted struggles against the corporations that poisoned their bodies and the government officials who obstructed protest and accused victims of local egoism. Their wave of protest and struggle for justice was, to a great extent, a response to the idiosyncrasies of the country's modern political and economic institutions, which endorsed essentially unrestrained industrial—and, for a time, military—expansion from the mid-nineteenth century onward. This postwar history of industrial pollution is also a story of how legislative and institutional changes ensued, how local governments flexed their progressive muscles, and, ultimately, how by the early 1970s a national pollution disaster was, if not eradicated, significantly ameliorated. To be sure, there were very important instances of industrial pollution in

Japan before this period, for instance at the Ashio and Besshi copper mines and at the Northern Kyushu Yahata Steelworks. But the postwar encounter with and reaction to industrial pollution was of a scale, intensity, and impact unique in modern Japanese and, perhaps, global history. For certain activists such as Ui Jun, it even portended the "destiny" of the whole world.

As Brett Walker, Timothy George, Ui Jun, Iijima Nobuko, Ishimure Michiko, and others have masterfully and sensitively shown, industrial pollution victims occupy a central place in this history.[24] According to Walker, the core of the national pollution experience in Japan was pain, especially pain inflicted on the weak, the old, the young, the unborn, the marginalized, and the politically disenfranchised. In order to legitimize its claims upon citizens to endure pain and even death for the nation, the Japanese state (but, of course, not only the Japanese state) has devoted a great deal of energy to what Walker characterizes as a process of "interpreting and contextualizing such pain as dignified national sacrifice." Yet, as Walker points out, not all forms of pain have been so easily absorbed into national narratives and mythologies of selfless sacrifice. In particular, "pain caused by industrial pollution is less easily interpreted and contextualized as dignified and so can prove . . . dangerously subversive to the nation and those who tell its stories."[25] Indeed, so subversive was the experience of pain and discrimination from industrial pollution in Japan, I argue, that it formed the foundations of a powerful environmental injustice paradigm that inspired some Japanese to take action even beyond the archipelago—to communicate the national experience of environmental injustice to the world. The groups I explore in this study took great care to conscientiously knit this local experience of pain and injustice into the very fabric of their movements to address environmental problems threatening other countries and the globe. They were convinced that local experience, sentiment, and suffering such as that at Minamata Bay or along the Jinzū River could be—in fact, *had* to be—translated across geographical, political, and cultural space to become the raw material for struggles elsewhere.

In this book I first want to show how Japanese transnational activists have practiced agency beyond, yet always in connection to, the national and the local. The Ghanaian philosopher Kwame Anthony Appiah has articulated this sentiment most eloquently in his musings on the plausibility of a "rooted cosmopolitanism." For Appiah, the rooted cosmopolitan experience is made possible not because of some "common capacity for reason" but via "a different human capacity that grounds our sharing: namely the grasp of a narrative logic that allows us to construct the world to which our imaginations respond."[26] For Japanese transnational activists this meant understanding narratives of pollution and resistance from abroad through the familiar lens of local experience, as if observing a different yet recognizable reflection in a mirror. As Appiah puts it, "Cosmopolitanism can work because there can be common conversations about these shared ideas and objects."[27] He prefers a "form of universalism that is sensitive to the ways in which historical context may shape the significance of a practice."[28] This is, admittedly, an elusive sentiment to pin down, hovering, as it does, between the particular and the universal. But it seems to me to best encapsulate the standpoint of most transnational environmental activists in Japan throughout the period under study.

The social movement scholar Sidney Tarrow offers an excellent characterization of this locally informed yet globally sensitive "rooted cosmopolitan" mindset that I see emerging and developing within Japanese activists and groups involved transnationally from the late 1960s onward. Tarrow defines transnational activists as "people and groups who are rooted in specific national contexts, but who engage in contentious political activities that involve them in transnational networks of contacts and conflicts."[29] Rootedness for Tarrow stems from the fact that, even as activists "move physically and cognitively outside their origins, they continue to be linked to place, to the social networks that inhabit that space, and to the resources, experiences, and opportunities that place provides them with."[30] It is not a process of activists "migrating" from the domestic to the international but, rather, activists deploying local "resources and opportunities to move in and out of international institutions, processes, and alliances."[31] In this way, transnational activists become the "connective tissue of the global and the local, working as activators, brokers, and advocates for claims both domestic and international."[32] This aspiration among some Japanese environmental activists to act as the connective tissue between geographically separated struggles and to project their worldview of environmental injustice onto movements in other countries and global initiatives is at the heart of the concept of agency I will illustrate throughout this book: specific local experiences of environmental injustice provided them with the raw material for a larger vision and mission. The activities of these rooted cosmopolitans provide a marvelous methodological tool for tracking the ways notions of environmental injustice were first absorbed within the activist community in Japan and then transmitted by some across borders.

## Transnational Activism and the Historical Development of Japanese Civic Activism

The second and related argument of this book is that a transnational historical perspective can tell us important new things about the trajectory of Japanese environmental activism—and, perhaps, Japanese civic activism more generally—after the country's massive wave of domestic environmental protest in the 1960s and early 1970s. Most obviously, this transnational history complicates notions of a social movement "ice age" in Japan from around the mid-1970s onward. Throughout the book I show the palpable influence of Japanese activism on environmental developments in countries as far afield as Finland and in international organizations such as the United Nations. Japanese activists injected their struggle against environmental injustice into a range of movements addressing issues such as chemical contamination in Canada, Italy, and Thailand; air pollution in the Philippines; radioactive waste dumping in Micronesia; deforestation in Malaysia; and global climate change. Moreover, a transnational perspective reveals how exogenous forces (i.e., extranational forces) may have shaped civic activism in the country in a kind of boomerang effect.[33] A key objective of this work is to show how transnational involvement stimulated ideational transformations within some leading civic activists and groups in Japan, especially with respect to notions of victimhood prevalent in many Japanese movements of the early postwar period.

Leading civic activists and scholars alike have spoken of an "ice age" for contentious activism in Japan after the high point of antipollution protests in the early 1970s.[34] Herein Japanese environmental activism—actually, contentious, advocacy-focused activism more generally—arguably entered a period of prolonged stagnation, only to reignite again in the 1990s fueled by the new political opportunities of a recessionary Japan and the influence of new norms supportive of civil society.[35] The ice age thesis is highly persuasive to the extent that it explains the mechanisms behind the waning of overt, widespread protest in the early 1970s. Robert Pekkanen, for instance, explains the mid-1970s transition from contentious activism to an "ice age" of "inward-looking consumer identity-focused groups" in terms of the "regulatory framework," which made it extremely difficult for most civic movements to grow and institutionalize.[36] In his classic study on the law and social change in Japan, Frank Upham pointed to the role of officials in formulating countermeasures to preempt and manage open conflicts like the one they faced at Minamata Bay.[37] From a different perspective, I have also identified the role of leading civic activists in endorsing noncontentious forms of associational activity after the turbulence of the late 1960s and early 1970s—in effect facilitating the "deep freeze."[38]

But, as Pekkanen, I, and many other scholars recognize and have shown, an ice age should not be interpreted as an extinction.[39] Just as some life survives—indeed thrives—in climatic ice ages, so too in social movement ice ages. After the cycle of protest receded (as all protest cycles do), contentious environmental activism continued in myriad ways both domestically and transnationally, albeit in a different and far less visible or widespread manner than the 1970s high point.[40] As I show in subsequent chapters, one of these historical trajectories played out transnationally in manifold movements that crossed the borders of the archipelago relatively unnoticed, only to become visible periodically when they confronted national and international political institutions and multinational corporations. In fact, the notion of a movement ice age is, no doubt, partially a by-product of our choosing a particular scale of analysis. Focusing on the national level and below has made the transnational movements I explore in this book virtually invisible to date and has arguably contributed to both activist and scholarly notions of an ice age for contentious civic activism from the mid-1970s onward. There was undoubtedly a waning of high-profile and widespread environmental protest in the early 1970s in Japan, but shifting the spotlight to transnational activism complicates the sense of complete rupture or disjuncture implicit in the idea of a movement ice age followed by a thawing in the 1990s. Indeed, the following chapters point to fascinating continuities in contentious environmental activism linking the era of pollution protest to the 1990s resurgence of civil society and the rise of movements advocating for the global environment in Japan.

By examining involvement beyond the archipelago, we discover how Japanese activists and groups contributed to a nascent environmental "transnationality" worldwide based on "the rise of new communities and formation of new social identities and relations" not definable "through the traditional reference point of nation-states."[41] As these activists searched globally for answers to Japanese pollution, they became part of the global environmental awakening of the 1960s and 1970s. They were drawn into what Sheila Jasanoff and Peter Haas have called "epistemic" networks and communities, and they became part of emergent environmental "transnational advocacy networks."[42] Some of these spaces Japanese activists helped to construct were actual physical places such as the parallel NGO forums at UN environmental conferences, while others were more like shared experiential spaces such as the meetings between Japanese Minamata disease sufferers and Canadian Indians poisoned by mercury in the 1970s. As Mathias Albert and others contend, such "transnational political spaces" become "crucial locations for the production of cultures and cultural spaces," and, even more significantly, they can also become "new political spaces above and beyond the nation-state framework."[43] At NGO conferences held parallel to UNCHE (1972) and the United Nations Conference on Environment and Development (UNCED, 1992), for example, Japanese activists played a role in the construction of an emergent transnational, even global, civil society in which participants were beginning to experiment with new forms of citizenship "beyond the state."[44] As I discuss further in the conclusion, the transnational engagement of the Japanese environmental groups analyzed in subsequent chapters was, in fact, part of a wider spectrum of Japanese transnational activism that began to expand and diversify from the 1970s. Along with environmental groups, activists involved in peace and antiwar issues, women's liberationism, Asian developmental assistance, and Japan–South Korean grassroots relations all became active from around the early 1970s. This study hopes to contribute to this largely unresearched history through its focus on transnational Japanese environmental activism.

Significantly, participation in these spaces emboldened and empowered Japanese groups to exert pressure back on to Japanese political and economic institutions and, in some cases, to force substantive modifications in behaviors, policies, and practices. Margaret E. Keck and Kathryn Sikkink's groundbreaking research on transnational advocacy networks is particularly important in this context.[45] As Keck and Sikkink explain, such networks are "bound together by shared values, a common discourse, and dense exchanges of information and services." They are influential on multiple levels—locally, nationally, regionally, internationally, and transnationally. They build "links among actors in civil societies, states and international organizations," thereby multiplying "the opportunities for dialogue and exchange." Importantly, through their engagement in advocacy networks, activists "bring new ideas, norms and discourses into policy debates, and serve as sources of information and testimony." By making "international resources" such as ideas about the environment available in domestic struggles, they blur "the boundaries between a state's relations with its own nationals" and, in the process, challenge the previously impermeable barrier of national sovereignty.

Keck and Sikkink also describe a "boomerang pattern of influence" of transnational networks, in which "international contacts can 'amplify' the demands of domestic groups, pry open space for new issues, and then echo these demands back into the domestic arena."[46] Faced with new pressures from without, unresponsive states are often left with no choice but to act. The Japanese government's abandonment of plans to dump radioactive waste in the Pacific Ocean in the early 1980s, which I explore in chapter 5, is a good example of Japanese activists shrewdly using transnational alliances to influence domestic policymaking.

But this boomerang pattern of influence operated not only at the level of political and economic institutions: activists often found themselves, their messages, and their movements transformed in the process of engaging abroad. Thus, another central objective of this study is to examine the ways Japanese environmental activists and their environmental injustice paradigm changed in response to transnational involvement and, moreover, the consequences of this for the development of civic activism in Japan more generally. In the following chapters I endeavor to show how transnationalism—"the ongoing interconnection or flow of people, ideas, objects, and capital across the borders of nation-states"—had a lasting effect on the way the Japanese activists involved contextualized and positioned local and national phenomena, most notably the trauma of industrial pollution in Japan.[47] Interactions  abroad forced them to think very carefully about the possible limitations of understanding environmental injustice through the lens of Japanese victimhood alone. As they engaged with activists throughout East Asia and the Pacific in the 1970s and 1980s, for example, Japanese activists learned that the success of their local struggles might even, and ironically, be contributing to the suffering of people elsewhere as Japanese companies relocated polluting industries offshore. I believe activists' reflexive awakening to their complicit "aggression" in this system marks an important ideational development in the mentality of postwar civic groups in Japan.

The kind of ideational change I am referring to becomes clearer if we consider what came before. Social movements (labor, student, antipollution, women, peace, and antiwar) flourished in post–World War II Japan in great part because of the legal and institutional reforms carried out by the US-led occupation from 1945 to 1951. In terms of popular political empowerment, these were critical reforms indeed because, until the enactment of the postwar constitution, legally there were no sovereign citizens in Japan, only subjects of a sovereign emperor. The postwar constitution, however, abolished imperial sovereignty and made almost all Japanese people fully enfranchised citizens of a liberal-democratic polity for the first time in the country's history. The constitution also guaranteed a space for Japanese people to legally engage in civic activism and protest without the fear of imprisonment. The country's conservative politicians and bureaucrats did their very best to stymie these newly won freedoms and to curtail the new civic movements, but they could not control popular energies as clinically and violently as had been possible under the prewar regime. So, in this sense, de jure (i.e., national state) citizenship in a democratized Japanese nation made possible—for the first time—citizenship as a normative project constructed through the collective and individual practices and ideas of individuals in a civil society. As Wesley Sasaki-Uemura and others have shown, the Japanese people embraced their new freedoms of association and speech and, through grassroots civic activism, they imagined new forms of citizenship beyond (and often in conflict with) national state citizenship—what we might call the citizenships of civil society.[48] These new imaginations of citizenship in turn served as the ideological foundations of social movements that challenged the state and its postwar drive for reconstruction and relentless economic growth.[49]

In their earliest formations, civic movements tended to adhere to a reactive or defensive model of activism premised on a model of victimized citizens mobilizing to resist the infiltration of powerful political and economic institutions into their daily lives.[50] Civil society was most often understood as the sanctuary inside which activists could form tight bonds of solidarity and mount their mobilizations of resistance. There was no gray area here: the state and corporations were aggressors and Japanese citizens were always victims. This imagination of victimhood based on "civil society versus the state and the corporation" bore the imprint of history, since it grew directly out of activists' experience of suppression under wartime militarism coupled with their visceral reaction to the reemergence of conservative rule in the postwar era.

But the late 1960s and 1970s marked a turning point in this mentality, thanks in great part to the influence of transnationally active groups and individuals. The earlier defensive model of citizenship based on defense of the local did not disappear as a motivating factor and key source of identity but, through transnational involvement, the activists involved now also recognized and advocated the need for a reflexive activist agenda cognizant of their ambivalent position as both victims and aggressors. The novelist and anti–Vietnam War activist Oda Makoto was the earliest and most vocal mouthpiece for this sentiment in his characterization of ordinary Japanese people as both victims and aggressors in the context of the Vietnam War. Prior to this conflict, Japanese antiwar pacifism was characterized by a strong sense of popular victimization by the wartime Japanese state, the American atomic bombings, and the continued US military presence in the country. This mentality carried over into the Japanese anti–Vietnam War movement to the extent that activists superimposed their past experience as "war victims" on to the current plight of the Vietnamese people. But seeing the multidimensional involvement of the Japanese economy and government in the Vietnam War prompted Oda to challenge this logic. As he explained in a seminal 1966 essay, "Heiwa o Tsukuru" (Making peace), Japanese citizens were certainly victims to the extent they had suffered in the latter stages of the Pacific War and afterward as residents of a quasi-US protectorate. But, according to Oda, to the extent Japanese benefited and prospered as citizens and consumers in this system, they also became accomplices and "aggressors" against the Vietnamese people—albeit indirectly.[51] Oda's presentation of Japan and, more importantly, Japanese civic activists as aggressors provided the ethical foundations for later mobilizations against so-called Japanese Hyena corporations profiting from the Vietnam War, but it also complicated seamless discourses of grassroots victimhood prominent in earlier movements.

Women's groups active transnationally from the early 1970s also expressed a growing sensitivity toward their complicity as Japanese citizens. Activists opposing so-called *kiseng* sex tourism by Japanese men in South Korea, for example, called on Japanese women to bravely face their "aggression" toward Asia both in the past as "women on the home front" who had supported the war and, in the present, as the mothers and wives of "corporate warriors" involved in sex tourism in South Korea and elsewhere. Among the various subcommittees at the 1974 Conference of Asians (discussed in chapter 4) was a women's group that addressed issues such as political oppression, labor discrimination, and the sexual exploitation of women in Asia. The group highlighted the "shocking reality" that the expansion of Japanese industry into Asia was forcing women to "live and work in even more oppressive circumstances" than in the past. Even worse, the "advance of Japanese capitalism" brought with it other forms of exploitation such as Japanese sex tourism in the Philippines, Thailand, and South Korea. In their resolution at the conference the women's group concluded that "the true liberation of Asia" was not "merely a matter of national economic and political struggle" but also depended on "the struggle to liberate women." To this end they resolved "to maintain even closer bonds of contact and cooperation among Asian sisters."[52]

We witness a similar shift in the mentality of environmental activists and groups involved transnationally. As the student activist Aoyama Tadashi observed in 1976, the Japanese people had waged many battles against industrial pollution in the country. As a result the living environment was now undeniably cleaner and the public strongly opposed to industrial pollution. Yet, despite all of this, the Japanese had been oblivious to those in foreign countries suffering in the shadows of Japanese affluence, especially throughout Asia.[53] "Haven't we essentially ignored the voices and existence of our neighbors up until now? I believe that it is necessary for us to listen to the appeals of our neighbors if we are to truly understand our position and the path Japan is attempting to set out upon."[54] Indeed, involvement in Asia and the Pacific encouraged—even demanded—that the activists involved engage in a critical, historically sensitive self-reflection on Japan's tainted legacy in Asia and the Pacific just as antiwar and women's groups were doing. In the process these activists discovered that fellow Asians and Pacific Islanders tended to understand Japan's environmental incursions into their regions in the context of a longer, agonizing history of Japanese imperialistic misbehavior. This was a completely unanticipated and unsettling perspective for the Japanese, who had not drawn connections between environmental problems and the country's militarist past. Thus, even more than in their global encounters, regional engagement encouraged the Japanese activists involved to fundamentally rethink the notion of victimhood underwriting their environmental injustice paradigm.

Transnational interaction thus became a vehicle for Japanese activists to relativize the local by positioning it in a much wider network of relationships and exchanges in which victims could simultaneously be aggressors and solutions were often no more than the offloading of problems onto others in localities across the sea. Activists too had to reconsider their own positions as a result of transnational engagement. It was not enough to see themselves as simply virtuous victim advocates. As citizens and consumers of a nation committing environmental injustices abroad, they also needed to acknowledge and deal with their simultaneous position as complicit aggressors—albeit indirectly and by association. As I discuss further in the conclusion, one outcome of this realization was the growth among some activists of a more reflexive, expansive, and multidimensional agenda and mentality. The anthropocentric and localistic foundation of their environmental injustice paradigm remained central, but the range of environmental victims in their field of view increased tremendously, as too did the reflexivity of their activism.

*Summary of arguments*

To summarize, then, this book argues, first, that the trauma of industrial pollution in Japan produced a potent environmental injustice paradigm among victims, activists, and environmental groups. This paradigm fueled the domestic movement, and it became the ideational and motivational basis for the transnational activities of some activists and groups—so called rooted cosmopolitans—from the late 1960s onward. Although this paradigm evolved in the course of transnational involvement, its focus on the marginalization and inequity experienced by environmental victims at the very base of society remained constant across geographical space and over time. Indeed, I argue that Japanese groups' advocacy of a justice-driven, rights-focused, emancipatory environmentalism represents their principal contribution to the contemporary global movement. Second, in historical terms, the book suggests that a transnational focus helps to explain important developments in Japanese civic activism after the high point of domestic protest in the early 1970s. In a kind of boomerang effect, involvement in environmental transnational advocacy networks in East Asia, Europe, and North America encouraged Japanese activists to reconsider and reposition their conceptualization of environmental injustice beyond notions of victimhood defined within the container of the nation. The result was a more reflexive and multidimensional activist identity and agenda, which arguably fed into a reimagination of civil society in the country from the late 1980s onward.

## Organization of the Study: Scalar Iterations of Environmental Injustice

As noted above, scholarship to date has carefully and sensitively documented the ways victims and their supporters mobilized against industrial pollution at home from around the late 1950s to the early 1970s. In the following chapters I focus on how the environmental injustice paradigm born in these domestic movements subsequently operated and evolved through activism at different scales of activity—in regional spaces such as East Asia and the Pacific, and in global spaces like UNCHE (1972) and UNCED (1992). The earliest transnational interactions were dominated by a handful of leftist social and natural scientists like Tsuru Shigeto and Ui Jun who had also been leading figures in the domestic environmental movement. But the activist networks these individuals established opened the door for other actors to become involved in the ensuing years—students, industrial pollution victims, former anti–Vietnam War activists, anti–nuclear power protesters, and, eventually, full-time activists in professional ENGOs.

Rather than charting a chronological history of one or more of these networks or groups from start to finish, however, the case studies that follow are designed to investigate the impact *of* and *on* Japanese activists' environmental injustice paradigm at and within different scalar imaginaries—local, national, regional, and global—from around the late 1960s to the turn of the century. For that reason certain actors will become prominent in the narrative at times only to fade to the background and then return later (which, as Sidney Tarrow notes, is actually how transnational activism tends to operate).[55] Although I certainly trace in detail the historical trajectory of specific Japanese activists and groups such as the Independent Lectures on Pollution (ILP) movement started by Ui Jun, my primary interest is in how these groups deployed their environmental injustice paradigm over time and at different scales of involvement and the resulting outcomes. How, for example, did engagement with environmental problems in the East Asian region—site of Japan's former colonial empire—influence the way those Japanese activists involved understood and articulated concepts of environmental injustice?

I move through six iterations of the environmental injustice paradigm: first, its emergence in the domestic pollution crisis and the response of the pioneering Research Committee on Pollution (RCP) in the 1960s; second, in RCP members travels and activism in North America and Europe from the late 1960s to mid-1970s; third, in Japanese pollution victims' and activists' involvement at the landmark UNCHE conference in 1972; fourth, in movements addressing Japanese corporate pollution in East Asia throughout the 1970s; fifth, in movements opposing the planned dumping of Japanese radioactive waste in Micronesian waters in the early 1980s; and sixth, in Japanese involvement in global-scale environmental problems beginning around the late 1980s and marked by events such as the Earth Summit (UNCED) in 1992 and the Kyoto climate conference in 1997.[56] Japanese activists mobilized their environmental injustice paradigm to great effect in each of these scalar iterations by informing discourse, imparting knowledge, and supporting movements. But each scalar iteration also served to complicate the notion of environmental injustice and push it in new directions beyond the defining core of Japanese industrial pollution and its victims. In the process, the environmental injustice paradigm arguably became richer and more reflexive, as too did the mentalities of the activists involved.

In terms of historical scope, I focus on the period from the 1960s to the turn of the century for three reasons. First, empirically speaking, this is when Japanese transnational environmental activism emerged, developed, and diversified from a state of almost nonexistence to a vibrant realm of transnationally engaged ENGOs. Second, this period witnessed a critical transition in environmentalism worldwide as the problems of localized industrial pollution were overlaid (although not replaced) by concerns for global-scale issues such as climate change. Third, in relation to Japanese civic activism, the period stretches from the era of heightened civic protest in the 1960s and early 1970s through to the apparent resurgence of civil society in the country from the 1990s onward. Needless to say, I believe these processes are interrelated although, as I show throughout the study, in more complex ways than a simple linear narrative of globalization might suggest.

In chapter 1, I begin in Japan, tracing the formative moment of the environmental injustice paradigm in the industrial pollution crisis at home from the mid-1950s to the mid-1970s. I show the intensifying attention to the horrific human costs of industrial pollution by the victims, the mass media, public intellectuals, the law courts, officialdom, and specialist groups like the Research Committee on Pollution (RCP) established in 1963. As I explain, although RCP members' initial interest grew out of their program to decipher the class dynamics of pollution, it was the environmental injustices experienced by victims that affected them most viscerally and shaped their agenda to find some kind of solution. Researchers such as clinician Harada Masazumi and engineer Ui Jun wanted desperately to understand not only the epidemiology of pollution but, more critically, the political and social "physiology" of environmental injustice. If orthodox Marxian class analysis could not explain phenomena on the ground, then new responses and modes of resistance would be required that perhaps crossed even class boundaries or national frontiers. As highly educated individuals with a cosmopolitan outlook, RCP members quickly recognized the global-historical significance of Japanese industrial pollution. Moreover, they realized that, as experts, they possessed knowledge that could potentially circumvent pollution in other places—even in other countries—and perhaps prevent further human misery at the hands of industry. It was through groups such as the RCP that the "local" began to take on an enhanced significance.

In chapter 2 I follow RCP members on their initial tours to polluted sites in Europe and North America and in their interactions with foreign pollution victims and environmental activists from the late 1960s to the mid-1970s. Such activities offered RCP members an opportunity to test their assumptions about industrial pollution and the roots of environmental injustice. For instance, were the advocates of socialism, who claimed that socialist states had solved the problem of industrial pollution, to be believed, and, if they were wrong, what would be the consequences for the popular struggle against industrial pollution? In fact, what RCP members discovered in socialist countries was horrific pollution equal to, and often worse than, that in Japan and other capitalist countries. Thereafter they became convinced that the battle against pollution worldwide would not succeed if left to atomized local movements or the traditional class protagonists of Marxian political theory. Instead, they concluded that local movements needed to be strengthened by the creation of new spaces for victims of environmental injustice that cut across class lines and national boundaries. This conclusion found concrete form in a historic transnational engagement facilitated by the RCP between Minamata disease sufferers in Japan and Native American communities afflicted by mercury contamination in Canada.

In chapter 3 I shift scale to one of the earliest moments of global environmentalism in the contemporary era, the landmark United Nations Conference on the Human Environment held in Stockholm in 1972. The RCP, the ILP, and Japanese industrial pollution victims figured prominently here, with the economist Tsuru Shigeto as an influential intellectual voice in elite academic and intergovernmental circles and pollution victims as vocal participants in the NGO forums run parallel to UNCHE. Together these groups and individuals made important contributions to fiery debates over economic growth and development. On the one hand, pollution victims used their experience of environmental injustice to emphasize the *human* as opposed to environmental "limits to growth," while, on the other, Tsuru Shigeto advocated a reformulation of development that transcended the narrow GNP index and included fundamental human welfare concerns. Both approaches advocated a strongly anthropocentric environmental agenda in keeping with the local experience in Japan.

In chapter 4 I turn to the region, analyzing Japanese movements opposing the relocation of pollutive industrial processes to East Asia in the 1970s. This regional awakening compelled activists involved in the ILP and other spin-off movements to problematize their position as victims (or spokespersons for victims) of environmental injustice. What did local victories against industrial pollution mean if Japanese industry simply relocated pollution and environmental injustice to Asia? If the nation-state became a tool to protect localities in Japan at the expense of those in Asia, were not those Japanese localities accomplices or "aggressors" in the overseas pollution of Japanese corporations? In the chapter I argue that engagement with pollution issues in Asia in the 1970s became a conduit through which the Japanese groups involved began to reflexively critique the aspect of local victimhood implicit in their environmental injustice paradigm. Within the "container" of Japan, the victims and perpetrators of environmental justice had been relatively distinct, but the discovery of Japanese pollution in Asia deeply complicated such distinctions.

Chapter 5 shifts to another regional imaginary, namely the Pacific, focusing on a particularly toxic and long-lived pollutant: radioactive waste material. With the commencement of domestic commercial nuclear-powered electricity generation in the late 1960s, Japanese nuclear officials became more and more concerned about the growing stockpile of both high-level and low-level radioactive waste material. Pressed for storage solutions for this growing mountain of radioactive waste, in the early 1970s nuclear officials hatched a plan to dispose of up to 60 percent of low-level radioactive waste in steel canisters in the Pacific Ocean near the Northern Mariana Islands. Outraged Pacific Islanders mobilized in opposition on learning of the plan in the late 1970s. Importantly, these protesters brought their struggle to Japan in the early 1980s, speaking at rallies, meeting with activists and officials, visiting nuclear power plants, connecting with local struggles against new plant constructions, and coordinating worldwide signature campaigns with their Japanese supporters. As with the earlier industrial pollution export problem in East Asia, this transnational involvement forced Japanese antinuclear activists (whether opposing A-bombs or nuclear power plants) to rethink the powerful narrative of local victimhood in their movements. After all, like the inhabitants of Hiroshima and Nagasaki, peoples of the Pacific had had their homes vaporized by nuclear weapons and their bodies poisoned by radionuclides. Moreover, Japanese nuclear power plants were contributing to the destruction of communities at both the front end (i.e., uranium mining on indigenous lands in Australia) and, potentially, at the back end (i.e., plans to dump radioactive waste in the Pacific) of the global nuclear fuel cycle. Such problems stimulated the Japanese antinuclear activists involved to rethink their movement in the context of a longer history of Japanese colonialism in the Pacific and the ongoing culpability of Japan in contemporary neocolonialism or, as one Pacific leader branded it, "nuclearism."[57]

In chapter 6 I shift scale to the global, examining Japanese activists' involvement in movements addressing global-scale environmental problems from the late 1980s onward. Stratospheric ozone damage, rainforest destruction, biodiversity depletion, and climate change posed environmental problems of an immeasurably larger scale than anything before. These were truly global problems that demanded globally coordinated responses if humanity was to secure its "common future" on the planet. But, as I explain, the Japanese activists involved approached these issues through the familiar paradigm of local environmental injustice, refined of course through many decades of domestic and regional struggle. Connecting their empathy for industrial pollution victims to victims in the marginalized peripheries of the developing world, Japanese activists proposed notions of local empowerment and endogenous development as the necessary starting points for any solutions to global-scale environmental problems. They challenged discourses of shared human fate like "our common future," calling instead for people and institutions in the rich "North" to reform their modern, convenient lifestyles built on ravenous consumption of resources, often sourced from the "South." The problems may have become global and, in a sense, everywhere at once, but through the lens of environmental injustice, it appeared obvious that the burdens were never so evenly dispersed.

In 1974, when Japanese antipollution activists were considering a study tour to pollution sites worldwide, some of them wondered if it was a necessary endeavor. After all, was Japan not a polluters' paradise full of "pollution department stores"? Why look abroad when all kinds of pollution problems remained in their own backyard? Opinions were divided, but eventually even the most reluctant decided to participate. After the tour one participant recounted just how valuable an experience it had been. Not only did it help him and others rethink Japanese pollution in a wider context, it also represented a historic recalibration of Japanese interactions with the outside world. Since the beginning of Japan's hurried rush to modernize in the mid-nineteenth century, international engagement—especially with the industrialized West—had been mostly about learning the secrets of growth, development, and so-called civilization. But this tour to connect with victims elsewhere and to explore the shadows of Western success signaled a new, more mature, engagement. More to the point, it involved communicating an important story of local environmental injustice to the world.

This book charts the emergence and evolution of that environmental injustice paradigm from its birth in Japan's pollution nightmare to the multiscalar transnational movements it subsequently informed and invigorated. On one level, it points to the transformations made possible by repositioning the local in spatial imaginaries that transcend the nation, but, on another, it also confirms the critical importance of the local as an ideational platform and motivating factor in environmental knowledge and transnational action in the modern world.

CHAPTER 1

# Japanese Industrial Pollution and Environmental Injustice

Japan had experienced its share of industrial pollution before the postwar era, but nothing of the scale and intensity of that which unfolded from the mid-1950s to the early 1970s. Particularly striking was the enormity of human destruction wrought by postwar pollution on livelihoods, living environments, human dignity, and human bodies. In most cases industry was to blame, but in large urban centers like Tokyo and Osaka ordinary citizens also contributed to environmental degradation through voracious consumption and ever-intensifying demands for convenience, construction, and mechanization. The results of this simultaneous surge in consumerism and unyielding industrial expansion were horrific for both the environment and the humans stricken with industrial diseases—not to mention the dent on national pride as the country became infamous worldwide as a polluters' paradise. So extreme was the crisis that it provoked a historic wave of grassroots resistance across Japan as local communities and victims expressed their anger in civic protest, in the media, and in the law courts. They were supported by a cadre of pollution-victim advocates—scientists, lawyers, physicians, politicians, local bureaucrats, and schoolteachers—for whom the pollution problem became an all-absorbing quest for justice. Throughout the period, various victim advocacy groups formed within Japan, like the medical researchers studying mercury poisoning at Kumamoto University, progressive lawyers in the Nihon Bengoshi Rengōkai (Japan Federation of Bar Associations, JFBA), and independent groups like the Research Committee on Pollution (RCP). Participants in these groups were among the first to communicate the story of Japanese environmental injustice to the world.

In this chapter I explore the ways human suffering in toxic spaces throughout Japan helped propel a paradigm of injustice to the very core of contemporary Japanese environmentalism, providing the ethical and ide-ational sustenance for subsequent generations of transnational activists. I trace the rising recognition of, and reaction to, environmental injustices in a range of groups, institutions, and media: the victims of industrial pollu-tion and their movements, the mass media, influential publications, the law courts, all levels of government, and specialist groups like the RCP. I then focus on RCP members' crucial involvement with pollution victims, in or-der to understand the intellectual and emotional factors that shaped their perspectives on environmental injustice and stimulated their subsequent transnational action. The horrific situation of victims was so shocking—so morally reprehensible—that the violation of victims' human rights and their protracted struggles for justice almost completely dominated the activism of such groups. We might usefully compare this environmentalism to other environmental imaginaries of the time, such as Rachel Carson's *Silent Spring* in the United States, which emphasized the violation of the rights of nature and living organisms like birds. In the case of polluted 1960s Japan, it was the degraded and poisoned human living environment and, more crucially, the humans located therein that monopolized attention. Once a tool for human nourishment, productivity, and leisure, the natural environment now became a silent conduit for the deadly chemical substances of human injury and injustice. In subsequent chapters I explore how this anthropocentric, justice- and rights-focused environmentalism would dominate the transna-tional action of Japanese environmental activists in the coming decades.

While the overwhelming majority of antipollution groups in Japan focused on their own local struggles, having neither the resources nor the inclination to address the wider implications, for groups like the RCP, whose members' were highly educated and internationally literate, tackling the deeper structural aspects of Japanese industrial pollution was a matter of pressing concern from the outset. Their membership's unique combination of scientific expertise, fury toward industry, and compassion for victims profoundly shaped the group's approach to environmentalism through the lenses of inequity, discrimination, and injustice. Moreover, this combination of factors also contributed to their sense of moral obligation to communicate Japan's experience to the world when the opportunity arose. As social and natural scientists with decidedly humanist leanings, they desperately wanted to understand the political and socioeconomic dynamics of pollution in

Japan. What caused it? Was it something to do with capitalism in general or Japanese capitalism in particular? What might be the most effective method to eradicate pollution and to secure some form of recompense for the victims? More than any other factor, it was the plight of pollution victims that put "fire in the belly" and "iron in the soul" of groups like the RCP.[1] Although all communities across the archipelago were enduring the consequences of pollution, antipollution advocates quickly recognized that it hit some groups more brutally than others. Indeed, the unborn, the young, the elderly, women, the poor, and peripheralized rural communities emerged as the martyrs of Japan's relentless drive for affluence and so-called development.

## Japanese Pollution and Its Victims

It is worth reiterating that, prior to the postwar pollution crisis, Japan already had a sorry track record of industrial pollution dating back to at least the mid-nineteenth century, when the country's samurai rulers abandoned relatively regulated involvement with Western countries for full-scale Western-style modernization and, later, imperialistic expansion. Areas of Japan had gone toxic long before the 1960s, especially air and river degradation in regions near copper mines and related processing facilities. The pre–World War II period was not totally devoid of environmental protest and official action either, with some instances of environmental regulation by local governments and pollution abatement measures by industry. But these prewar developments were promptly sidelined when the country mobilized for war in the 1930s and they were essentially abandoned in the postwar reconstruction years.[2]

With the transition from early post–World War II deprivation to the affluence of high-speed economic growth from the mid-1950s, Japan entered its darkest moment of industrial pollution in the modern era. As early as 1955—when overall economic growth had recovered to prewar highs— newborns were poisoned by arsenic mistakenly introduced into powdered infant formula manufactured by the Morinaga Milk Company. The poisoning caused fever, severe diarrhea, skin spotting, and, in some cases, death. For those infants who survived, the prognosis was dim. Studies revealed that victims were still suffering the effects over a decade later, with impeded bone development, proteinuria (elevated urinary protein), abnormal brain activity, hearing loss, and lower IQ levels.[3] Over eleven thousand were affected, and 133 infants died in 1955 alone. Similar food poisoning occurred in 1968

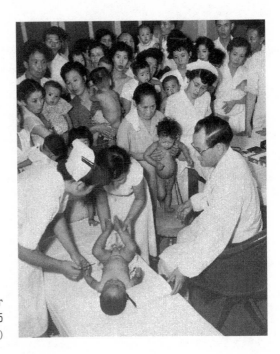

Infants being examined for
arsenic contamination, 1955
(The Mainichi Newspapers)

when people consumed Kanemi Rice Bran Oil contaminated with poly-chlorinated biphenyls (PCBs). Victims suffered with painful eye discharge, acne-like eruptions on the skin, pigmentation, respiratory difficulties, joint and muscle pain, and general lethargy. Because of the skin pigmentation and skin eruptions, many victims withdrew from social life and the workplace altogether. The so-called cola babies born of mothers poisoned by the oil had dark-brown pigmented skin and were found to have lower IQs. Compound-ing victims' misery and sense of injustice, eight months earlier some five hundred thousand chickens had died and one million were made sick after consuming feed containing oil by-products produced by Kanemi in the same manufacturing facilities. At the time the company had denied any wrong-doing and government officials refused to follow up, with disastrous effects for some ten thousand human victims just months later.[4]

Industrial waste contaminated air, land, rivers, and seas—most shock-ingly in the Big Four pollution incidents at Minamata Bay, Yokkaichi City, and the Jinzū (Toyama) and Agano (Niigata) Rivers. In the mid-1950s patients living around Minamata Bay in Kumamoto Prefecture began to present at local hospitals with abnormalities of the central and peripheral nervous systems, which had been first observed as strange dancing, seizures,

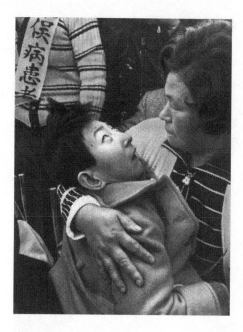

A congenital Minamata disease
sufferer and her mother, 1973
(The Mainichi Newspapers)

and sudden death among local cats. Investigations revealed the source of the pollution to be effluent dumped into the bay by the Chisso Corporation.[5] The etiology of this disease, called Minamata disease, lay in consumption of seafood containing the bio-accumulative organometallic compound, methyl mercury. Typical symptoms included concentric constriction of the visual field, sensory disturbances, speech impediment, hearing loss, motor coordination disturbances, and convulsions. Tragically also, methyl mercury is a developmental neurotoxin that can cross the placenta. Infants born of women who ate polluted seafood exhibited severe symptoms, including mental retardation, involuntary reflexes, and coordination disturbances. As one report later explained, "They have no mental world and in their crying existence they have been condemned to a subhuman existence by the dumb inhuman forces of society."[6] Needless to say, these innocent victims of congenital Minamata disease became focal symbols of environmental injustice in Japan, most notably in the sensitive yet heartrending photographs by Eugene Smith that shocked the world in the 1970s.[7]

Around the same time, residents living downwind from a petrochemical complex in Yokkaichi City in Mie Prefecture began to complain of breathing difficulties and severe asthma. Subsequent investigations revealed the cause to be noxious gases emitted from the complex. This second of the

Big Four pollution incidents, called "Yokkaichi Asthma," became synony-
mous with the tragic downside of regional development in the postwar period. People living nearby suffered from bronchitis, sore throats, and colds at
rates 220 percent higher than average. Many contracted chronic obstructive
pulmonary disease, which caused severe breathing difficulty, sore throat, painful coughing seizures, and sometimes death. An influential 1964 publication
described the condition as follows: "Asthma is the 'citizen's disease' in Yokkaichi. In the middle of the night an attack suddenly occurs. The only way
to escape the pain is to leave this petroleum city."[8]

The third of the Big Four surfaced in the late 1950s when a local doctor in Toyama Prefecture confirmed that cadmium dumped into the Jinzū
River by the Mitsui Mining and Smelting Company caused the debilitat-
ing condition known as Itai Itai (It Hurts It Hurts) disease. The cadmium
made victims bones brittle and prone to fracture, caused damage to major
organs, and resulted in an excruciatingly painful death. The caption of one
photo of a shockingly deformed infant stricken with the poisoning read,
"Cadmium in my bones from the water and food make my legs break in a
dozen places. I suffer from the dread[ed] Itai Itai disease and there seems no
hope for me."[9] The highest recorded number of bone fractures in the body
of an individual sufferer was seventy-two, of which twenty-eight fractures
were in the rib cage alone.[10] If all this was not enough, in 1964 another case
of methyl mercury poisoning occurred, this time in Niigata Prefecture,
caused by effluent dumped into the Agano River by the Shōwa Denkō
Company.[11]

Residents of Tokyo and Osaka also suffered from deteriorating air and
water quality. In 1960 Osaka experienced choking smog for 165 days out of
the year, and Tokyo fared no better. As late as 1969 Mount Fuji, about sixty
miles (approx. one hundred kilometers) from central Tokyo, was visible for
only thirty-eight days; reports from a century earlier had the number at over
one hundred days of visibility per year. Air quality became so bad in the
nation's capital that in April 1970 forty children in Tokyo's central Suginami
Ward collapsed from photochemical smog inhalation, with some requiring
hospitalization.[12] The city's rivers were in no better condition. A 1971 report
by the Tokyo metropolitan government described how, "in the decade from
1955," the Sumida River "was contaminated with factory effluents and domestic water to such an extent that it had turned into an open sewer, not
only prohibitive for fish and other aquatic life but also giving off unpleasant
and obnoxious odors."[13]

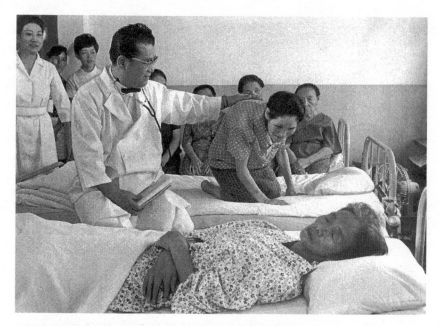

Itai Itai disease sufferers and their physician, Dr. Hagino Noboru, 1972
(The Mainichi Newspapers)

Japanese citizens did not suffer in silence. Antipollution protest movements appeared as early as the late 1950s when irate fishermen in Tokyo
(1958) and Minamata (1959) stormed the premises of polluting factories and
demanded recompense. Such local movements were greatly encouraged in
1964 when protesters led by schoolteachers in Shizuoka Prefecture south of
Tokyo forced local politicians to abandon plans for a petrochemical complex
similar to the noxious Yokkaichi facility. Selected as a special industrial region
by the central government in 1963, the area was slated for a major petrochemical development in 1964. By this time, however, local residents knew
about lethal pollution-induced asthma in Yokkaichi, and they quickly mobilized into an opposition movement to stop construction. Their scientifically
savvy and well-organized movement proved successful: by late 1964 local
officials, under intense public pressure, decided to shelve the project.[14] The
Shizuoka opposition movement proved to be a boon for industrial pollution victims. Enamored by this victory and supported by progressive
lawyers and victims' advocates, beginning in 1967 victims of the Big Four
pollution incidents instigated civil law proceedings against offending companies, and from 1971 to 1973 courts delivered monumental victories in

their favor. In the long run the Shizuoka movement also contributed to a softening of corporate and bureaucratic hypersensitivity to regulation, opening the way for a wave of environmental legislation from the late 1960s. Rather than resist regulation, industrial and government elites learned from Shizuoka that steering legal change might be more strategically savvy than resisting protest head on.

Antipollution and antidevelopment movements continued to mobilize around the nation throughout the 1960s and early 1970s, hitting a peak of around three thousand local mobilizations in 1973. Pollution victims began to forge rudimentary movement networks and publish their own newsletters or *minikomi* (mini communications), which increased eightfold during the period.[15] Inspired by the Shizuoka success, other high-profile prevention movements mobilized to stop construction of a freight line in Yokohama City and a new international airport in Chiba Prefecture—the latter drawing in radical leftist student activists.[16] Both mobilizations began in 1966, and although both ultimately failed, they confirmed just how sensitive local communities were becoming to environmental disruption in the name of economic development. Some even heralded this rising "wave of resistance" as a new stage in the democratization of Japan.[17] True or not, all of these movements contributed to a growing sense of dissatisfaction with unbridled economic growth dependent on the sacrifice of the living environment and human health.

Together with grassroots protest, the rise of a public discourse on industrial pollution also contributed greatly to anger over environmental injustices in 1960s Japan. Journalists led the way here by exposing the shocking consequences of pollution and reporting on the abysmal situation of victims. In the late 1960s, for example, the newspaper *Asahi Shinbun* took the unprecedented step of forming a "pollution team" of reporters to work exclusively on the issue. For eighteen months, beginning in 1970, the team wrote pollution- and environment-related articles for their respective departments and collaborated on a special series called "Kankyō o Mamoru" (Protecting the environment).[18] The newspaper followed up in 1971 with the provocative book *Kutabare GNP: Kōdo Keizai Seichō no Uchimaku* (To hell with GNP: The lowdown on high-speed economic growth). A sardonically titled chapter, "Kokumin Sōkōgai" (Gross national pollution), argued that, rather than simply "shifting the burden onto victims," the human and environmental costs of growth should be deducted from the GNP to give a more accurate picture of so-called growth.[19] Buzzwords made popular in the media also capture the tenor of the moment: *shokuhin kōgai* (food pollution) in 1961, *kōgai* (pollution) in 1965, *hedoro* (industrial sludge) in 1970, and Minamata in 1973.[20] The foreign media also chimed in. The *New York Times* explored Japan's pollution problems in a 1968 article, "Not All Is Serene in Cities of Japan" and, more comprehensively, in a multipage 1972 special headlined "Students in the elementary schools grow up suffering from Asthma. Plants wither and die. The birds around Mount Fuji are decreasing in number. They no longer visit the town."[21] So consequential had this discourse become by the early 1970s that even conservative politicians found it necessary to couch their designs for the country in environmental language. In his best-selling 1972 work *Nihon Rettō Kaizō Ron* (*Building a New Japan: Plan for Remodelling the Japanese Archipelago*), Liberal Democratic Party (LDP) heavyweight Tanaka Kakuei imagined a "renaissance" for Japan "in which man and sunshine and verdant surroundings" would "replace big cities or industries as the rightful master of society."[22]

Public intellectuals played a crucial role in forcing questions of environmental injustice onto the public agenda in the 1960s. In terms of sophisticated multidisciplinary analysis of environmental problems worldwide during this period, these Japanese public intellectuals stood on par with, or were even ahead of, their counterparts elsewhere. In the context of American environmental thought, scientists such as marine biologist Rachel Carson, entomologist and population specialist Paul Ehrlich, and antinuclear campaigner and ecologist Barry Commoner immediately come to mind. In Europe it was "small is beautiful" proponent E. F. Schumacher (UK), deep ecology founder Arne Naess (Norway), and ocean explorer Jacques Cousteau (France) who took the lead. In the case of Japan, however, antipollution campaigners and victim advocates took center stage: economists Miyamoto Ken'ichi and Tsuru Shigeto, chemical engineer Ui Jun, jurist Kainō Michitaka, and writers Ishimure Michiko and Ariyoshi Sawako. Concern for victims profoundly influenced the public statements and activities of these individuals and, moreover, helped propel notions of injustice to the very forefront of environmental debate in Japan at the time.

The 1964 book *Osorubeki Kōgai* (Fearsome pollution) is a case in point. Coauthored by Miyamoto Ken'ichi and environmental hygienist Shōji Hikaru, this best-selling volume was the first important mainstream publication documenting the extent, nature, and causes of industrial pollution in Japan. Hardly light reading, *Osorubeki Kōgai* sold an amazing 430,000 copies and can be likened to Carson's *Silent Spring* (1962) in the United

States or André Gorz's *Ecologie et Politique* (1975) in France.[23] What made the book unique, however, was its focus on the mechanisms of victimization and injustice inherent in Japan's high-growth development model. *Osoru-beki Kōgai* became a powerful mouthpiece for Miyamoto and Shōji to propagate the viewpoint that industrial pollution was, above all, a story of how human welfare and human rights had been flagrantly trampled in the relentless march for intensive capitalistic accumulation. Thanks to their book, the two authors found themselves transformed into industrial pollution authorities almost overnight.

While Miyamoto and Shōji provided the first scientific treatment of pollution for a mainstream audience, writer Ishimure Michiko gave it a human face with her heartrending 1969 work, *Kugai Jōdo: Waga Minamatabyō* (published in English as *Paradise in the Sea of Sorrow: Our Minamata Disease*). Ishimure had actually written about pollution victims earlier, but it was not until *Kugai Jōdo* that she gained national attention. In 1970 the book was awarded the first of many prizes, which Ishimure resolutely declined in respect for the victims' ongoing struggle. Although somewhat later, another female writer, Ariyoshi Sawako, made a similar impact on the environmental debate with her serialized documentary-novel *Fukugō Osen* (Compound pollution), which ran in the newspaper *Asahi Shinbun* from October 1974 through June 1975.[24] Week by week, and somewhat more accessibly than Miyamoto and Shōji's earlier work, Ariyoshi laid out the shocking health risks of insecticides and pesticides such as DDT, in the process producing a kind of manifesto for the alternative food movement in Japan. One is tempted to portray Ishimure and Ariyoshi as the Japanese equivalents of Rachel Carson. The similarities are undeniable: they were both women writing for a mainstream audience on environmental issues at around the same time. But unlike Carson, neither Ishimure nor Ariyoshi were scientists by training, nor did they single-handedly start the environmental debate in Japan as Carson had done in the United States in 1962. Rather, these two Japanese women further clarified and cemented the outrageous injustices of environmental pollution in the public mind, and Ishimure's work, coming as it did in 1969, fortified the growing pressure for substantive environmental legislation to address these injustices.

Faced with such pressures, government officials began to react, first at the local level. In 1964 Yokohama City signed a landmark pollution prevention agreement with local industry that set voluntary emissions standards and formalized processes of citizen participation and oversight. In nearby

Tokyo, progressive Governor Minobe Ryōkichi established a dedicated Pollution Research Office in 1967, and in 1969 passed a landmark pollution prevention ordinance with the strictest standards for air and water quality in the nation.[25] In contrast to the Minobe administration's proactive posture, the response to pollution at the national level came only in agonizingly cautious—some would say patently reluctant—steps, which only added to a popular sense of inaction and injustice. In terms of legislative remedies, the national government's approach until the 1970s was based on harmonization, not justice. For example, after the Honshū Paper Mill polluted Tokyo Bay in 1958, a law passed to regulate water quality was deliberately weakened by a clause specifying that pollution control measures should proceed in "harmony" with "sound economic development"—in effect providing a loophole for polluters.[26] The 1962 Baien no Haishutsu no Kisei tō ni Kansuru Hō (Law for the regulation of smoke and soot), passed in response to air pollution in Yokkaichi City, contained a similar clause, as did the 1967 Kōgai Taisaku Kihonhō (Basic law for environmental pollution control)—touted by officials as an epoch-making piece of environmental legislation. While officials were probably not intent on willfully destroying the environment or poisoning citizens, in hindsight, the harmonization approach reveals a callous disregard for pollution and its hapless victims. There can be no doubt that this stance only added to a growing sense of environmental injustice nationwide.

By the same token, not all national bureaucrats were cut from the same cloth. Given its portfolio, the Ministry of Health and Welfare (MHW) was among the earliest ministries to pay serious attention to the industrial pollution problem. In 1959, only months after Kumamoto researchers identified methyl mercury as the culprit in Minamata disease, the MHW's Food Hygiene Research Committee reached the same conclusion.[27] Similarly, in 1965, MHW tests pointed to fish in the Agano River as the cause of the second Minamata disease outbreak in Niigata. By early 1967 another MHW research team was pointing the finger directly at the Shōwa Denkō factory upstream.[28] Along with this pollution monitoring, the MHW also provided funding for nongovernmental groups. Significantly, from 1963 to 1967 the MHW provided critical start-up funding for Tsuru Shigeto's group of anti-pollution campaigners, the Research Committee on Pollution. Given the later contribution of RCP members to the Japanese and global environmental movement, this official state funding for a pioneering ENGO deserves recognition.

Other ministries also responded, although perhaps not always with the same level of genuine concern. An industrial pollution division was established in the Ministry of International Trade and Industry (MITI) in 1963, an interministerial coordination committee for pollution control at the vice-ministerial level in 1964, and a Kōgai Shingikai (Deliberative Council on Pollution) in 1965.[29] More concretely, the government-owned Kōgai Bōshi Jigyōdan (Pollution Prevention Corporation) was established in 1965 with the objective of averting future siting disputes through the procurement of environmentally suitable sites, construction of green belts, installation of abatement equipment, and loans for pollution control and prevention measures.[30] Of course, such countermeasures did little to alleviate suffering on the ground, and well-intentioned officials were often thwarted by the prevailing consensus on "harmonizing" environmental protection with industrial development.

Nevertheless, mounting pressure from protest movements and a worried populace eventually forced national lawmakers and bureaucrats to respond. By 1968 the MHW was in a sufficiently strong position to officially recognize the Itai Itai and Minamata conditions as pollution diseases—decisions that bolstered the ongoing lawsuits and opened the way for official compensation.[31] At a historic session of parliament in 1970—later called the Pollution Diet—fourteen laws were either newly passed or amended, giving Japan one of the strictest environmental regulation regimes in the world. The strengthening of the Kōgai Taisaku Kihonhō of 1967 was emblematic of this Diet session. Notably, lawmakers deleted the pro-industry clause in Article 1 of the law, which had required environmental protection to proceed "in harmony with sound economic development."[32] Complementing these historic legislative reforms, in 1971 the Environment Agency of Japan (EAJ, Kankyōchō) was established and a nationwide system for pollution dispute resolution put in place. Two years later, in 1973, the Diet passed the Kōgai Kenkō Higai Hoshō Hō (Law for the compensation of pollution-related health injury), creating the world's first governmental compensation scheme for pollution victims. Japan could now boast a hefty suite of antipollution regulations and an environmental bureaucracy staffed by a cadre of ostensibly green officials. The creation of this environmental bureaucracy is also interesting for what it says about the official response to years of environmental injustice. Rather than leaving disputes between polluters and victims to be resolved by the courts, as was done in the Big Four, officials thereafter preferred to keep this process informal through bureaucrat-led resolution mechanisms that kept control firmly in bureaucratic hands.[33]

There is no doubt that environmental conditions in mid-1970s Japan were much improved compared with those a decade earlier. Of course, industrial and other forms of pollution were by no means eradicated and, as others have noted, significant environmental problems remained unsolved.[34] Moreover, after the court cases were over, the lawmaking done, and the media hype exhausted, it was the victims of pollution and their families who were left to cope with the aftereffects of contamination—very often for the rest of their lives. Indeed, the victims embodied the very essence of environmental injustice wrought by industrial pollution, and as we will see, their plight and their symbolism authenticated and invigorated the environmental injustice paradigm Japanese activists first formulated at home and then took to the world.

## Understanding Environmental Injustice: The Research Committee on Pollution

Pioneering antipollution and environmental advocates played a catalytic role in the national response to pollution by connecting the dots between contamination, industry, politics, injustice, and injury and by supporting the movement for victim recompense. Together with pollution victims, these individuals helped fashion Japan's environmental injustice paradigm. No group was more influential in this connection than the Research Committee on Pollution formed in 1963 by eight leftist academics.[35] Above all, the RCP shared a commitment to the plight of pollution victims and an unrelenting determination to expose the perpetrators—an anthropocentric perspective that, as I have noted, came to dominate contemporary Japanese environmentalism and deeply informed later transnational involvement. As the RCP's founder, economist Tsuru Shigeto, later explained, these eight academics represented almost the entire reservoir of pollution expertise in Japan at the time, and, working in isolation, each had struggled greatly to piece together a comprehensive picture of the crisis. Once united, however, the group generated powerful synergies in terms of multidisciplinary perspectives, investigative methodologies, and social networks. The openness of group members to diverse and often contradictory strategies helped sustain their ongoing collaboration. For instance, while Tsuru, Kainō, and Shōji sometimes worked inside the system as pollution czars and government advisers in progressive local governments, Ui waged a public crusade against conservative political leaders and national ministries. Notably, in 1970 Ui was arrested for storming the MHW—a financial patron of the RCP—on behalf of Minamata disease sufferers.[36]

From the late 1950s, RCP members began to visit suspected sites of pollution such as Minamata Bay and the petrochemical complex in Yokkaichi City. Their fieldwork experiences forced them to think carefully about the politics and economics of pollution and, for a number of them, matured into a systematic project to identify and clearly articulate the essential elements of Japanese pollution as a first step toward its eradication. From the mid- to late 1960s, members' activities expanded beyond site observations and public advocacy to include court appearances, local government service, and activist network building. In the law courts, Miyamoto Ken'ichi, Shōji Hikaru, and legal scholar Kainō Michitaka supported Yokkaichi asthma plaintiffs in their civil action (1967–1972) against the six polluting petrochemical companies.[37] Miyamoto testified as an expert witness for the plaintiffs, providing the court with a detailed history of postwar Japanese pollution, while Shōji and Kainō acted as special advisers to the plaintiffs' attorneys. Miyamoto and Kainō also joined Ui as special advisers to the plaintiffs in the Niigata methyl mercury poisoning case (1967–1971). Ui's background in the etiology and pathology of industrial pollution proved invaluable in this intensely scientific lawsuit, as too did Miyamoto's persuasive closing argument for the ultimately victorious plaintiffs.[38] Apart from the Big Four pollution cases, RCP members appeared as expert witnesses and legal advisers in a myriad of pollution suits over airport noise, land reclamation, coastal access rights, auto emissions, and bullet train vibration. In the process they contributed to a minor revolution in Japanese environmental common law, including innovations such as the principle of absolute liability in the Itai Itai disease case, joint tortfeasance and corporate negligence in the Yokkaichi case, and the concept of maximum permissible limits in the Osaka Airport night-flights case.[39]

As they fought alongside victims in the courts, RCP members also fanned out as advisers in the many progressive local governments elected from the mid-1960s. In Western Honshū, Shōji Hikaru served as chairman on pollution advisory boards for Osaka, Kyoto, Kobe, and Amazaki Cities, where he drafted pollution prevention ordinances that dramatically improved air and water quality. Shōji's pollution strategy for the smog-ridden Osaka City was a crucial ingredient in the successful two-term governorship (1971–1979) of the socialist constitutional scholar Kuroda Ryōichi, elected on a promise to "restore Osaka's beautiful skies."[40] Even more influential in the

Photochemical smog and noise pollution meter installed in downtown Tokyo by the Minobe administration, 1973

(The Mainichi Newspapers)

local antipollution cleanup was the Tokyo governorship (1967–1979) of Marxian economist Minobe Ryōkichi, who swiftly mobilized Tsuru Shigeto and Kainō Michitaka into his pollution brain trust. Tsuru served on a specialist urban planning panel that, in 1969, recommended a sweeping strategy to address pollution through public housing, urban transport, and land redevelopments.[41]

Kainō Michitaka shouldered an even greater responsibility as chief of the innovative Tokyo City Pollution Research Bureau, which assembled bureaucrats responsible for town water, sanitation, and waste disposal alongside medical practitioners, biologists, botanists, public works specialists, meteorologists, and chemists.[42] As the capital city's pollution czar, Kainō sent factfinding missions to China, South Korea, and the United States, convened international conferences, strengthened municipal regulations, and formulated a citywide strategy involving source prevention, industrial relocation, and greenbelt construction. Like Miyamoto and Shōji, Kainō was enamored by Chinese and Soviet communism, and hoped to inject some elements into Tokyo governance. He was particularly impressed by reports from Russia describing state-of-the-art automobile factories operating at only

30 percent capacity because communists apparently only made what they needed.[43]

Two of Kainō's initiatives as pollution czar had nationwide effect: the 1970 volume *Kōgai to Tōkyōto* (Pollution and Tokyo city), and the Tōkyōto Kōgai Bōshi Jōrei (Pollution prevention ordinance) of 1969. A weighty seven hundred pages long, *Kōgai to Tōkyōto* represented a cutting-edge statement on urban environmental policymaking, covering the causes of air, water, sound, and vibratory pollution; their health effects; remedial regulatory and legal mechanisms; and the role of civic activism.[44] Given that it was an official publication, the volume's advocacy of vigorous civic opposition to pollution was particularly striking, yet understandable given the extent of Tokyo's problems and the ideological proclivities of Kainō and others in the Minobe administration. The message was that, although Revolution with a capital "R" was impossible, through people power a smaller pollution revolution could really happen. Despite its length, *Kōgai to Tōkyōto* sold an impressive thirty thousand copies, becoming required reading for local officials nationwide.[45]

A year before publication of that book, Kainō and his bureau made an indelible mark on environmental law in Japan with their brainchild ordinance, the Tōkyōto Kōgai Bōshi Jōrei. What distinguished this ordinance from those in other municipalities was its provocative disregard for national standards. Unlike national pollution regulations diluted by economic harmony clauses, the Tokyo ordinance set unprecedented emissions standards for sulfur and other noxious oxides. Pro-industry bureaucrats and politicians initially resisted, citing national legal supremacy, but, faced with a potential electoral backlash, a wave of protest, and numerous lawsuits, they eventually relented, and the ordinance survived intact.[46] When the Pollution Diet convened in the following year, the ordinance became a minimum standard that vote-sensitive national politicians could not simply ignore. Indeed, this ordinance represented one of the RCP's most noteworthy regulatory achievements, substantively influencing both local and national regulation. More prosaically, life in Tokyo improved as a result: by the mid-1970s annual average levels of sulfur dioxide, carbon monoxide, and suspended particulates had dramatically decreased, while photochemical oxidants and nitrogen dioxide were leveling off.[47]

While Kainō and other RCP members tackled Japan's regulatory deficiencies, others such as Ui Jun focused on grassroots network building. In the evening of October 12, 1970, Ui convened the first of his Independent

Lectures on Pollution (ILP) at the Urban Engineering Department of Tokyo University. Coming at the height of the pollution crisis, these public lectures attracted hundreds of students, office workers, housewives, small business owners, and local administrators. Ui presented thirteen lectures during the first term, covering the history and current state of Japanese industrial pollution, the situation in European countries, and strategies for resistance. The second term featured guest speakers such as Minamata activist Ishimure Michiko, Itai Itai disease researcher Dr. Hagino Noboru, and socialist stalwart Arahata Kanson, who captivated a one-thousand-strong audience with his talk on the legendary prewar antipollution activist Tanaka Shōzō who had fought for the rights of locals.[48]

Just as important as the lectures were the publications and activism generated by the ILP movement. After Ui's initial 1970 lecture, ILP participants spontaneously formed an executive committee that meticulously transcribed proceedings for a monthly newsletter, *Jishu Kōza* (The independent lectures). This publication subsequently became a mouthpiece for environmental movements across Japan. Ui's first-term presentations were later published in the volume *Kōgai Genron* (The principles of pollution), which sold one hundred thousand copies and was named among the ten most influential books of postwar Japan by the influential weekly *Asahi Shūkan*.[49] Among the most important contributions of Ui's lectures was his characterization of industrial pollution not only as technical problem to be solved but, more fundamentally, as a critical component in a system of discrimination and injustice against the very weakest in society and, moreover, a phenomenon that implicated not only government and industry but also ordinary citizens, who benefited from the suffering of pollution victims and contributed to discrimination against them.[50]

Operating from a small apartment in Tokyo, the ILP executive committee served as a contact point between local activists and urbanites keen to join the antipollution struggle. As Ui explained, many initially came out of curiosity but, deeply inspired, joined on as supporters in various initiatives such as the movement of Minamata disease sufferers.[51] Moreover, from 1972 onward, Ui and the executive committee expanded their activities transnationally, protesting with activists outside UNCHE in Stockholm, publishing English-language materials, and guiding foreign journalists around Japan's pollution sites. The ILP also became a seedbed for movements opposing Japanese industrial pollution in Asia in the 1970s and radioactive waste dumping in the Pacific in the 1980s. In this way, a domestic network

Ui Jun presenting at the Independent Lectures on Pollution, 1973
(The Mainichi Newspapers)

established to oppose Japanese industrial pollution, teach about its causes, and seek justice for its victims also served as a launchpad for Japanese activists to take their environmental injustice paradigm to the world.

Throughout the 1960s RCP members feverishly strove to comprehend the mechanisms of industrial pollution and, more pointedly, to fashion some kind of political strategy for victim recompense. Most members brought a decidedly Marxian perspective to the pollution problem, beginning with the general assumption that industrial capitalism, ipso facto, produced pollution. But, as professional social and natural scientists, RCP members were also resolutely committed to studying the causes and manifestations of industrial pollution as it occurred in actual places and communities. This was an important commitment because empiricism demanded a rigorous testing of ideology in the field and ultimately, for some in the group, a modification of their deepest political commitments. For example, members' investigations into Japanese cases of pollution revealed that labor unions were not necessarily the natural allies of industrial pollution victims and, in some cases, could even exacerbate injustices. Moreover, in contrast to the impoverishment of the working class typical of early-stage capitalism, "immiseration" under contemporary advanced capitalism manifested in different groups and phenomena such as "pollution, urban congestion and decay, or chronic inflation."[52] Such differences implied the necessity for modifications in both theory and strategy. Although members never completely abandoned their belief that pollution was more likely under capitalism than socialism, the realities of actually existing industrial pollution encouraged them to rethink strategy beyond rigid class lines. Important also, by disrupting the stability of their ideological universe, RCP members' engagement with the problem of Japanese industrial pollution raised the question of industrial pollution elsewhere, especially in socialist and communist countries where, theoretically, it should not have existed. To be sure, their Marxist leanings gave them a cosmopolitan and international perspective to begin with, but I believe that the theoretical, ethical, and strategic challenges posed by Japanese industrial pollution also planted the seeds of their later willingness to travel and connect across borders. In a sense, discovering that the local was not operating as it should have been theoretically sowed the seeds of a project to reimagine and reposition that local.

Consider first the trajectory of Miyamoto Ken'ichi. Miyamoto (1930–), an economist and scholar of public finance, was a founding member of the RCP with Tsuru Shigeto. His approach to pollution and the environment had the most palpable Marxian flavor of the group, a result of what Miyamoto described as his early "baptism" into Marxism, which for many years enjoyed a quasi-religious status among Japanese social scientists.[53] Miyamoto became concerned about industrial pollution at the 1961 meeting of the socialist Zen Nihon Jichi Dantai Rōdō Kumiai (All-Japan Prefectural and Municipal Workers Union, or Jichirō), where he learned of officially censored data evidencing severe air and water contamination around the new petrochemical complex in Yokkaichi City, located in Mie Prefecture around 230 miles (370 kilometers) south of Tokyo. This data diverged sharply from a glossy pamphlet from the Urban Engineering Department at Tokyo University (involved in the project), which eulogized Yokkaichi as an "ideal industrial city of sunlight and green space" supplanting the asphyxiating coal-powered centers of old. Intrigued, Miyamoto traveled to Yokkaichi twice over the coming months where he was deeply shocked to discover over eight hundred asthma sufferers and a foul-smelling bay with malodorous, inedible fish. In mid-1962 on a guided tour of the complex Miyamoto observed wastewater treatment facilities and interviewed factory officials who insisted the pollution originated from a sunken ship in the bay. Infuriated

The "hellish skies" over Yokkaichi City, June 1970
(The Mainichi Newspapers)

by these denials and mindful of the victims, Miyamoto decided to gather more data on the "insidious" and "fearsome" villain at Yokkaichi.[54]

Later in the same year, Miyamoto traveled farther south to the Yahata Ironworks in northern Kyushu, where he was shocked again—this time by the gray, smog-choked sky and the blackened Dōkai Bay. Coal or oil power irrespective, he came to see these industrial cities as hotbeds of tyrannical monopoly capital, modern "corporate castle towns" like the feudal castle towns of old ruled by sword-wielding samurai warriors.[55] With the establishment of the RCP in 1963, Miyamoto, Tsuru, and other members intensified their field research: Yokkaichi again in 1964 and 1967, the planned Shizuoka petrochemical plant in 1964, and myriad other cities such as Minamata, Kisarazu, and Mizushima. At each site they met with activists, victims, medical doctors, and industry representatives, carefully documenting the devastating progression from industrial irresponsibility to contamination and, ultimately, human suffering and injustice.[56]

Deeply disturbed by the human costs of industrial pollution, members began communicating their findings publicly almost immediately. In December 1962 an incensed Miyamoto penned what would be the first postwar essay to use *kōgai* (pollution) in its title. In the essay, "Shinobiyoru Kōgai"

(Insidious pollution), Miyamoto lambasted the "hellish skies" over Japan's industrial towns and condemned pollution as the new "king of human rights violations."[57] As mentioned, most widely read and influential was his best-selling 1964 book, *Osorubeki Kōgai* (Fearsome pollution), coauthored with fellow RCP member Shōji Hikaru.[58] As fellow RCP member Ui Jun later explained, *Osorubeki Kōgai* was more than an alarm bell like Carson's *Silent Spring*; it also became the "how to" manual for victims, advocates, and antipollution movements nationwide.[59] Inside its covers readers encountered a shocking compendium of images and statistics. Along with photos of smoggy industrial cities, polluted lakes, and distraught victims, Miyamoto and Shōji provided a "pollution map" of Japan, identifying contamination in almost every prefecture nationwide. A "pollution diary" based on newspaper clippings from 1961 to 1962 painted a similar picture. Shōji marshaled his natural science expertise in chapters on the causes and consequences of air and water pollution, while Miyamoto discussed the political economy of pollution and strategies for resistance. *Osorubeki Kōgai* went through thirty-six reprints and sold close to half a million copies; although it was but one part of a wider awakening, it must be credited with shaping a public language and debate on environmental injustices in Japan where there had been relative silence before. That the major Japanese dictionary, the *Kōjien,* at that time contained no entry for the term *kōgai* attests to *Osorubeki Kōgai*'s landmark significance.[60] Miyamoto and Shōji also found their own lives transformed, deluged thereafter with requests for assistance from protest movements, local governments, and environmental litigation attorneys.[61]

*Osorubeki Kōgai* had an overtly Marxist tone and was littered with blanket assertions such as "the history of pollution" is "the history of capitalism," "pollution is a symptom of class conflict," and the "capitalist class" is the "pollution aggressor."[62] The book singled out Japan as a special case of pollution, pointing to collusion between conservative politicians and industry executives. In the absence of an effective regulatory framework and driven by a catch-up mentality, Japanese capital concentrated in the highly polluting heavy and chemical sectors, whose firms devoted almost no funds to pollution prevention.[63] Miyamoto and Shōji also highlighted the imbalances both within public spending and between public and private expenditure. They noted that, although public spending in Japan for 1960 was 1.6 times higher than that of a comparable nation (the United Kingdom), outlays for public housing, for example, were 72 percent less than the United Kingdom, while outlays for industrial infrastructure were more than three times greater.[64] Both the national and local governments in Japan poured public funds into ports, freight lines, roads, power plants, and airports, while disregarding daily life infrastructure such as sewerage, cleaning and waste management, and hospitals.[65] Indeed, rather than portraying a neutral arbiter of social and economic interests, Miyamoto, Shōji, and other RCP members portrayed a *kigyō kokka* (private enterprise state) managed by economic technocrats and conservative politicians, ever ready to violently defend corporate interests.[66]

In a Marxian tone, *Osorubeki Kōgai* concluded that Japanese pollution caused by industry cutting corners was a "social disaster" inherent in the "relations of capitalist production." It was about "class conflict," with the "contemporary aggressor" being large corporations and the state, and the victims being workers, farmers, and fishermen.[67] Of course, this observation that pollution affected groups beyond the working class did not fit neatly with classical Marxian theory, nor did it translate easily into revolutionary strategies centered on the proletariat. Nor were such implications lost on the orthodox left, and Miyamoto and Shōji found themselves the target of severe criticism from the Japanese Communist Party and labor unions for their "bourgeois liberal" discourse of rights.[68] For his part, Miyamoto eventually concluded that antipollution movements need not be ultimately subsumed back into the historical struggle of the proletariat but would have their own unique role to play under future socialism.[69] Here he shared an affinity with later global discourses on human rights and post-Marxist visions, in which groups subject to injustices because of race, gender, sexuality, or even the environment would become part of a "chain of equivalence," without the need to surrender their unique identities for a shared subjectivity of class.[70]

Moreover, although *Osorubeki Kōgai* unequivocally linked industrial pollution to monopoly capitalism (especially its Japanese configuration), the book did not ignore reports—sketchy though they were—of pollution in socialist countries. Miyamoto and Shōji briefly discussed UN reports of the time that documented air pollution in the Slezsko coal fields in the Ostrava region of Czechoslovakia, which rivaled the worst cases in Japan. They also noted urban pollution in the Soviet Union and communist China as large numbers of people moved from rural areas to cities.[71] In the final passages of the book Miyamoto and Shōji admitted that the history of pollution in Japan and its relationship to Japanese capitalism—which they had so confidently explained in earlier chapters—really needed to be contextualized through comparison to foreign countries, especially socialist ones.[72] This nagging question about the systemic roots of pollution—was it all about (Japanese) capitalism, or perhaps something more?—would be one factor behind RCP members' transnational involvement from the late 1960s onward.

While Miyamoto observed the hellish skies and excruciatingly painful asthma at Yokkaichi, fellow RCP member Ui Jun (1932–2006) discovered a different kind of hell in Minamata Bay and Niigata Prefecture, produced by the chemical methyl mercury. Ui had studied applied chemistry as an undergraduate at the University of Tokyo and, after a brief stint in industry, returned to the university in 1959 as a graduate student working on plastic manufacturing processes. It was around this time (late 1959) that Ui first read reports linking the strange disease in Minamata to methyl mercury. He was immediately intrigued because Nihon Zeon, the company he had worked for from 1956 to 1959, regularly dumped a similar kind of mercury in its factory effluent. Ui promptly began to conduct research on Minamata disease in his free time, and in 1963, he decided to quit the chemical engineering program at Tokyo University and reenter as a graduate student in civil engineering, where he could concentrate on the methyl mercury issue. By 1963 Ui and a fellow pollution researcher, the photographer Kuwabara Shisei, had confirmed beyond doubt that methyl mercury in factory effluent was the cause of Minamata disease. But, lacking the courage, the pair decided not to publish their findings—a decision that Ui greatly regretted later, because he believed it might have diminished, if not averted, the second outbreak of Minamata disease in Nagano Prefecture in 1965.[73]

Ui Jun is arguably the most important figure in transnational environmental activism in postwar Japan. As a scientist he asked questions that could only be answered by looking abroad, as an activist he helped mobilize movements with the knowledge and resources to go transnational, and as an individual he was thoroughly committed to preventing a repeat of the Japanese disaster anywhere else in the world. It also helped that Ui was, for want of a better term, an indomitable individual. Although he was not a confident English speaker, on many occasions Ui plucked up the courage to speak about Japanese pollution before foreign audiences and in television and radio interviews. He was willing to travel to foreign countries and contact people out of the blue. And he had no hesitation about directly confronting managers of polluting companies, whether in Japan, Italy, Canada, or elsewhere. Supporting this resolve was Ui's commitment to the victims, especially the sufferers of Minamata disease, who he felt he had let down. As Ui

Ui Jun arrested as he attempts to
enter the MHW in support of
Minamata disease sufferers,
May 1970
(The Mainichi Newspapers)

commented after an arduous 1969 visit to Finland, "I thought to myself that it was the memory of the sufferer's pain which supported my activities during this tense week."[74] Indeed, Ui came to see himself as a kind of "special foreign envoy for Minamata," charged with telling the victims' tragic story to the world.

Like Miyamoto, Ui's transnational motivation initially stemmed from a desire to understand why such terrible things had happened to innocent Japanese people—to fishermen, to young mothers, and to children. With its extensive coastline, massive tidal fluctuations, high rainfall, fast-flowing rivers, strong winds, and absence of land borders, Japan appeared to possess the perfect conditions for averting pollution. Nevertheless, the country had become a polluters' paradise. For Ui there were at least two explanations for this situation. First, he believed that, institutionally, the incestuous relations between business and government and the resulting consensus on economic growth above all else facilitated and exacerbated pollution. The Japanese government was not a watchdog but a handmaiden of industry.[75] Second, he pointed to the relative weakness of human rights consciousness in Japan, where people perceived rights not as benefits won through struggle but almost as gifts bestowed from above by the US occupiers after the war. He singled out discrimination against Minamata disease sufferers as a typical example of this weak rights consciousness. After all, what group better typified an appalling violation of human rights than the Japanese people poisoned by methyl mercury? Yet, the reality for victims once they fell ill was discrimination, social exclusion, and poverty. Sufferers found it difficult to find work or to get married. To announce that one was a Minamata sufferer, argued Ui, was often tantamount to asking for discrimination. And, the fact that others could so easily discriminate against pollution victims proved for him that the Japanese had a "very weak conceptualization of their own rights and the rights of others." Only by discriminating against others could they suppress the nagging anxiety that they too were being discriminated against in one way or another.[76] Like Miyamoto, then, Ui's conceptualization of Japanese industrial pollution was profoundly shaped by the discrimination against local communities and poisoned victims he witnessed at Minamata and elsewhere. In fact, he spent as much time trying to understand the roots of environmental injustice and victim discrimination as he did the science of environmental pollution. The encounter with this discrimination and injustice instilled in Ui, even more so than in Miyamoto, a strong sense of obligation to ensure that the facts of the Japanese tragedy were correctly communicated abroad and that the voices of the victims were heard—both as a warning to the world and as a pathway to victim empowerment. Importantly, this stance deeply colored the activities of the ILP movement as well as subsequent spin-off movements involved in environmental problems throughout Asia and the Pacific in the 1970s and 1980s.

The career trajectory of Harada Masazumi (1934–2012), a medical researcher and clinician at Kumamoto University on Kyushu Island, offers yet another important insight into the development of an environmental injustice paradigm among leading Japanese antipollution activists in the 1960s. It was in 1960 that the twenty-six-year-old Harada, a new graduate student in the university's neuropsychiatry laboratory, first learned about the compound methyl mercury and its effects on living organisms. For his first six months as a graduate student, Harada was assigned to laboratory work in which he conducted mercury experiments on cats, rodents, rabbits, and chickens. It was only in mid-1961 that he was permitted to conduct an examination on a human sufferer of methyl mercury poisoning at Minamata Bay. As Harada later recalled, this visit to the home of a young victim determined how he would live the rest of his life.[77] Interacting with a Minamata

Harada Masazumi examines slides of
Minamata disease victims, 1972
(The Mainichi Newspapers)

disease sufferer firsthand—especially a child—affected him on a deeply emotional level. But just as distressing for the young physician were the social and economic conditions in which these victims were forced to live. Similar to Ui, Harada also discovered, along with terribly poisoned human bodies in Minamata, horrendous poverty and appalling discrimination.

As a young physician fresh out of university, this terrible situation was almost impossible to comprehend, and it immediately provoked within Harada a deep sense of resentment and even rage. The victims had done nothing more than consume fish, yet now they faced pitiless discrimination and were forced to lead their lives hidden away from society.[78] As he put it, "The world I saw through Minamata was a configuration of the complicated fissures and discrimination which haunt all of human society. I too had become used to this world in which people no longer considered others as humans. I was able to see [through Minamata disease] how I had positioned myself within that structure of discrimination. I concluded that the fundamental cause of Minamata disease was the condition of people not considering others as humans. . . . I also recognized that the damage was expanding and that the lack of any relief measures was due to human discrimination in which people did not view others as humans."[79] Harada would later describe Minamata disease sufferers and their families as a "discarded" or "abandoned" people, victimized by a cruel structure of dehumanization.[80] Chisso Corporation, owner of the offending factory, was certainly to blame, but the "condition of dehumanization" involved many more people— including Harada himself.

Like Miyamoto and Ui, Harada also became convinced that, to understand industrial diseases in all their complexity, researchers had no choice but to visit polluted spaces directly. Reading or hearing about pollution secondhand might be useful in relaying certain basic facts, but only by seeing toxic environments and interacting with victims firsthand would advocates truly comprehend the complex structure of discrimination in which pollution unfolded. Pollution was about much more than toxic chemicals and gases contaminating ecosystems and human bodies; it was also about the processes of dehumanization that made this possible, and such things could only be understood by physically entering into the world of victims.

Harada's commitment to understanding pollution on the ground and to meeting victims in their own localities was further strengthened by an emotional encounter he had with the mother of a young Minamata disease sufferer. As the woman explained, she was extremely grateful for the many examinations undertaken by Harada and his colleagues at the university, but what she really needed after six long years was an answer. "Every time I'm asked to bring him in, it takes a full day and I lose a whole day's wages which makes life very difficult."[81] To this Harada had no reply, but after the encounter he made a commitment that, thereafter, all his consultations with Minamata disease sufferers would be conducted in their homes, even if this meant laborious hours of travel for himself. Importantly, Harada's commitment to meeting and treating pollution victims in their own spaces seems to have made him receptive to helping pollution victims anywhere, even if this meant traveling outside Japan, which he would begin to do from the mid-1970s.

Moreover, like Ui, Harada's transnational impulse was fueled by a deep sense of responsibility and even remorse as a researcher and clinician from polluted Japan. In his and others' efforts to short-circuit the denials of Chisso officials and their governmental supporters about the causes of Minamata disease, Harada and fellow clinicians and researchers had been left with no choice but to formulate a watertight set of "typical" symptoms for the disease that could not be rebutted or denied. While such definitional clarity had undoubtedly assisted many Japanese victims in their battle for retribution and compensation, Harada also recognized how this clarity may have too-narrowly demarcated the health effects of mercury poisoning, which stretched from milder neurological side effects to absolute incapacitation. This sense that he may have somehow unwittingly contributed to the disempowerment of certain mercury-poisoning victims served as a powerful motivating factor behind his transnational activities from the mid-1970s onward.

What we encounter in the cases of Miyamoto Ken'ichi, Ui Jun, and Harada Masazumi, then, are three highly educated and empathetic social and natural scientists whose involvement with industrial pollution and its victims in Japan profoundly shaped their understanding of the phenomenon within a paradigm of environmental injustice. In Minamata, in Yokkaichi, and at contaminated sites all over Japan, they discovered human suffering and discrimination that they desperately wanted to understand, explain, and eradicate. Each of them harbored a personal sense of remorse and responsibility as scientists from a terribly polluted nation about which the rest of the world knew very little. They realized that they possessed knowledge that could potentially circumvent pollution in other places—even in other countries—and perhaps prevent further human misery at the hands of industry.

Admittedly, these factors by no means predetermined that RCP members would become active transnationally, but I suggest that, when the opportunity to go abroad presented itself, such factors made them more receptive than they may otherwise have been. Moreover, one lasting outcome of pollution protest, media attention, court cases, public activism, and, of course, suffering industrial pollution victims was the production of a potent environmental injustice paradigm in 1960s Japan, most visible within groups such as the RCP and ILP, but also evident in the media, in public discourse, in governmental legislation, and even within national bureaucracies such as the MHW. In the following chapters I trace the ways Japanese activists deployed this paradigm in their various transnational involvements beginning in the late 1960s. Although the various scalar iterations (e.g., regional, global) of this paradigm would demand modifications and enhancements, environmental victims, the violation of their rights, and the mechanisms of injustice harming them would remain central in the message that the Japanese activists involved relayed abroad, as well as in the ways these activists approached and understood environmental issues beyond the archipelago.

CHAPTER 2

# The Therapy of Translocal Community

Transnationalism can have vastly different connotations, ranging from the relatively informal diffusion of ideas or practices across borders to highly co-ordinated mobilizations among activists from different countries. I am receptive to the many shades of transnationalism along this definitional spectrum but want to give priority to material or physical connections, because it is the face-to-face meetings between people from different countries that very often stimulate meaningful changes in the ways those involved think, how they act, and the kinds of changes they produce when they return home. Particularly important here is Sidney Tarrow's idea of transnational activists as "connective tissue"; in other words, the ways in which such actors move to forge physical, emotional, and intellectual connections between people, communities, and movements separated by geography and national borders.[1] Like the dynamic connective tissue within living organisms, these rooted cosmopolitans are far more than passive conduits, because they are the ones actively creating the network of interconnections and becoming the carriers of meanings, of human experiences, and of shared struggles. I imagine them as the very life force of transnationalism, helping to "oxygenate" the system, so to speak. Ui Jun, Harada Masazumi, and other RCP members appear to have realized very early on that their role in the creation of transnational—or more accurately, perhaps, trans*local*—interconnections could be of real value in pollution victim empowerment.

The sinologist and social theorist Arif Dirlik has proposed this idea of "translocal" to signify how geographically rooted struggles and identities can become springboards for mobilizations, interconnections, and exchanges that transcend national borders. For Dirlik, trans*local* is far more than a terminological modification of trans*national* because it challenges us to reconsider the capacity of places to disrupt the ideological hierarchies of scale that can serve as strategies of containment in a historical field monopolized by the national panorama.[2] As the geographer Ash Amin puts it, places have the potential to become "more than what they contain, and what happens in them [can be] more than the sum of localised practices and powers, and actions at other 'spatial scales.'"[3] Some, such as the geographer Sally Marston, even propose a post-national "flat ontology" of the world that "discard[s] the centring essentialism that infuses not only the up–down vertical imaginary but also the radiating (out from here) spatiality of horizontality."[4] Instead, Marston and fellow geographers envision a world in which "all contemporaneous lives . . . are linked through the unfolding of intermeshed sites."[5] What interests me in such observations is the suggestion that the local is not—and never was—a nationally bounded space, and, more significantly, that within the local there exists a potential for universal vision, consciousness, and action transcending the local while remaining attached to it. Indeed, one argument I develop in this and the following chapters is that local experience and attachment served as powerful stimuli for transnational action in the contemporary Japanese environmental movement, even when attention shifted to problems of the globe in the 1980s.

At the height of Japan's pollution crisis in the late 1960s, Ui Jun made a number of pioneering visits to Europe to collect information on local instances of industrial pollution and to report on the grave crisis facing Japan. Encouraged by one of his superiors at Tokyo University, who feared Ui might be drawn into the rising tumult of student protest, for fifteen months from August 1968 Ui traveled throughout Europe as a research fellow with the World Health Organization (WHO). While in Europe, Ui delivered many lectures; gave media interviews; met with scientists, activists, and government officials; and conducted pollution site investigations in countries such as Sweden, Hungary, Finland, Italy, the Netherlands, England, France, Switzerland, West Germany, Austria, Czechoslovakia, and Belgium. The trip was eye-opening for him. In the midst of a bitterly cold Hungarian winter, he saw how the "blue" Danube River had become a "blackened stream" due to toxic industrial sludge, and he experienced firsthand the terrible air pollution of Budapest caused by citizens burning low-grade coal for heating. Ui estimated that Budapest's brown tap water—which he had no choice but to drink—had a maximum visibility of only twenty centimeters.[6] He witnessed similar pollution in the Soviet Union and in other East European socialist states such as Czechoslovakia and could only conclude that, while it was true many of these states had pollution measures in place before Western nations, claims that they had eradicated pollution were simply wrong. In fact, based on his field experiences, Ui concluded that the political and economic system of socialism might even delay the discovery and exacerbate the effects of pollution—a conclusion greatly at odds with many advocates of state socialism in Japan.[7] Miyamoto Ken'ichi came to a similar conclusion during a visit to Czechoslovakia in 1967. After a conference in Prague, he was permitted to visit the industrial region surrounding Ostrava City near the Czech-Polish border, where he discovered the same "hellish skies" he had seen in northern Kyushu in 1961.[8] Seeing pollution in socialist countries and interacting with social scientists revealed for Miyamoto the "errors of Japanese Marxian theories on pollution" and contributed to his rethinking of political strategies to address the injustices of environmental pollution he had first discovered at home.[9]

In this chapter I retrace RCP members' visits to pollution sites worldwide and their meetings with foreign activists and victims from 1968 until the mid-1970s. I am interested in what they learned through these visits and how they were affected, especially with regard to their evolving ideas about the causes of and remedies for industrial pollution and its resultant injustices. I also show how this group began to communicate Japan's history of environmental injustice to the world. I begin with the early travels of Ui Jun and Miyamoto Ken'ichi in Europe in the late-1960s where they encountered water and air contamination equal to, if not worse than, that in Japan, and came face-to-face with the reality of pollution in socialist countries. I then explore the World Environment Investigative Mission funded by the newspaper *Chūnichi Shinbun* and organized and led by RCP members in 1975. Visiting sixteen countries and forty pollution sites, this mission was the most extensive endeavor to study worldwide pollution in modern Japanese history. Particularly important were the linkages RCP members forged with Native American communities in Canada afflicted by mercury poisoning. Individuals such as Harada Masazumi offered their scientific expertise and also acted as bridges between the Native Americans and Minamata disease sufferers in Japan. Emboldened by this support from Japan, the Native Americans subsequently pursued their grievances with the Canadian government and in the courts.

To invoke Keck and Sikkink's concept, transnational involvement also had a "boomerang" effect on the activists themselves, especially with regard to their attitude to overseas engagement. As we will see, Ui, Miyamoto, Harada, and other RCP members walked away from these travels with a heightened appreciation for the fundamental discrimination feeding environmental injustices against minorities, the poor, women, children, the disabled, the politically disenfranchised, and those depending most directly on nature for survival worldwide. They became committed to forging alliances of victims—regardless of political systems—based on translocal communities of resistance and mutual therapy. Initially skeptical about the tour, Miyamoto even went so far as to declare that the Japanese pollution experience would not be of any real value for the world unless Japanese victims actually met with victims elsewhere, and then only if those researching pollution physically traveled to and conducted research at pollution sites abroad. Individual cases of pollution in particular spaces might be solved, Miyamoto opined, but without direct interaction they would be repeated elsewhere.[10] More personally, RCP members' travels filled them with a deep sense of remorse and responsibility as scientists from the most polluted nation on earth. They were shocked to discover how little was known about Japanese pollution, and they lamented their complicity in the global development of "typical" (*tenkeiteki*) diagnoses of pollution maladies such as Minamata disease, which tended to recognize only the most acute presentations.

Involvement with Native American communities and other pollution sufferers worldwide presented RCP members with an opportunity to recalibrate and enhance their environmental injustice paradigm. This certainly involved the formulation of a new attitude to the outside world, which broke with well-established Japanese patterns of lauding the shining successes of the advanced nations while ignoring the shadows. But, more significantly, it also involved recognizing the global-historical significance and applicability of the Japanese encounter with industrial pollution and environmental injustice—in other words, repositioning the environmental injustice paradigm in contexts and problems beyond Japan. This recognition continued to grow in the coming years as subsequent Japanese groups injected their local experience into a diversity of environmental issues worldwide. Ui Jun and others in the RCP can be credited with taking the first steps in this direction.

## The Discovery of European Pollution

Ui traveled first to Sweden in 1968, where he learned of the country's long-time struggle with mercury pollution. Since the early twentieth century it had been known that mercury compounds were highly effective as grain fungicides, and they were extensively utilized for this purpose in Europe from the 1940s—albeit in small doses—on barley, wheat, corn, and beets. After numerous instances of poisoning, in the 1950s the Swedish authorities (and other governments throughout Europe) decided that all grains treated with such fungicides had to be marked with a red dye, Rhodamine B, and specially handled. At least in Sweden, poisoning instances declined thereafter, but the problem of mercury already released into the environment was not solved. Ui learned how new technology developed by Swedish scientists in the mid-1960s uncovered elevated levels of mercury in fish taken from various lakes throughout the country, leading to concerns about their safety for human consumption.

As an expert in methyl mercury poisoning, Ui arrived in Sweden at an opportune moment. In 1968 Swedish scientists first realized that they had been misinterpreting the research findings of Japanese Minamata disease specialists. The Swedish scientists had overlooked a critical footnote explaining that the reported safe mercury concentration levels were based on yield-to-weight ratios for *dried* samples, and that *fresh* fish would naturally yield lower ratios but with similar levels of toxicity. The Swedish scientists had been mistakenly comparing mercury levels in their samples of fresh fish to the safe levels for dried fish in the Japanese report, in effect greatly underestimating toxicity. Compounding the problem, Ui's imminent arrival in Sweden forced government officials to admit that they had kept confidential a report on Niigata Minamata disease sent to them by a research team from the Japanese Ministry of Health and Welfare. As the officials had feared, Ui brought a copy of the report with him. The high-circulation Swedish daily, *Svenska Dagbladet,* immediately latched on to the story, running a front-page interview with Ui titled "Persistent Struggle Reveals Truth about Minamata." Thanks to the media attention, the Alliance of Swedish Freshwater Fishing Industries presented Ui with a letter for Japanese fishermen that criticized haphazard economic growth and called for a grassroots alliance against mercury worldwide. Ui was also invited to present on the history of Minamata disease at a mercury problems symposium in Stockholm.[11]

Ui's visit to Sweden proved valuable for him and for his Swedish hosts. To begin with, Swedish scientists' constantly raised the issue of why research from Japan only dealt with typical (i.e., severe) cases of mercury poisoning, when it seemed there was a spectrum of symptoms depending on the level of poisoning. For Ui Jun, Harada Masazumi, and other Japanese Minamata researchers, such questions prompted a critical rethinking of their earlier work and even a sense of remorse. Investigating mercury in Sweden also made Ui all the more indignant about mercury contamination in Japan. In Sweden, methyl mercury in the environment stemmed from multiple sources, such as factory effluent and grain fungicide runoff and, hence, was hard to trace to a single source. But, in the cases of Chisso at Minamata Bay and Shōwa Denkō in Niigata Prefecture, the perpetrators were clear, yet it still took over a decade for official government and judicial recognition. Ui later described his shame and embarrassment over this situation in Japan and recalled wanting to "jump into a hole in the ground" every time foreign scientists confronted him with such questions. But, despite his sense of embarrassment, Ui's Swedish visit unquestionably helped open up the debate about mercury contamination in that country and, for Ui personally, posed challenging questions that led to new transnational connections. Notably, after his presentation in Stockholm, a Finnish biologist invited Ui to examine mercury pollution in that country, which he promptly agreed to do.[12]

Before traveling to Finland, however, the trail of European mercury contamination led Ui to Italy. At a conference on water quality in Switzerland in May 1969, Ui approached the organizers after learning there would be no presentations on water quality problems in Japan, by then a global economic power and, as Ui well knew, a polluters' paradise. He was given permission to screen his documentary film, *Polluted Japan,* followed by a presentation on mercury and cadmium poisoning in the country. As he had hoped, the film and presentation sparked an immediate response from European scientists, who were only beginning to appreciate the dangers of environmental mercury contamination. Three Italian scientists approached Ui after the presentation saying that they suspected at least three sites of mercury contamination in Italy, which they promised to show him if he visited the country.[13]

Ui had been hoping to make contact with Italian scientists working on mercury ever since a colleague at the Yokohama National University alerted him to reports about industrial contamination from factories in the Italian province of Ravenna and near the cities of Milan and Venice. These factories engaged in similar industrial processes to those of Shōwa Denkō, the company responsible for Minamata disease in Niigata Prefecture, so Ui was eager to see conditions firsthand. One of Shōwa Denkō's early refutations had been that worldwide there were many factories using the same processes yet nowhere had there been reports of mercury contamination, a claim that Ui and many other antipollution protesters found wholly unconvincing.[14] The meeting with Italian scientists in Switzerland thus provided him with a golden opportunity to test out Shōwa Denkō's claims.

In Italy, Ui traveled with his hosts to a petrochemical complex on the outskirts of Milan that reminded him of scenes back in Japan: "As we approached the factory I began to notice the sour odor I was used to smelling each time I visited the Kyushu Minamata Factory. There was no doubt this factory was producing plasticizing agents, butyl alcohol, or acetic acid from acetaldehyde."[15] Although officials at the plant denied the acetaldehyde was synthesized using a mercury catalyzer, Ui's own investigations revealed that most of its technology came from the Chisso Corporation. On his third day in Italy Ui took the bold step of calling on the company headquarters in central Milan, where he was able to air his concerns with the manager of technology. As in Sweden, these provocative activities by a famous mercury researcher from Japan elicited an immediate response in the media and among Italian scientists. Ui once again found himself front-page news when the progressive Catholic Italian newspaper *Avvenire* ran an interview with him ominously titled "'Chemical Death' to Us as in Japan?"[16] At a conference on oceanic medicine in Naples, Ui shocked his audience with what was perhaps the first scientific presentation on mercury contamination in the country and, as he quipped, "the fact they were hearing it from a little yellow Japanese shrimp" made it all the more impressive.[17]

Ui encouraged Italian scientists to focus on mercury levels in fish, not water, since the latter would usually be low or negligible and hence could mistakenly be overlooked as insignificant. He also suggested that the suspect factories in Milan, Ravenna, and Venice immediately be required to install treatment facilities to ensure no leakage of mercury in their effluent. As in Sweden and Switzerland, Ui again found himself the main focus of discussion and attention at the Naples conference, which clearly gave him a great sense of vindication and accomplishment: "The applause I could hear as I wiped the sweat from my brow and stepped down from the podium felt wonderful. My struggles of the past year faded away completely."[18] That he was also somehow representing the victims—or the potential victims—made his efforts seem worthwhile. "If my investigations result in preventing an outbreak [of mercury poisoning] in Italy, I'll be able to say that my ten years of struggle were rewarded," he concluded. His aim was by no means to "frighten people" but to "communicate the cries of individuals murdered by Japanese pollution." And, for Ui, they were "literally murdered." Although his investigations ultimately uncovered no individuals with typical symptoms of Minamata disease, Ui was thoroughly satisfied: if he could prevent a repeat of such crimes elsewhere, then the agony of presenting in tortured English and of facing off with combative company officials would all have been worth it.[19]

Ui next traveled to Finland, where his hosts took him to the city of Kotka on the country's southwest coast to meet with local fishermen and investigate mercury contamination from upstream pulp mills. At the request of the fishermen Ui agreed to take dried samples of fish back to Japan for testing. As he had done in Italy, at every opportunity Ui appealed to the Finnish people to learn from the Japanese experience. In an interview with a television crew accompanying him on his investigations in Kotka, Ui was asked about Finnish government assurances that mercury levels in fish stocks were within safe limits. To this he replied that, although such levels may not immediately result in symptoms of Minamata disease, once brain cells were destroyed by mercury they could not be regenerated. Moreover, even in Japan, where mercury-contaminated fish were no longer consumed, sufferers were still being diagnosed because symptoms often took longer to develop or to be recognized. As he explained, "We [in Japan] put production before all else and were concerned only about filling our stomachs, hence in the beginning we didn't realize the dreadfulness of industrial wastewater. Please don't ignore our experience. It's too late once a sufferer appears." He told the reporter that learning of the mercury contamination in this "magically beautiful scenery" only made him feel more terrible. "We don't want the people of this country to make the same mistakes we did. Let me repeat. Please don't repeat our terrible precedent."[20]

Ui repeated this mantra in a Helsinki meeting organized by his hosts with Finnish government officials and specialists responsible for the country's water quality. He urged the officials not to use occupational safety limits when setting public health standards for mercury and other environmental pollutants. As he explained, occupational limits balanced the advantages and disadvantages of using a particular substance in industrial processes and implicitly accepted certain levels of poisoning. But, in the case of public health, he argued, the rule of thumb must be that it is unhealthy to absorb any level of mercury above that occurring naturally. In his final appeal to the officials, Ui again invoked the image of Japanese victims: "I would like to relay to you a request from Minamata sufferers. This disease is so painful it is beyond the imagination of healthy people. Among the sufferers was one who died saying that, short of contracting the disease, there was no way for others to understand the pain. But when I left Japan the sufferers who came to see me off said they hoped my activities [abroad] would prevent this disease from occurring again elsewhere in the world. It is with their request that I conclude." Indeed, as he later wrote of his week in Finland, "I thought to myself that it was the memory of the sufferers' pain which supported my activities during this tense week."[21]

On his return to Japan in mid-1969 Ui delivered lectures and published numerous books and articles based on his European travels.[22] Apart from the knowledge he gained about specific forms of pollution, Ui came back convinced that government bureaucracies and other configurations of centralized political power, whether socialist or capitalist, could not be relied upon to defend people from the threat of pollution. On the contrary, the modern nation-state helped to exacerbate pollution by shielding those responsible, so the only option was for victims and their supporters to mobilize on their own initiative. This was an important insight because not only did it confirm and legitimize the logic of self-help and localism among many environmental protest groups in Japan, but it also suggested that building horizontal alliances could even mean joining hands with pollution activists beyond the borders of the nation. Ui personally began to sense a global role for himself and other Japanese scientists: "Whether or not my activities equaled the efforts of Minamata and Niigata sufferers and their supporters hinged on what I did after returning to Japan. The truth is that I felt confident that, if I could continue on in Japan, then Japanese scientists could become world scientists."[23]

Ui wasted no time planning for the next phase of transnational engagement. On the plane flight back to Japan he began to conceive of an ambitious investigative mission by Japanese scientists, journalists, and pollution disease sufferers to study pollution and environmental degradation and meet with victims worldwide. The mission would travel the world for a thousand days, it would be independent of government and industry, and it would comprise individuals fiercely committed to autonomous and dispassionate research. The aims would be twofold: to correctly understand the state of pollution in various parts of the world, and to correctly communicate this information to people in Japan and in other countries. Participants would first write essays on aspects of Japanese pollution, which would then be translated into English and sent to various countries with requests for cooperation. A plan for the mission would then be formulated based on a review of the existing literature on pollution from abroad. During the mission, participants would form small groups of five, spending one to two months in each country investigating the full array of pollution problems. Thereafter they would coauthor an encyclopedia of pollution problems in the late twentieth century, which could serve as a handbook for scientists and officials on how to prevent further cases of pollution worldwide. Ui became convinced that, if his plan succeeded, Japan could fulfill its responsibilities as the world's most advanced polluted nation.[24]

RCP members were not immediately responsive to Ui's grand proposal, however. Shōji Hikaru, Miyamoto Ken'ichi's coauthor on *Osorubeki Kōgai*, for example, wondered if the time was right to take pollution researchers away from Japan where they were most needed.[25] Even Miyamoto was initially noncommittal: Japan had some of the worst pollution in the world, and moreover, the country was beginning to show leadership in dealing with pollution, in regulating industry, and in scientific research, so why the need to go abroad now?[26] For Ui, however, there was no more timely moment than in the midst of this pollution crisis. What better opportunity could there be for Japanese scientists, journalists, advocates, and victims to shape global opinion on the environment? But Ui found an ally in RCP leader Tsuru Shigeto, who likened pollution research to cartography and suggested that "those who study pollution must visit and walk these sites at least once, just like the people who make maps."[27] An unexpected request from abroad also bolstered Ui's plan. In the early 1970s Aileen Smith contacted Miyamoto with a request from the National Indian Brotherhood and Barney Lamm, a tour operator in Canada, to investigate cases of methyl mercury contamination in the English-Wabigoon river system and related poisoning among indigenous communities on nearby reservations.[28] Aileen Smith and her photographer husband, W. Eugene Smith, came to international attention in the early 1970s with their shocking yet sensitive photographic portrayals of Minamata victims.[29] Miyamoto later recalled the transformative effect on him of Smith's request that they go and "teach" not "learn."[30] Miyamoto suddenly realized that, instead of simply borrowing foreign ideas, as had been common practice in Japan from at least the mid-nineteenth century, the pollution crisis offered Japanese scientists a unique opportunity to use their knowledge to influence events abroad in a progressive and positive way.

With the support of most members, then, Ui's plan finally came to fruition in 1975. Although the undertaking would not be as extensive as he had originally envisaged, it was the most comprehensive fact-finding mission on pollution in modern Japanese history and a key moment in connecting the Japanese environmental injustice paradigm to environmental struggles and issues worldwide. With financial sponsorship from the newspaper *Chūnichi Shinbun*, the so-called Sekai Kankyō Chōsadan (World Environment Investigative Mission, or WEIM) conducted two tours abroad in 1975. The first departed on March 8 and spent fifty-two days visiting sixteen countries and forty pollution sites worldwide (mainly in Europe and North America but also in Southeast Asia), while the second departed on August 10 and spent sixteen days engaged in a focused study of mercury poisoning among native Indian communities in Ontario, Canada.[31] The first tour in March was divided into two groups: one devoted primarily to mercury contamination throughout the world, consisting of Miyamoto, Ui, Harada, and Karaki Kiyoshi (a reporter with the *Chūnichi Shinbun*), while the second focused on urban pollution and activism in Europe and North America, and included economists, engineers, local government officials, and specialists on nuclear power. Ui and Harada led the second tour to Canada in August 1975 and were accompanied by two young scholars from Tokyo University, engineer Nakanishi Junko and sociologist Iijima Nobuko; two Minamata disease researchers, Akagi Taketoshi of the Kumamoto University Medical School and Fujino Tadashi of the Minamata Medical Office; and Shigeno Toyoji, an editor with the *Tokyo Shinbun* newspaper.[32] The aim of the mission was fourfold: to visit countries with pollution issues similar to those in Japan and witness conditions on the ground firsthand; to study environmental regulations in other countries; to communicate the story of Japanese pollution through film screenings and presentations; and, most importantly, to interact with foreign researchers, victims, and local residents opposed to industrial contamination.[33] Throughout the tours participants filed regular field reports to the newspapers *Chūnichi Shinbun* and *Tokyo Shinbun*, and afterward Tsuru Shigeto edited a two-volume series titled *Sekai no Kōgai Chizu* (A pollution map of the world), which summarized the experiences and main findings of participants.[34]

Apart from the mercury investigations, (discussed further below), mission participants examined an impressive range of issues and networked with many leading activists in the battle against industrial pollution worldwide. For nature conservation they studied the US National Park system and the British National Trust and, for restoration initiatives, they looked to grassroots initiatives against eutrophication in Lake Erie in North America. In the field of environmental law they scrutinized regulatory regimes in France, Germany, and the United States, focusing particularly on automobile emissions regulations. During a meeting with biologist Barry Commoner at Washington University in Saint Louis, the world-renowned environmental campaigner pessimistically told the group that there was no incentive for US automakers to produce environmentally friendly vehicles because recalibrating production lines would cost too much. Commoner did, however, express hope in the CVCC engines developed by the Honda Motor Company, which easily met the rigorous emissions standards of the US Clean Air Act.[35] More viscerally, during their visit to Los Angeles the group experienced noise and air pollution from automobiles firsthand. Kayama Ken, an engineer from the Tokyo Institute of Technology, wryly observed that shopping malls were about the only places to "escape" from auto fumes but, ironically, the only way to get to a shopping mall was by car.[36] Participants involved in the project also traveled to Budapest, London, Moscow, and New York to study the strengths and weaknesses of urban waste disposal systems. And, although participants did not travel extensively throughout Asia, the mission's published reports also showed recognition of "pollution export" from developed to developing countries, which became a central focus for Ui's ILP movement and various spin-off groups throughout the 1970s. Essentially no stone was left unturned.

When the mission arrived in Finland, a local nature protection association asked the Japanese group to investigate a state-run petrochemical complex. Ui and Miyamoto were taken to the plant by a member of parliament, where they received briefings from a pollution countermeasures official and an ecologist from Helsinki University. To their great surprise, the guide at the complex explained how its designers had learned from the Yokkaichi experience, making significant improvements and design modifications as a result. Miyamoto was skeptical at first but changed his mind during the tour. Unlike the Yokkaichi complex, located beside a city, planners carefully chose a site around twenty-eight miles (forty-five kilometers) north of Helsinki in the center of a 1,500 acre (625 hectare) pine forest. Smokestacks had been purposely built short so as to contain emissions within the pine forest buffer zone and to preserve the scenic view. To avoid water contamination and the infamous smelly fish of Yokkaichi, factories in the complex recycled water and filtered all effluent through a treatment pond before releasing it into the Gulf of Finland. Fish were also raised in the treatment ponds to monitor pollution levels. Miyamoto was generally impressed by these pollution countermeasures and, in fact, concluded that foreign countries seemed to have learned more lessons from Yokkaichi than the Japanese government or industry.[37]

Among the more interesting findings for participants was the prevalence and strength of anti–nuclear power movements abroad. As Hōsei University economist Nagai Susumu described it, a "storm of antinuclear power movements" was "sweeping across Europe and America."[38] During their visit to Switzerland, mission participants traveled to the city of Basel in the Rhine Valley, where they met with residents protesting the construction of a nuclear power plant. They learned from the worried protesters that some nine nuclear facilities were located in a fifty-kilometer radius of the city.[39] Determined to stop construction of the tenth facility, the opposition group had occupied the planned site, pitching their tents and hoisting protest flags atop a mountain of dirt excavated for the foundations. The Japanese visitors were impressed by the transnational composition of the group, which included activists from Switzerland, France, and Germany.[40]

Antinuclear fervor was no less apparent in the United States. In California, participants met with the former state governor, Edmund Gerald "Pat" Brown, who identified nuclear power plant siting and construction as the most contentious and difficult problems facing California. He described how the utility company, Pacific Gas and Electric, was forced to abandon construction of a nuclear power plant in Bodega Bay in 1964 after residents protested the company's inability to guarantee the safety of the facility in this seismically active area. In the wake of the 1973 oil shock, however, Brown sensed moves to rethink the place of nuclear power in the country.[41] At the offices of the Ralph Nader Group in Washington, DC, activists told their Japanese visitors that the anti–nuclear power movement was the very core of the antipollution movement in the United States and that their ultimate aim was to halt construction of all nuclear power plants nationwide. The Nader activists put forward three critical reasons for opposing nuclear energy: the grave threat of radioactive materials for the environment, given their half-life periods in the hundreds and thousands of years; the particular risks of fast-breeder reactors using plutonium, one of the most toxic substances for human beings, which could also be utilized in nuclear weapons; and, more prosaically, the simple fact that nuclear power was not a cheap source of energy, as proponents claimed.[42]

The encounter with anti–nuclear power movements was at once unanticipated and challenging for the mission participants, whose own country was on the verge of a nuclear power revolution in the mid-1970s. Officials, activists, and scientists they met in the United States were eager to learn from the group just how Japanese officials had been able to convince the Japanese public about the necessity and safety of nuclear power given the country's terrible experiences with atomic energy and radiation at Hiroshima and Nagasaki.[43] To that question the Japanese visitors could provide no answer, and, quite unexpectedly, they were forced to seriously consider this issue of nuclear power, which had been largely sidelined by their concerns about more immediate pollution threats. As Karaki Kiyoshi from the newspaper *Chūnichi Shinbun* observed, the Japanese media often spoke of a "nuclear allergy" in the country, and many citizens believed that both they and officials were being extremely careful about the commitment to nuclear power. But, from the perspective of outsiders, the situation looked very different: the Japanese seemed to have bypassed serious discussions about safety and were moving full steam ahead on nuclear power plant construction. Some foreign scientists even wondered whether Japan's energy challenges were so serious as to demand such an uncritical commitment to nuclear power.[44] In light of such questions, Nagai Susumu suggested that now was the time for Japanese citizens to seriously reconsider the safety of nuclear power, the social structure supporting its promotion, and Japan's future economic and energy policies.[45]

Despite the best intentions of mission participants, however, nuclear power was relegated to the realm of NIMBY (not-in-my-back-yard) confrontations and the peripheralized voices of a few stalwart opponents and was never subjected to broad and intensive political debate in Japan until a major disaster in 2011. One possible reason for activists' relatively lukewarm attention to the issue within Japan lay in the difference between nuclear power and the other environmental pollution issues they were addressing. There were certainly many thousands of radiation victims from Hiroshima and Nagasaki, but unlike Minamata, Yokkaichi, and other pollution incidents, nuclear power plants had no victims, or at least, no victims with harrowing stories of environmental injustice and suffering powerful enough to elicit a widespread grassroots and public response. Indeed, as I show in chapter 5, it was beyond Japan's borders that the environmental injustice paradigm connected with antinuclear issues, notably in protests against planned radioactive waste dumping in the Pacific Ocean.

## Following the Trail of Mercury

So, as much as they appreciated the message of antinuclear activists worldwide, it was not the risks of radiation but the visible human injustices of mercury and other chemical pollutants that most concerned mission participants in the early 1970s. Ui, Harada, Miyamoto, and others followed the trail of mercury pollution throughout Europe and North America, with particular emphasis on cases in Finland, New Mexico in the United States, and Ontario Province in Canada. Just as with Ui's earlier European journey in the late 1960s, these investigations into mercury resulted in some of the most fruitful and substantive exchanges of the RCP's transnational involvement. The experiences also stimulated the Japanese travelers to rethink the causes of pollution, the dynamics of discrimination, the responsibility of scientists, and the potential of border-crossing communities of victims and advocates.

While Ui and Miyamoto investigated the petrochemical industry in Finland, their colleague, clinician and Minamata disease researcher Harada Masazumi, delved into the Finnish struggle with mercury.[46] On his first day in Finland, Harada joined scholars at Helsinki University in a workshop on environmental pollution and the health effects of poisoning from heavy metals such as cadmium and mercury. Harada learned how, in 1966 alone, Finnish pulping industries had used up to 3.6 tons of organic mercury as a sterilizing agent in their manufacturing processes. Finnish authorities instituted countermeasures beginning in 1968, after which environmental levels of mercury slowly began to fall, but numerous sites of contamination remained, such as Lake Kirkkojärvi in the municipality of Hämeenkyrö in southwest Finland. Individuals tested in that area exhibited elevated mercury levels in their hair and blood samples, but there had been no officially diagnosed cases of typical Minamata disease. The Finnish scientists did, however, tell Harada about one possible case of poisoning, so, with a microbiological chemist as his guide, Harada immediately traveled to Lake Kirkkojärvi to investigate.

In Hämeenkyrö, Harada met with an old couple who lived by Lake Kirkkojärvi in a small wooden structure that looked to him "like something out of a fairy tale."[47] The couple had come to live there in 1962 after the husband retired from the railway company. Of modest means, the couple had been supplementing their food requirements with fish from the lake, beekeeping, and by raising chickens. Unfortunately, their cabin was located some twelve miles (twenty kilometers) south of a pulp mill responsible for dumping organic mercury into the lake and surrounding river systems. Authorities prohibited fishing in the lake in 1967, but in 1970 local residents began to observe strange behavior among cats, which were seen convulsing and on occasion diving from bridges into the lake and nearby rivers. These cats had, of course, been poisoned by organic mercury after consuming fish from the lake and were displaying typical symptoms of Minamata disease. Harada was shocked to learn that the old couple had not been tested for poisoning until very recently, despite the testing of others in the region—probably, he assumed, because they were poor and lived a somewhat peripheral existence in their small cottage.

Clinical reports based on hair and blood sample tests eventually confirmed that the husband, at least, had mercury poisoning. Nevertheless, medical authorities had attributed his various maladies to other conditions such as coronary disease, angina, asthma, diabetes, hyperlipidemia (high blood cholesterol), arthropathy (joint disease), and functional damage to the stomach. Harada's own examinations of the man revealed numbness around the mouth and hands, a loss of sensation in the legs, minor convulsions in various muscles, a loss of hearing and smell, and a heightened sensitivity to cold—all suggestive of mercury poisoning yet not conclusive. Indeed, the case of this Finnish man was emblematic for Harada of a tendency among clinicians—regardless of the country—to explain pollution disease away by attributing it to other diseases and conditions that actually arose as complications of the initial poisoning. The standard medical practice of using differential diagnosis to specify a particular disease based on symptoms also explainable for any number of other diseases was not only ineffective in the case of pollution disease, but also tended to obscure the seriousness of the situation from a public health perspective. Pollution disease, Harada concluded, was "an entirely new experience for humankind," and medical science was yet to formulate new methods and diagnostics to correctly identify it.[48]

As a Japanese specialist on Minamata disease, Harada could not help but feel implicated in this worldwide misapprehension of pollution disease, especially among those in the medical fraternity. He felt that Japanese scientists had helped to solidify a medical definition of Minamata disease based strictly and narrowly on the typical symptoms of the so-called Hunter-Russell syndrome, and the result was that victims of mercury poisoning, like the old man he examined in Finland, were being incorrectly diagnosed with other diseases.[49] From the early 1970s, Harada and other researchers, in cooperation with sufferers at Minamata Bay, had begun to show that, apart from the typical symptoms, mercury poisoning induced other systemic conditions such as angiosclerosis (hardening of the blood vessel walls), muscular pain, heart disease, and diabetes. Harada's research also revealed that mercury poisoning victims were more susceptible to infectious disease even though a causal relationship between the poisoning and the susceptibility to infection could not be categorically displayed.[50] According to Miyamoto Ken'ichi, Harada and his colleagues were essentially engaged in a project to undo or, at least, modify the groundbreaking work of early Minamata disease researchers in Japan who "should have constructed a medical diagnosis from the conditions of Japanese sufferers."[51] Instead of simply importing the Hunter-Russell diagnosis for Minamata disease, Miyamoto felt that Japanese scientists should have built their own diagnosis based primarily on their own field observations in Minamata and then communicated these findings to the world.

After examining many victims of mercury poisoning worldwide, Harada could only agree, suggesting that there were really no "typical" cases of pollution diseases such as mercury poisoning, just stages along a spectrum of severity. Typicality was also problematic from a public health perspective, because it only recognized the severest presentations of a disease and, hence, only stimulated a response from officials once poisoning had reached dangerous levels.[52] What Harada, Miyamoto, Ui, and others on the mission discovered as they traveled the world was how a "decades-old diagnosis shaped by political conditions in Japan" had disseminated worldwide.[53] They realized that now Japanese scientists had an obligation to undo this situation by correctly and swiftly communicating the facts about Minamata disease to an international audience so that victims elsewhere, like the old man and his wife, would not be abandoned and ignored.[54] Japanese scientists had to communicate a "complete picture of Minamata disease" by establishing the absolute minimum symptoms of organic mercury poisoning in the human body.[55] Ui was even more specific in his prognostications: at least once or twice a year, Japanese researchers had to publish their findings in high-circulation English-language scientific journals such as *Nature* and *Science* so as to reach a global audience of scientists.[56] Ui was convinced that the current situation of mercury contamination worldwide could have been avoided if Japanese scientists had been more active in the international scientific community, for example, by presenting their findings at international conferences in English.[57]

From this perspective, the face-to-face meeting and interaction with the elderly couple in Finland was of deep significance for Harada because it was a positive step by a Japanese scientist to address the diagnostic problem of mercury poisoning worldwide. After sharing some honey, cheese, and crackers with the couple, the man passed some frozen fish to Harada, telling him to use them for research but *not* consumption. As the man explained, no doctor had ever shown such concern for him before, and the fact that a Japanese doctor had come so far to examine him was the "proudest moment" of his life.[58] Harada left the meeting with an even stronger sense of responsibility, concluding that "we are all brothers, and the problem of environmental contamination is a shared problem around the world. We must make the most of the lessons of Minamata."[59]

If the case of the couple in Finland spoke to Harada and other participants' responsibility as Japanese scientists, then their experiences in North America confirmed their learning from the domestic struggle that pollution affected and discriminated against the very weakest and marginalized members of society. Before traveling to Canada, Miyamoto and Harada visited New Mexico in the United States to investigate the case of an African American family afflicted with mercury poisoning. The case was quite straightforward, and there was no doubt methyl mercury was to blame for the poisoning. But what interested and concerned Miyamoto and Harada was the apparent structure of discrimination that caused the poisoning in the first place. The incident, involving the Huckleby family of Alamogordo City, New Mexico, was first reported nationally in 1970 in the *New York Times* and on NBC television. After consuming pork from a family-owned pig in 1969, four members of the Huckleby family began to display various degrees of mercury poisoning symptoms. Ernestine, the eight-year-old daughter, was stricken first, initially experiencing back pain and difficulty walking and then falling into a coma, although doctors were initially unable to diagnose her condition. A few days later the thirteen-year-old son, Amos, began to experience constricted vision and ataxia (loss of voluntary muscle coordination), followed soon after by the twenty-year-old daughter Dorothy, who displayed similar symptoms. All three were hospitalized. The children's mother, Lois, was pregnant at the time, and when the child, Michael, was

born, he displayed limited movement functions along with sensory disturbances to smell, sight, and hearing—symptoms typical of fetal methyl
mercury poisoning.

The source of the contamination was quickly traced to waste grain that
the father, Ernest Huckleby, had acquired free of charge when it was discarded by a granary in the nearby town of Texico. The grain had been treated
with the highly toxic mercurial fungicide Panogen 15, used to prevent mold
growth on seed and grain. Ernest used the contaminated grain to feed eighteen pigs over a four- to six-week period. He later recalled that after a few
weeks some of the animals began to display erratic behavior: fourteen piglets
went blind and were unable to walk. Within a month twelve had died and
those that survived continued to show impeded development. In the mean-
time Ernest slaughtered one of the pigs for family consumption.[60]

The Huckleby family eventually sued the grain company on the basis
that, being illiterate, Ernest Huckleby was unable to read the warning labels on the fifty-four-gallon (204 liter) storage drums, nor did he understand
why the grain had been dyed pink. The suit was unsuccessful, however, with
the court finding that the company had indeed fulfilled its legal responsibility by attaching a label clearly warning that the contents were for seeding
only, had been treated with a toxic substance, and should not be consumed
or used as feed under any circumstances. Specifically, the court noted the
label's caution that the contents contained a "Category I poison," "highly
toxic to man," that the word "poison" was printed prominently in red, and
that the label included a skull-and-crossbones mark.[61] As Miyamoto cyni-
cally observed, ultimately the court rejected the lawsuit on the basis that
a poor, uneducated, illiterate black man was in the wrong; that it was his
deficiency and his fault for being unable to read or understand the warnings.[62] But from Miyamoto's perspective, a completely different interpretation
seemed plausible. The company knew that a large population of underprivileged and illiterate African Americans living in the region raised their own
animals on grain, hence it had a greater responsibility to inform them of the
dangers and to ensure that contaminated grain was not used for feed.[63]

The plight of the family affected Miyamoto and Harada on a deeply
emotional level, especially in their capacity as so-called Japanese pollution
experts. Here was a clear instance of how the horrors of Minamata had not
been effectively and persuasively communicated to the world. After all, if
people outside Japan had truly understood Minamata, such incidents would
not have been repeated and companies would not have continued to use such

toxic chemicals. Miyamoto was in no doubt that if Americans had known more about Minamata disease they would certainly have abandoned the use of dangerous mercury and the Huckleby children would have been spared their brutal suffering.[64] It was a clear example of how Japanese scientists had not fulfilled their responsibility to the world, so they too were liable. After consulting with the children's doctors and examining their medical records, Harada and Miyamoto met with the son, Amos, who was receiving special care at a county school for the disabled. They observed that, although he was blind, his speech impaired, and his mobility limited, "his mind was clear." "The thing he wanted to know most from us was about Japanese Minamata sufferers' rehabilitation back into society. He wanted us to tell him about any cases of people blinded [by the disease] who had found a job and were working. This was a clear sign of his powerful mentality and desire to live. But we had no answers to his impassioned questions."[65] Nor could they provide Amos's mother Lois with the answer she so desperately wanted to hear—that Minamata disease could be cured. "It was the most important question in the life of this woman caring for four victims. But the pity is that there is no cure for Minamata disease at present. With the most pained expressions we answered 'current medicine cannot cure the disease. But with appropriate care certain functions can be restored.'"[66]

Traveling on the road from Alamogordo to El Paso with its "never-ending sand dunes," Miyamoto and Harada reflected on their encounter with the Huckleby family: the young children, lying helplessly prostrate in their hospital beds just like the severely poisoned children in Minamata, the courageous Amos who dreamed of a bright future, and the anguished mother with no other option but to "pray to God every day."[67] "Her somberness and the warmth of her hands is something we will never forget," Miyamoto and Harada later wrote of their meeting with Lois.[68] They could provide no relief or remedy to this woman and her family, but stepping across national borders and reaching out to other human beings fighting the same battle as those in Japan redefined "Minamata" in ways Harada and Miyamoto could not have imagined even five years earlier. The injustice of industrial pollution knew no borders, so neither could their struggle against it.

## Connecting Minamata and Ontario

The culmination of the investigatory mission was participants' study of mercury poisoning at two Indian reservations in Canada. Not only did members meet, examine, and interact with the Indians as they had done with pollution victims elsewhere, they also accompanied them to negotiations with Ontario and Canadian government officials, facilitated historic meetings in Canada and in Japan with sufferers from Minamata Bay, and encouraged the Indians to instigate court proceedings for compensation. Here, more than anywhere else, the Japanese participants fulfilled their self-assigned responsibility as scientists from the world's most polluted nation, and here too they witnessed the potential of transnational action in the global struggle against discrimination and injustice—for them the root causes of pollution.

During March and August of 1975, mission participants conducted investigations at both the Grassy Narrows and White Dog Indian reservations, located along the English-Wabigoon River system about sixty-two miles (100 kilometers) northwest of Kenora City in the Canadian province of Ontario. The source of the mercury contamination was a pulp mill located around 124 miles (200 kilometers) upstream from the reservations in the city of Dryden. The pulp mill operator, the Dryden Paper and Pulp Company, was a subsidiary of a joint venture between Canadian business interests and the British multinational, Reed International.[69] Of the approximately seven thousand inhabitants of Dryden, some 1,600 either worked in the factory or were engaged in activities associated with it, prompting Miyamoto to liken the city to the "corporate castle towns" in Japan such as Yokkaichi City.[70] Although the company initially denied it was the cause of the contamination, claiming that natural levels of mercury in the region were high, tests on river fish showing elevated concentrations closer to the factory quickly invalidated such claims.[71] Flying into the area, mission participants were shocked by the extent of effluent from the factory's pipes, with clumps of frozen brown debris visible for at least sixty miles (97 kilometers) downstream. In a report for the newspaper *Chūnichi Shinbun*, Karaki Kiyoshi described the thick smoke plume bellowing from the factory's smokestacks into the clear blue sky and the "reddish-brown effluent" spewing into the Winnipeg River, turning the melted ice brown.[72]

The Dryden pulp mill began operations in 1962, but it was not until 1969 that the Ontario government initiated a study on possible contamination and poisoning in the river system, primarily in response to the rising global concern over mercury but also in response to the grassroots work of tour operator Barney Lamm. Blood and hair samples were taken from eighty-eight Indians on the reservations, of which nine individuals with elevated mercury readings—some with up to one hundred parts per million (ppm) in their hair samples—were hospitalized for further tests. The official 1971 report concluded that, while these individuals did indeed register high bodily mercury concentrations, no physiological effects had been identified, and there were no typical cases of Minamata disease.[73] Nevertheless, the Ontario government ordered the factory to stop dumping mercury-laden effluent (which it did not do until after the 1975 visit of the Japanese mission). The government also immediately banned commercial fishing in the region, and it advised tour operators to ensure that sport fishermen did not consume their catch.[74]

The Indian communities were decimated by the contamination of their waterways, and most working in the fishing and tourism industries lost their jobs. The spiritual and physiological devastation engendered depression, alcoholism, violence, poverty, and suicide, not to mention a deep animosity toward white Canadians. As the Indian chief explained in his welcome speech to the Japanese mission, "The earth is our father, the water is our mother. God told us to live by drinking the water of mother earth. Then the white man poisoned mother earth with mercury. After we are dead, the white man will die too. Never forget that, white man!"[75] Moreover, the contamination of fish stocks not only eliminated a key source of cash income, it also compromised an indispensable source of protein for the community. Mission participants learned that, in the absence of another food source, many Indians were left with no choice but to continue consuming contaminated fish. Tour operators also demanded that Indians employed as guides cook and eat the fish caught by sport fishermen to avoid alarming tourists. Miyamoto and Harada summed up the desperate conditions on the reservations as follows: "The Indians receive their social security payments once a week after which they drink until they drop or even die. On the reservations they resort to hair spray, perfume, and insecticides in search of alcohol, mixing these with water. Then, when they get drunk they fight and commit arson. When they wake up the next morning they have no job, just like every other day, so they light a cigarette and sit in the sun. They spend the whole day sitting in the same way with lethargic hollow expressions."[76]

Harada Masazumi conducted clinical medical examinations on eighty-nine Indians during his visits to the reservations, working side by side with a local doctor and advocate for the Indians, Peter Newberry, during the March tour, and with the Rochester University toxicologist Thomas W. Clarkson during the August visit.[77] Harada's surveys of the Indians revealed that, although most no longer consumed fish, close to one-third continued to do so. His clinical tests did not uncover any serious (i.e., typical) cases of Minamata disease, but thirty-seven individuals presented with sensory disturbances and nine others with constriction of the visual field—both of which are symptoms consistent with heavy metal poisoning.[78] On the basis of these examinations, Harada concluded that there was a very high likelihood of mercury poisoning among inhabitants of the reservations. When Harada and mission participants confronted the Dryden Paper and Pulp Company with these results, they were stunned by the nonchalance of company representatives, who declared, "Our factory has faithfully followed government thresholds. So, if damages have been suffered within the thresholds then the government must pay compensation [to the victims]. If we are found liable for negligence in a court of law we will take responsibility but, in that case too, the government will bear some responsibility."[79]

Government agencies proved no more hospitable, but the arrival of the Japanese group did force a number of concessions, including a historic meeting between Indian representatives, the official government mercury countermeasures committee, and members of the Japanese mission. Amazingly, although this government committee was four years old, only under pressure from the Japanese mission did its members relent and agree to meet with the Indians in person. Moreover, thanks again to the Japanese visitors, prior to the historic meeting, the committee released previously classified reports on scientific investigations conducted by the Canadian National Institute of Hygiene to determine the toxicity of fish in the region. The reports revealed that primates and cats fed a diet consisting of 35 percent of fish from the area contracted Minamata disease in around fifty days, and animals from both species subsequently died.[80] At the meeting the Indians confronted committee members with difficult questions that hit at the heart of discrimination: "We have been crying out for four years, but the Canadian government has not listened at all. But our voices reached far off Japan and these four scientists came to help. This was not because the Canadian and Japanese governments paid, but with their own funds. But now we've learned that a massive $600,000 has been used on research, and that you have written research papers. Is this research to ease our concerns or is it only so you can profit? Tell us the truth."[81] In his presentation, Harada appealed to the committee members' responsibility as scientists and pointed out the risks of using "typical" diagnoses: "We've had the same debate in Japan over and over. While we were debating about whether or not 'typical' sufferers had surfaced or if the causal chain was clear . . . a terrible tragedy occurred." As Harada explained, by the time a "typical" case was identified, multiple other cases of fetal poisoning and nonspecific cases would have occurred, so there was no time to wait. Based on his work on the reservations, he told the committee there were four indisputable facts: contaminated fish, inhabitants with elevated mercury levels in blood and hair samples, cat deaths caused by mercury poisoning, and a variety of nonspecific cases. These facts, he demanded, meant that the discovery of a "typical" sufferer was "only a matter of time."[82] The government committee was unmoved, however, and announced there would be no cooperation with the Japanese mission because, at this stage, no patients had presented with typical symptoms of mercury poisoning.[83]

For Ui, Miyamoto, and Harada, this official response confirmed the universal law that discrimination was the principal cause of environmental destruction, psychological devastation, and human illness. Mission members were convinced that, had white people been poisoned, this incident and its cover-up would never have occurred.[84] How else was the dismissive attitude of Dryden Paper and Pulp Company to be explained, or the meeting with government officials, which Ui described as a "venue for racial discrimination"?[85] And what of the local doctors, who advised that the Indians had no medical problem other than alcoholism and that the Japanese group would do best to focus on that issue? As Miyamoto and Harada observed, "Such conditions not only made us realize the difficulties of our investigations, they also bore a striking resemblance to Minamata in the 1960s."[86] Observing the "the desperate pleadings" of this "yellow race" in their broken English to white government officials transported mission participants back to Japan and the struggles of Minamata disease sufferers.[87] Regardless of the place, pollution seemed to materialize at the very apex of a chain of discrimination, the final step in the rapid destruction of the traditional lives of local people such as farmers, fishermen, people of color, and indigenous communities. Indeed, it seemed that the destruction of community and tradition were critical prerequisites for pollution to occur and to inflict its devastation on innocent human bodies. Harada expressed this sentiment most poignantly as follows:

> The root of pollution lies in the destruction of lifestyle and culture produced when a discriminated group is forced to accept a certain set of values—whether between nations, races, or classes. In Canada too, the

Indians were forced further and further to the peripheries by the whites and, driven on to reservations, their traditional lifestyle and unique culture was completely destroyed. One result was the occurrence of mercury contamination. Locals could no longer fish and lost their jobs as tour guides. Over 80 percent of the population started receiving social security and, with nothing to do, drowned in a sea of alcohol. Pollution disease not only ravages human flesh; it is also a social disease which destroys the spirit. Wherever pollution occurs in the world, in the background there are always victims who belong to the discriminated and powerless masses; defenseless people who have been spiritually wounded.[88]

Harada's was a bleak assessment of the mission's experience in Canada indeed, but the story of this exchange between Japanese scientists and Canadian Indians does not end so pessimistically. This border-crossing engagement instilled both sides with a sense of hope and the vision of a new, translocal community capable of transcending the isolation and alienation of discrimination and injustice. In July 1975, nine representatives from the Grassy Narrows and White Dog reservations visited Japan to see the polluted Japanese archipelago firsthand and to meet directly with mercury poisoning victims in Minamata and Niigata. They were greeted at Haneda Airport in Tokyo by members of Ui Jun's ILP network, Tokyo supporters of Minamata disease sufferers, and Kawamoto Teruo, leader of the Chisso Minamatabyō Kanja Renmei (Chisso Minamata Disease Sufferers Alliance). Traveling to Minamata Bay in Kumamoto Prefecture, the Indians met with Japanese victims and explained how they too lived off fish and were at the same risk as Minamata residents. In a tender exchange, an Indian named Tom took the hand of a bedridden fetal mercury poisoning victim, Chizuru, saying softly "Hello, I'm Tom. I'll send you a letter from Canada."[89] Outside the Chisso factory, the same Tom scooped up a handful of sludge from a pipe and, smelling the material, concluded it was no worse than sludge from the Dryden pulp mill. At an event for the Indians held at the Minamata public hall with three hundred guests, the chief, Andy, spoke of their shock but also of their inspiration: "What we have experienced at Minamata is beyond imagination. Seeing the destructive power of mercury was a heartbreaking lesson for us. The Canadian government denied Minamata disease at Dryden. Why, despite possessing the knowledge of modern medicine and science, did they not clearly advise people on the reservations of the danger? But we will not give up our struggle against the government. The real struggle has just begun."[90] As the Indians explained to Ui during his March visit to Canada, not until the Japanese came did the government react, so now the onus was on the Indians themselves to stand up and build on the energy from their Japanese friends.[91] At a press conference prior to their departure from Japan, their leader struck an optimistic note, commenting, "We were extremely shocked and frightened because we had not thought that mercury poisoning could so totally destroy human beings. But thanks to the warm cooperation of all in Japan, we now have the confidence to win the long and difficult battle against mercury pollution and racial discrimination."[92]

Following the Indians visit to Japan, in October 1975, four Minamata victims and their supporters visited the Grassy Narrows and White Dog reservations. While in Canada, the Japanese group joined the Indian sufferers in their negotiations with the Dryden Paper and Pulp Company, Reed International, and Ontario state officials. In the meeting the Minamata group screened excerpts from Tsuchimoto Noriaki's disturbing documentary *Igaku toshite no Minamatabyō* (Minamata as medicine) and presented a letter of appeal asking Reed International to take responsibility for dumping the mercury, to pay compensation, and to negotiate directly with the affected Indian communities. At the Grassy Narrows reservation, two hundred members of the community came out to celebrate the Minamata group's visit.[93] Ui best summed up the historical significance of these exchanges in a December interview with the progressive magazine, *AMPO: Japan-Asia Quarterly Review*. As he explained, "for poor and minority peoples, who are nearly always the first victims," the process of overcoming "their isolation by getting together and concretely realizing the worldwide polluting effects of multinational corporations" was a development of truly "great significance."[94] Knowing that people thousands of miles away shared in their struggle gave victims strength and the reassurance of belonging to an authentic community opposing environmental injustice.

## Conclusion

The overseas travels of Ui Jun and Miyamoto Ken'ichi in the late 1960s and the encounters of the World Environment Investigative Mission in the 1970s taught Japanese activists a great deal. While confirming Japan's unenviable position as a global "pollution laboratory," activists also learned that Japan was no outlier: pollution was rapidly spreading and becoming more and more complex in both developed and developing countries alike. Established political paradigms and ideologies could no longer adequately explain pollution and environmental injustice, which occurred under socialism as commonly as under capitalism. Going abroad helped Japanese activists realize that contemporary pollution demanded new interpretations and innovative political strategies that responded to the spatial and technological realities of modern industry and the complex relationships between humans and their living environments in an urbanized world. The conflicts over nuclear power that Japanese activists witnessed in Europe and the United States, although never adequately grasped at the time, alerted them to the complicated intersection of energy, the environment, and economic growth that would become so central to subsequent debates about the "limits to growth" and "sustainable development." In particular, their experiences with mercury in Canada, Finland, and, earlier, in Japan itself, raised troubling questions about the geopolitics of pollution and environmental injustice. Mercury contamination hit hardest in geographically peripheralized and impoverished communities, which were literally sacrificed for the affluent, globally connected metropoles they serviced. In Ontario, Kotka, Minamata, and Niigata they witnessed similar processes at work.

Investigating mercury contamination in other national settings greatly expanded their framing of the problem. What was previously understood as "Chisso Corporation versus the residents of Minamata Bay" or "Shōwa Denkō versus people along the Jinzū River" could now be positioned within a framework of global, multinational capitalism: executives of Reed International wreaked havoc in indigenous communities in Ontario from boardrooms a world away in the United Kingdom, factories in Milan borrowed technology from Chisso Corporation in Japan, and government officials in Finland concealed reports from the Japanese Ministry of Health and Welfare. As we will see in chapters 4 and 5, opposing "pollution export" by Japanese corporations would come to dominate Japanese transnational initiatives throughout the 1970s and 1980s.

Yet, while travel abroad alerted Japanese activists to the intensification and interconnectedness of industrial pollution worldwide, it confirmed the importance of local communities as the building blocks of effective resistance to environmental injustice. Ui, Miyamoto, Harada, and others came away convinced that the first step toward stopping pollution and discrimination lay in the forging of human-to-human ties between affected local communities. The Japanese term *kōryū*—meaning exchange, interchange, or mingling among people—appears again and again in their writings of the time. Despite the different social, linguistic, cultural, and political conditions of countries, Ui saw great value in exchange and interaction as a way to inspire pollution victims to act for themselves. After all, only when the Canadian Indians met with Minamata sufferers and saw polluted sites in Japan firsthand did they understand the seriousness of the issue and make a firm commitment to act.[95] Harada similarly observed that, while Japanese corporate and government elites feared the negative repercussions of communicating the story of Japanese pollution abroad, from a long-term perspective, such "negative exchange" or "mutual interchange among victims" represented the best way to forge authentic international friendship and goodwill.[96] Pollution was certainly a "fearsome" phenomenon built on the foundation of human discrimination and injustice, but through it new transnational communities of resistance, trust, and mutual therapy had begun to take root.

Indeed, it was in the very creation of such communities that these Japanese scientists envisioned a new international responsibility for themselves as the representatives of victims from the world's most polluted nation. As we have seen in this and the previous chapter, Harada, Ui, and others harbored a deep sense of remorse for their own self-perceived failures, for example, in the worldwide propagation of the typical symptoms required to diagnose Minamata disease. But their travels and missions abroad demonstrated a new way of seeing the outside world radically at odds with the intellectual conventions of modern Japan. As Miyamoto explained, for Japanese from the Meiji era (1868–1912) onward, foreign journeys—especially to the West—were all about learning. "But ours was not this kind of passive journey," he observed; it was about "communicating the Japanese experience" and "seeing conditions abroad with our own eyes, and mutually exchanging information." In this sense, "learning" took on a slightly different meaning from that to date.[97] Meiji-era statesmen, for instance, were only interested in the "bright" aspects of the countries they visited and how these could be useful for an emerging nation. According to Miyamoto, they completely ignored the "shadows" of Western development, primarily because they were part of the elite ruling classes and were oblivious to the "voices of the people."[98] But, as Miyamoto reflected, "Our journey is about listening to the voices of the people. What we are 'learning' is not only about . . . the environmental policies of central and local governments, but we are also listening to the voices of victims and to the opinions of the very few scientists and politicians who are struggling with and helping them."[99]

Miyamoto admitted that he was still not confident to speak about the necessity and value of their journeys abroad, especially given his limited linguistic ability and the very short time spent overseas. But, when they "visited a rainy Los Angeles suburb located beside an oil refinery," and when they met with Nicky, the principal physician for the Huckleby family in El Paso, Miyamoto "keenly felt" the significance of their journey, which knit together a therapeutic translocal community against discrimination and injustice.[100] The reality was that they were not alone, and this was a remarkably invigorating discovery for pollution victims and their indefatigable advocates. The final statement of the Canadian Indian visitors after their 1975 visit to Japan captured this sentiment perfectly:

> We came on the invitation of the Minamata disease patients' alliance.
>
> Our hearts have been warmed by the beauty of the land and the warmth and hospitality of our hosts.
>
> But, we came to learn about a horrible truth: Minamata disease—industrial methyl mercury poisoning in human beings.
>
> We have seen the destruction caused by this industrial pollution on the human body and the suffering of entire communities. And as fellow human beings we are deeply hurt.
>
> We are also horrified at the similarities of the Minamata experience in the early stages, and our present situation at Grassy Narrows and Whitedog in Canada.
>
> The facts of our situation in Canada are quite simple. The Dryden Chemical Company has polluted our waters and fish with mercury. They have destroyed our food and livlihood [sic]. During this time they have made increasing profits and received millions of dollars in government aid.
>
> We suffered for five years without relief from either the Dryden Chemical Company or our government.
>
> Now support and help is coming from our brothers and sisters, the Minamata disease patients, some seven thousand miles away.
>
> The struggle of Japanese victims has been difficult enough. Our struggle is compounded by a history of racism.
>
> This beginning of contact with the Minamata disease patients is the beginning of our struggle in Canada.[101]

CHAPTER 3

# The Human Limits to Growth
## Japanese Activists at UNCHE

In a famous speech to the Economic and Social Council of the United Nations in Switzerland in 1965, US ambassador to the UN Adlai Stevenson articulated an embryonic vision of globalism characterized by a "heightened sensitivity to the fragility of the life-support system of the planet" and a "sense of human solidarity in a world of increasing interdependence."[1] Invoking the imagery of a spacecraft, Stevenson observed how "we travel together, passengers on a little space ship, dependent on its vulnerable reserves of air and soil; all committed for our safety to its security and peace; preserved from annihilation only by the care, the work, and, I will say, the love we give our fragile craft."[2] One year later the economist Kenneth Boulding penned his influential essay, "The Economics of the Coming Spaceship Earth," in which he argued passionately for a transition from the "cowboy economy," based on a frontier mentality of rampant consumption, to the "spaceman economy" informed by prudence and respect for the limited resources of the planet.[3] A combination of images, ideas, and events nurtured this perspective, none more so than the photographs of the Earth taken from the Lunar Orbiter satellites and Apollo missions throughout the 1960s.[4] As Ursula Heise has argued, this early moment of global environmental sensitivity was the point when it became possible—for some, at least—to comprehend the whole planet "as one's backyard."[5] For the science fiction writer Arthur C. Clarke, this was the historic moment when "the Earth really became a planet."[6]

Of course, romantic spaceship imagery and communitarian visions of "One Earth" were but one aspect of a global environmental movement marked by a good deal of pessimism, accusation, and disagreement. Much of this discord revolved around the seeming clash between human activity, on the one hand, and the long-term well-being of the planetary environment, on the other. So-called environmental prophets of doom, for example, warned about the dire implications for the planet of population growth, over-reliance on technology, depletion of resources, and reckless economic growth.[7] In his 1968 bestseller, *The Population Bomb,* biologist Paul Ehrlich cautioned that there were too many people on the planet, that their numbers were increasing too quickly, and that the outcome would be environmental catastrophe, international conflict, starvation, death, and, ultimately, nuclear war.[8] In the midst of the Cold War, the "bomb" of the book's title adroitly blended fears about nuclear annihilation with concerns over the heaving millions of the Third World and the looming environmental crisis. Striking a different yet nonetheless similarly pessimistic chord was another biologist, Barry Commoner, who argued in his 1971 book *The Closing Circle: Nature, Man, and Technology* that the problem was neither population nor economic growth but the technology utilized by the rich nations in achieving development.[9] Commoner singled out pesticides, herbicides, synthetic chemicals, fossil fuels, and nuclear power, and he pointed the finger accusingly at developed nations, which he blamed for the bulk of environmental degradation and resource depletion. The rich countries had a moral responsibility, he said, to compensate and support developing nations—many of which were former colonies—because only through development could population stasis be achieved. On this point, Commoner's neo-Marxist, postcolonial environmental agenda contrasted starkly with the neo-Malthusian approach of those like Paul Ehrlich. Moreover, it resonated with other emancipatory environmentalisms emerging from the developing world and among antipollution campaigners like those from Japan.

A defining statement in this early debate on the environment and development appeared in 1972 with the release of *The Limits to Growth,* prepared by a team of scientists at the Massachusetts Institute of Technology (MIT) for the think tank, the Club of Rome. The report outlined possible future scenarios based on the most sophisticated—if controversial—computer modeling techniques of the time. It suggested that, given current trends of exponential economic growth, there was a high likelihood of environmental and social crisis if not collapse in the near future. Advances in technology and productivity could slow or even reverse such trends, but the report's authors warned that there were grave risks in nonchalantly relying on some future technological fix that may or may not appear: "Faith in technology as the ultimate solution to all problems can . . . divert our attention from the most fundamental problem—the problem of growth in a finite system."[10]

In this chapter I turn to the involvement and influence of Japanese activists and pollution victims in this early moment of environmental globalism, culminating in the UN Conference on the Human Environment in Stockholm in 1972. An examination of UNCHE and the years leading up to it offers a fascinating insight into the ways Japanese activists became actors in the emergent "transnational political spaces" of the global environmental movement.[11] In a classic instance of what Saskia Sassen characterizes as "local initiatives" becoming "part of a global network of activism without losing the focus on specific struggles," Japanese pollution victims and activists took their stories of pollution and environmental injustice to a world audience at UNCHE, giving these struggles a human face and relevance for many people unfamiliar with the specificities of domestic political struggles in Japan.[12] At the same time, these activists and victims were able to skillfully utilize transnational spaces to "boomerang" pressure back on the Japanese government, forcing officials such as EAJ director Ōishi Buichi to make astonishing admissions before a world audience.

Japanese activists, such as Tsuru Shigeto and Ui Jun, also emerged as quintessential rooted cosmopolitans who used their knowledge and experience from Japan to influence global debates about industrial pollution, economic development, and international inequity. Involvement in this global environmental upsurge also proved challenging for the Japanese participants. The conflicts among the developed and developing nations forced Japanese activists and victims to think seriously about the role of Japanese industry in environmental destruction abroad, especially in East Asia. If Japanese pollution was merely being "exported" in response to domestic opposition, was this really a solution?

In this chapter I concentrate on the involvement of Japanese activists in the emergent global debate on the environment during the 1960s and 1970s. Where did they stand and what did they advocate? As we have seen, the encounter with environmental injustices in Japan deeply influenced RCP members' overseas activities. Although they expressed interest in a great many issues, ranging from waste disposal to nuclear power, ultimately it was environmental problems with clearly discernable human victims that RCP members studied most intensely and supported most vigorously. A combination of fury and obligation informed this agenda: fury that pollution had victimized people in Japan and a sense of obligation to stop its spread elsewhere. Recall members' relatively lukewarm reaction to the Ralph Nader Group's warnings about the growth of nuclear power worldwide compared with their deeply emotional response to the plight of an obscure community of Native Americans in the Canadian wilderness. Degradation of the natural environment alone was not enough. For groups such as the RCP, socialized in the crucible of Japanese industrial pollution, the presence of human victims was also a critical ingredient for engagement.

Nowhere is this stance clearer than in Japanese groups' interventions into the early debate over the environment and economic development. Whether as insiders or outsiders, the Japanese activists involved tended to view the problem through an anthropocentric lens of injustice and human rights. The issue for them was not so much the natural environment versus human activity but, rather, who or what controlled the natural environment and economic development and, moreover, who did and did not benefit. This perspective tended to position Japanese groups in the camp of individuals like Barry Commoner and advocates from developing nations who were also pursuing a rights-focused, emancipatory environmental agenda. Needless to say, it was a perspective that grew directly out of their experience with very localized environmental injustices in Japan.

I trace the development of this localistic Japanese perspective in two narratives. The first charts the involvement of Japanese pollution victims and their supporters at the United Nations Conference on the Human Environment in Stockholm in 1972. Scholarship to date has paid almost no attention to this involvement despite the fact that Japanese pollution victims and the country's environmental problems became centerpieces of debate during this historic conference. Here I emphasize the Japanese delegation's cogent human-centered interpretation of the "limits to growth" idea. Whereas most debate at UNCHE focused on the limited capacity of the natural environment to sustain humanity, the Japanese group stressed the *human* limits to growth. Japanese pollution victims offered their damaged bodies as living proof that unbridled economic development was having immediate human costs as grave as any long-term depletion of, or damage to, the environment. Industrial pollution in Japan, they argued, spoke to a different kind of limitation: not with respect to natural resources but with respect to balancing economic activity with concern for human health and dignity. That this argument came from the mouths of Japanese victims themselves afforded it an urgency and authority that captured the attention of journalists, delegates, and activists alike at the conference.

The second narrative of the chapter traces the international activities of Tsuru Shigeto in the lead-up to UNCHE. While Japanese pollution victims presented to the world a rights- and justice-based critique of economic growth based on local experience, Tsuru set about articulating a bold reinterpretation of the idea of "development" itself. At influential gatherings in the early 1970s he argued that the environment-development dilemma could only be solved by expanding the concept of development, which had been defined too narrowly in terms of the GNP index. Instead Tsuru proposed a broader concept of development inclusive of human welfare concerns. This concept would take into account negative externalities such as pollution that were generally absent in GNP calculations. Tsuru's attempt to redefine development was quite innovative, given that most debates at the time tended to gravitate around the definition of the environment. Of course, Tsuru's thinking about development had deep roots, drawing extensively on his encounter with industrial pollution in Japan. He presented Japan as a quintessential example of the tragic environmental and human costs realized when human welfare was divorced from economic development. Reuniting the two, however, offered a way forward, because a model of development inclusive of human welfare would implicitly recognize the necessity of a habitable living environment while accepting certain necessary levels of economic growth. Tsuru seems to have believed that this expanded concept of development could simultaneously satisfy the growth demands of developing nations while eliminating the human costs of GNP economics in the rich countries. Although he did not use the term at the time, his thinking here in many ways anticipated the later concept of sustainable development, which would similarly attempt to chart a middle way between the environment and development.

## UNCHE 1972: Communicating Japanese Environmental Injustice to the World

It was against the backdrop of worsening industrial pollution worldwide in the 1960s and early 1970s that political leaders and concerned citizens around the world began to pay attention to the environment in their backyards and beyond. Internationally, the most important event of this era was UNCHE, convened in Stockholm in 1972. No other event better encapsulated the potential and the complexities of global environmentalism in a world fragmented into nation-states and divided by palpable differences in ideology, geography, resources, and stages of development. Barbara Ward and René Jules Dubos's *Only One Earth: The Care and Maintenance of a Small Planet*, prepared especially for the conference, expressed the desire of organizers that the national delegations think about the environment as a global issue, transcending borders and the specific conditions of individual countries. But such lofty aspirations proved difficult to achieve in the face of violent disagreements between developed and developing nations, not to mention the ideological discords of the Cold War.

On the positive side, historian of the modern environmental movement John McCormick describes UNCHE as "the landmark event in the growth of international environmentalism."[13] UNCHE certainly broke ground in terms of UN history, being the organization's first international conference on the environment and, in fact, its first international event devoted to a single issue.[14] The event undoubtedly propelled the environment to an unprecedented level of global attention and concern. For two weeks beginning on June 5, 1972, one hundred and fourteen countries, nineteen intergovernmental agencies, and over four hundred nongovernmental organizations converged on the city of Stockholm to participate in the formal UN conference and in many other parallel symposia, rallies, and events. They were accompanied by an army of print and electronic media representatives from around the world, who dispatched detailed daily reports on debate both within and outside the conference. Thanks to extensive preconference preparations, such as the Founex conference discussed below, delegates were able to finalize and approve the Declaration on the Human Environment, with its list of twenty-six principles, and an action plan that outlined specific measures individual countries could voluntarily adopt.[15] The original draft of the Declaration drew extensively on ideas from the Tokyo Declaration authored by Tsuru and others at a 1970 symposium in that city, especially its assertion that all people have "a fundamental right with respect to the environment." Opposition from Switzerland and Austria, however, forced this clause to be changed in its final—arguably watered-down—version to all people have "the fundamental right to freedom, equality and adequate conditions of life, in an environment of a quality that permits a life of dignity and well-being."[16] Conference delegates also negotiated a number of international treaties on the environment relating to cultural and natural heritage, marine pollution, endangered species, and pollution from commercial shipping.

Formal agreements aside, UNCHE was a conference riven with controversy, disagreement, and contradiction. Despite an agreement to stop contamination of the oceans, on the day UNCHE ended, the private ship *Topaz,* loaded with 7,600 drums of industrial waste from Europe, resumed dumping operations in the Atlantic Ocean as observers from Japan, Ireland, and elsewhere looked on.[17] Cold War politics also greatly weakened the conference. Apart from Romania, all of the Soviet Bloc countries boycotted the conference in support of the German Democratic Republic (East Germany), excluded from participation because it was not a member of the United Nations.[18] The Vietnam War also caused sparks after the Swedish prime minister—supported by NGOs and the Chinese delegation—condemned the United States, saying that "the immense destruction brought about by indiscriminate bombing, by large-scale use of bulldozers and herbicides is an outrage sometimes described as ecocide, which requires urgent international attention."[19] Controversy over the proposed ten-year moratorium on commercial whaling proved to be a thorn in the side of the official Japanese delegation, which refused to compromise despite almost total support for the ban among participating countries. The only consolation for the Japanese was that they were supported by the boycotting Soviet Union, itself still a commercial whaling nation. Even progressive Japanese observers such as Matsui Yayori, a feminist, environmentalist, and journalist with the left-leaning newspaper *Asahi Shinbun* found the uproar over whaling somewhat puzzling. Speaking to a Japanese audience of environmental activists after UNCHE, Matsui wondered if "whales" were "more important" than "yellow people" to Americans, given the ongoing "ecocide" under way in Indochina.[20] Matsui's observation was an interesting one indeed, inadvertently revealing the deeply anthropocentric perspective of Japanese environmentalism encapsulated in the stories of injustice Japanese victims would relate with such poignancy throughout UNCHE.

Most divisive in terms of the environmental debate, however, was the simmering "North-South" problem, which dominated debate both inside and outside the conference. Along with Indira Gandhi, Robert McNamara of the World Bank, and the Brazilian delegation, the People's Republic of China emerged as the champion of the global South. In strongly ideological language the Chinese declared that the "major cause of environmental pollution" was "capitalism," which had "developed into a state of imperialism, monopoly, colonialism and neocolonialism—seeking high profits, not concerned with the life or death of people, and discharging poisons at will."[21]

The Chinese asserted that "each country" had "the right to determine its own environment standards and policies in the light of its own conditions, and no country whatsoever should undermine the interests of the developing countries under the pretext of protecting the environment."[22]

Events outside the formal conference proved to be just as provocative and controversial—not to mention haphazard. Invoking a famous Swedish culinary image, one observer likened the activity in and around Stockholm city to an "environmental smorgasbord," while another suggested that "history may not find it clear which was the main event and which the sideshow."[23] As McCormick correctly observes, UNCHE represented "the beginning of a new and more insistent role for NGOs in the work of governments and intergovernmental organizations," and it connected national NGOs transnationally as never before.[24] Not until the Earth Summit (UNCED) in Rio in 1992, with its attention to global-scale environmental problems such as ozone depletion and climate change, would NGOs be involved in such a moment of heightened concern for and controversy over the global environment.

When the delegation of Japanese pollution victims and their advocates stepped off the airplane in Stockholm, they became part of a remarkably diverse array of unofficial and semiofficial events that, one way or another, addressed the burning question of the environment and economic growth. Closest in terms of affiliation to UNCHE was the Environmental Forum, financially supported by the Swedish government and approved by the UN conference secretariat as the official venue for nongovernmental organizations. As one attendee later wrote, the Environmental Forum involved "exhibitions, films and slide shows, panel discussions, lectures, and workshops on some fifty subjects. Books were sold, pamphlets distributed, and petitions signed. There was music and biodynamic food (including 'poison free' soft drinks sold in non-returnable bottles, which shows how difficult it is to live as one teaches)."[25] Contrary to organizers hopes that the forum would be a compliant and unobtrusive space for congenial NGOs, the heated debates over the causes of environmental degradation at times even upstaged the main event. Notably, the Environmental Forum served as the venue for the famous Ehrlich-Commoner debate over whether it was population or technology driving global environmental destruction. While Barry Commoner criticized the affluent countries for irresponsible use of technology and neocolonialism, Paul Ehrlich invoked the ire of developing nations in his vocal assertion that population growth was one of the most significant contributors to environmental degradation.[26]

More radical in conception and practice was the Dai Dong Conference, named after the Chinese notion of the whole world as a family. Familial imagery aside, however, Dai Dong served as a vocal and often militant mouthpiece for an emancipatory environmentalism advocating the rights of developing nations. Dai Dong included scientists and other specialists from Europe, the United States, Asia, Africa, and Latin America. Ui Jun participated as the official delegate from Japan. In speeches and panel discussions he spoke passionately about the country's severe pollution and the courageous struggles of victims. Ui also took part in a public dialogue with Barry Commoner that was widely reported in Japan and worldwide. Both activists agreed that environmental problems would not be solved without accompanying solutions to "poverty, discrimination, and war." As Commoner argued, because environmental degradation was a "social problem," it was not enough to treat it as a "biological issue" or through the lens of "nature conservation" alone. Ui could only agree, noting how his involvement with Minamata disease had forced him to expand his perspective from "natural science" to "social science."[27] Given its advocacy of environmental rights and justice, Dai Dong thus served as the perfect venue to showcase Japanese industrial pollution and the stories of its hapless victims. As a self-proclaimed "transnational peace effort" committed to global consciousness, transnational cooperation, and economic justice, Dai Dong participants addressed environmental degradation through the lens of wider social, political, economic, and cultural inequities worldwide—an emancipatory focus that resonated closely with the agenda of Ui and Japanese pollution victims. The United States came in for particular criticism for its "ecocidal" war in Indochina, while developed countries were lambasted for having "shortchanged" the Third World by monopolizing technology and plundering natural resources.[28]

Japanese activists' involvement in the UNCHE process began in mid-1971 when Ui Jun and others in the ILP movement obtained a draft copy of the official Japanese national report for the conference prepared by bureaucrats at the Ministry of Foreign Affairs.[29] What they discovered was a document largely devoid of detailed discussion about Japanese pollution, and instead filled with what they viewed as page after page of bureaucratic "trumpet blowing."[30] Ui was particularly irritated by the total absence of specific discussion about Minamata disease, Itai Itai disease, Yokkaichi asthma, and other infamous incidents of pollution in the country.[31] Only in a very short section did the report mention how heavy metals such as cadmium and methyl mercury had "caused health effects" in humans in some areas. The bulk of the report focused on the official responses and institutional and regulatory developments.[32] As Ui pointed out, no scientific specialists or victims were consulted during the drafting process, resulting in a bland and abstract document that gave readers little sense of the advanced nature and horrific human consequences of pollution in Japan.[33] The phrase "caused health effects," for instance, obfuscated the reality that industrial pollution had killed, and was still killing, many innocent Japanese citizens.[34] Nowhere in the report was there any sense that many Japanese people re-gretted their path to economic affluence, nor was there any indication that some of them were now reconsidering the benefits of so-called growth.[35]

The ILP responded immediately. On the suggestion of Ui, beginning in December 1971 the executive committee began to prepare its own inde-pendent "alternative" national report on Japan, which was to be circulated as widely as possible in Stockholm the following June. A working party con-stituting students and numerous ordinary citizens set about compiling data for case studies on some twenty instances of pollution in Japan. The origi-nal text was then translated into English by a group of seventeen Japanese volunteers and subsequently polished for publication by Anthony Carter, an American missionary involved in the movement.[36] Volunteers from the Women's League for Peace in the lay Buddhist organization Sōka Gakkai helped raise funds for the publication.[37] The resulting pamphlet, *Polluted Japan,* proved to be a landmark English-language document on the tragedy of Japanese industrial pollution, to which even the Japanese government was forced to respond. On learning of the pamphlet, the government quickly supplemented the first version of its report with three new sections dealing more specifically with instances of air and water pollution.[38] The high-circulation newspaper *Asahi Shinbun* also publicized the pamphlet's release in late February 1972 in an article titled "No More Minamatas."[39]

Throughout UNCHE, the ILP delegation distributed around 2,500 copies of the pamphlet to activists, NGOs, bureaucrats, journalists, and ordinary citizens from around the world.[40] Inside *Polluted Japan*'s covers, readers discovered page after page of photographs, maps, sketches, tables, charts, and text documenting industrial pollution and horrific human injustice. The cover presented readers with a human hand shockingly de-formed by mercury contamination, accentuated on subsequent pages by photos of fetal mercury poisoning victims, Yokkaichi asthma sufferers, PCB contamination victims, and casualties of cadmium poisoning. The images are unnerving: a young Minamata sufferer in bed with a terribly distorted hand and glass-eyed stare, a woman's back covered in literally hundreds of painful eruptions caused by PCB-contaminated rice bran oil, and the deflated body of an infant victim of cadmium poisoning whose barely recognizable limbs are warped into terrifying angles from multiple bone fractures. Here indeed was the chilling reality of the "health effects" so non-chalantly referred to in the government's national report.

*Polluted Japan* presented readers with detailed studies on eighteen forms of pollution in Japan including Minamata disease, Itai Itai disease, Yokkaichi asthma, arsenic and PCB contamination, farming chemicals, automobile fumes, garbage, paper and pulp, oil, and radioactivity. No stone was left unturned.[41] In his introductory essay, Ui repeated his mantra on Japanese pollution for an international audience: namely, that pollution should not be understood as an unexpected and unfortunate outcome of economic growth but as something intentional that facilitated Japanese economic development.

It is often said that "kōgai" is a side effect or distortion related to development. But this type of thinking comes from those who are primarily responsible for the generation of "kōgai." The facts indicate that "kōgai" is not such a trifling matter as to simply be called a side effect or distortion of a rapidly developing economy. To simply say that it is a "distortion" is to indicate that if economic development were carried out rightly, or managed in such a way so that it would follow a natural course without any distortion, then the "kōgai" would not appear. But the fact is that "kōgai" is one of the most powerful and central factors in a rapidly developing economy. Japanese economists have pointed to a number of factors that have spelled success for Japan's capitalist economy and the factors most stressed have been low wages and trade protectionism. But a third factor must be added and that is the neglect of the "kōgai" problem or permitting the economy to dirty its own clothes. The "kōgai" problem is an essential part of the structures of the capitalist economy of Japan.[42]

Ui and the ILP also organized a delegation of pollution victims and environmental advocates to travel to Stockholm and participate in the various parallel NGO conferences.[43] Ui and the executive committee decided on victims of Minamata disease and Kanemi Rice Bran Oil contamination because their symptoms, being externally visible, would have the greatest impact.[44] Traveling from Minamata were thirty-six-year-old sufferer Hamamoto Tsuginori, wearing a cloth bib reading, "AN INDIVIDUAL CANNOT BE REPLACED," and fetal mercury poisoning victim Hashimoto Shinobu, fifteen years old, accompanied by her mother, Fujie.[45] Sasaki Shigemitsu and Kinoshita Tadayuki represented Kanemi Rice Bran Oil victims, while Shibushi Bay resident Tōgo Sōbei spoke for the anti–industrial development movement in Japan. Supporting these victims and activists—in what was the first trip abroad for most—were Ui Jun, Harada Masazumi, Itai Itai disease specialist Dr. Hagino Noboru, filmmaker Tsuchimoto Noriaki, and missionary Anthony Carter.[46]

The group was astounded by their reception in Stockholm. Matsui Yayori of the newspaper *Asahi Shinbun* described how "ordinary citizens are showing much more interest in Japan than was expected. TV news is constantly running stories about how Tokyo City was forced to pass traffic regulations to address the terrible photochemical smog in the city. Major newspapers are running stories on the Minamata and Kanemi incidents. Japanese pollution has become a 'dining room' topic for Swedish people."[47] On June 5, Ui and the ILP delegation addressed an audience of some hundred journalists at their hotel in central Stockholm. With the four victims seated beside him, Ui Jun announced that "these people's bodies show the horrors of Japanese pollution."[48] The victims themselves sat with banners draped around their necks reading "only one life," "MINAMATA," and "KOGAI HANTAI."[49] Hamamoto Tsuginori told the reporters that he wanted to express his rage and let the world know the "double damage" inflicted on Japanese pollution victims by a government that took "sides with polluting corporations" and did "nothing until victims protested." He spoke about the arduous life of Minamata disease sufferers and, with cane in hand, shuffled around the room to show the physical challenges of living with Minamata disease. Hashimoto Fujie spoke for her daughter Shinobu, terribly incapacitated by fetal mercury poisoning. Fujie said that she wanted to communicate the agony of a mother whose eldest daughter had been killed by Minamata disease and whose younger daughter (Shinobu) was afflicted with the fetal variety. She confessed her worry about Shinobu's future and, in a poignant admission, said she wanted people to understand the agony of a mother who hoped her child would die before she did. Kanemi PCB victim Sasaki Shigemitsu set the room alight with flashbulbs when he removed his shirt to reveal a torso covered in excruciating skin eruptions. "Look at my body," he announced, "These may look like pimples but they are actually eruptions caused by PCBs."[50]

Following the press conference the Dai Dong group, in cooperation with the People's Forum, organized a "Japan Night" attended by the press and around five hundred people. During the evening filmmaker Tsuchimoto Noriaki screened his confronting documentary, *Minamata: The Victims and Their World*, which was rescreened by popular demand some days later. The newspaper *Asahi Shinbun* reported how the audience cheered loudly during scenes of Minamata victims and activists directly confronting executives of the Chisso Corporation.[51] Ui acted as master of ceremonies for the evening, while Drs. Hagino and Harada presented slideshows, films, and talks on the nature and development of industrial pollution in Japan.[52] On June 6, the first day of UNCHE, the ILP delegation led a street demonstration in front of the hotels of national delegates and then to the Japanese embassy. Ui, Hagino, and Harada also conducted slideshows and led a panel discussion at the Environmental Forum on heavy metal poisoning worldwide.[53] On June 14, Dr. Lars Friberg, the renowned environmental medicine researcher, invited the ILP group to speak on the topic of Japanese industrial pollution at the Karolinska Institute, after which they were presented with the Karolinska Medal in recognition of their scientific research and a donation of 140,000 yen for the movement. Hagino Noboru's presentation on Itai Itai disease at the institute was subsequently recognized as the moment when cadmium gained general scientific acceptance worldwide as the primary causal agent of the disease.[54]

Although they were unable to gain access to the main conference, the victims and activists of the ILP group were generally satisfied with their achievements. Hamamoto Tsuginori of Minamata later observed that "the Japanese government wasn't happy we disabled people participated. It would have been nice to have said even something short at the main conference." Nevertheless, Hamamoto concluded, "I'm really glad I came."[55] For Ui, the most surprising and worrying revelation was just how little the world knew about Japan's pollution nightmare compared with the country's economic miracle. The reaction of delegates from developing countries who had previously looked to Japan as a successful, non-Western role model of development was particularly startling. Ui could not forget the look of disbelief on the face of a young woman from Iran as she learned of Japan's terrible pollution situation.[56] Indeed, the Stockholm experience imbued the ILP group with a renewed commitment to communicate the lessons of Japanese pollution and injustice to the world. Participants from Minamata and elsewhere were astounded to discover that their local experiences offered a sobering corroboration of arguments about the limits to economic growth. What made their message unique and all the more striking was the way Japanese pollution victims physically embodied their critique. As living evidence of the human limits to growth, their message had a visceral and emotional immediacy that captured the attention of activists, journalists, and conference delegates alike at UNCHE. This was a reaction the Japanese group had not anticipated, and it alerted them to the international significance of their very local experiences of physical suffering and injustice.

## Tsuru Shigeto: The Quintessential Rooted Cosmopolitan

Pollution victims and their supporters like Ui Jun were not the only Japanese voices audible in this early 1970s upsurge of environmental concern worldwide. While the ILP and other groups were pursuing their agendas in the spaces of an emergent global civil society, others like Tsuru Shigeto were simultaneously utilizing their status and connections within academic, scientific, and political circles to articulate a Japanese perspective on environmental problems. In Tsuru's case this perspective revolved around a critique of GNP and a fundamental redefinition of development as human welfare—in a sense, becoming the theoretical expression of victims' emotional and embodied critique of environmental injustice.

*The Limits to Growth* neatly encapsulated the sentiment driving environmental concern in the years leading up to UNCHE—especially before the developing countries began to vociferously challenge what they saw as a debate unfairly skewed in favor of the rich. As the title of that book candidly pronounced, "growth"—in population and consumption—was the primary cause of environmental degradation and resource depletion and, given that it was likely to continue in an exponential way, the prospects for humanity were grim unless people somehow brought these processes under control. As the MIT team ominously concluded from the output of their "World Model" (what one skeptic later ridiculed as "The Computer That Printed Out W*O*L *F*"), "*We can thus say with some confidence that, under the assumption of no major change in the present system, population and industrial growth will certainly stop within the next century at the latest.*"[57] Although based on their own independent computer modeling, the MIT team's conclusions dovetailed with other contemporary analyses of the long-term consequences of global resource depletion by economists, biologists, and demographers.

As an internationally recognized economist and antipollution campaigner, Tsuru Shigeto joined this chorus of criticism against growth, although his position on "development" was more moderate than groups such as the MIT team. As noted at the outset, Tsuru was not opposed to development per se, just its narrow definition as an increase in GNP. This approach to development undoubtedly had to do with his longtime theoretical interest in developmental economics, but it also drew on his experiences in the progressive Tokyo administration of Governor Minobe Ryōkichi in the 1960s, where he helped craft policies for clean living environments and citizen participation—in other words, policies based on guaranteeing civic rights to enjoy and utilize a clean living environment (as opposed to policies focused solely on limiting human effects on the natural environment). Similarly, his desire to deal with environmental protection within the more important (for him) issue of human welfare drew on a Japanese environmental injustice paradigm constructed around pollution victims whose welfare had been willfully and ruthlessly ignored. Such experiences profoundly shaped Tsuru's vocal international critique of the GNP index, which he saw as a numerical expression of environmental disruption caused by reckless growth insensitive to human welfare.

Tsuru Shigeto, it should be noted, was a thoroughly cosmopolitan individual years before he became an environmental activist, and his formative experiences in these earlier years provided the theoretical basis and human connections necessary for his involvement in international environmental issues in the 1970s and beyond. A remarkably intelligent and contemplative youth, Tsuru traced the roots of his environmental concern to the 1917 best seller *Binbō Monogatari* (Tales of poverty) by the Marxian economist Kawakami Hajime, which he read in middle school. Tsuru recalled being particularly enamored by an episode Kawakami recounted from his days as a university student. The young Kawakami had traveled to the Ashio copper mine, located around one hundred miles (160 kilometers) north of Tokyo in Tochigi Prefecture and site of one of Japan's most infamous and destructive cases of industrial pollution in the late nineteenth and early twentieth centuries. Kawakami explained how he had been overwhelmed with sympathy after hearing speeches from victims of pollution from the mine and, in a display of spontaneous altruism, donated some of the clothes he was wearing.[58] Although Tsuru never went so far, he did develop a similar commitment to the plight of marginalized pollution victims in his own environmental activism. Moreover, the Ashio copper mine pollution incident served as a crucial reference point for Tsuru a couple of decades later when he was attempting to rethink development as a process *inclusive* of human welfare concerns.

The tenor of the times in early twentieth century Japan also played a role—albeit inadvertently—in shaping Tsuru's approach to environmental problems. Tsuru's father, Nobuo, president of the Toho Gas Company, then the primary gas supplier in the Nagoya region of central Honshū Island, had been deeply disappointed with Japanese diplomats after the country's momentous victory in the Russo-Japanese War of 1904–1905. His father felt that, despite the historic achievements of the Japanese armed forces, diplomats had let the country down by not securing a more generous postwar settlement from the Russians. When Tsuru was born in 1912 Nobuo determined that his son would become an effective foreign diplomat with all the necessary skills to pursue Japan's national interest on an international stage. To this end he began preparations by arranging for private English-language lessons for the young Tsuru from his second year of middle school.[59] Although Tsuru would never fulfill his father's dreams and become a diplomat, years of English-language study positioned him well for a cosmopolitan life and career in the coming years.

In the late 1920s Tsuru entered the Number 8 Higher School in Nagoya (the predecessor of present-day Nagoya University), where he continued his language study in the English Speaking Society and, significantly, threw himself into a program of leftist activism on campus that would have life-altering consequences. Tsuru became involved in a reading group called Shaken (social research), which included both faculty and student members. Although a largely moderate association, the group had been banned in 1927 by order of the Japanese Ministry of Education as part of the state's more general crackdown on leftist elements nationwide. The group continued to operate in secret, however, reading works such as the German-language version of Karl Marx and Friedrich Engels's *The Communist Manifesto* and becoming involved in various democratization movements on campus.[60] Among these, in 1929 Tsuru and his fellow members established a campus division of the Japan branch of the Anti-Imperialist League and began publishing a monthly newsletter called *Iskra,* after the Russian Social Democratic Workers' Party bulletin of the same name.[61]

Tsuru Shigeto, 1972
(The Mainichi Newspapers)

The "inevitable"—as Tsuru later described it—came in early December 1930, when Tsuru and thirty-five other students were arrested for organizing speaking events critical of the Japanese army's incursions into China as well as for pasting political pamphlets outside a number of Nagoya factories on the request of the National Council of Japanese Labor Unions.[62] Tsuru spent the next three months in police detention and on his release learned that he had been expelled from the Number 8 Higher School. Aware of the peril his son faced as an identified "thought criminal," Tsuru's father suggested that he go overseas to continue his studies. Although most Japanese students traveled to Germany at the time, Tsuru's father felt that the Marxist influence was too strong there, with the Social Democrats as the largest political party and a powerful Socialist Party. If Tsuru was agreeable, his father promised to pay for travel and two years of study and living expenses in the United States. Somewhat surprised but not resistant, Tsuru boarded the Japanese mail steamboat *Taiyōmaru* in August 1931, bound for the United States.[63] After an initial period at Lawrence University in Wisconsin, Tsuru transferred to Harvard University, where he graduated with honors in 1935 and then went on to complete doctoral studies in economics in 1940. His advisers and colleagues at Harvard included some of the most influential figures in twentieth-century economics such as Joseph Schumpeter, Wassily Leontief, John Kenneth Galbraith, and Paul Samuelson. Among non-economists, Tsuru became close friends with the Marxian historian of Japan and Canadian diplomat E. H. Norman—a friendship that ultimately resulted in an order to testify about Norman before the House Un-American Activities Committee in the late 1950s and accusations from the left that he had somehow contributed to Norman's untimely suicide.[64]

With the outbreak of the Pacific War in 1941, Tsuru was repatriated to Japan with other Japanese living in the United States, and throughout the war years he served in the Ministry of Foreign Affairs (MOFA) and very briefly in the army. At war's end, Tsuru was invited to join the Strategic Bombing Survey of the Supreme Commander of the Allied Powers (SCAP) on the request of two of its members, John Kenneth Galbraith and Paul Baran, who were close associates from his days at Harvard.[65] In 1946 Tsuru was again seconded to SCAP from his post in MOFA by order of then Foreign Minister Yoshida Shigeru, this time serving in the influential Economic and Scientific Section (ESS). In an interesting twist of circumstances, while at the ESS Tsuru was charged with drafting and translating a letter from General Douglas MacArthur to Yoshida Shigeru (by then, prime minister) ordering that the Japanese government immediately adopt measures to bring rampant inflation under control.[66] On his return to the Japanese public service in 1947, Yoshida appointed Tsuru to the Keizai Antei Honbu (Economic Stabilization Headquarters, later the Economic Planning Agency, EPA, or Keizai Kikakuchō) where he was involved in the preparation of the first postwar economic white paper.[67]

By the age of thirty-five, then, Tsuru had over a decade of experience living and studying abroad, where he had associated with some of the most influential economists of the time. In two short years after the war he had served at the highest levels of the Japanese bureaucracy and within the powerful economic sections of SCAP. This experience as an insider at the most elite levels of politics and the academy served Tsuru well when he embarked on environmental activism beginning in the 1960s. It also fed into his project to rethink the notion of development. Most directly, while a student in the United States in the 1930s, Tsuru had developed an interest in development economics and conducted some research into the Tennessee Valley Authority (TVA). Remarkably different from the Ashio copper mine region in Japan, which had been terribly polluted by mining operations, the Tennessee

Valley project appeared to Tsuru to have effectively integrated development and the environment, because the region had an upstream copper mine similar to Ashio but without the pollution. Tsuru was intrigued by the contrast and became convinced that the TVA model of nonpollutive (i.e., human-welfare-sensitive) development could be imported into Japan. In October 1946 Tsuru organized the TVA Research Colloquium, which met monthly to consider how the TVA principles might be adapted for regional development projects in Japan. Members came from across the bureaucratic and industrial spectrum and included many technical specialists involved in transport, heavy industry, and electrical utilities. Among prominent individuals in the colloquium was Okita Saburō, an influential economist, government official, and, later, member of the Club of Rome who, many decades hence, would play a key role in making the notion of "sustainable development" environmental common sense worldwide.[68]

Given Japan's subsequent torrent of regional development throughout the 1960s, and the resulting pollution and environmental destruction, Tsuru's TVA Colloquium can be viewed only as a resounding failure with respect to its direct influence on government policy and industrial development. Nevertheless, for Tsuru, Okita, and other specialists in the group, it was a transformative experience, representing their first opportunity to think about development in post-defeat Japan from a comparative perspective. It was through the TVA Colloquium that Tsuru was able to conduct a field survey of the Ashio copper mine region in 1953 as a member of the governmental consultative committee, the Shigen Chōsakai (Natural Resources Survey Committee). The environmental damage and human misery Tsuru witnessed was shocking and convinced him of the need for thorough economic planning, attentive to both the profitability of individual economic actors and the wider macroeconomy as well as to the welfare of ordinary citizens and their living environment.[69] Although the colloquium ended in 1949, it served for Tsuru as a prototype for the Research Committee on Pollution with its focus on field research, interdisciplinary exchange, and cross-national consideration of local development.[70]

Tsuru began to tackle environmental issues in earnest from the early years of the 1960s while a faculty member and later president of Hitotsubashi University in eastern Tokyo. As we saw in chapter 1, in 1963 Tsuru and others established the RCP in response to the unfolding domestic environmental crisis. After resisting insistent pleas to run for the Tokyo City governorship, for two years from 1968 Tsuru served in a consultative capacity on the Tokyo Problems Research Committee, which advised the progressive governor, Minobe Ryōkichi (who ran for office when Tsuru declined), on issues relating to housing, land, new town development, redevelopment, urban transport, and public finance. Tsuru used the opportunity to advance his embryonic environmental vision, most notably in the committee's influential 1969 policy proposal *Tōkyō e no Teigen* (Recommendations to Tokyo), which sketched out not only an environmentally friendly but also a democratically organized vision of urban life in the capital, in which local residents would have a large role in shaping their living environments.[71]

In the early 1970s Tsuru became more and more involved in the global environmental movement as an opinion leader and as an organizer of influential international conferences. These were the years when his earlier studies and contacts overseas came to fruition, providing him with opportunities to build alliances of like-minded scientists and to communicate his critique of GNP and vision of development to an international audience. In terms of transnational alliances, Tsuru's first standout achievement was the International Symposium on Environmental Disruption held in Tokyo in 1970, which he organized with the environmental economist Allen Kneese of Resources for the Future in Washington, DC. Formally named "Environmental Disruption in the Modern World: A Field of Action for the Social Scientists," the Tokyo symposium was a landmark event in the formation of a transnational movement of natural and social scientists committed to the central tenets of environmentalism. For assistance Tsuru drew on his connections in industry and government, arranging financial and logistical support from Tokyo City, the Osaka and Mie prefectural governments, the Japanese Ministry of Education, and the Tokyo Electric Power Company (TEPCO).[72] Symposium participants read like a who's who of international environmental specialists at the time. On the Japan side were members of the RCP, Tokyo and Osaka City officials, and representatives from the MHW. Overseas participants included Allen Kneese, who proposed a theory of market systems sensitive to common property resources; Harvard economist Wassily Leontief, who advocated national accounting reflective of negative externalities (like pollution); Wellesley College economist Marshall Goldman, who described widespread pollution in the Soviet Union; Michigan University legal scholar Joseph Sax, who championed environmental litigation; and the German American economist and founder of ecological economics Karl William Kapp, who provided the framing opening remarks for the symposium. As Kapp observed, "I consider it as particularly appropriate that this first international symposium on the disruption and possible destruction of man's environment takes place in a country that had to endure the horrors of Hiroshima and Nagasaki. Moreover, Japan today has one of the most rapid rates of industrialization and of economic development with all its disruptive consequences on the environment."[73] Among the many issues debated at the symposium, participants paid great attention to the problem of incorporating the costs of pollution into calculations of GNP and to methods for making polluters pay for environmental degradation caused by industrial processes—both vitally important issues for Tsuru.

Along with the presentations and debates, participants in the conference also signed the Tokyo Declaration, which famously asserted that all people and future generations have "a fundamental right with respect to the environment"—a Japanese-inspired idea of environmental rights that would carry over to the UN conference in Stockholm two years later. Tsuru and other RCP members' notions of environmental rights (to fresh water, sunlight, clean air, and the like) drew heavily on their commitment to environmental justice, which, as explained, emerged from their earlier struggles against domestic industrial pollution. The Tokyo Declaration closely mirrored their anthropocentric concept of environmental rights by stressing the entitlement of humans to certain minimum standards in their living environments as opposed to what might be called the intrinsic rights of nature.

RCP members underscored this emphasis on the environmental rights of humans by taking their foreign guests on a "pollution tour" of the country. In Tokyo, for instance, they visited the city's polluted bay, a smelly trash processing facility, a public housing project built on reclaimed land, and a sewerage treatment station.[74] Thereafter the group traveled to Osaka, Yokkaichi, and Minamata, where they saw—and breathed—pollution firsthand.[75] All these visits were designed to leave the foreign participants with an indelible appreciation for the human costs of industrial development, which Tsuru and colleagues viewed as the key issue in the environmental debate. Their intentions did not go unanswered: deeply moved by the experience, the legal scholar Joseph Sax obtained a copy of the distressing documentary *Minamata kara no Sakebi* (Cries from Minamata) that he later screened for specialists at the influential American think tank Resources for the Future, in Washington, DC.[76] Tsuru's prominence in international environmental circles also increased dramatically after the symposium, which he skillfully utilized to mount an attack on GNP economics and to advocate a welfare-centric vision of development.

## Tsuru Shigeto: Defining Development beyond the GNP Index

Most notable in this connection, in the months leading up to UNCHE, Tsuru delivered two highly influential lectures that clarified his critique of GNP and his position on the environment-development dilemma. The first, In Place of GNP, he delivered in July 1971 at Maison des Sciences de l'Homme (MSH) in Paris, and the second, North-South Relations on the Environment, he delivered in April 1972 at the Columbia-United Nations Conference on Economic Development and Environment in New York.

At the New York conference in early 1972, Tsuru explained how, in the days of mass global unemployment during the Great Depression, economists had begun to closely associate GNP growth with improvements in economic welfare. Thanks to the Keynesian revolution in economic theory, they concluded that "any measure that would expand effective demand, even including the nonsensical digging and refilling of holes in the ground," represented "a positive step towards increasing welfare so long as it brought about a net increase in employment."[77] Although unquestionably appropriate for the acute unemployment of the Great Depression, the notion that GNP growth equated to increased welfare gained such a position of "dominance" and "prestige" that "it acquired the status of orthodoxy" and came to be universally applied thereafter to all institutional configurations and economic circumstances.[78] But with the onset of widespread industrial pollution and severe degradation of the human living environment, cracks appeared in this seemingly rock-solid orthodoxy and, for Tsuru, presented an opportunity for economists and political leaders to reconsider the dictum that an increase in GNP is, ipso facto, an increase in welfare.[79]

As Tsuru wryly observed in his speech, although called Gross National *Product,* the index was not really about production, since the most common method of its calculation—the expenditure method—totaled outflows for consumption, investment, government spending, and net exports and, in this sense, reflected gross national *costs.*[80] Tsuru gave the example of trash. Intuitively, disposing of more trash might be considered an increased burden or "cost" for society, but in expenditure GNP accounting, increased government spending on waste disposal (for example, increasing the number of garbage trucks) was recorded as a positive addition to economic growth.[81] But, more to the point, different from the "heyday of competitive capitalism," when the link between GNP and welfare was "free of seriously misleading connotation," in advanced economies of the contemporary era Tsuru identified two fundamental changes that had severed this link once and for all.[82] First, technological advances had "heightened the possibility of negative external effects of gigantic proportions," most discernibly in environmental degradation and human disease from industrial pollution and contamination. Second, affluence had also transformed popular preferences such that people now valued "goods" not accounted for in calculations of GNP, such as public amenities, clean air, beautiful scenery, and a healthy living environment.[83] Many developed societies may have achieved full employment, but the appearance of these negative factors and the changing preferences of consumers (i.e., now more post-materialist), paradoxically, had served to divorce the GNP index from actually perceived welfare. GNP was, according to Tsuru, no more than a "one-dimensional quantitative measure of growth" that tended to conceal "all kinds of concrete problems of social and economic reform which usually constitute the contents of *development.*"[84]

Of particular interest to Tsuru and other environmental advocates were the so-called negative externalities or diseconomies born of GNP-centered economic growth. As we have seen, Tsuru had been interested in the negative effects of industry since the prewar years and through his postwar involvement in the TVA Colloquium. An invited lecture at Harvard University in the early 1960s on the role of cities in technological innovation and economic development further sparked his theoretical interest in the phenomenon of externalities. There he had argued, rather intuitively, that industry will tend to agglomerate near large urban centers because cities offer many positive externalities such as a ready workforce and various forms of infrastructure such as ports and railroads.[85] Applying this same logic in a negative way, in 1961 he published an essay appropriately titled "Kōdo Seichō e no Hansei" (Reconsidering high-speed growth) in which he observed, "If an automobile travels at full speed on a muddy road it will throw up mud. The faster it goes the worse the spattered mud will be," alluding, of course, to the pollution produced as a result of industrial activity.[86] Indeed, the emergence of pollution confirmed for Tsuru a number of troubling realities about the free market system. At the microeconomic level, firms tended not to internalize the costs of negative externalities (especially those they were responsible for, such as air pollution) but the very shrewdest ones moved quickly to internalize positive externalities.[87] Extrapolating this to the macroeconomic level, Tsuru observed how the advanced capitalist nations were thus able to grow by "squandering human stock and disregarding human decency of the working class (both at home and in colonies)" and by "taking full advantage of the economic usefulness of common property resources without paying for them at the time of use."[88] Tsuru could only agree with Ui Jun, who similarly argued that pollution was not merely a *by-product* of economic growth but a fundamental—if counterintuitive—*apparatus* of growth under capitalism. As a crude index of growth, GNP failed to account for negative externalities like pollution or degradation of lakes, seas, and forests, and, as Tsuru explained to a 1971 audience in Paris, "Just as I can increase my monthly expenditure by drawing upon my past savings, we can make our GNP larger than otherwise would be the case by depleting our store of resources without replacing them."[89]

Therein lay the rub for Tsuru. When development was left to the vagaries of the free market, the "built-in bias for market goals" with all the associated negative externalities would inevitably come to dominate.[90] The free market, by its very nature, was not capable of reflecting depletion, degradation, or other deleterious effects on so-called public goods like air, water, and scenery. Just as the MIT team predicted, economic activity within the GNP regime would continue unchanged regardless of decreasing resources, increasing population, or environmental degradation because the free market encouraged self-interested (and often socially irresponsible) behavior at the level of the firm. But once people began to question the logic and ethics of this dynamic—once the "failure of the market" was "admitted"— the fallacy of GNP would be revealed and people would recognize "that the 'invisible hand' does not work and that 'someone' has to take into his own hands the task of guiding the economy towards certain specific normative goals. . . . In other words, economics has to become political economy again with all its normative aspects concretely specified and the strategies spelled out."[91]

Tsuru was not alone in his critique of GNP economics. At the Tokyo Symposium Tsuru convened in 1970, for instance, fellow economist Uzawa Hirofumi had also referred to the problem, observing how, "traditionally, the concept of real national income [i.e., real GNP] has been used as a measure of economic welfare. But this concept is an aggregation of only those goods and services which have positive prices. In order to use that concept as a measure of economic welfare, we have to deduct the cost involved in eliminating external diseconomies, but this is easier said than done because of the absence of market prices on them."[92] As Erik Dahmén put it, "Expressed in ordinary language, it is a question of considering damage to the environment as a cost just like any other cost of doing business. But this formulation does not solve the problem, even theoretically."[93] One solution, according to Dahmén and many other economists, was to charge a fee, tax, or levy for negative externalities. In this system "no strict limitations would be set for the costs in the form of environmental damage that would be acceptable. Instead, a bill would be presented, the amount of which would be reduced or increased proportional to the reduction or increase in environmental damage."[94] At the level of national accounting, Uzawa Hirofumi proposed some kind of adjustment—similar to depreciation methods used in firms—for "deterioration or depreciation of social and natural capital," hence making the GNP index a more accurate indicator of "welfare-oriented real national income."[95] Tsuru agreed, pointing to the "polluter pays principle" (PPP) proposed by the Organization for Economic Co-operation and Development (OECD) in which externalities were internalized as *ex post* or *ex ante* costs "within the atomistic accounting of . . . originating industries or individuals."[96]

But as Tsuru and other critical economists from wealthy developed countries soon discovered, their proposals to address pollution by imposing a charge on economic actors—effectively increasing the cost of operations and impeding growth—attracted vociferous and indignant opposition from the advocates of developing countries who, quite understandably, pointed to the hypocrisy of the wealthy nations. In a nutshell, these advocates argued that it was not fair that developing countries be forced to balance economic growth with environmental responsibility when the First World countries had done just the opposite in their own paths to advanced development. As the Indian prime minister, Indira Gandhi, noted in her speech at UNCHE, "We do not wish to impoverish the environment any further and yet we cannot for a moment forget the grim poverty of large numbers of people. . . . How can we speak to those who live in villages and in slums about keeping the oceans, the rivers and the air clean when their own lives are contaminated at the source?"[97] "When it comes to the depletion of natural resources and environmental pollution," observed Gandhi, "the increase of one inhabitant in an affluent country, at his level of living, is equivalent to an increase of many Asians, Africans or Latin Americans at their current material levels of living."[98] The *ECO* newsletter, published by Friends of the Earth (FoE) and the *Ecologist* magazine, through UNCHE, acknowledged this criticism and suspicion about environmentalism among developing countries, noting that it was "seen by many as a plot by the rich to hang on to wealth won by despoiling the environment, while depriving the poor of the fruits of development, in the name of ecological purity."[99] The reality, as Nigerian politician Adebayo Adedeji put it, was that "we may have one earth but we certainly do not have one world economy. We have instead an economically segmented world—a world polarized more than ever before into the 'haves' and the 'have nots.' "[100] The Brazilians, for example, scoffed at discussion about industrial pollution, labeling it a "rich man's" concern, while the Ivory Coast declared that it would welcome pollution if this meant higher growth.[101] This remarkably different perspective on the environment among the "have nots" by no means diminished Tsuru's commitment to stopping environmental degradation from industrial pollution. But its focus on injustice and inequity also resonated with Tsuru's theoretical leanings and his activist experience in Japan. The challenge, of course, was to formulate a solution responsive to both of these objectives—somewhere between a critique of GNP and the developmental rights of the Third World, so to speak.

Fearing that the developing nations might boycott the Stockholm conference, UNCHE secretary general Maurice Strong hastily brought together a group of twenty-seven eminent economists, sociologists, and environmentalists in the Swedish city of Founex in June 1971 to discuss the environment-development dilemma or, as it was often described, the "North-South" problem. Along with Tsuru, other participants included development experts such as the Egyptian Marxian economist Samir Amin, the Polish-born French eco-socioeconomist Ignacy Sachs, the Chilean economist and socialist Felipe Herrera, the Sri Lankan economist and civil servant Gamani Corea, and the noted Swedish macroeconomist Jan Tinbergen. After two weeks of intensive and productive discussion—what Strong later described as "one of the best intellectual exchanges" he had ever been involved in—the group produced an influential publication, *The Founex Report on Environment and Development,* which not only helped secure the participation of the developing nations at UNCHE the following year, but also shaped the future direction of the global environmental debate by laying the foundations of the idea of sustainable development.[102]

By substantially expanding the definition of the environment and by recognizing that the relationship between the environment and development was essentially different for developed and developing nations, the Founex group was able to argue that the environment and economic development need not necessarily be incompatible and that, accordingly, the developing nations would not be penalized in any future environmental protection regime.[103] The *Founex Report* argued that, while it was appropriate to understand development as a *cause* of environmental problems in developed nations, in developing countries development actually represented a *cure* for environmental problems. This was because the environmental problems of developing nations were of a "different kind" to the "quality of life" issues informing the developed countries' environmentalism and reflective of "poverty" and the "lack of development" such as "poor water, housing, sanitation and nutrition . . . sickness and disease, and . . . natural disasters."[104]

Although he participated in the Founex conference and helped craft the report, Tsuru was not completely satisfied with the outcome. He felt that broadening the concept of the environment to include problems such as soil erosion and human health was more about "strategic expediency," to bring the developing nations on board, than about dealing with environmental destruction "in a straightforward way."[105] Founex solved the tension between the North and South, Tsuru argued, by creating two definitions of the environment, one for the developing nations and another for the developed, differentiated by their stages of economic development.[106] As he explained in early 1972,

> The choice before us, it seems to me, is either (I) to encompass all the conceivable major environmental issues under our purview, including, for example, such matters as soil erosion, urban plight, public health problems, etc., or (2) to focus more sharply on those phenomena which can be clearly defined as environmental problems exemplified typically by air and water pollutions and noise. The inclination to take the first of these alternatives appears to be motivated by strategic judgment . . . that the current environmental concern on the international scale can be taken advantage of to load onto that concept as many problem areas as possible so that aid activities in such fields can be intensified. Those who take this choice apparently fear also that the second alternative, if emphasized too sharply, will result in the recognition that the environmental concern, at least in some areas, conflicts with development objectives.[107]

In keeping with his critique of GNP-centered growth, Tsuru suggested, conversely, that it was the concept of "development" and not the "environment" that needed to be rethought. On the one hand, he believed the environment and environmental problems should be defined "precisely" and narrowly so that "counter-measures" at the local, national, and international levels would "have a well-defined focus."[108] But, on the other hand, as he had been advocating to international audiences since well before Founex, he felt that development had to be reconceptualized as something far broader than the blunt measurement of the GNP index and more attuned to human welfare.[109] To the extent that development was understood as the sum total of expenditure in the free market, the environment and development would be in conflict and there would be external diseconomies such as pollution.[110] But what if the "failure" of market-led growth was finally accepted and "development" fundamentally reconceptualized within the "rubric" of "welfare-focused development planning"?[111] In this rubric there would be no conflict between the environment and development, nor would there be any need for developing and developed nations to have different definitions of the environment.[112] "The unifying philosophy here is that development has an aspect which has to transcend the market mechanism in the sense that public goods of both types—for producers and for consumers—have to be provided. It is in this sense that 'development' can subsume 'environment'; and to the extent that 'environment' is subsumed under 'development,' it competes for limited funds available for various concrete needs of 'development.'"[113] The Brundtland Report of 1987 would later popularize this notion of environmentally informed development as "sustainable development," but it was Tsuru and his contemporaries at events such as Founex and UNCHE who lay the foundations. Indeed, although Tsuru was critical of the Founex conference for expanding the scope of environmental problems, he was actually doing something similar in his reconceptualization of the idea of development. Indeed, the report of the Founex conference replicated, more or less, the same revision of development Tsuru advocated in New York, Paris, and elsewhere in the months before UNCHE. As the *Founex Report* stated,

> Whilst the concern with human environment in developing countries can only reinforce the commitment to development, it should serve, however, to provide new dimensions to the development concept itself. In the past, there has been a tendency to equate the development goal with the more narrowly conceived objective of economic growth as measured by the rise in gross national product. It is usually recognized today that high rates of economic growth, necessary and essential as they are, do not by themselves guarantee the easing of urgent social and human problems. Indeed in many countries high growth rates have been

accompanied by increasing unemployment, rising disparities in incomes both between groups and between regions, and the deterioration of social and cultural conditions. A new emphasis is thus being placed on the attainment of social and cultural goals as part of the development process. The recognition of environmental issues in developing countries is an aspect of this widening of the development concept. It is part of a more integrated or unified approach to the development objective.[114]

Of course, Tsuru recognized that redefining development away from its market focus to include welfare aspects would involve costs, especially for developing nations. Given that developed nations produced most global pollution, he concluded that there was an "overwhelming" moral duty for the North to pay for the "clean up" and for "any extra costs imposed on developing nations by the introduction of nonpollutive technology ahead of local saturation." Rather than "aid," Tsuru said such transfers from the wealthy to the poor must be seen as obligations for technological excesses and for past injustices such as the gratuitous and immoral siphoning of natural resources by imperial powers from their colonies.[115] Stockholm would be an opportunity to "consolidat[e] international public opinion towards acceptance of the general principle that developed countries should assume, at least for the coming decade or so, the major cost of keeping the pollutions [sic] with international consequences within permissible thresholds."[116]

By the eve of UNCHE, then, Tsuru Shigeto had played a major role in rallying a transnational alliance committed to tackling the problem of environmental degradation worldwide. The Tokyo Symposium's advocacy of "environmental rights" and Tsuru's international activities from the late 1960s onward helped propel a worldview shaped by a specific national experience of environmental injustice to the very center of global debates about the environment and development. In his attempt to reconceptualize development as a process inclusive of human welfare considerations, Tsuru not only helped secure the participation of developing nations at Stockholm, but, just as significantly, he also contributed to the rudimentary formulation of a new—yet no less controversial—idea of sustainable development. It seems fair to conclude that, coupled with the impact of Japanese pollution victims at UNCHE, Japanese environmental activists like Tsuru contributed in significant ways to this defining moment of global environmentalism in the early 1970s. Importantly, they did so by drawing on a very local experience of industrial pollution and environmental injustice.

## Conclusion

In a sardonic twist on the UNCHE slogan "Only One Earth," the day after the conference the *New York Times* ran an article titled "One Confused Earth," in which it offered an understandably ambivalent analysis of the event.[117] On the one hand, a participant interviewed for the article observed that what this "frustrating event for idealists" lacked was a "Thomas Jefferson—someone who could lift the delegates above their parochial concerns and rally them behind a contemporary equivalent of the call for life, liberty, and the pursuit of happiness." On the other hand, however, although no such Jeffersonian savior emerged, the article still pronounced UNCHE a modest success; primarily because it happened at all, but also because the rich countries "learned in a very direct way" how differently the developing nations understood the "environment" and "development." As the article observed, "One persistent theme heard from the underdeveloped countries was the obligation of the rich few to help them pay for the costs of environmental protection as they develop. That may sound strange in Washington, but it is the way much of the world feels."[118] According to historian John McCormick, UNCHE helped fashion a "more comprehensive view of human mismanagement of the biosphere," and environmentalism arguably shifted from "the popular, intuitive, and parochial form" of that in rich countries to something more "rational and global in outlook" and, hence, more acceptable to nations at different stages of economic development.[119]

For environmental NGOs such as the group from Japan, UNCHE represented the beginning of a new phase of transnational interconnectivity and global influence that would continue to intensify thereafter. UNCHE showed Japanese activists the value of transnational activism as a political tool—a "boomerang" of influence, to use Keck and Sikkink's idea—for exerting pressure back on the Japanese government. The effect of *Polluted Japan* on the Japanese government's involvement at UNCHE revealed this potential most graphically. In the transnational activism of Tsuru Shigeto we also glimpse how Japanese transnational activists influenced the evolution of key concepts and debates on the environment. Tsuru's critique of GNP and his attempt to reconceptualize "development" helped shape a wider debate about North-South inequities and the conflict between environmental protection and economic development. Tsuru's privileged, cosmopolitan background also made it possible for him to move seamlessly between the worlds of officialdom, scientific experts, international organizations, and grassroots movements, in effect giving voice to the concerns of Japanese environmentalists at multiple levels. As Ui Jun observed in the ILP monthly newsletter, hereafter Japanese environmental movements needed to forge ever more intensive overseas connections. The day will undoubtedly come, he said, when a "blue-eyed stranger will approach us at a sit-in or a demonstration and ask for an explanation."[120] In order to cope with this future, the movement had to spread its network beyond the archipelago—which indeed it would do.

But engaging in the global environmental movement did not mean abandoning the local. As their involvement at UNCHE reveals, Japanese victims and activists drew on local experiences with industrial pollution to offer a distinctive interpretation of the limits to growth, which spoke forcefully to the horrendous human costs of economic growth. With their words and their injured bodies they argued that these human limits mattered as much as—if not more than—the limited capacity of the natural environment or the need to limit population. Tsuru Shigeto's critique of GNP and his concept of welfare-focused development provided the theoretical framework for this discourse on humane limitations. Like the victims' bodies, his appeal to human welfare as a guiding principle of environmentalism bore the undeniable imprint of a national trauma in which economic development had proceeded on the back of physical agony and multifaceted injustice.

CHAPTER 4

# Pollution Export and Victimhood

The UN conference in Stockholm was an eye-opening experience for the Japanese pollution victims and their supporters, thanks in part to the remarkable media and public attention they received, but also for what the group learned about Japanese corporate pollution worldwide. Activists, journalists, and delegates from other countries—especially East Asia—confronted the Japanese with troubling reports about the environmentally destructive activities of Japanese industry: pollutive mining operations in the Philippines, logging in Malaysia and Indonesia, and industrial plants in Singapore.[1] As Ui Jun frankly admitted, until Stockholm he and others had not really thought about the Japanese "economic invasion" of Asia, overwhelmed as they were with their concern about pollution at home and their desire to communicate this story abroad. But the conference had forced them to carefully reconsider Japan's role in bolstering and perpetuating injustices elsewhere; the ways, for example, Japan was buttressing authoritarian regimes in East Asia, supporting the US war in Vietnam, and damaging living environments and human health—all to support an affluent daily life back home.[2] As sociologist Isomura Eiichi opined in an essay after UNCHE, "From the perspective of Asians, Japan is a 'factory owner' and Asians are the 'workers.' This factory owner takes resources from Asia back to the Japanese archipelago where they are processed and then sold back to the 'workers' at a high price. In the process, the resources of these workers' countries are ravaged, the natural environment is destroyed, and the standard of living does not necessarily improve."[3] Addressing this "pollution export" from Japan to Asia would become the primary focus of Japanese transnational environmental activism throughout the 1970s. It would involve establishing new connections with East Asian activists and movements, communicating the story of Japanese industrial pollution throughout the region, and implementing a range of transnational initiatives to address the problem head on. It would also necessitate a fundamental rethinking of strategy and objectives on the part of Japanese groups involved.

In this chapter I focus on the ways the pollution export problem complicated ideas of environmental injustice fashioned in the domestic struggle. In its international iteration before and during UNCHE, the Japanese environmental injustice paradigm spoke powerfully to the human limits to growth. Japanese pollution victims served—quite unproblematically—as living proof of these limits. But the effect was somewhat different when this local Japanese experience of injustice was projected on to a regional canvas. In the first place, it forced the Japanese activists involved to carefully reconsider the supposed "resolution" of Japanese industrial pollution in the early 1970s, exemplified, for instance, by victories in the Big Four pollution law suits, the 1970 Pollution Diet, and visibly cleaner living environments. Activists began to wonder about the legitimacy of local victories if they resulted in industry simply relocating pollution, environmental destruction, and human injustice to some locality overseas. If the state and its regulatory framework had simply become tools to protect Japanese localities at the expense of those abroad, were not these localities implicated in the overseas pollution perpetrated by Japanese corporations?

Such questions destabilized a powerful assumption that had galvanized the struggle against environmental injustice from its origins in the domestic pollution crisis of the 1960s: namely, that the activists or the people they spoke for were necessarily and unproblematically positioned on the side of victims. As they reached out to the sufferers and opponents of Japanese pollution export throughout East Asia, these activists encountered, again and again, a troubling narrative that connected the country's colonial and military legacy to its contemporary pollutive activities—a continuous, unbroken history of injustice and discrimination toward the region. Indeed, pollution export exposed the limitations of an environmental injustice paradigm permeated by a consciousness of victimhood anchored in a distinctive national experience. To be sure, empathy based on the shared experience of environmental injustice continued to be a source of motivation and transnational solidarity for the Japanese groups I examine in the chapter. But the fact that those others happened to be in a region formerly colonized and brutalized by the Japanese military and now ravaged by Japanese industrial activity disrupted any seamless notions of an alliance of victims. This tension between solidarity and aggression in the regional iteration of environmental injustice proved to be one of its most challenging and, I would argue, transformative moments.

I begin the chapter with some background on the spread of Japanese industry into East Asia in the 1970s, followed by analysis of the landmark Conference of Asians held in Tokyo in 1974. This defining event brought together activists from antipollution groups, the anti–Vietnam War movement (Beheiren), and from East Asia. Activists such as Oda Makoto of Beheiren encouraged antipollution activists to consider the limitations of environmental injustice framed through the lens of victimhood alone. Instead, Oda pushed his environmentalist colleagues to consider their simultaneous "aggression" toward Asia. Mobilizations against specific instances of pollution export in the early 1970s further encouraged this reconsideration of victimhood. I analyze four seminal examples in the chapter: the 1973–1974 action against the Asahi Glass Corporation in Thailand; two actions against the Toyama Chemical Company and the Nippon Chemical Company in South Korea, both beginning in 1974; and the protest against Kawasaki Steel's sintering operations in the Philippines from late 1975. All four cases provide fascinating insights into the ways regional involvement encouraged activists to rethink domestic "victories" and notions of victimhood. In Thailand and the Philippines, Japanese groups discovered a troubling replication of Japanese corporate pollution, while in South Korea they had to face the troubling continuities between pollution export in the present and Japanese colonialism and aggression in the past. One concrete outcome of these encounters was the establishment of the Han-Kōgai Yushutsu Tsūhō Sentā (Antipollution Export Information Center, AEIC) in 1976. Born as an alliance of antipollution export groups, the AEIC became the organizational hub for activists committed to transforming their earlier campaign as environmental "victims" into a proactive and reflexive program opposing Japanese industrial "aggression" in Asia and beyond. Once again, leading activists like Ui Jun played a key role as rooted cosmopolitans, forging intellectual and organizational connections between movements at home and in Asia. They were the ones who encouraged local groups to reposition the local in wider and often unsettling frameworks of inequity. Moreover, by shining a light on pollution export, they helped to "boomerang" pressure back on to responsible corporations such that by the late 1980s the costs to corporate public image tended to outweigh the benefits.

## From Pollution Miracle to Pollution Export

As T. J. Pempel and others have noted, Japan's economic links with Asia began to intensify in the 1970s thanks to the collapse of the Bretton Woods monetary system in 1971, the dramatic increase in crude oil prices following the first oil shock of 1973, and the subsequent regulatory easing on capital outflows.[4] What had previously been a relationship based on simple trade now began to encompass more foreign direct investment (FDI) by Japanese industry. In the period between 1973 and 1976, Japanese FDI into Asia essentially doubled that of the previous twenty years combined.[5] Significantly, the composition of this FDI changed in the early 1970s, with greater emphasis on "energy-intensive, highly polluting sectors like chemicals, iron and steel, and nonferrous metals."[6]

Antipollution activists recognized that various factors were fueling the growth of Japanese FDI in Asia. In 1974, Ui Jun stated unequivocally that cheap wages and resources were the primary factors driving Japanese FDI growth in Asia and that stricter domestic antipollution regulations were only a "minor" factor in the corporate decision-making matrix.[7] Broadly speaking he was correct, but there is no doubt that tougher regulation, coupled with a wave of domestic protest, played a role in the relocation decisions of corporations involved in the more pollutive industries such as petrochemicals and extractive metallurgy. Thanks to research by Derek Hall, we know that pollution export was a deliberate state and corporate strategy in the 1970s, and, for a time, that elites in both sectors were "remarkably forthright" about this.[8] In mid-1970, for example, the Ministry of International Trade and Industry (MITI) partially justified a new fund for the relocation of petrochemical industries offshore by pointing to the restraining effect of pollution opposition on new domestic constructions.[9] Just one month later, the giant Mitsubishi Corporation confirmed this evaluation, noting site acquisition difficulties in Japan as a factor in its decision to build an oil refinery in Southeast Asia.[10] As late as 1975, an official from Kawasaki Steel (hereafter Kawatetsu [as known in Japan]) made the following blatant admission during civil proceedings to stop the company constructing a sixth blast furnace at its Chiba Prefecture plant:

> Although a sintering plant is an indispensable part of a steel plant, it also produces more air polluting materials than any other part of the plant. Therefore, we at Kawatetsu have decided to build the new sintering

plant which is needed for the no.6 blast furnace in a foreign country instead of within the Chiba plant. . . . This decision . . . will enable us to drastically reduce the amount of discharge of polluted materials. The new sintering plant is now under construction in Mindanao [in] the Philippines, as part of Japan's economic aid to that country.[11]

At the receiving end, Asian leaders and dictators welcomed Japan's polluting industries with open arms. South Korean president Park Chung-hee actively supported the entry of these industries into the country through a combination of watered-down pollution regulations and suppression or co-optation of local protest.[12] In 1973 Park nonchalantly stated that "for the purposes of the industrial development of our country, it will be best not to worry too much about pollution problems."[13] Elite attitudes were no more enlightened in Southeast Asia. In the Philippines the corrupt dictator, President Ferdinand Marcos, allowed Kawatetsu to have 100 percent ownership of a highly polluting sintering plant (alluded to in the quote above) on Mindanao Island. A 1974 report by the activist publication *AMPO: Japan-Asia Quarterly Review* noted how Marcos unilaterally approved the plant even though the Philippines Board of Investment was still considering its economic merit and environmental impact. By the time Japanese prime minister Tanaka Kakuei visited the country in early 1974, the establishment of the Kawatetsu-owned and -operated Philippine Sinter Corporation was essentially a done deal.[14] Like his kindred spirit President Park in South Korea, Marcos told the Japanese in 1976 that the Philippines would "be happy to take . . . polluting industries off your hands."[15]

So, while domestic environmental regulation and protest and hospitable foreign governments do not totally explain Japan's economic advance into Asia in the 1970s, there is no doubt they were a consideration, especially for the dirtiest industries. More pertinently, many Japanese activists became convinced that corporate pursuit of pollution havens lay at the core of the country's FDI boom in the region, and this conviction formed the basis of their mobilizations against it.

### Regional Solidarity: The Conference of Asians, 1974

In response to this wave of Asian FDI, and on the initiative of the charismatic antiwar campaigner and novelist Oda Makoto, in June 1974 activists from the Japanese anti–Vietnam War movement Beheiren, Christian groups, and Ui Jun's ILP movement organized the inaugural Conference of Asians to bring together progressives from the region to consider the nature and extent of Japan's relationship with other Asian nations.[16] Apart from opening their eyes to a range of inequities and injustices throughout the region, the conference also served as a critical opportunity for some activists associated with the ILP to reconsider the notion of "victimhood" deeply informing ideas about injustice in the Japanese environmental movement. Oda Makoto and other Beheiren activists played a critical role in stimulating this reconsideration, because they had spent the better part of a decade thinking about Japanese complicity in the Vietnam War and, hence, offered environmental activists a sophisticated analysis of Japan's simultaneous "victimhood" and "aggression"—as a quasi-colony of the United States on the one hand, and as an active supporter of the US campaign in Indochina on the other. Indeed, the conference is worth considering in detail because it was an important 1970s moment of transnational connection between local Japanese groups and their Asian counterparts, which stimulated significant ideational transformations relating to understandings of the local, injustice, and victimhood. We can see in it the ways transnational interaction fostered new ways of thinking within domestic civic movements in Japan.

The Conference of Asians ran for seven days from June 8 to 16, 1974, and involved around 250 participants, forty of whom traveled from six countries throughout East Asia, including South Korea, the Philippines, Singapore, Thailand, and Malaysia. Participants represented a variety of progressive organizations such as labor unions, antipollution movements, community groups, Christians, and student societies.[17] On the Japanese side, ILP activists were joined by stalwarts of the Beheiren movement like Oda Makoto, who helped articulate the conceptual parameters of the event. The conference was divided into three discrete phases. On the first two days, the foreign participants were taken on a "pollution bus tour" in and around Tokyo, similar to the one Tsuru Shigeto had organized for the Tokyo Symposium in 1971. At Sanrizuka, in nearby Chiba Prefecture, they met with Tomura Issaku and comrades involved in a movement to stop construction of the New Tokyo International Airport (Narita Airport). While in Chiba the group observed the Kawatetsu Steel mill with its five (and soon to be six) blast furnaces, as well as the massive Keiyō Industrial Region on the shores of Tokyo Bay. At the Asahi Glass factory in Chiba a participant from Thailand could not hold back his tears on coming face-to-face with the company responsible for shocking pollution in Bangkok.[18] Visits were not limited to environmental hot spots either: Paul Chamniern, an activist from the slums of Bangkok, traveled with others to meet Japanese volunteer groups working in Tokyo's working-class San'ya slum.[19] One Malaysian delegate admitted that before the conference he viewed Japan's antipollution struggle as little more than a fashionable activity of well-to-do people who simply shouted slogans. But, coming to Japan, meeting Minamata victims, and hearing firsthand reports made him realize that it was actually the poorest and most underprivileged people in Japan who were carrying the weight of the movement on their shoulders.[20]

After the bus tour, participants traveled to the six-hundred-year old Yugyōji Buddhist temple in Fujisawa City an hour south of Tokyo, where they engaged in a two-day "teach-in." Discussions ranged from the structure of American domination in Asia to the exploitation of workers in Singapore to the Thai labor movement and the legacy of British colonialism in Malaysia.[21] As the progressive magazine *AMPO* later recounted, "After the day's discussions were carried on informally into the night, all slept in the large common room. One participant commented, 'this is like a parliament called by anarchists.' The evenings were sometimes turned over to songs and local dances, a welcome relief from the seriousness of discussions of the Asian scene. In the whole process there developed an unmistakable feeling of participating in something unprecedented."[22] Oda Makoto was swept up in the emotion of the moment, recalling, "When we went out on the [bus tour] we all slept side by side at small inns. I became convinced that sleeping on futons laid side by side and without regard to nationality was the best and the most Asian way of doing things."[23]

For the main conference, participants moved to Hachiōji City in Tokyo, along the way observing a US munitions supply facility in Sagamihara and the Mitsubishi Caterpillar factory. Like the teach-in, the wide-ranging discussions at the conference all in one way or another touched on violations of human rights throughout Asia. Japanese participants, for instance, addressed the "mechanism of Japan's economic invasion" and the responsibility of ordinary Japanese for corporate pollution export, while Hamamoto Tsuginori and Ishimure Michiko, advocates for Minamata disease victims, repeated their cautionary tale about corporate irresponsibility within Japan.[24] Breakout sessions dealing with regional labor conditions, political prisoners, and women's liberation reinforced the themes of injustice, inequity, and rights. On the final day, which was open to the public, participants ratified the Joint Declaration of the Asian People authored by Oda Makoto, and they made a range of commitments and resolutions to oppose political imprisonments and discrimination against women in Asia, confront Japanese corporate polluters, and meet in conference as often as necessary or possible.[25] The declaration reiterated participants' main objective of collectively overcoming injustices and violations of human rights throughout Asia—often perpetrated by the United States and Japan.

As the proceedings of the conference declared, "We want to tease out in concrete detail the nature of [Japan's] economic invasion and its pollution export. We want to fundamentally rethink things, and through solidarity with the peoples of Asia, whose daily lives have been stolen, build a network of struggle to steal back these daily lives."[26] More specifically, delegates hoped the gathering would expose the nefarious activities of Japanese companies and the various facilitating policies of corrupt governments in Asia and, through exchange of information, become the first step in a multipronged attack on this structure of domination. For his part, Oda Makoto saw the conference as a historic display of unity among Asians and an opportunity for them to once again announce to the world "Asia is One."[27]

Importantly, for the Japanese participants—especially environmental groups like the ILP—the creation of such "oneness" would first require a frank engagement with their complicity in Japanese corporate behavior in Asia, as consumers and Japanese citizens. Oda made this point loud and clear, explaining how in the course of the anti–Vietnam War movement he had realized that Japan was no longer or simply a victim nation. For Oda, earlier Japanese antiwar and peace movements had been based almost entirely on the perspective of victims—in other words, the mentality of having suffered terribly in the war and not wanting to experience such suffering again. But, while ordinary Japanese were indeed victims of their state in the previous war, they were also perpetrators, said Oda. For example, what the Japanese did to the Chinese or what Japan did to Korea was an issue for every Japanese person. "In other words, the logic that because we are victims we cannot be perpetrators does not hold. We are perpetrators because we are victims."[28] In the context of the pollution export problem, this meant that ordinary Japanese needed to scrutinize the source of their affluent daily lives—how these lives might be connected to Asian suffering and the kind of action needed to "stop walking all over Asian people," as Oda put it.[29]

Again and again foreign delegates called on Japanese activists to recast domestic struggles in the wider Asian struggle or risk replaying the tragic history of Japanese aggression in Asia. From the perspective of economic imperialism, it was clear to the foreign delegates that victories in antipollution struggles within Japan actually intensified the export of pollution. Just as Japanese unionists' struggle for higher wages encouraged Japanese corporations to look abroad in search of cheaper labor markets, pressure from domestic antipollution movements forced industry to find more hospitable locations abroad. These were "urgent problems for the Japanese movement," which would be solved only through an "Asia-wide perspective."[30] A delegate from Thailand articulated this desire for Japanese accountability in the clearest of terms: "What we want is responsibility not charity. Those of us who came from Asian countries [to participate] and all the people in Asia right now do not want to receive charity from Japan. What we want is responsibility. We are aware of our own responsibility and wish to cooperate and to build an organization within which we can struggle together. So please don't treat us like little children."[31]

Indeed, at a deeper level, the event proved more transformative than a mere exposé on Japanese economic transgressions in Asia; it was an opportunity for participants—especially Japanese environmental groups like the ILP—to know and understand other Asians, not on the basis of an amorphous civilizational "Asianness" but within a progressive imaginary knit together by commitment to a new struggle for the defense of human rights and living environments; a critical and contentious regionalism constructed from below and based on mutual responsibility. For their part, ILP activists left the conference both inspired and challenged. On the one hand they were able to repeat—for an all-Asian audience—the cautionary tale of Japanese environmental pollution. Ui Jun hoped they would recognize and work to avoid Japan's mistaken and "uncritical importation of Western culture since the Meiji era." He did not want to see Asian countries "suffer in the same way" as Japanese pollution victims had.[32]

On the other hand, however, Japanese delegates—many of whom would become deeply involved in the pollution export problem—began to rethink environmental injustice from their position as citizens of an "aggressor" nation. Hirayama Takasada, a member of the ILP movement and staunch opponent of pollution export, is a case in point. For Hirayama, Japanese pollution in Asia simply had to be connected to a longer history of aggression and domination in the region. As he explained,

> Japanese lead a daily life stained with the blood and sweat of Asian people. Today Asia is integrated into Japan's industrial structure like a rubbish heap of contradictions. We (latent) victims of Japanese pollu-

tion must recognize our position as accomplices in and beneficiaries of Japanese imperialism and we must engage in the struggle to slice into the inside of Japanese imperialism—removing pollution from within Japan and stopping the export of pollution to . . . Asia. Failure to do so will inhibit the formation of strong ties with the people of Asia and all those countries dominated by Japanese imperialism.[33]

Hirayama emphasized that the motivation for this struggle emerged from the Japanese people's "regret for 100 years of incessant invasion of Asia from the Meiji era." Their challenge in the present was to connect this history of invasion to the "voices of Minamata disease suffers" and, ultimately, to the realities of Japanese corporate misbehavior in Asia.[34] While any transnational movement against pollution export would certainly require "shared emotion" as Asians or empathy as "victims" of environmental injustice, Hirayama stressed the necessity of connecting that emotion and empathy to a recognition of the "aggression" by Japan against Asia in the past and present. Needless to say, this reconsideration of victimhood and recognition of complicity marked an important intellectual development in thinking about environmental injustice largely absent in the 1960s. It would be reinforced by various concrete mobilizations against pollution export, four decisive instances of which I turn to now.

## Polluted Japan in Bangkok: Beyond the Logic of "Old Maid"

In an important 1977 essay, Inoue Sumio—a former Beheiren activist now leading the struggle against pollution export—criticized what he called the "Old Maid logic" in Japanese antipollution protest. He was referring here to the card game Old Maid, in which the aim is to *not* be the one left holding the unpaired queen of spades (the joker card in the Japanese version, Babanuki) by skillfully shifting it to other players. In terms of pollution protest, the metaphor symbolized the ways local communities had expelled pollutive industry from their localities without the slightest concern for its next destination—what might now be described as NIMBY (not-in-my-back-yard) logic.[35] As I have shown elsewhere, this Old Maid logic held sway among many local Japanese antipollution movements of the 1960s and early 1970s, with one prominent advocate even arguing that the wider public interest was best served when antipollution groups adhered to a resolute "local egoism."[36]

But, as Inoue's critique of Old Maid logic evidences, by the mid- to late 1970s a growing number of Japanese environmental activists had rejected local egoism, primarily on ethical grounds, in response to pollution export. For Inoue and others, the oppressive political conditions under which many Asians lived often precluded Japanese forms of grassroots resistance, which benefited from a democratic constitution and the rule of law. The self-gratifying logic of some Japanese activists that the aggregate of their local egoisms would produce a greater overall good collapsed completely when pollution crossed national borders. To be sure, protesting communities in Japan could, with a degree of confidence, count on other communities nationwide to do the same, effectively stranding polluting industries and serving a greater overall *national* good. But what about in countries where dictatorial regimes suppressed all expressions of local resistance? When polluting industries set up operations there, the chain of resistance linking local egoisms broke down and the troubling question of responsibility resurfaced: if the next community could not continue the struggle, then who would help them offload the pollution card? Moreover, that such questions involved Japan and other Asian countries added a whole other dimension to the issue of responsibility, connecting pollution export to the sins of an imperial past and a fragile mentality of victimhood.

A sensitivity to this Old Maid logic was evident among some Japanese antipollution groups almost immediately after UNCHE. Stimulated by their interactions with other Asian activists at the conference, members of the ILP executive committee started an English-language publication, *KOGAI: The Newsletter from Polluted Japan,* with a 140,000-yen donation received from the Karolinska Institute. This newsletter was distributed free of charge (mainly throughout East Asia) on a seasonal basis, beginning in summer 1973. Ui Jun's opening statement in the first edition succinctly articulated the new task antipollution activists had set themselves: "Our purpose is to place emphasis on the Asian environmental situation and through this emphasis and cooperation come to the aid of various peoples' movements working on the same problems throughout Asia. . . . We feel that in this way we can in some small respect compensate for the great damage that Japanese imperialism has done in the past and will continue to do in the future." Ui wanted *KOGAI* to be a voice for antipollution movements around Asia and a source of inspiration for groups as they saw their local struggles communicated to activists across the region. *KOGAI,* Ui and others hoped, would evolve into a vehicle for genuine transnational solidarity based on mutual recognition and common struggle—an Asia in which the people were united and not just the elites.

The ILP executive committee also established an Asia group dedicated to investigating Japanese economic activity in the region, and the movement's Japanese-language publication, *Jishu Kōza*, began a new column titled Ajia no Mado (Window on Asia), which ran dedicated articles on Asian issues. These initiatives served as important vehicles for activists involved in the ILP movement to begin a discussion about Japanese environmental injustices in a regional context. In late 1972, for example, ILP activist Matsuoka Nobuo reported on his travels throughout Malaysia and Thailand where he reconnected with contacts forged at UNCHE. Matsuoka reported how young Malaysian intellectuals were extremely skeptical, if not cynical, about so-called Japanese economic and technical assistance, which was often no more than a euphemism for Japan procuring cheap labor and materials. As Matsuoka put it, "If we fail to carefully reconsider what assistance really is, Japanese run the risk of losing the good faith of our Asian friends to a point where it is irrecoverable." While in Malaysia, Matsuoka spoke about Japan's environmental problems to his hosts, and he investigated the health risks of Japanese pesticides used in Malaysian farming. He also promised to send copies of *KOGAI* to Malaysian activists.[37] In Thailand, Matsuoka visited Chulalongkorn University in Bangkok, where he learned of student initiatives to clean up the city's rivers.[38] As in Malaysia, he gave an hour-long presentation with slides on Japanese pollution (Minamata, Itai Itai) to faculty members and students (many belonging to nature conservation clubs), and he distributed copies of *Polluted Japan*.[39] After the presentation at Chulalongkorn, the moderator commented that this was the first time many had heard about Japanese pollution, and hence it would serve as a warning and something none of them would forget. Matsuoka recalled how, on hearing this, he was "overtaken" with the sense that from now on all Japanese activists "must be prepared to shoulder another heavy responsibility."[40] "Can we silently watch as Japanese pollution crosses the sea and spreads throughout Asia?" he asked. "The time has come for us to act on the realization that we have another heavy responsibility. Each and every one of us should think about what we can do."[41]

Matsuoka's interaction with Thai environmental groups was propitious, because only months later, suspicions about Japanese pollution export to Thailand became realities. Under the ominous headline "No Repeat of the Minamata Tragedy," on August 5, 1973, the Thai daily, *Siam Rath,* began a series of articles on contamination of Bangkok's Chao Phrya River by the Thai Asahi Caustic Soda Company (TACS), a Thai-Japan joint venture established in 1966, with the Asahi Glass Company of Japan (part of the Mitsubishi Group) providing 49 percent of the capital and all of the technical expertise.[42] According to the *Siam Rith,* testing conducted by Thai authorities in September 1973 revealed that river water contaminated by caustic soda dumped from the TACS factory had completely destroyed farming crops. More worryingly, for a six-month period beginning in May 1973, effluent dumped from the factory containing chlorine, hydrochloric acid, and traces of mercury resulted in a massive die-off of fish and shrimp, which local residents had unwittingly consumed.[43] As early as May 1973, people along the river had contracted various skin afflictions and bouts of diarrhea of unknown cause. Fearful of the river water, many resorted to digging makeshift wells.[44] For its part, TACS denied dumping any contaminated waste and refused all responsibility for the fish kill and human health effects, saying that its effluent was "smelly" but not toxic.[45] The company's Japanese general manager admitted to the use of inorganic mercury in production processes but said the utmost efforts were made to remove any traces from effluent and, in any case, this was *inorganic* mercury and not *organic* mercury, the culprit in Minamata.[46] Asahi Glass's environmental track record in Japan, however, suggested otherwise. In summer 1973, as the company faced a brewing controversy in Bangkok, irate fishermen from Chiba blockaded Asahi Glass and other factories responsible for polluting the waters of Tokyo Bay. Tests conducted in waters near the Asahi Glass plant revealed high levels of both inorganic and organic mercury.[47]

In Thailand, environmental activists mobilized almost immediately to address the Chao Phraya contamination. From August 26 to 31, 1973, nature conservation clubs at Thammasat, Kasetsart, Chulalongkorn, and Mahidol Universities organized an urgent nature conservation exhibition on the campus of Thammasat University, which devoted considerable attention to the Japanese pollution experience and its implications for Thailand.[48] Thanks to their earlier interactions with Japanese activists at UNCHE and, later, with Matsuoka Nobuo, the students were armed with a battery of powerful resources such as *Polluted Japan* and other disturbing slideshows and documentaries on the Japanese tragedy.[49] Concerned officials from both the Thai Ministry of Industry and of Public Sanitation attended the screening of Tsuchimoto Noriaki's *Minamata: The Victims and Their World,* which no doubt played into their decision to begin investigations into TACS the following month.[50]

Building on Matsuoka Nobuo's interactions with Thai students before the crisis, Hirayama Takasada—also of the ILP Asia group—visited the Kasetsart University nature conservation club on August 6, 1973, to give another slide presentation on Japanese pollution.[51] His timing could not have been better. Activists at the university greeted Hirayama with the *Siam Rath* newspaper article of the previous day on the TACS pollution controversy.[52] His reaction was one of shock and indignation.

> What this!? The evil hand of mercury contamination has reached Thailand! My naïve assumption that full-scale pollution export was yet to occur had been betrayed with consummate easy by these cold, hard facts. Utterly surprised, for a time I was speechless. I was thrown into utter despair by a piercing reality: "pollution export had begun! Thai Asahi Caustic Soda was just the tip of the iceberg." Yet I was quickly filled with rage. I could not allow this. I simply could not allow it. Once again I engraved in my mind the purpose of this visit: to communicate the situation of Japanese pollution and to find a way to mobilize an antipollution movement based on cooperation between Japanese and Southeast Asian people.[53]

Back in Japan, activists moved quickly against Asahi Glass. Determined not to "silently watch the foreign economic invasion and pollution export of corporations and the Japanese government," on September 14, 1973, around 150 protesters from groups including the ILP, Beheiren, and the Mitsubishi Heavy Industries Antiwar Shareholders Committee demonstrated outside the Tokyo headquarters of Asahi Glass with placards—in Japanese and Thai—reading "Asahi Glass, Stop Exporting Pollution!" and "the Japanese people will not allow contamination of the Chao Phraya River by Asahi Glass."[54] This demonstration was widely reported in major Thai media outlets such as *Siam Rath*, which ran interviews with protesters and printed large photos of the event. Thereafter, the Japanese groups received a deluge of letters from Bangkok citizens expressing gratitude and asking for more information on pollution.[55]

One month later, on October 14, 1973, Inoue Sumio and fellow activists established the Nichi-Tai Seinen Yūkō Undō (Japan-Thai Youth Friendship Movement), which served as the central node in the transnational mobilization against Asahi Glass.[56] Thereafter, grassroots exchange between activists in both countries intensified, at first primarily through the mailing of materials such as the *KOGAI* magazine and, later, via mutual visits and coordinated protest events. Most impressive of these transnational phenomena was the simultaneous protest of September 1974 held in Tokyo and Bangkok. This action was the brainchild of Hirayama Takasada and Sutatip Inthon, a young sociologist and member of the nature conservation club at Thammasat University. During his August 1974 visit to the university, Hirayama told Inthon about their demonstration against Asahi Glass headquarters planned for September of that year, and, in response, she determined to hold a major environmental exhibition at the same time, to be called "The Pollution Export of Polluted Japan."[57] The combined actions, the two activists hoped, would become a powerful "two-front attack" (*hasamiuchi*) on the company and pollution export more generally.

On September 14, 1974, a modest group of around eighty protesters marched on the headquarters of Asahi Glass in central Tokyo, again with Thai- and Japanese-language banners reading "Asahi Glass, Get Out of Thailand!" More than the protest of a year earlier, the Japanese were acutely aware of the historical significance of the event as a moment of border-crossing solidarity. In spite of their geographical separation, in this moment, at least, they shared a common space with Thai compatriots fighting for the same cause. Telegrams from Thailand heightened this sense of joint struggle. A telegram from the organizers of the Thai event told the Japanese that "we struggle together with you in order to survive."[58] The Federation of Independent Students of Thailand (FIST), an organization at the forefront of the country's historic October Revolution of 1973, concluded that "people around the world are slowly realizing that the greatest obstacle to the real development of mankind is imperialism" and hence "our historic mission is to cooperate in the destruction of the destructive system called imperialism."[59] Inoue, Hirayama, and the other organizers were somewhat disappointed at the turnout in Tokyo, coming just months after the buoyant emotion of the Conference of Asians.[60] But, in the broader context of Japanese environmental activism, the movement was of historic import. This was one of the first times Japanese and other Asians had protested together—albeit in different countries—against an instance of Japanese corporate pollution outside Japan.

Developments at the Thailand node of the demonstration were of a different scale altogether. Students and faculty involved in nature conservation clubs at Thammasat, Chulalongkorn, and Ramkhamhaeng Universities held their exhibition on "Pollution Export from Polluted Japan" at the Thammasat University auditorium for three days, September 14–16, 1974. The aims of the event were threefold: first, to raise consciousness of the dangers of environmental pollution by reference to the Japanese experience; second, to pressure the Thai government to think about effective methods for regulating waste material from factories; and, third, to caution companies planning to construct new facilities.[61] Okuda Takaharu of the ILP Asia group, who was in Thailand for the exhibition, observed how it represented the first serious attempt to think about pollution problems in Thai history.[62] Visitors to the exhibition were greeted by a large banner at the entrance reading "POLLUTED JAPAN," under which was placed a coffin and a photograph of a child victim of fetal Minamata disease.[63] The lobby of the auditorium displayed photographs—supplied by the ILP—of Yokkaichi City, Minamata Bay, PCB contamination victims, nuclear power plants, and Okinawa US military bases, all with accompanying explanations in Thai. A series of panels dealt with the Japanese economic penetration into Asia and the collusion between Japanese and Thai political leaders. There was also a satirical cartoon titled "The Japanese Monster Dying from Pollution" and a panel asking visitors to sign a petition opposing Japanese-led construction of a petrochemical plant in Si Racha on the Gulf of Thailand.[64] Copies of the declaration made at the Tokyo protest against Asahi Glass were also distributed to visitors.[65]

Okuda described how Japan was severely criticized throughout the exhibition, encapsulated by the comment of one individual who bluntly concluded, "Japanese imperialism is nastier than American imperialism."[66] But there were also positive moments for Japan during the event, such as the outburst of applause when the organizers announced that activists in the Japan-Thai Youth Friendship Movement were holding a simultaneous demonstration in Tokyo.[67] Okuda observed that "through this simultaneous demonstration the citizens of Thailand and Japan are finally being connected by a still-delicate thread. In order to strengthen this connection it is nothing more than a matter of conscientiously monitoring pollution export. Such a movement is already underway in Thailand."[68] Speaking to Okuda after the event, Sutatip Inthon could only agree that the exhibition was a great success but, in a tone of realism, added that "this movement is still a very small minority."[69]

Small, no doubt, but the simultaneous transnational protest of September 1974 had lasting effects. In the three days of the event, an unprecedented fifteen thousand Thai citizens came face-to-face—through presentations, debates, slides, films, and photographs—with the realities of Japanese pollution and its export to their country.[70] Thereafter the Mitsui and Mitsubishi Corporations announced that plans to construct the petrochemical plant at the Si Racha district were to be shelved for at least three years. In their press release, the two companies admitted that one reason was Thai students and intellectuals increased attention to the pollution risks of petrochemical complexes.[71] Activists on both sides also walked away transformed. Sutatip Inthon observed that the exhibition was about much more than the TACS problem because it introduced the Thai people to broader questions of economic development, industrial pollution, and human health. "Momentous" also for Inthon was the transnational coordination with the Tokyo protesters.[72]

Okuda Takaharu was correspondingly impressed by the energy and optimism of the Thai students in the wake of the revolution of October 1973. He was pleased and proud to see members of the nature conservation club at Thammasat University diligently translating *Polluted Japan* into Thai.[73] As he explained, the efforts of these students to tell the Thai people about an "insignificant" antipollution movement started in Japan by "ordinary citizens" four years ago was of "great encouragement" for those Japanese "seeking genuine connections with the people of Asia and an end to pollution export."[74] Okuda believed that the way forward for the diversified antipollution movement in Japan was, on the one hand, to communicate the valuable experience of the domestic movement—unique in world history—to the peoples of Asia and, on the other hand, to obtain as much information as possible from the people of Asia. "Only then will 'solidarity' cease to be an obsolete concept." "There are many things we need to communicate. And there are so many things we need to learn. It is clear that the process of building connections between Thai and Japanese citizens has just begun. But to the extent that we pursue the common objective of 'eliminating pollution and that which produces it,' there is a potential for us to build connections with the people of Asia. . . . The task from here on is to further strengthen diverse and substantive connections. This is necessary for our mutual survival."[75]

### Pollution Export to South Korea: Don't Let the Pollution Escape

As Hirayama, Inoue, and other activists scrambled to gather information and organize a response to the TACS incident in Thailand, their unnerving sense of Japanese pollution export already "well underway" was confirmed in early 1974 when another instance in nearby South Korea came to light.[76] Even more than pollution export to Thailand, its occurrence in South Korea disrupted the close association Japanese groups had drawn between environmental injustice and their own victimhood. As they keenly recognized, lurking beneath the South Korean pollution export problem was a troubling legacy of colonization and brutal aggression on the Korean peninsula. In a sense, pollution export to South Korea coalesced with these unresolved historical issues to produce a doubled or compounded sense of aggression in the consciousness of activists. Most immediately this recognition inspired action in the form of resisting any further violation of Korean human rights by Japanese industry and its South Korean patrons. But it also provoked a reconsideration of the ethical foundations of environmental injustice. As the following two movements against the Toyama Chemical and Nippon Chemical companies reveal, Japanese activists' engagement in pollution export to former colonies like South Korea not only expanded the geographical scope of their struggle against environmental injustice, it also fashioned a new reflexivity, in which victims recognized their simultaneous position as aggressors—just as Oda had done in the context of the Vietnam War and repeated at the Conference of Asians. To be sure, these transnational movements were small scale and involved but a handful of activists. But together with contemporary antiwar, minority, and women's liberation groups involved in Asia, they were pushing Japanese civic activism in new directions and into relatively uncharted geographical and ideational terrain.

Japanese activists first became aware of pollution export to South Korea via a February 15, 1974, article in the newspaper *Tōyō Keizai Nippō*, published by the resident Korean community in Japan. According to the article, headlined "'Pollutive Plant' Export, South Korea?!," the Japanese company Toyama Chemical Industries planned to sell its Toyama mercurochrome plant to a Korean entrepreneur after having being forced to cease its Japanese operations in 1973 because of mercury contamination. The new owner, Mr. Koe, a Japanese resident Korean and president of the Sanwa Chemical Corporation, intended to dismantle, transport, and then reconstruct the plant in Incheon City, eventually exporting the mercurochrome back to Japan for use by Toyama Chemical. Mercurochrome, of course, is a powerful topical antiseptic containing up to 25 percent mercury content. Despite reassurances from the company, there had long been concerns that effluent from the production process might contain traces of mercury, which it indeed did.[77] The move to South Korea appeared to be a convenient way to continue production of mercurochrome while avoiding annoying regulations and noisy protest in Japan.

Incheon residents—mostly members of the Young Women's Christian Association (YWCA)—learned of the planned facility from the *Tōyō Keizai Nippō* article, which served as an important vehicle for information exchange between Korean activists in Japan and their South Korean counterparts. The Incheon YWCA quickly convened an emergency meeting at which members passed a resolution of opposition, devised a plan of action, and issued a warning to Sanwa and Toyama Chemical. The women also petitioned the Incheon municipal mayor to stop construction of the mercurochrome plant and to immediately revoke Sanwa Chemical's company registration.[78] Given the repressive political atmosphere under the Park Chung-hee dictatorship, their decision to directly lobby officialdom was a bold one indeed.

Unaware of the Incheon YWCA movement, in Japan the ILP Asia group, led by Hirayama Takasada and his colleague Inoue Sumio (both students at Tokyo University), swung into action. In Tokyo they conducted searches on Toyama Chemical at the Japan Patent Information Organization, the Patent Agency, the National Diet Library, and the Government Printing Center. Their investigations into mercurochrome production revealed that inorganic mercury was indeed a by-product of the manufacturing process. Hirayama and Inoue also traveled to Toyama Prefecture, where they met with two grassroots groups: the Kōgai o Kokuhatsu suru Shimin Rengō (Citizens' Alliance to Expose Pollution) and the Toyama Kyūenkai (Toyama Relief Association), both of which had been established to support industrial pollution victims in that area.[79] Representatives of these groups explained the background of Toyama Chemical's decision to close its mercurochrome facility in Toyama. In September 1973 the company had been forced to halt production after authorities measured elevated levels of mercury in Toyama Bay—in some places equivalent to levels in Minamata Bay. The company voluntarily installed an extra mercury extraction device, but in December 1973 the Toyama prefectural government advised that mercury exceeding safe limits had again been detected in industrial sludge near the factory's drainpipes. MITI officials also announced that some sites in the bay were still dangerously polluted with mercury.[80] It was at this point that Toyama Chemical's executives hatched their scheme to sell the plant to Mr. Koe and import mercurochrome from Incheon.[81]

On returning to Tokyo, Hirayama and Inoue wrote up the results of their investigations in a report, *Toyama Kagaku no Suigin Tarenagashi Sangyō to Kankoku e no Kōgai Yushutsu ni tsuite* (Toyama chemical's mercury-dumping operations and pollution export to South Korea) and on April 5, 1974, they established the Toyama Kagaku no Kōgai Yushutsu o Yamesaseru Jikkō Iinkai (Executive Committee to Stop Toyama Chemical's Pollution Export, hereafter Stop Toyama).[82] Although it would undergo numerous name changes, this movement and its monthly publication, *Kōgai o Nogasuna!* (Don't let pollution escape!), continued essentially uninterrupted for the following twenty years, in many ways becoming the backbone of transnational environmental activism in the country during this period. The publication's title is symbolic of the transformation under way in some Japanese activists' understanding of environmental injustice. Whereas earlier the objective had been to simply eradicate industrial pollution from local living spaces in Japan, now the task also entailed apprehending pollution before it "escaped" overseas—that is, dealing with environmental injustice at the source rather than shifting it elsewhere, Old Maid style.

Around two hundred participants took part in the movement's first demonstration outside Toyama Chemical's headquarters in Tokyo's Nihonbashi area on April 27, 1974. Protesters carried banners in Korean and Japanese reading "Mercury Polluter Toyama Chemical, Stop Exporting Pollution!" Accompanying the Stop Toyama group were Kawamoto Teruo, an advocate for Minamata disease sufferers; Park Cheonsoku and Park Soncheon of the Zai-Nihon Daikanmin Kokumindan (the Korean Residents Union in Japan, or Mindan); and Shimizu Tomohisa, leader of the colorfully named Haena Kigyō o Kokuhatsu suru Kai (Association to Expose Hyena Corporations), which was a veteran of the anti–Vietnam War struggle.[83] The demonstration had special significance for the resident Korean participants. As their appeal noted, the rally was "a moment of historic import as . . . Koreans seeking the democratization of South Korea and opposing Japanese economic invasion and the imposition of pollution united— on a common battlefield—with Japanese people opposed to pollution export." It represented a "great opportunity for joint struggle in the future."[84] To coincide with the Tokyo protest, activists in Toyama Prefecture conducted simultaneous demonstrations outside of Toyama and Takaoka train stations and the Toyama Chemical Factory, where they handed out leaflets to passers-by and company workers.[85] The following extract, drawn from one of these leaflets, is typical of the sense of complicity and responsibility developing within some environmental groups in Japan at this time: "We cannot ignore this mechanism in which our 'affluence' is built on the sacrifice of the South Korean people. . . . Come on, let's stop from within Japan the economic invasion and export of pollution into Asia by Japan, exemplified by Toyama Chemical's corporate activity."[86]

It was at this April demonstration that the Japanese activists first learned of the Incheon YWCA movement. A member of the Japan YWCA participating in the protest read out an article translated from a South Korean Christian newspaper detailing the activities of the Incheon YWCA movement, which was met with warm applause.[87] As the *KOGAI* newsletter later recounted, "Probably the sisters in Korea had more difficulties and were placed under worse conditions than us to express their protest against the 'import of pollution' from Japan. But they were brave, and we must learn from their anti-pollution movement. On our part though, we have changed gradually through our movement. We have really come to think seriously that we must change the present Korea-Japan relationship from its foundation. The present relationship is only serving the interests of the LDP . . . and Park regimes."[88] Inoue Sumio observed how, different from the joint struggle with students in Thailand, the Park dictatorship made it "next to impossible" for South Korean activists to come out in open protest or to form direct transnational linkages. But, although they were not in direct contact, for all intents and purposes, the Toyama Chemical movement was indeed a "joint struggle" with the women of the Incheon YWCA. As he concluded, "even if we cannot form strong direct links with the people of South Korea, . . . if we can accomplish a 'de facto joint struggle' then that is just fine."[89]

On April 30, 1974, just three days after the demonstrations in Tokyo and Toyama, NHK television news announced that the Toyama Chemical board of directors had unanimously decided to abandon its plan to sell the mercurochrome facility. When Hirayama and Inoue subsequently visited the company headquarters, officials reiterated their decision of the previous year to stop production of mercurochrome altogether, although they carefully explained the decision on the basis of "lower profits," and not because of the protests in Japan and South Korea, or the damning report of the Toyama Prefectural Pollution Department, which concluded that the company had dumped close to 2,200 pounds (approximately one ton) of mercury into Toyama Bay.[90] Given such recalcitrance—even in defeat—activists decided to keep their movement afloat as a watchdog on Toyama Chemical and, indeed, on any other company that dared to export pollution. A letter by the group to Toyama Chemical explained that, although the company had "wisely" decided against the plan, opponents "did not consider the matter to have been solved."[91]

> The reason you wanted to take [the plant] all the way to South Korea was because you feared the antipollution movement in Japan. If there was no pollution you would have had absolutely no reason to be afraid. In other words, weren't you afraid because you had been dumping pollution? [ . . . ] So, even if your company says it will 'cease all production, development, and export of mercurochrome' we cannot believe you. Together with other antipollution movements, resident South Koreans, and the people of South Korea, we will continue to closely monitor the activities of your company and Sanwa Chemical.[92]

## Ulsan, South Korea: Local Responsibility and Historical Debts

Members of the Stop Toyama movement did not have to wait long for a new challenge. The second South Korean incident surfaced in June 1974, as the Toyama Chemical protest was drawing to a close and activists were preparing for the Conference of Asians. Similar to the Toyama mobilization, local antipollution groups in Tokyo also joined this second mobilization out of a sense of responsibility to communities at the receiving end of Japanese pollution export. They drew explicit connections between South Korea and their own peripheralized status within Japan. Moreover, they began to express a sense of historical responsibility as citizens of a country that had formerly colonized and brutalized the Korean people. Needless to say, rooted cosmopolitan activists like Hirayama and Inoue played no small role in the development of this multidimensional and reflexive consciousness among local groups. As the "connective tissue" between local protests, they helped such groups reposition their struggles on a broader regional canvas and within a longer historical trajectory.

On June 3, 1974, the newspaper *Nikkei Sangyō Shinbun* reported that the Nippon Chemical Company intended to establish a joint venture with a South Korean company in the Ulsan Industrial Region to manufacture sodium bichromate and mirabilite anhydride. The article noted that the joint-venture company, Ulsan Inorganic Chemicals, already had approval from the Park government and in quite candid language described the undertaking as "a new direction in the development of production bases through the international dispersion of pollutive industries."[93] At the time, Nippon Chemical manufactured sodium bichromate in factories at Komatsugawa, in Tokyo's downtown Edogawa ward, and in Tokuyama City, located in Yamaguchi Prefecture on the Southern tip of Honshū Island. Like Toyama Chemical, Nippon Chemical was a company with a checkered past both as a polluter and an accessory in Japanese wartime imperialism. The hexavalent chromium Nippon Chemical used in the production of sodium bichromate is a highly toxic substance that was (and is) listed in the Dokubutsu oyobi Gekibutsu Torishimari Hō (Poisonous and deleterious substances control act) of Japan. Poisoning symptoms include stomach pain, bloody diarrhea, and, in more serious instances, convulsions and coma. Inhalation of particles containing the substance can result in asthma, pharyngitis, conjunctivitis, and, in the long-term, lung cancer.[94] During the manufacturing process, toxic hexavalent chromium slag is produced in large quantities and must be properly disposed of to avoid environmental contamination. Nevertheless, in 1970 Nippon Chemical shamelessly sold slag containing hexavalent chromium to Ichikawa City in nearby Chiba Prefecture that was used as landfill on rice paddy fields being converted into residential neighborhoods. The company also sold slag-contaminated land—including the site of its Komatsugawa plant in Edogawa Ward—to the Tokyo municipal government for some US$40 million, the profits of which were used to finance construction of the new factory in South Korea.[95] Soon after the Chiba landfill project commenced, local residents noticed a strange yellow substance leaching from the ground, and ensuing tests by a Tokyo University professor revealed dangerously elevated levels of hexavalent chromium, some of which was washing into Tokyo Bay.[96]

Under pressure from the media and local residents, in February 1972 Nippon Chemical shifted all manufacturing of sodium bichromate to its Tokuyama factory, but in August of that year a ship carrying slag from the factory sank in waters off the coast of Shimonoseki in Yamaguchi Prefecture, exposing Nippon Chemical's surreptitious dumping of toxic waste at sea. Investigations revealed that the company had ocean-dumped some eleven thousand pounds (approximately five tons) of waste material despite a promise—in the form of a pollution prevention agreement with Tokuyama City—that it would convert all waste material into insoluble trivalent chromium (and despite two levels of bureaucratic oversight).[97] Consequently, in September 1972 the Tokuyama Municipal Assembly ordered a temporary suspension of production at the Komatsugawa factory.[98] In late June 1974, a citizens' group conducted further tests on pools of water to the south of the Komatsugawa factory in Tokyo that revealed levels of chromium 1,300 times above the regulatory limits. In 1975, water testing conducted near the factory again revealed chromium hot spots with contamination up to 2,200 times above regulatory limits.[99] Hirayama and Inoue's own testing around the Tokyo factory in 1974 also confirmed ongoing chromium contamination problems. As Inoue explained, this sorry history of lies and cover-ups made the logic behind Nippon Chemical's decision to go to South Korea crystal clear: "If Tokyo isn't possible, there is always the countryside," and "if Japan isn't possible, there is always South Korea."[100]

But the Nippon Chemical incident was about more than pollution and its export—it was also about a history "stained with the blood and sweat of Asian people," as Hirayama graphically put it. The company began operations in 1893 as Tanahashi Pharmaceuticals, and in 1915 started to manufacture sodium bichromate, a key ingredient in explosives.[101] During World War II the company used large numbers of forced Korean laborers to mine chromium for use in the production of munitions to fuel Japan's military adventures in Korea and China.[102] Nippon Chemical's remorseless commitment to profit over ethics continued into the postwar era. Throughout the Vietnam War the company brazenly imported chromite from the Soviet Union, which was in turn used to manufacture explosives subsequently used by the United States in the Vietnam conflict—in a sense allowing Nippon Chemical to profiteer on Cold War rivalries.[103] Anti–Vietnam War activists often referred to Mitsubishi Heavy Industries as a "merchant of death" and a "hyena corporation" for its production of armaments, but these labels seem equally applicable to Nippon Chemical. *Kōgai o Nogasuna!* was even less forgiving, describing the company's move to South Korea as part of a longer "Asian invasion" built on Nippon Chemical's remorseless "sucking of the South Korean people's blood."[104]

Members of the Stop Toyama group held their first demonstration against Nippon Chemical at Kamedo Station in downtown Tokyo in late August 1974, and they continued to do so almost monthly until the South Korean plant commenced operations in 1976 and intermittently thereafter. The group also held public slide shows on hexavalent chromium contamination and pollution export, and members distributed leaflets in neighborhoods around the Komatsugawa factory explaining the link between local pollution and Japanese industrial expansion into South Korea. Throughout the mobilization, *Kōgai o Nogasuna!* continued to report in great detail on developments in South Korea, and editions carried clippings from South Korean newspapers accompanied by Japanese translations, commentaries, and clever political cartoons. In August 1975, at the height of a hot and humid summer, the group engaged in a month of daily demonstrations to display its resolute opposition to pollution export.[105] During these demonstrations protesters often formed a human chain around the Komatsugawa factory to symbolize the movement's objective of surrounding and obstructing Nippon Chemical's operations in Japan and abroad. For Hirayama and his colleagues, the movement was always about far more than pollution export; it was about preventing the resurgence of an expansionist Japan only very recently tamed by war defeat. As activists gathered to protest Nippon Chemical in 1975—the thirtieth anniversary of the war defeat—some even had the sense that their country was "leaning in the direction of militarism," moving toward an "Asian invasion" externally and "suppression of the [Japanese] people" internally.[106] An overreaction perhaps, but activists' linking together of Japan and Korea, and the militarist past and the pollutive present, clearly transcended earlier imaginations of environmental injustice based on local victimhood alone.

The involvement of local Tokyo groups such as the Bokutō kara Kōgai o nakusu Kumin no Kai (Residents' Association to Remove Pollution from Bokutō) evidenced Hirayama and others' success in nurturing a more nuanced understanding of environmental injustice among some local grassroots groups in Japan.[107] Established to deal specifically with pollution from Nippon Chemical's operations in their downtown Tokyo neighborhoods, the Bokutō Association attracted a great deal of media attention in mid-1975 after obtaining documents from the Tōkyōto Kōgai Kyoku (Tokyo Municipal Pollution Bureau) that identified the company's illegal hexavalent chromate slag dumping site.[108] Matsuoka Yūji, one of the group's leaders, explained how he became involved when his two young children suddenly developed asthma after relocating to Kōtō Ward near the Nippon Chemical factory. It was not until attending a slideshow organized by local activists, however, that he first heard about the factory and began to suspect a connection to his children's ailments. At the gathering Matsuoka met with disgruntled company employees, who explained how they had developed holes in the cartilage of their nasal cavities after working in the factory and inhaling its noxious fumes.[109]

A Nippon Chemical employee with a
nasal cavity hole from hexavalent
chromium poisoning, 1975
(The Mainichi Newspapers)

But it was not only self-interest, local egoism, or even paternal instinct
that fueled Matsuoka and others' activism; they were also clearly motivated
by a sense of injustice. Along with the pollution itself, the group pointed to
the "structure of discrimination" in which those in uptown Tokyo discarded
all of their unwanted things on downtown Tokyo, like trash processing facilities and chemical factories. It was this sense of injustice that made the
Bokutō Association's members all the more receptive to Hirayama and others'
calls to oppose Nippon Chemical's move into South Korea. After all, wasn't
Japan treating Asia in much the same way as uptown Tokyoites were treating people downtown? And, if this was the case, didn't members of the
Bokutō Association have an ethical responsibility to stop Nippon Chemical
from inflicting pain on the South Korean people—a pain they knew only
too well?[110] At a June 1975 demonstration against Nippon Chemical, members of the association articulated this position unequivocally, declaring
that "there could be nothing more disrespectful to South Korea and its
people than to impose this [pollution] on them simply because it is not
possible in Japan. Nippon Chemical must not be allowed to replicate the

same 'imperialist mentality' from the war when it forcibly brought Koreans to Japan and imposed abusive labor on them. We will fight until pollution export is stopped and until the realization of normal ties of friendship and goodwill between South Korea and Japan which endure for 100 years, 200 years, or forever."[111]

The Bokutō Association's pledge reverberated across the Sea of Japan. During August 1975 the South Korean newspaper *Dong-A Ilbo* ran a series of articles on the opposition to pollution export in Japan.[112] An August 18, 1975, editorial in the paper noted how many Japanese "social organizations" and "conscientious citizens" had come out to protest against companies like Toyama and Nippon Chemical because they felt it would be a "national shame to export to neighboring countries pollutive industries which ran the risk of mercury poisoning." "Their claim is that 'we will absolutely not allow [Nippon Chemical] to export pollution to South Korea without having solved the chromium contamination at their own factory.'" The editorial carefully reminded readers that this opposition to pollution export began first among citizens in Japan, "a fact which should leave us [South Koreans] with 'red faces.'"[113] For Matsuoka and the Bokutō Association, however, if pollution kept escaping to Asia, the only red faces would be theirs, and, worse still, red too would be their hands, stained with the blood of other Asians. As the *KOGAI* newsletter of spring 1975 announced to its predominantly Asian readership,

> We Japanese have been too indifferent to the existing exploitation system within which we and the Asian people around us are entrapped. Surely we are now living in an expanding "empire." We have not been aware of the economic relations between Asia and Japan, in which the present "prosperity" of Japan stands on the sacrifice of Asian people. The more Japanese (or more exactly, the more a small number of Japanese) become wealthy, the poorer the other Asian people become. And what is more important, we haven't realized that Asians are developing their own movements and their own socio-economic development and independence. Now we must have the perspective not of what we can do for them, but what we must not do to them.[114]

Nowhere is this emergent sense of responsibility toward fellow Asians more evident than Chiba residents' mobilization against the industrial giant Kawatetsu. Their movement reveals how by the late 1970s many domestic environmental protesters were both aware of and prepared to act against instances of pollution far beyond their own backyards.

## Mindanao: Translocal Empathy

Like the movements against TACS, Toyama Chemical, and Nippon Chemical, the mobilization opposing Kawatetsu's pollution export to the Philippines offers an invaluable insight into the process by which some local protest movements in 1970s Japan escalated into transnational actions on the basis of activists' expanding sense of injustice and responsibility. The Kawatetsu issue traced its origins to 1951, when the company constructed Japan's largest integrated steelworks in Chiba City with the strong backing of the government and industrial financiers. The first blast furnace became operational in 1953, and by 1965 the facility had five furnaces, making it the largest in Japan and the sixth largest worldwide.[115] In its early days, Kawatetsu was seen as a beacon of modernity and postwar reconstruction. A local school even composed a song celebrating the steelworks' billowing smokestacks, proclaiming "smoke rises up to dye the vast heavens, silver in daytime and gold at night, the sound of steel-making is the note of civilization."[116] The "smoke," of course, had horrific effects on human health, because it contained a poisonous cocktail of iron oxide, cadmium, nitrogen and sulfur dioxides, sulfurous acid gas, and arsenous acid.[117] Tests by the Chiba City authorities in 1970 recorded concentrations of sulfur dioxide in five sites around the city far exceeding national regulatory standards, while data on sulfurous acid gas density for the period between 1963 and 1973 revealed increasing concentration levels closer to the Kawatetsu facility. A 1972 report by the EAJ on sulfur dioxide gas pollution listed four sites in the vicinity of Kawatetsu among the worst ten nationwide.[118] As the *KOGAI* newsletter explained to its readers, residents near the facility "cannot hang out their washing to dry and are not able to open windows in spite of the heat of summer days because of the sooty and smoky air created by the steelworks. They suffer not only from such difficulties as these in their daily lives but also from diseases such as acute inflammation of the eyes, bronchitis, Kawasaki asthma, pulmonary emphysema, and lung cancer because of the air pollution caused by KSC [Kawatetsu]."[119] In 1972 Yoshida Akira of the Chiba University Medical School issued a damning report on the health condition of people living around the facility, revealing instances of respiratory disease exceeding those in Kawasaki and Fuji Cities, both notorious as "pollution department stores."[120] In response, Chiba City hastily established a pollution-disease certification scheme that by 1974 had recognized five hundred victims, nineteen of whom were already deceased. By 1977 the number of officially recognized pollution suffers had risen to 699 persons.[121]

Chiba residents first mobilized in 1972, forming the Chiba Kōgai Juku (Chiba Pollution Academy), which, as the name suggests, was initially not for protest but to gather objective data on the pollution problem in the city. To this end, local housewives kept "pollution diaries" while others built simple devices to measure sulfurous acid gas densities and levels of metal corrosion. Other members observed plant and animal life to gauge air pollution levels. All of this data was then collated and made public in a series of reports.[122] According to the progressive *AMPO* magazine, in 1974 around a hundred people regularly attended monthly meetings and participated in grassroots monitoring initiatives associated with the academy.[123] But the activities of the group began to change when Kawatetsu announced plans to construct a new—and sixth—blast furnace in May 1973.[124] At this point the academy shifted from citizen science to vigorous opposition to Kawatetsu. In May 1975, two hundred Chiba residents instituted court proceedings against the company. The plaintiffs sought an injunction on construction of the sixth blast furnace, compliance of existing facilities with national environmental pollution standards, and compensation to forty-seven pollution victims or their bereaved families.[125] Members of the Chiba Pollution Academy became involved in this initiative via the Chiba Kawatetsu Kōgai Soshō o Shien suru Kai (Chiba Kawatetsu Pollution Lawsuit Support Group), established to assist the plaintiffs and their families.[126]

Up to that point, the battle with Kawatetsu had been a local one, largely between the company and residents living within a three-mile (five-kilometer) radius of the facility. But all of this changed at the first public hearing at the Chiba district court in September 1975, when a Kawatetsu official stated during testimony that the sintering factory—an extremely pollutive stage in steel production—would be relocated to Mindanao Island in the Philippines and, hence, Chiba residents need not worry about pollution. Activists in the Chiba Pollution Academy now faced a conundrum similar to that of activists opposing the Toyama and Nippon Chemical companies. They had to choose between local egoism and transnational responsibility. Was it ethically acceptable to simply stop construction of the sintering plant in their own backyard, Old Maid style, or was something more fundamental at stake?[127] By early 1976 they had made up their minds: Kawatetsu's pollution export plan was—in and of itself—ethically wrong, and they had a responsibility to oppose it whether at home or abroad.

Rooted cosmopolitan activists knowledgeable about the plight of the Filipinos played a vital role in convincing local Chiba activists to reach this decision and, moreover, to stay committed to a struggle across the sea. They relayed a story not only of pollution but also of political corruption and communal displacement that bore striking similarities to Kawatetsu's disregard for human health and the environment in Chiba. Needless to say, the Chiba activists needed no lessons in the detriments of sintering, which is a preparatory treatment of iron ore in which pulverized ore is burnt with limestone and other minerals at extremely high temperatures to produce iron sinter suitable for blast furnace use. The burning process results in various waste products that cause air pollution and related detrimental environmental and human effects. Sulfur and nitrogen dioxide, for instance, cause human asthma and, in combination with atmospheric moisture, become acids that return to the ground as corrosive acid rain. Along with the gases, sintering also produces large quantities of dust, dioxins, and heavy metals such as zinc, cadmium, and lead, which, if not properly disposed of, can contaminate the ground and water.[128]

From spring 1974, Kawatetsu began construction of the sintering facility at Cagayan de Oro in the north of Mindanao Island. Thanks to the strong hand of the Philippine president, Ferdinand Marcos, it did so with absolute impunity.[129] Marcos created a free trade zone for Kawatetsu that allowed it to fully own and control the newly established Philippine Sintering Corporation. He also gave the company tax-free and duty-free status on the importation of capital equipment, raw materials, and supplies, and exempted it from any export tax. As the *KOGAI* newsletter noted, "For good measure, there is cheap land and a cheap labor force and freedom to discharge pollution. . . . In a matter of speaking, the [free trade zone] is a nationalized territory of the foreign capitalists."[130] Kawatetsu brought plenty of corporate allies on board, contracting "every aspect of construction" to Japanese enterprises including Kobe Steel, Nippon Conveyor, and Hitachi Shipbuilding & Engineering.[131] Marcos also paved the way for Kawatetsu politically by ratifying the Japan-Philippine Treaty of Amity, Commerce, and Navigation, which had lain idle for close to thirteen years because of strong domestic opposition in the Philippines. In talks with Japanese prime minister Tanaka Kakuei, Marcos also stated that "in order to promote the country's industrialization and to develop the economy," the Philippines was willing to "accept the polluting plants which could not be permitted to expand any more in Japan."[132]

The residents of Cagayan de Oro did not fare so well. Reports from the area that filtered back to Japan explained how some 1,500 households were given the "choice" of relocating to a government-provided alternative or otherwise fending for themselves in the shadow of the sintering plant.[133] The government alternative was a newly constructed village on 215 acres (eighty-seven hectares) of denuded land in the mountains twenty miles (thirty-two kilometers) from Cagayan de Oro. Authorities called the new community "Andam Mouswag," meaning "ready for progress" or "ready for take-off" and the "neat and modern housing development" was widely promoted as a "microscopic" version of the "New Society" Marcos and his "new breed of technocrats" envisioned for the Philippine nation.[134] But in reports for *AMPO* and the Japanese-language monthly *Gendai no Me,* in late 1975, the Filipino activist Wilfredo Salvatierra described a very different situation, characterizing the "Alice in Wonderland" project as an attempt to "rewire" the community.[135] Salvatierra observed that the whole scheme looked "very much like a copy of Mao's ideas in China, except for one important detail: the people themselves have no say in what is done. They are similar to laboratory specimens, and Andam Mouswag is the laboratory. They were ordered out of their original barrio [neighborhood] of Nabacaan so that the Kawasaki Steel Corporation could build an iron sintering plant there. They were offered the choice of going to Andam Mouswag or fending for themselves."[136] Salvatierra described how coconut farmers were being retrained as carpenters, masons, and heavy equipment operators to work on the Kawatetsu construction site. Already by late 1974, some 70 percent of the men were employed there.[137] Nevertheless, the displaced people were discontented with the shift from an earlier seaside subsistence lifestyle to a modern housing development where they were now compelled to engage in wage labor in order to pay the rent and feed their children. People still living in the vicinity of the sintering factory were also upset about the coming pollution. As one resident bluntly said to Salvatierra, "Do the Japanese people think we are idiots? Do they think we will open our arms and welcome 'filth?'"[138] Such opposition notwithstanding, construction of the sintering facility finished on time in January 1977 and, three months later, President Marcos and his wife Imelda attended the official opening ceremony.[139] As nearby residents had feared, pollution ravaged the surrounding environment. Fishing stocks were hit particularly hard. What had previously been a 130-pound (59 kilogram) daily catch shrank to a measly 6.5 pounds (three kilograms).[140] Even President Marcos's executive director for the relocation project, Alejandro Melchor, was equivocal about the wider benefits for the Philippines, saying "I don't know, but it's certainly benefiting certain people in the Philippines."[141]

Alerted to these developments in Mindanao, in November 1975 activists in the Chiba Pollution Academy complemented their domestic struggle with a new initiative called "Don't Make Mindanao Island a Second Chiba!," which the journalist Sakakibara Shirō described as an attempt to "transcend local egoism" by supporting the movement to oppose Kawatetsu's export of polluting processes to Mindanao.[142] Activities included leafleting and media campaigns, lobbying Kawatetsu directly, public rallies and marches, numerous exchanges with Filipino activists, and fact-finding missions to Cagayan de Oro and Andam Mouswag. In September 1976, a handful of activists in the Pollution Academy led a street march from the Chiba prefectural government office to the front entrance of Kawatetsu's iron mill in Chiba.[143] Participants included Yamada Keizō, a Sophia University academic and pastor who had visited Mindanao on a fact-finding mission in August, along with schoolteachers, office workers, students, and housewives. In response Kawatetsu closed the iron gates at the entrance to the facility and stopped workers from entering or leaving. Observers at the time suggested that such measures "proved how threatened" Kawatetsu was "by the possibility of the people of Chiba and Mindanao joining together to raise their voice against pollution."[144] During the rally Yamada Keizō relayed the unfortunate experiences of people living near the Kawatetsu plant in Mindanao, and he appealed for a transnational grassroots solidarity movement to oppose Kawatetsu's pollution export.

Filipino visitors also confirmed the story of far-off Japanese corporate environmental injustices during their visits to Japan. In November 1976 a Catholic nun and two priests from the Good Shepherd movement in Mindanao visited the Chiba factory to see the sintering process with their own eyes.[145] Surveying the once-venerated "silver smoke" rising from Kawatetsu's smokestacks, the nun wondered out loud: "Is this pollution?"[146] In their meetings with the Chiba residents, the Filipino visitors were eager to learn about the health effects from the steelworks and also the kinds of political pressures faced by activists. With Yamada acting as interpreter, an elderly Chiba man suffering from pollution disease warned the Filipino visitors to be suspicious of leaves unseasonably changing color and falling off trees.

Holding back his tears, the usually reticent old man finished by saying "Thank you so much for coming here on such a cold day. I want to express my respect and gratitude to you all."[147] One of the Filipino priests used the opportunity to both thank and entreat his Japanese hosts: "First of all, I would like to express my deepest thanks on behalf of the Philippine people to the Japanese people for acting in solidarity with the residents of Cagayan de Oro in this Kawasaki Steel problem. . . . Together with you we intend to struggle to minimize the exploitation of Japanese capital." The priest noted that all media—radio, TV, newspapers—were under the strict censorship of Marcos and how "the arrival of Japanese and American capital" was making the dictatorial regime "happy."[148] Under such conditions of political suppression the Filipino people were not able to easily resist the Kawatetsu project or any others, but the priest explained that the Marcos regime was very sensitive to criticism from without, especially from civic movements in Europe, North America, and Japan. "So, it will be of great support to us if the people of Japan communicate the situation of many people in the Philippines and the crimes of Japanese corporations through demonstrations and rallies and via the mass media. . . . We want all citizens movements [in Japan] to recognize that, regardless of the pollution, they should not be relieved when the contamination stops in Japan because there is a mechanism by which such harm is exported intact to other countries. . . . We pray for the growth of your movement and for solidarity with the people of the Philippines."[149]

Japanese activists helped fortify this transnational solidarity through numerous visits to the Philippines. In the period from February 1975 to August 1976, Yamada Keizō traveled to Mindanao four times, where he consulted with people at the Cagayan de Oro construction site and with the residents of Andam Mouswag.[150] Japanese Catholic priests used their institutional ties to communicate environmental knowledge from Japan, for example, by screening slideshows for locals on the human health effects of industrial pollution in Japan. For their part, the Filipinos were grateful, but some wondered—quite realistically—just how much the Japanese could achieve. During a 1976 visit to Cagayan de Oro, a local schoolteacher described the reality to Tsukamoto Hiroki of the ILP as follows: "We don't want Kawatetsu to come but there is nothing we can do. At the very least we want them to properly install pollution prevention equipment. . . . We are extremely grateful that Japanese people have heard our voices. But will you be able to do anything in Japan to stop Kawatetsu setting up here?"

Tsukamoto was left nonplussed, admitting later that, "honestly speaking," he "didn't have the words to respond to this question."[151]

Like Thailand and South Korea, the situation in the Philippines forced Japanese activists to reconsider the troubling entanglement of the local, the regional, and the historical. As the July 1976 edition of *Jishu Kōza* asked its readers, "How are we to answer such voices? What should we do? The voices of these Filipinos seeking independence accuse not only Kawatetsu but also we Japanese. By pushing forward with pollution export and economic aggression, this country and we too are once again becoming enemies of the people of Asia."[152] *Jishu Kōza* reminded its readers that the prosperity of Kawatetsu and Japan were "built on the destruction of Japanese people's daily lives and through the sacrifice of Asian people's blood."[153] Japanese industry was "actively exporting pollution to South Korea, Thailand, the Philippines, and even far-off Africa and South America, and planning its 'economic invasion' of these countries." Ethical Japanese people could simply "not ignore" this "reality" nor the "demand of people from the Third World" to "live as human beings."[154]

## From South Korea to the Third World

Building on the momentum of these movements, in April 1976 the various Japanese movements protesting pollution export to South Korea, Thailand, the Philippines, and elsewhere gathered in Tokyo for the Ajia e no Kōgai Yushutsu o Kokuhatsu suru Shimin Daishūkai (Citizens Rally to Protest Pollution Export to Asia). The event attracted around 550 people from forty-six associations nationwide and was extensively covered in the national daily newspapers.[155] Discussions about the relocation of polluting industries dominated, but activists also considered the broader issue of Japan's so-called economic invasion abroad.[156] Activists in the South Korean mobilizations and the Chiba Pollution Academy organized the event with the assistance of prominent groups involved in other specific cases of Japanese pollution export worldwide. By 1976, it should be noted, movements were pursuing Japanese corporate transgressions in all corners of the globe. For example, activists in the Afurika Kōdō Iinkai (African Action Committee) were actively opposing Japanese corporate involvement in Namibia, a country administered by the racist apartheid regime in South Africa in direct contravention of a resolution putting the country under UN trusteeship. Despite this blatant breach of international law, the Japanese Kansai Electric Power Company (KEPKO) continued to import uranium from Namibia.

On top of this, the Mitsubishi Corporation was also developing plans to sell nuclear power plants and related technology to South Africa.[157] On the other side of the world, activists in the Raten Amerika Kōdō Iinkai (Latin American Action Committee) were opposing Japanese involvement in the Amazon Development Program in Brazil, which was desolating indigenous Indio communities through deforestation to make way for a highway.[158] All in all, the 1976 event was a testament to the expanded vision that had developed within the Japanese environmental movement since activists' first encounter with the pollution export problem at UNCHE in 1972. According to *AMPO*, "Report after report [at the rally] presented a ghastly picture of how the Japanese mini-Empire operates. The audience shared the understanding that Japanese capitalism came to flourish with the fertilizer of Korean and Vietnamese blood and is maintained by the blood and sweat of Third World people today."[159]

Discussion and debate at the rally reiterated many of the themes explored throughout this chapter, especially the ways pollution export made ordinary Japanese and even activists complicit aggressors—albeit passive—in the environmental transgressions of Japanese industry abroad. Advocates for Minamata disease sufferers at the rally expressed a renewed appreciation for the transnational reach of Japanese industrial pollution. They noted how the struggle against pollution export had prompted them consider anew the blood-soaked history of their "foe," the Chisso Corporation, which led the advance of Japanese capital onto the Korean peninsula and made profits through the sacrifice of the Korean people in the prewar and wartime years. "This characteristic of Chisso continued thereafter in the form of Minamata disease and the suppression of its sufferers."[160] Of particular note is the way activists at the rally were now conceptualizing the movement and their own role in it as part of a broader struggle against environmental injustice worldwide. Consider the following extract from the *Kyōdō Sengen* (Joint declaration) at the 1976 rally:

> We have rediscovered the shocking fact that our daily lives are built on the sacrifice of people of the Third World. The aggression did not end on August, 15, 1945, but revived through Japanese economic complicity in the Korean and Vietnam Wars. The Japanese ruling class called this affluence. But now we want to walk a new path which rejects affluence built on the sacrifice of our friends in the Third World. This difficult path involves a commitment to fundamentally reconstructing the

mechanism in which the Japanese economy cannot operate without economic aggression toward the various countries and ethnic groups of the Third World. . . . We can no longer be concerned only with the wellbeing of the Japanese people. We must start a new movement based on a new set of values in which anything that disadvantages the people of the Third World is something that we too must repudiate. In order to destroy all mechanisms which are obstructing the realization of both their and our common wellbeing, we want to join hands with them and struggle together with them.[161]

To this end, participants agreed to establish the Han-Kōgai Yushutsu Tsūhō Sentā (Anti-Pollution Export Center) as an organization to expose Japanese pollution export from the "inside."[162] They called on the support of courageous corporate whistle-blowers and people of the Third World, and committed the newly created center to conducting investigations that would "strike a concrete blow on the Japanese government and business world."[163] As the declaration concluded, "By clarifying the totality of our connections with the peoples of Asia and the Third World we at once become aware of our situation and our position and, moreover, just how important such awareness is right now."[164] In keeping with this new sentiment, activists updated the subtitle of the movement's monthly, *Don't Let the Pollution Escape: Exposing Pollution Export to South Korea,* by replacing "South Korea" (Kankoku) with "the Third World" (Daisan Sekai).[165] This change in title not only spoke to an expanded geographical perspective but also, just as significantly, it signaled the evolution of a richer appreciation of the mechanisms of environmental injustice that overlaid victimhood with aggression—the fundamental contradiction haunting Old Maid or NIMBY logic. As I explain in the concluding chapter, I believe this melding of aggression with victimhood in Japanese groups' struggles against pollution export marked an important transition in postwar civic thought in Japan. It broke with powerful mentalities of victimhood in earlier antipollution and pacifist thought and fashioned a new, more multidimensional, and reflexive basis for activist consciousness. In the following chapter, we see this consciousness further refined in the early-1980s struggle against environmental injustice in the Pacific involving a stubbornly long-lived pollutant: radioactive waste.

CHAPTER 5

# Pacific Solidarity and Atomic Aggression

If we remain silent now, little by little we will become "atomic aggressors."

Japanese antinuclear activist (1981)[1]

Just what kind of place is one that can't be accessed for twenty-four thousand years? What kind of life is there?

Belauan antinuclear activist,
Roman Bedor, Tokyo (1981)[2]

"A house with no toilet" is one of the less flattering ways critics have described commercial nuclear power in Japan since its beginnings in the 1960s.[3] Indeed, not only in Japan but worldwide, the disposal of radioactive waste from nuclear power plants has been the Achilles heel of this industry, and as much as proponents speak of a nuclear fuel "cycle," the reality is a nuclear dead end of radioactive waste material that continues to accumulate and, in some cases, will remain toxic to human beings essentially forever. As early as 1951, the eminent chemist and Harvard University president James B. Conant even predicted that humanity would eventually turn away from nuclear power not because of the inherent dangers of nuclear fission but because of the conundrum of radioactive waste disposal.[4] Some countries did subsequently abandon nuclear power but over half a century later there are still hundreds of commercial nuclear power reactors operating worldwide and the issue of safe management and disposal of radioactive waste remains unresolved. According to a Japanese Cabinet Office report of March 8, 2011, in 2009 Japan had in its possession some 1,692 canisters of high-level radioactive waste and a startling 1,616,910 steel drums (fifty-three-gallon/200-liter capacity) of low-level waste, which is provisionally stored at nuclear power plants and various other facilities throughout the archipelago.[5] Low-level waste, it should be noted, does not mean radioactive material harmless to humans. On the contrary, some of this material is so radioactive it must be shielded with lead. All of it must be stored for varying periods ranging from tens to hundreds of years until it is no longer toxic to humans and other life on earth. Since the 1990s, the Japanese government has planned to permanently bury most of this material, but critics question the wisdom of this method in a country where the ground is predisposed to seismic disruptions. Furthermore, few communities are willing to accept a radioactive graveyard in their backyard regardless of how deeply and securely the waste is buried. The bitter reality—as the "no toilet" metaphor implies—is that there is no easy method to flush this material away, at least not within the terrestrial borders of the archipelago.

That Japan has a ballooning radioactive waste dilemma today because of its enthusiastic embrace of nuclear power over the past half century or so is a self-evident fact.[6] As long as the country's nuclear reactors are producing electricity, the mountain of radioactive waste in need of storage continues to grow, in the case of low-level waste on average at a rate of about 110,000 canisters per year.[7] A lesser-known aspect of this situation, however, is that the amount of low-level radioactive waste material in need of storage would be considerably less today had it not been for a highly successful transnational mobilization in the early 1980s involving Japanese antipollution export groups, local communities opposing nuclear power plant construction, anti–atomic weapons organizations, and protesters from island nations throughout the Pacific Ocean. Just as the United States, the United Kingdom, and nuclearized states throughout Europe had done from the earliest days of the post–World War II era, during the early 1960s Japanese nuclear officials began to devise plans to dump up to 60 percent of the low-level radioactive waste from nuclear facilities (mainly future power plants) into the Pacific Ocean.[8] They realized that doing so would help mitigate if not solve many of the problems they faced at the so-called back end of the nuclear fuel cycle, such as terrestrial storage costs and disputes over location. Moreover, they assumed no one would care about waste dumped into the Mariana Trench, one of the deepest areas of the Pacific Ocean some 560 miles (900 kilometers) from Tokyo.

Actually, there were many people living on surrounding Pacific Ocean islands who cared immensely, and it is their opposition movement in solidarity with Japanese groups that I investigate in this chapter. Different from the industrial pollution export of the 1970s, which was often camouflaged beneath the image of corporate Japan bestowing the light of industrial progress on developing Asian nations, there was really no credible justification for dumping radioactive waste beyond the country's borders other than the simple fact that no Japanese wanted the material in their backyard—in other words, another undeniable case of NIMBY logic. Nowhere was this more conspicuous than in government officials' inability to answer a question posed again and again by Pacific activists: If the material was as safe as they claimed, then why not dump it in Japanese coastal waters or, as one protester acerbically put it, "in the moat at the Tokyo Palace"?[9]

In this chapter I look closely at the rise of this protest movement among Pacific island nation activists and its uptake and resonance among Japanese antipollution and antinuclear communities in the early 1980s. The movement is interesting for two reasons. First, it evidences the continuing and, indeed, expanding transnational involvement of Japanese environmental groups led by rooted cosmopolitan activists in the early 1980s—now in concert with antinuclear groups and involving nuclear issues in the Pacific. Activists and political leaders from Guam, Saipan, Tinian, and elsewhere found Japanese allies with extensive transnational experience and a shared worldview, such as the ILP network, the Antipollution Export Information Center (AEIC), and the Pacific Asia Resource Center (PARC), publisher of the influential *AMPO: Japan-Asia Quarterly Review*. Activists in these Japanese organizations subsequently connected the Pacific protesters to anti-A-bomb movements in Japan such as Gensuikin (Japan Congress Against A- and H-Bombs), the Genshiryoku Shiryō Jōhōshitsu (Citizens Nuclear Information Center, CNIC), and even local struggles against nuclear power like the one at Kubokawa in Kōchi Prefecture. To invoke Keck and Sikkink's terminology again, this transnational alliance managed to "boomerang" sufficient pressure back on to Japanese nuclear officials such that they were forced to halt and eventually abandon their ocean dumping plan.

Second, ideationally, the protest speaks to the ongoing potency of environmental injustice as a motivational factor within Japanese environmental activism in the early 1980s—but with interesting twists. Activists in the ILP, AEIC, and PARC supported the Pacific activists' movement because it resonated with their own struggle against environmental injustice, initially in the domestic crisis of the 1960s and later in the anti–pollution export movements of the 1970s. In this sense, the movement against radioactive waste disposal represented an extension and elaboration of their vision of environmental injustice. Social movement scholars have referred to this phenomenon as "narrative fidelity"—in other words, the ways in which an issue "strikes a responsive chord" and "rings true with extant beliefs, myths, folktales, and the like."[10] "The more central or salient the espoused beliefs, ideas, and values of a movement to the targets of mobilization"—in this case to the Japanese groups—"the greater the probability of their mobilization."[11]

But two aspects of this transnational mobilization distinguish it somewhat from the iterations of environmental injustice I have explored in earlier chapters. The first is the commanding presence of Pacific activists in relaying their experience of injustice—environmental and historical—in Japan. Different from public protests and publications of the early 1970s, in which Japanese activists largely spoke for their overseas allies, in this mobilization Pacific voices permeated the discourse in speeches, newspaper reports, essays, and protests. The influence of these (potential) Pacific victims cannot be underestimated in the context of a postwar Japanese movement culture animated by the condition of victimhood.

The other distinguishing factor of this mobilization was the way it blended—sometimes uncomfortably—notions of environmental injustice, nuclear power, and atomic victimization. Pacific protesters came to Japan primarily to advance their own agenda, but in the process of building a transnational movement, they encouraged the Japanese groups involved (including anti-A-bomb groups like Gensuikin) to rethink the nuclear issue—in much the same way pollution export to Thailand, South Korea, and elsewhere in the 1970s stimulated Hirayama Takasada, Inoue Sumio, and other activists to question notions of victimhood in earlier antipollution protests. The radioactive waste dumping controversy complicated the victim consciousness animating antinuclear protest in postwar Japan. Opponents of nuclear weapons in particular had based their ideology on the victimhood of residents in Hiroshima and Nagasaki at war's end and, later, of Japanese fishermen exposed to radioactive fallout after the US hydrogen bomb test at Bikini Atoll on March 1, 1954. In the anti–nuclear power plant movement gathering steam from the late 1970s, local communities forced or otherwise cajoled to accept nuclear power plants in their backyards were also portrayed as victims of the nuclear power industry in Japan.

Pacific activists complicated both of these narratives. People in Hiroshima and Nagasaki were certainly victims of the two American bombs, but residents of Micronesia had been victimized by close to seventy atomic and hydrogen weapons tests in the 1940s and 1950s alone. Some had lost their homes (their islands and atolls were vaporized) and many were made sick by radioactive fallout and their offspring struck down with lymphatic cancers, leukemia, and genetic defects. On top of this, radioactive waste from nuclear power plants in Japan was now to be dumped into their waters. Clearly the Japanese were not the only victims of the nuclear age and, even worse, their nuclear power industry now threatened to make them "atomic aggressors" in the Pacific.[12] Just as pollution export had made some Japanese activists think about Japan's troubled place and history in Asia, this Pacific iteration of environmental injustice opened the eyes of many antinuclear advocates to the ways Pacific activists connected the radioactive waste issue to a longer struggle for independence and the obliteration of nuclear neocolonialism or, as the prime minister of Vanuatu, Walter Lini, labeled it in 1983, "nuclearism."[13] The dumping controversy and transnational movement against it exposed a cycle of nuclear discrimination and injustice that began with the extraction of uranium—often on indigenous peoples' lands—continued with enrichment and power production in local communities in Japan, and ended with the disposal of radioactive waste material at sea. To the extent Japanese antinuclear activists failed to comprehend this cycle and to reposition their individual struggles within it, they remained open to criticisms of hypocrisy and complicity in Pacific nuclearism.

## Radioactive Waste: The Pacific Solution

The Japanese government's plan to ocean dump low-level nuclear waste in the early 1980s drew on long-established practices among other nuclearized nations.[14] From 1946 to 1970, the United States dumped close to ninety thousand canisters of low-level waste near the Farallon Islands off the coast of San Francisco in Northern California and in the Atlantic Ocean near the states of Massachusetts and Texas, in what became a "fairly routine" process by the 1950s.[15] As Alley and Alley explain, dumping operations "did not always run smoothly": some canisters were carelessly dumped outside of designated disposal sites, while others resurfaced in unexpected places, sometimes in fishermen's nets or, in one instance, floating two hundred miles off the coast of New York City. Canisters that did not sink were sprayed with bullets until they did.[16] US dumping slowed considerably—although it did not stop—in June 1959 when the *New York Times* ran a story with a map showing radioactive dumping sites "off every major seaport region from

Boston to Corpus Christi, Tex."[17] People living in cities such as Boston were incensed to learn that radioactive materials had been dumped in shallow areas close to shore that were known breeding grounds for lobsters and other sea life. In October 1980 Jackson Davis, a biologist at the University of California at Santa Cruz, reported to a House of Representatives subcommittee on the environment that at least one-third of the 47,500 canisters dumped off the Northern California coast were leaking "extremely high level" radiation, some of which he had detected in fish samples.[18] Davis's findings directly contradicted the generally accepted assumption that any discharged radiation would be diluted to insignificant levels in the ocean rather than concentrating locally. As we will see, Davis and his research later became important factors in the movement against planned Japanese waste dumping on the other side of the Pacific.

European countries also enthusiastically discarded their radioactive wastes at sea. Under the supervision of the European Nuclear Energy Agency (ENEA), beginning in 1967 the Netherlands, Belgium, France, the United Kingdom, and West Germany dumped low-level radioactive waste, mostly in the Atlantic Ocean.[19] In 1960, the French Atomic Energy Agency even toyed with the idea of dumping waste into the Mediterranean Sea, but this plan was scrapped after a major public outcry led by Prince Rainier of Monaco and the famed conservationist and marine photographer, Jacques-Yves Cousteau.[20] Like the US dumping, the ENEA-supervised process was often a messy and dangerous business. In 1976, for example, the specialist disposal vessel *Topaz* was contaminated and its crew exposed to radiation when canisters on board were damaged en route to a dumping site.[21] Along with the media, the Soviet Union loudly criticized the United States and its Western allies for this dumping and contamination of the ocean, but even this criticism turned out to be a hollow deceit: the Soviet Union and later Russian Federation actually dumped twice the amount of all other countries combined during this period.[22]

As early as 1955, Japan was a player in the shady global practice of ocean dumping. Even before the commencement of commercial nuclear power generation in the country in 1966, Japanese officials were concerned about the buildup of radioactive waste material from medical and research facilities. In 1954 the Nihon Hōshasei Dōigensō Kyōkai (Japan Radioisotope Association, JRA), then responsible for the import, distribution, and management of radioactive byproducts, consulted with the government's Kagaku Gijutsu

Chō (Science and Technology Agency, STA), which advised that there was really no domestic or international regulatory framework in place and that standard international practice was to ocean dump low-level radioisotopes in concrete-filled canisters.[23] Low-level radioactive waste dumping commenced soon after, in July 1955, when twenty-seven makeshift oil cans filled with cobalt 60 were dumped into Sagami Bay just south of Tokyo. Two years later, in September 1957, the JRA dumped a further ten cans of concrete-solidified cobalt-60 into nearby Suruga Bay off the coast of Shizuoka Prefecture.[24] But the bulk of ocean dumping occurred at sites off the coast of Tateyama in Chiba Prefecture beside Tokyo. From 1955 to 1969, some 1,661 canisters of low-level radioactive waste were dumped to a depth of 8,200 feet (2,500 meters) at these sites.[25] In 1977, the Suisan Chō (Fisheries Agency, FA) conducted tests at thirteen points around the Sagami Bay disposal area, revealing elevated radiation in two places: cobalt-60 up to thirty-two times safe levels at one place and cesium-137 up to twelve times acceptable standards at the other.[26] Subsequent ocean sediment tests by the STA in 1980 revealed ongoing contamination at the Sagami Bay sample points, but tests at the dumping site off the coast of Tateyama revealed no abnormalities.[27]

More than the JRA, however, it was the Genshiryoku Iinkai (Japan Atomic Energy Commission, JAEC) that took the lead in formulating and attempting to implement an ocean dumping regime in anticipation of the commencement of commercial nuclear power in the country. Japan's first test reactor reached criticality in October 1963, and the earliest commercial reactors came online at Tōkai (No.1) in July 1966, Tsuruga (No.1) in March 1970, Mihama (No.1) in November 1970, and Fukushima (No.1) in March 1971. In February 1961 the JAEC established a subcommittee to study the feasibility of ocean disposal, which issued its report in June 1964 to committee chairman Satō Eisaku, who also headed the STA, MITI, and the Hokkaidō Kaihatsu Kyoku (Hokkaido Development Agency), and would become prime minister only months later.[28] Building on the 1964 report, in 1969 the STA established the Hōshasei Kotai Haikibutsu Bunkakai (Subcommittee on the Management and Disposal of Solid Radioactive Wastes), which was charged with identifying potential disposal sites in the Pacific Ocean.

After two years of investigations, the study group identified four candidate disposal sites, the closest 560 miles (900 kilometers) from Tokyo and the farthest 1,056 miles (1,700 kilometers) away. The JAEC formally articulated its stance on low-level waste disposal in its 1972 Genshiryoku Kaihatsu Riyō Chōki-Keikaku (Long-term plan for the development and use of nuclear power), which concluded that ocean dumping up to a certain level of radioactivity was safe and that the country's low-level radioactive waste should be disposed of both at sea and on land.[29] After consulting with officials in the FA, the Kaijō Hoanchō (Japan Coast Guard, JCG), and the Kishō Chō (Japan Meteorological Agency, JMA), the JAEC decided that site B (coordinates: 30N 147E), located roughly 560 miles southeast of Tokyo and 620 miles (1,000 kilometers) north of the Northern Mariana Islands was the most appropriate because of ocean depth, currents, and prevailing weather patterns.[30] Interestingly, the JAEC's subcommittee charged with coordinating the disposal program stated unequivocally in its 1974 report that, since it would not be possible to manage or monitor materials once dumped into the deep ocean, it was of the utmost importance that the authorities conduct a trustworthy and comprehensive safety assessment before commencing any disposal program.[31] But no such safety assessment was ever carried out. Instead, in its 1976 Hōshasei Haikibutsu Shori no Kihon Hōshin (Basic policy on the management and disposal of radioactive waste material), the JAEC announced that trial disposals at site B would begin in 1978 and full-scale dumping from 1980.[32] As they searched for candidate disposal sites from the late 1960s, government nuclear officials also diligently prepared the regulatory framework to enable ocean disposal.

The 1970s were heady days indeed in the Japanese nuclear power industry. Arisawa Hiromi, the influential economist and chairman of the Japan Nuclear Power Industry Council, even imagined Japan becoming the center (and apex) of an "Asian nuclear fuel cycle," declaring at a conference that "if Japan is asked by foreign countries to provide services (enrichment, reprocessing) as part of its nuclear fuel cycle, it should do so." Specifically, Arisawa wanted Japan to become the central hub for the enrichment of uranium and the reprocessing of spent nuclear fuel from power plants throughout Southeast Asia and the Western Pacific.[33] For a time, officials in the nuclear power industry even envisioned the creation of a "Pacific Rim Nuclear Energy Community," with, needless to say, Japan leading the way. With the regulatory framework and infrastructure in place for ocean dumping, for a brief moment in the late 1970s all of this must have seemed possible.

What nuclear officials initially failed to appreciate, however, was the potentially disruptive backlash from people living on islands in the vicinity of site B—not to mention from scientists and technicians long skeptical about the safety of ocean dumping. In their rush to ready the legal and logistical infrastructure, Japanese nuclear officials did not seek the approval of, nor did they notify, people living on western Pacific islands such as the Marianas and the Ogasawaras, which were located closest (311 miles/500 kilometers) to site B. As the *AMPO* newsletter reported, when the Japanese government was finalizing the plan in 1979, it merely sent a letter to the Australian government, a partner in the Pacific Basin Community Scheme, requesting its approval.[34] Of course, Japanese officials were acutely aware that any request for "approval" from governments and people in the Marianas and Ogasawaras ran the risk of accusations of duplicity and contradiction. After all, if this was a lawful process of disposal in international waters using supposedly fail-safe techniques, why the need for approval from states or communities hundreds of miles away?

Nuclear authorities knew only too well that serious questions remained with respect to the reliability and safety of ocean disposal and that these questions threatened to undermine the whole scheme if they escalated into a widespread public debate. In fact, in 1972, years before ocean disposal even became an official plan in Japan, the Zenkoku Genshiryoku Kagaku Gijutsusha Rengō (National Alliance of Nuclear Power Scientists and Technicians) writing in the RCP's journal *Kōgai Kenkyū* (Pollution research) had pointed out that, in the case of ocean dumping, canisters needed to be properly weighted to ensure sinkage but that as weight increased so too did the risk of rupture on impact. "The chance of damage is high," the article concluded.[35] Furthermore, even if the steel canisters survived the ocean-floor impact, over time they would most certainly deteriorate as a result of deep ocean pressure and corrosion. The discovery of damaged canisters and surrounding contamination off the coast of San Francisco in California and in Sagami Bay in Japan only corroborated these warnings.[36] Given such data, nuclear officials' failure to advise and seek the approval of Pacific residents is hardly surprising. As they realized, guarantees of safety paradoxically yet inevitably led back to the simple yet unanswerable question: If the material was so safe, why not dump it in Japanese coastal waters?

### Pacific Furor and Japanese Responses

Despite Japanese officials' best attempts to keep the project inconspicuous if not clandestine, political leaders and nongovernmental groups on Pacific islands eventually learned of the dumping plan in 1979, to which they reacted with immediate and fierce antipathy. As Alley and Alley point out, they "had good reasons to be distrustful" about governmental guarantees of safety. In 1954, people of the Rongelap and Utirik Atolls suffered serious radiation exposure after the Castle Bravo hydrogen bomb test at Bikini Atoll because they were not evacuated or even advised of the dangers by the US military. The people of Bikini Atoll returned home in 1968 based on assurances that the region was safe, only to learn in 1978 that their foods— and, hence, their bodies—were being contaminated by radionuclides.[37] The French government showed a similar indifference toward people living near its nuclear weapons test site at Mururoa (also Moruroa) Atoll in the south Pacific. When the Belauan antinuclear activist Roman Bedor met with the French deputy foreign minister in 1983 to present an anti-bomb petition, the deputy minister said that opponents were completely "misinformed," because French testing was safe whereas US testing was not.[38] According to Bedor, the deputy minister advised "that no one had yet been affected by the testing [and] that he himself had swum in the lagoon in Mouroa [sic] and was still in good health." Bedor asked the deputy minister if the tests were so safe why they were not conducted in France, but he received no satisfactory response.[39] Japanese officials were no less condescending. In a meeting with an official delegation from Guam and the Northern Marianas in 1981, STA director Nakagawa Ichirō condescendingly announced that the nuclear waste canisters to be dumped were "completely safe" and that he "wouldn't mind embracing them" or "sleeping with them" in his "bed."[40]

Pacific protest against the Japanese dumping plan began in 1979 in the Northern Marianas, the closest place to site B other than the Ogasawaras. In late November 1979 the governor of the Northern Marianas, Carlos Camacho, sent an urgent telegram to the United States ambassador to Japan, Mike Mansfield, expressing grave concerns over the possibility of radioactive contamination from nuclear waste disposal and asking him to request further information from the Japanese government.[41] Camacho heard nothing until late January 1980, when the Japanese STA formally advised the US embassy of the plan. In response, Camacho sent another telegram to Mansfield in February 1980, asking him to relay the official opposition of the Commonwealth of the Northern Mariana Islands.[42] Protest spread throughout Pacific island nations after the *Pacific Daily News* published out of Guam ran an article on the Japanese dumping plan on February 9, 1980.[43] In Guam, Governor Paul Calvo and the Guam legislature promptly passed a resolution of opposition on February 14, while two days later, on February 16, the Northern Mariana Islands House of Representatives passed a "Declaration of the Northern Marianas as a Nonnuclear Area." Thereafter, similar resolutions were passed in the Republic of Belau (Palau), Yap State in the Caroline Islands, the Hawaiʻi state legislature, and various other Pacific nations.[44] The far-off Independent State of Samoa even sent an official telegram to the Japanese government expressing absolute opposition to the disposal plan.[45]

Nongovernmental groups also joined the chorus of opposition. On Saipan, the largest of the Northern Mariana Islands nature conservation groups quickly mobilized a protest movement, as too did activists in Guam, who established the Mariana Alliance Opposing Nuclear Waste Dumping on April 10, 1980.[46] Led by the sixty-nine-year-old mayor of Tinian, Felipe Mendiola, the alliance started a signature campaign and immediately began to build a transnational opposition movement throughout the Pacific and beyond.[47] Significantly, the alliance was quick to forge connections with Japanese groups. In an October 1980 letter to the ILP movement, the alliance explained:

> The peoples and governments of the Pacific Islands have been opposing the Japanese Government's plan to dispose of nuclear waste material in the Pacific and we have called on all Japanese people with heart to rise up in opposition with us. . . . We have learned that, in response, voices opposing oceanic dumping have appeared throughout Japan and that numerous civic and residents groups have started a signature campaign demanding an immediate cancellation of the ocean disposal plan. This news is very pleasing to us and gives us great encouragement. Japanese and people of Pacific Islands uniting in struggle across the ocean for a shared objective—this is indeed an event of deep significance.[48]

Opposition to the dumping plan further intensified at two transnational gatherings of Pacific activists in 1980. At the third Nuclear-Free Pacific Conference (NFPC) held in Hawaiʻi in May, Pacific activists unanimously passed a resolution opposing the Japanese plan.[49] The follow-up conference, the Nuclear-Free Pacific Forum, held in Sydney, Australia, in September 1980, passed a similar resolution.[50] This latter forum was sponsored by the Australian communist-pacifist group, the Association for International Cooperation and Disarmament, and attracted some twenty NGOs and labor groups from around the Pacific, including anti–uranium mining groups, antinuclear groups, Aboriginal groups, the Australian Railway Workers Union, the School Teachers Union, and Greenpeace, as well as delegates from Papua New Guinea, West Papua, Vanuatu, Belau, Fiji, Hawai'i, Samoa, and New Zealand. Japan was also strongly represented at the forum, with participants and/or statements from the rival organizations Gensuikin and Gensuikyō (Japan Council Against Atomic & Hydrogen Bombs), the ILP Nuclear Power Group, PARC, and the AEIC.[51] Thanks to such meetings, by late 1980 Pacific activists had mobilized a high-profile transnational movement that drew together an impressive array of labor, antinuclear, pacifist, and environmental groups from around the Pacific region. It was a mobilization that Japanese nuclear officials had not anticipated, and they were left scrambling to respond to angry officials and activists in all corners of the Pacific.

In the first instance, Japanese nuclear officials had simply ignored expressions of opposition. The STA, for example, delayed its response to Governor Camacho's initial letter for some two months and, when it did reply, directed the response to the United States government on grounds that the Northern Marianas were under US control and hence had no formal diplomatic ties with Japan.[52] But by mid-1980, pressure from the Pacific movement was too intense to ignore, and on August 6 the Japanese government announced it would be sending a specialist "explanatory team" to the south Pacific to allay residents' apprehensions.[53] The STA explanatory team—or "persuasion team" as critics branded it—faced a difficult task. As the newspaper *Mainichi Shinbun* explained, the Japanese government's failure to consult with Pacific residents had resulted in them presenting Japan with an ultimatum: "Fish or atoms." Potentially affected nations were threatening that, if Japan proceeded with the dumping, they would revoke fishing rights in their waters, significantly affecting Japanese catches of tuna and bonito.[54] On August 9, just days before the explanatory team arrived in Guam, Governor Calvo told Japanese television reporters, "I assume these representatives will stress the safety of the disposal plan. But if it were really safe why don't you Japanese store it in the backyard of your own territory. Our Pacific Ocean is not a dumping ground for radioactive waste from your country. The people of Guam are opposed to this plan and will unite in opposition."[55]

During 1980, the explanatory team traveled to five Pacific islands: Saipan, Chuuk Lagoon (formerly Truk), Yap, Kosrae, and Guam. They also intended to visit the Cook Islands and Niue but, in a display of opposition, were refused visas to enter into these countries.[56] According to Kawana

Hideyuki, then an environmental reporter with *Asahi Shinbun*, the initiative was ultimately a spectacular debacle, simply failing to convince the people of the Pacific that the disposal process would be safe, that discarded radioactive material could be monitored and managed, that there would be no radioactive leakage, or that the canisters could be salvaged in an emergency.[57]

The explanatory team faced its first skeptical audience in Guam, where members gave a presentation at the Pacific Islands Conference of Leaders (PICL) meeting on August 14 and 15, 1980.[58] Using colorful slides and a host of impressive statistics, the team stressed the overall safety of the process and the Japanese government's commitment to act in strict accordance with the regulations of the LDC. But their supplications fell on deaf ears.[59] Governor Calvo was the most vocal and trenchant in his questioning: "You explained that it is necessary to isolate [the material] from the human environment. But doesn't the fact that you have to isolate it mean that [the material] is dangerous? Isn't it a contradiction to be isolating something which is safe?"[60] Calvo made explicit comparison to Japanese mercury poisoning, arguing that pollutants (like radioactive material) can have a major impact when they enter into the food chain and concentrate through bioaccumulation. Lacking a satisfactory response from the Japanese team, on August 15, 1980, the PICL officially rejected the plan, concluding that ocean dumping would destroy the ecosystem and threaten marine resources.[61] Leaders from nine Micronesian states and territories issued a formal statement requesting that the Japanese government abandon the plan.[62]

The team faced similar hostility in Saipan, where they gave a two-hour presentation to Governor Carlos Camacho and thirty government representatives. The Japanese were surprised to discover that Governor Camacho had engaged the services of University of California biologist W. Jackson Davis, who had detected radioactive contamination in sea life at a nuclear waste dumping site near the Farallon Islands off the coast of San Francisco. Davis again raised the issue of bioaccumulation, stating unequivocally that "the assumptions on which the Japanese are basing their appraisals of safety are flawed. Radioactivity is not diluted in sea water but remains on the ocean floor from where it reaches our mouths via fish."[63] The reception was no less hostile when the team visited the Ogasawaras in late September 1980 to address village leaders, farmers, and fishermen. Indeed, if government officials had hoped for a kinder reception from their fellow countrymen, they were poorly mistaken. Island leaders and fishermen expressed their staunch opposition to the dumping of nuclear waste a short 311 miles (500 kilometers) from their islands, with fishermen threatening to use their boats to blockade any vessels attempting to transport radioactive waste material for disposal.[64] More than "Japanese" or even "Ogasawarans," the islanders understood their opposition in the context of a wider struggle of Pacific Ocean peoples opposed to nuclear power. As they explained in the *Hangenpatsu Shinbun* (Antinuclear power newspaper) in 1980, "We won't be satisfied if the waste is simply not dumped near the Ogasawaras. We believe that there is a problem with nuclear-powered electricity generation itself."[65]

The proximity of the Ogasawaras to the proposed disposal site and to other potentially affected islands such as Guam and Saipan undoubtedly encouraged islanders' sense of being part of a wider antinuclear struggle in the Pacific. But even antipollution and antinuclear activists on the main islands came to share this Pacific perspective on the nuclear issue—a perspective, in fact, that was developing even before the dumping controversy arose and against a backdrop of rising anti–nuclear power protest within Japan. As early as May 1975, two activists from the ILP movement participated in the "Ride Against Uranium" organized by the NGO Friends of the Earth (Australia), in which participants cycled for ten days from Sydney to the Parliament House in Canberra to protest the mining and export of this element. Activists back in Japan supported the protest by staging a simultaneous demonstration outside the Australian embassy in Tokyo.[66] The title changes of activist publications during this period also indicate the broadening transpacific consciousness among Japanese groups throughout the late 1970s and 1980s, as well as their rising consciousness of nuclear power as a regional and global issue. Recall how the subtitle of *Don't Let the Pollution Escape! Exposing Pollution Export to South Korea* was changed to *Exposing Pollution Export to the Third World* in November 1976. In 1982 the subtitle was again changed to *Resisting Japanese Aggression Together with the Peoples of Asia and the Pacific*.[67] In June 1986, in the wake of the Chernobyl nuclear power plant disaster, the main title *Don't Let the Pollution Escape!* was abandoned altogether, the new title becoming *Antinuclear Pacific Ocean PACIFICA: Resisting Japanese Aggression Together with the Peoples of Asia and the Pacific*.[68]

Expanding interactions between Japanese and Pacific activists throughout the 1970s were also broadening the perspective of domestic antinuclear movements. After participating in the second Nuclear-Free Pacific Conference on the Micronesian island of Pohnpei in 1978, the ILP activist Yokoyama

Masaki organized the Taiheiyō kara Kaku o Nakusō! 3–1 Tōkyō Shūkai (Tokyo rally to rid the Pacific of nuclear energy) on March 1, 1979.[69] This year marked the twenty-fifth anniversary of Bikini Day, which in Japan was most directly associated with the radiation exposure of Japanese fishermen on the ship *Daigo Fukuryūmaru* (Lucky Dragon No. 5) after the Castle Bravo hydrogen bomb test in 1954. But thanks to his participation at the Pohnpei conference, Yokoyama and participants agreed to a new designation for the Bikini Day event: "Nuclear-Free Pacific Day." In other words, the commemoration was to be not only for Japanese but for all victims of "nuclearism" in the Pacific, including, for instance, Australian Aborigines, whose traditional lands were being decimated by uranium mining.[70] Thus, by the time of the ocean dumping controversy in 1980, some Japanese antipollution and antinuclear groups were already beginning to think about nuclear power and atomic weapons within processes of discrimination and injustice beyond the borders of the archipelago and, by consequence, beyond the national narrative of nuclear victimhood.

Japanese opposition to the dumping plan began on August 9, 1980, the same day Governor Calvo and others commenced their mobilization in Guam. Some forty civic groups including the ILP, the Nihon Shōhisha Renmei (Consumers' Union of Japan), and the Fujin Minshu Kurabu (Women's Democratic Club) established the Hōshasei Haikibutsu no Taiheiyō Tōki Keikaku Hakushi Tekkai o Motomeru Jikkō Iinkai (Executive Committee for the Cancellation of the Plan to Dispose of Nuclear Waste Material in the Pacific), which submitted an open appeal to Prime Minister Suzuki Zenkō demanding an immediate end to the plan and commenced a nationwide signature campaign.[71] The executive committee declared, "We [Japanese] cannot make the people of Pacific Island nations pay the price for Japan's nuclear energy development."[72] The newspaper *Mainichi Shinbun* noted that, although there were already many local groups opposing nuclear power plant construction within Japan, this was really the first time individual Japanese citizens and civic groups had taken concrete action with respect to the overseas effects of the country's nuclear power industry.[73] The signature campaign turned out to be a resounding success, with over forty-five thousand signatures collected by December 1980, all of which were subsequently delivered by hand to the assistant cabinet secretary.[74] Building on the success of this domestic campaign, from September 1981 the ILP antinuclear group, with the cooperation of the Belauan antinuclear activist Roman Bedor, helped coordinate a worldwide signature campaign against both French nuclear weapons testing in the South Pacific and the Japanese dumping plan, which were both understood as variations of the same contemporary "nuclearism."[75] Other domestic groups also joined the protest. In February 1981, Christian Bishop Aima Nobuo, Father Yamada Keizō (earlier involved in the Kawatestsu sintering plant opposition on Mindanao), Father John Binsko, and Yokoyama Masaki of the Nihon Kirisutokyō Kyōgikai (National Christian Council in Japan) met with Honami Minoru, a bureau chief in the Nuclear Power Safety Bureau at the STA. The group expressed their deep opposition and determination to stop Japan, a "nuclear victim nation," disposing of nuclear waste in the Pacific Ocean.[76] But Honami, a member of the failed explanatory team that had visited Guam the previous year, was unresponsive, telling the group that the STA was keen to start dumping as soon as possible and would do so after gaining approval from the Japanese cabinet and the relevant international nuclear oversight bodies. He advised that the government was "treating this issue as a problem of national security."[77] Fishermen—who potentially had the most to lose economically—also joined the fray. In late June 1981, leaders of fishing cooperatives and those in related industries nationwide gathered in Tokyo to discuss their opposition to the dumping plan. As with Christians and other civic groups, the expressed basis of their opposition was that the Japanese government had no right to force radioactive waste on peoples of the Pacific. But there was also a self-interested motive behind the fishermen's opposition: visitors from various Pacific nations such as Belau, while reaching out to fishermen as natural allies, also made it patently clear that if the Japanese government plan proceeded, Japanese fishing rights in their seas would be promptly revoked.[78]

Japanese opponents of the dumping plan also traveled to Pacific island nations. Notably, in January 1981 a Japanese group visited Belau and Guam in reciprocation for a visit by activists from those countries the previous October. The Japanese group included Yasusato Kiyonobu of the Kinwan o Mamoru Kai (Association to Protect Kin Bay) in Okinawa; Aramoto Hirofumi of the Hankōgai Uken Mura Sonmin Kaigi (Uken Villagers Antipollution Conference) on Amami Ōshima Island; Maeda Toshihiko of the Narita Airport opposition movement in Chiba Prefecture; and Arakawa Shunji and Ōkawa Hōsaku of the ILP movement, who served as guides.[79] During their visit the group attended meetings with local activists, gave media interviews and public speeches, and, in Belau, attended the inauguration ceremony of Haruo Ignacio Remeliik, the first president of the nuclear-free republic.[80] In television appearances on two local stations in Guam and in interviews with the *Pacific Daily News*, the group offered detailed updates on the antidumping movement in Japan. Yasusato, from the Kinwan group, carefully pointed out that the Ryūkyūan Islands and the Marianas were essentially the same distance from the proposed dumping site and, hence, this shared predicament meant that the two communities should struggle together.[81] To coincide with this visit, activists on Amami Ōshima Island started an English-language newsletter, *Kuroshio Tsūshin* (The black tide correspondence), which they translated and sent to fellow activists in Belau to provide updates on the movement and to build solidarity.[82] Such engagements reinforced a growing sense of recognition, responsibility, and even Pacific sentiment among Japanese activists, evident, for example, in the following appeal by "the people of Japan, Amami, and Okinawa" delivered at the Tokyo antidumping rally in October 1980: "Friends around the world! Friends in the Pacific! In the midst of a violent, reactionary storm we can hear the cries of Pacific peoples. Those voices are piercing through the dark clouds and jolting the very base of our hearts. . . . We cannot express [the extent of] our shame over forcing nuclear power plant waste on the people of the Pacific merely for the 'affluence of Japan alone.'"[83]

## Pacific Activists in Japan

Much of the activity I have explored in earlier chapters involved Japanese activists traveling abroad to other countries or to international events to communicate their experience of environmental injustice. As the travels of Okinawan and Amami islanders attest, the movement against nuclear dumping was no exception, with Japanese activists conscientiously traveling to Guam, Saipan, and other potentially affected Pacific countries. But what really distinguished this movement was the Pacific activists who came to Japan to engage with local antinuclear activists—in effect creating transnational spaces within Japan, much the same as Canadian Indians had done briefly in Minamata a few years earlier. Although some Japanese were already attuned to the regional and global ramifications of nuclear power in their country, these Pacific activists brought such issues into much sharper focus by drawing troubling connections between earlier Japanese colonialism in the region and the country's role in contemporary nuclearism. In particular, they helped disrupt two dominant, albeit erroneous, assumptions in the postwar antinuclear movement in Japan: namely, that the problems of nuclear-powered electricity generation were essentially domestic in nature and, second, that nuclear power and nuclear weapons were largely unrelated. To challenge these assumptions, the Pacific visitors tied together two disparate narratives: one a history of Japanese and Western injustice toward them, the other a vision of Pacific community to which they and the Japanese both belonged.

The first wave of Pacific activists arrived in Japan in late July 1980, in time for the annual events to commemorate the atomic bombings of Hiroshima and Nagasaki in August. At the World Conference against Atomic & Hydrogen Bombs held in Hiroshima on August 3, Pacific participants included Governor Paul Calvo and Marianas Alliance leader David Rosario from Guam; the mayor of Saipan, Francisco Diaz; Northern Marianas parliamentarian Joaquin Pangelinan; and Belauan antipollution and antinuclear activist Moses Weldon. Their attendance brought an entirely new flavor to the annual rally, which had focused on nuclear weapons rather than nuclear power and, especially, the symbolism of Japanese nuclear victimhood in the global campaign to abolish nuclear weapons. Now the issue of low-level radioactive waste dumping took center stage. The Pacific visitors shrewdly appropriated the narrative of national victimhood, pointing out that Japanese people—"atomic victims" at Hiroshima, Nagasaki, and Bikini—were about to become "atomic aggressors" in the Pacific.[84] In front of rallies in Hiroshima and Nagasaki, they asked "How can Japan, which experienced Hiroshima and Nagasaki, pollute our sea with nuclear waste?!"[85] Saipan mayor Francisco Diaz even posed this question to puzzled nuclear officials at the STA, where he was assured that there was "no chance of radioactive materials leaking" and, in the unlikely event of leakage, that radiation levels in the material were five thousand times lower than safe annual exposure limits, so there was no need to worry at all. In response Diaz again confronted officials with the thorny question: "If it is so safe then why don't you dump it in Tokyo Bay?"[86]

From the beginning of 1980 to the end of 1983—the high point of the movement against Japan's proposed dumping—foreign activists visited the country to participate in rallies, protests, debates, signature campaigns, and to lobby government officials. The majority came from potentially affected areas such as Belau, Saipan, and Guam, but their numbers also included Australian Aboriginals and American Navaho Indians who opposed uranium mining at the front end of the nuclear fuel cycle. These activists' encouraged

Japanese protesters to reconsider their local struggles and, indeed, their society more generally, in the context of wider configurations of discrimination and injustice throughout the Pacific.

In this connection, during October and early November 1980, two native Chamorros of the Mariana Islands traveled throughout Japan to communicate their people's opposition to the planned disposal of radioactive waste in their waters. The eldest of the two was Felipe Mendiola, the seventy-year-old mayor of Tinian Island, located roughly halfway between Guam and Saipan in the Northern Marianas. He was accompanied by David Rosario, a twenty-seven-year-old activist from Guam who was back again after the August events in Hiroshima and Nagasaki.[87] During their time in Japan, Mendiola and Rosario spoke to groups in Niigata, Fukui, Hiroshima, and Nagasaki, and they addressed two major rallies in Tokyo: the Taiheiyō o Kaku no Gomisuteba ni suru na! Tōkyō Shūkai (Don't make the Pacific a nuclear garbage dump! Tokyo rally) on October 22, and the 10.25 Hangenpatsu Kokumin Daishūkai (October 25 national antinuclear power plant rally), which adopted three positions: "A temporary stop to nuclear power plants, withdrawal of the plan to dispose of radioactive waste material at sea, and an end to Japanese nuclear armaments."[88] Tinian Island and the cities of Hiroshima and Nagasaki, of course, shared a fateful nuclear connection because it was from this small Pacific island that the B-29 aircraft loaded with their deadly atomic payloads had departed for Japan in August 1945. But Mendiola was determined to speak about a different history; a history not many Japanese knew of, and one he hoped might reinforce or even intensify their growing opposition to the dumping issue.

In fluent Japanese, Mendiola told audiences that he had come to appeal not so much to the government but to the Japanese people because he felt he knew them very well. From 1914, when Mendiola was just three years old, until 1945, when he was thirty-three, Tinian had been a colony of Japan. At school he was told to worship an emperor he neither knew about nor cared for, and the Japanese he spoke so fluently was a remnant of this imperial iteration (one of many) in his island's history.[89] The Pacific War only further complicated this sense of detachment. Mendiola explained that, being "neither Americans nor Japanese, we felt the war had nothing to do with us." But the Japanese military "conscripted all men and forced them to construct military bases and to perform nothing but military duties."[90] During the war, Tinianese accused of spying were either brutally murdered by the Japanese or, if they were spared, "treated worse than animals."[91] Yet, despite this discrimination and cruel treatment during the colonial years and despite the great suffering of the war—a war they were drawn into despite having no interest in it whatsoever—Mendiola stressed that the Tinianese were "resigned to the fact that the events of the Pacific War era were over" and they had decided to hold no grudges, letting Japanese come back to their island.[92]

But reading in the newspaper that Japan intended to dump atomic waste in the Pacific released a flood of painful memories, not to mention a new sense of anxiety. Despite its commitments after the war, the reality was that the Japanese government had paid only 16 percent of the reparations owed to the people of Micronesia, and now that same government intended to dump radioactive waste in their backyard. As Mendiola concluded, "Based on this, it is only natural that we do not trust the [Japanese] government when it says it will compensate us if there are damages [from radioactive waste dumping]."[93] Mendiola said that many islanders were beginning to speak about Japan's plan to dump nuclear waste in the context of a long history of "domination" by Spain, Germany, Japan, and the United States. He felt that the current movement was an expression of Micronesians' long-suppressed fury over this history of oppression.[94] Moreover, it was a movement determined to confront Japan head-on. Since war's end, for instance, the people of Tinian had faithfully maintained the graves of fallen Japanese soldiers and civilians, but the combination of many centuries of outside domination and the current nuclearism of powerful countries had caused islanders' bottled-up fury to erupt. They had decided that, should the dumping go ahead, these graves were to be bulldozed to the ground and all Japanese remains dumped into the Pacific, together with Japan's graveyard of radioactive waste. Furthermore, Japanese fishermen, who benefited so much from Micronesian waters, would no longer be welcome.[95] The Japanese and other foreign powers may well have trampled all over Micronesians in the past, but in the new postwar era of self-determination, human rights, and minority empowerment, it was they who would push back. Indeed, for Mendiola and others, the struggle of Pacific peoples' was not merely against nuclear waste dumping or even weapons testing but, more fundamentally, for the recognition of their basic rights and dignity as human beings.

Younger Pacific activists repeated Mendiola's mantra of rights and recognition for audiences throughout Japan in the early 1980s. Particularly important were two young Belauan activists: Ignatio Anastacio and Geldens

Meyer. Their extensive and exhaustive schedule of meetings, speeches, rallies, and site visits speaks volumes of their determination to connect with
and influence Japanese people at all levels of society, from the grassroots to
the Diet. Twenty-nine-year-old Ignatio Anastacio, newly elected to the Belau
National Congress, toured Japan from late February 1980 with his partner
and fellow activist Carol Kesolei. He was inspired after hearing about the
visits of Felipe Mendiola and David Rosario of the previous year. Assisted
by ILP activists, Anastacio first traveled to Niigata Prefecture, where he
addressed a local group opposing (ultimately unsuccessfully) the construction of a nuclear power plant in the towns of Kashiwazaki and Kariwa. In
Tokyo, Anastacio met with Japan Socialist Party Diet member Yoshida
Masao, himself a native of Niigata, to discuss the dumping issue, and in
successive days he gave speeches outside Shimbashi Station in downtown
Tokyo, at two anti–nuclear power rallies, and before activists involved in
a protracted protest against construction of the new Tokyo International
Airport at the Sanrizuka farming area in Chiba Prefecture. On his final
day, Anastacio toured the heavily industrialized region of Kawasaki just
south of Tokyo, which had no nuclear power plants but was then one of the
most polluted regions in the country. In the evening he met with representatives from the Amami Islands and Okinawa, and together this group authored a joint statement that pledged allegiance in the struggle against the
dumping plan. "Faced with a common enemy," the statement declared, "we
must join forces as members of the Pacific."[96]

  The highlight of Anastacio's visit was his deeply moving speech at the
February 28 Tokyo rally against nuclear power, nuclear fuel reprocessing,
and ocean dumping. He told attendees how "the lives and aspirations of the
Pacific islanders ha[d] always been a small part of their conquerors' considerations" and that "for centuries their good will [was] abused and they [had]
suffered greatly for it." "Japan ruled Belau for one quarter of a century. We
learned much from our Japanese rulers. They inflicted much suffering on
us. Many human lives were lost."[97] But now Belauans were fighting for true
independence, of which their antinuclear constitution represented a first
step.[98] "The time is past when the big powers can have their way with the
little people."[99] "If Japan wants to use nuclear power, it must assume its own
responsibility for the waste."[100] And if it failed to do so there would be consequences: "There is one thing I will do on returning to Belau after this trip.
As a member of parliament I will make a recommendation to the legislature
to reconsider the fishing agreement between the Japanese fishing industry

and Belau. Along with scrapping the fisheries agreement, I have decided to start a movement to boycott Japanese products. I am also considering a total halt to Japanese tourism. I believe that these [measures] should stay in place until the Japanese government publicly announces its intention to scrap [the plan] for nuclear waste dumping."[101] For Belauans and, indeed, for all Pacific Islanders, the position was simple: "Dispose of your own trash! We do not want that kind of material."[102] Anastacio called on all conscientious Japanese people to "rise up together with the very strongest bonds of solidarity. The peoples of Asia and the Pacific must join hands and live together in this beautiful natural environment, and to ensure that our lifestyle can continue."[103]

Geldens Meyer, a thirty-year-old fellow Belauan, came to Japan the following month (March 1981) and, during his three-week stay, engaged in a grueling schedule of rallies, official meetings, and speech-giving in the towns and cities of Kubokawa (Kōchi Prefecture), Sagamihara and Yokosuka (Kanagawa Prefecture), Shizuoka (Shizuoka Prefecture), Nagoya (Aichi Prefecture), Kyoto (Kyoto Prefecture), Osaka (Osaka Prefecture), and Iwanai (Hokkaidō).[104] In Kubokawa (now Shimantō) Meyer met with local fishermen, housewives, and residents involved in a (successful) struggle to stop the construction of a nuclear power plant.[105] At a rally organized by a Kubokawa women's group, Meyer called for a joint struggle between people opposing nuclear power in the town and Belauans opposing Japan's radioactive waste in their backyard. Meyer told the locals that he appreciated the Kubokawa struggle all the more now because of his movement's prolonged campaign for an antinuclear constitution in Belau, realized just a few months earlier.[106] Speaking at an event organized by Sanrizuka activists in Sagamihara—an area in central Kanagawa Prefecture with numerous munitions and storage facilities of the US military and Japanese Self-Defense Forces (JSDF)—Meyer repeated his call for grassroots solidarity in the face of neocolonial expansion throughout the Pacific, prompting one Japanese participant to observe how "it has become extremely difficult for we Japanese, of course, but also for the people of the Pacific to see just what the problem is, where the contradictions are, and who the enemy is. Together with the people of the Pacific we must work to disentangle these similar threads. I believe one starting point is nuclear dumping in the Pacific. We should work together in this endeavor."[107] In Yokosuka City, some fifty kilometers south-west of Sagamihara and home to both US and JSDF naval ports, a local antinuclear group showed Meyer canisters filled with radioactive waste material stored outside the Kurihama factory of Japan Nuclear Fuel Limited. They explained how they held protest rallies once or twice a year to oppose the transportation of nuclear fuel from the factory. In fact, just days before Meyer's visit, some members of the group had been arrested during a protest outside the factory to stop transportation of nuclear fuel to a nuclear power plant in Fukushima Prefecture in the north.[108] One of Meyer's hosts said she felt that Japan had "forgotten" about the "important" yet "obvious" things like the risk of accidents, pollution of the sea, and the effects of radioactive material on the unborn. Indeed, Japan had become the kind of country that quite "nonchalantly" dumped waste from its "own garden" into "neighboring gardens." "I feel ashamed and saddened by this," she admitted. "Each and every one of us needs to think more seriously about nuclear energy as the Belauan people are."[109]

At a rally with antinuclear activists in Shizuoka, Meyer attempted to contextualize the nuclear waste dumping issue in the wider structure of Pacific neocolonialism, explaining, for example, how vegetable oil extracted in Belau was exported to the United States, where it was manufactured into synthetic soap and then sold back to Belauans at great profit. Similarly, he pointed to the ways Japanese tourists flew in to Guam on Japanese airlines, stayed at Japanese hotels, and spent money at Japanese-owned stores "so all the profits return to Japan." As one participant later opined, the invasion of Japanese capitalism was happening much faster and deeper than the ties now being formed between the residents of the two countries.[110] During the rally, numerous Japanese participants referred to dumping in the "far-off" Pacific Ocean but Meyer reminded them that, on the contrary, Japan was itself an island nation of the Pacific. He startled a few by pointing out that the distances from the proposed dumping site to Shizuoka and to Belau were really not that different. Moreover, the fact that this area was a popular fishing ground for Shizuoka fishermen made his point about proximity all the more convincing. Indeed, the encounter with this young Belauan made Shizuoka antinuclear activists rethink their rather parochial mentality. As one leader later wrote, "From now on we want to deepen ties with the people of the Pacific Islands (deeper than the ties of Japanese and American capital there), and create an open movement in Shizuoka [different from] the somewhat insular [movement to date]."[111]

The final stop of Meyer's journey was far to the north, in the city of Iwanai in Hokkaidō, where he met with local citizens and members of the local fishing cooperative opposed to the construction of a nuclear power plant in the nearby city of Tomari (the plant was eventually constructed). In a gathering with sixty local residents, one elderly participant offered an emotional response, in which he explained how, during the Pacific War, he had been injured and taken to Belau. "As a Japanese I want to apologize for causing trouble to Belauan citizens who had nothing to do [with the conflict]. I will spend the rest of my life opposing nuclear power."[112] Anastacio, Meyer, and other Pacific activists encountered similar emotive reactions in towns all across Japan in the early 1980s, and they left the country convinced of the groundswell of opposition to ocean dumping at the grassroots and even among some local officials.

The visits of Pacific activists reached a crescendo in mid-1981, when a broad spectrum of officials from around the Pacific fanned out across Japan. In May an official delegation from the Northern Marianas and Guam arrived in Tokyo to submit a petition to the Japanese Diet on the ocean dumping plan. The group included many individuals from the delegation of the previous year, such as Governor Carlos Camacho, Northern Marianas House of Representatives speaker Joaquin Pangelinan, Saipan mayor Francisco M. Diaz, Tinian mayor Felipe C. Mendiola, Guam lieutenant governor Joseph Ada, and a number of other officials from Guam.[113] With the assistance of JSP chairman Asukata Ichio, the delegation submitted their petition to the Diet on May 18 with the endorsement of sixty-two NGOs and governments worldwide and reinforced with the scientific analysis of Professor Jackson Davis.[114] The petition harshly criticized "worldwide policies promoting peaceful uses of nuclear power without first developing adequate technology to dispose of the waste."[115] At a citizens' rally on the same day in Tokyo, attended by leading nuclear opponents such as Takagi Jinzaburō, Governor Camacho received enthusiastic applause for his speech pointing to the global structure of discrimination behind nuclear power. As he explained, "For the people who enjoy nuclear energy, it is immoral and even barbaric to force the danger upon presumably 'unsophisticated people' with little contact with the news media."[116] The group also had a thirty-minute meeting with STA director general Nakagawa Ichirō, at which he made his outrageous claim that the radioactive waste–filled canisters would be safe enough to "cuddle" and "go to sleep beside."[117] He also attempted to address the "not-in-my-backyard" issue, saying that "though the waste drums can be safely stored anywhere in the world, international law [i.e., the LDC] declares that they should not be disposed of on land or in waters near it, but be done at the bottom of very deep ocean regions out of the reach of humans. Some people say that our proposal means dumping one's garbage in other people's yards, but we don't think so because the dump site is in waters a little to our side of the mid-line between Japan and the Northern Marianas."[118]

What became clearer and clearer to Japanese in these encounters was the direct link Pacific Islanders drew between the Japanese nuclear power industry, the ocean dumping issue, and the neocolonialism of large nations. As Roman Bedor explained to Japanese audiences, "Our struggle is without a doubt a struggle for survival. Just as people in America and other countries want to live, we want to live too. Nevertheless, on the one side America has designs for a nuclear military base, and on the other side the Japanese government is considering disposing of radioactive waste in our ocean. . . . France has also tested the neutron bomb in the Pacific at Moruroa near to us. Moreover, another big country, China, is unilaterally using the Pacific as a target for ICBMs [Intercontinental Ballistic Missiles]."[119] Put simply, "The last 400 years of history in Belau and Micronesia" had been "a history of colonization and exploitation," and only now were the people of the Pacific Islands "beginning to raise their voices in pursuit of independence and a nuclear free region, breaking 400 years of enforced silence."[120]

Such observations laid bare the reality that this was a problem far more complex than the dumping of radioactive waste material in the Pacific. Japanese nuclear power was entangled in a global nuclear architecture that could be truly comprehended and addressed only through a new transnational perspective and politics that integrated local struggles into the larger battle against nuclearism. As the Australian Aboriginal activist Mick Miller put it during a 1980 visit to Japan, "The uranium dug up from our lands not only destroys us, ultimately the nuclear waste material Japan is attempting to forcibly dispose of in the ocean threatens the lives of Pacific island peoples, and it will come back [to haunt] Japan which relies on fishing resources of the Pacific Ocean."[121] Roman Bedor from Belau saw things similarly, commenting at a 1981 rally against the US-Japan Security Treaty that "the struggle that we are in, whether we are from the Pacific islands or you are from Japan, is the same struggle. We want to survive."[122] The Japanese government may have become an "atomic aggressor," but Bedor and many other activists from the Pacific were convinced the Japanese people were not. Bedor felt nothing but gratitude and even a sense of brotherhood with fellow Japanese activists: "Our country is only a small nation of 15,000 people. Receiving support from Japan in the midst of various arduous struggles was almost like finding a long-lost sibling. This was how we felt."[123]

## Pacific Victory

Although the movement against the Japanese government's plan to ocean dispose of low-level radioactive waste began initially among officials and civic activists on Guam and in the Northern Marianas in 1979, it quickly grew to include antinuclear activists within Japan after Pacific activists began visiting the country. From 1981 onward, the movement expanded even further thanks to transnational cooperation between Belauans and Japanese groups. In early 1983, Bedor embarked on a lecture tour of Europe with Australian Aboriginal activist Shorty O'Neill and Yokoyama Masaki of the ILP.[124] The three were warmly received in Berlin, West Germany, where the staunchly antinuclear Green Party, Die Grünen, was on the verge of a major breakthrough in federal politics in the upcoming election of March 6, 1983. In an article for the *No Nukes News Japan* newsletter, West German activists in Friends of the Earth Berlin described how antinuclear struggles a world away in the Pacific Ocean were garnering great support in their country, with many people signing on to the petition against nuclear weapons testing and Japanese dumping.[125]

Despite this growing international pressure, for a time Japanese officials attempted to maintain the government's stance. Meeting with a group of Japanese activists in 1983, one STA official stated that "we would like to proceed with nuclear waste ocean dumping as soon as possible since its safety assessment has already been completed as far as Japan is concerned. We are investigating the possibility of land disposal, but for a country like Japan where land is limited, ocean dumping is an important disposal method."[126] But officials at the STA knew only too well that by 1983 the dumping plan was doomed thanks to the vigorous transnational civic response. Indeed, the improbability of the plan was apparent to STA officials as early as 1981, when they advised representatives from the Japan Catholic Council for Justice and Peace, who were visiting to submit ten thousand signatures of opposition, that there would definitely be no dumping in 1981 (despite the initial plan to commence that spring) because of opposition from the Pacific.[127] In meetings with the Australian prime minister Bob Hawke in January 1984, Japanese prime minister Yasuhiro Nakasone advised that his country had postponed the commencement of dumping until at least 1985.[128] During a tour of the South Pacific later the same year, Nakasone went even further, telling the prime ministers of Papua New Guinea and Fiji that the plan would "not be implemented against the wishes of concerned countries."[129]

Japanese activists—whether A-bomb opponents or nuclear power plant protesters—walked away from their encounters with Pacific activists with a new perspective on the issue of nuclear energy in their country. As the declaration of a 1986 Tokyo rally for nuclear-free Pacific noted, "Our eyes were opened to the peoples of the Pacific in the midst of our opposition to Japan's planned ocean dumping of nuclear waste material. . . . The people of the Pacific were forced to suffer when [their islands] became the battlefields for U.S.-Japan hostilities during the Second World War. After the war they suffered nuclear harm as the large nations conducted over 200 nuclear weapons tests."[130] Closer to home, Japan—itself a victim of atomic weapons—was also implicated in this architecture of nuclearism and the associated injustices against the people of the Pacific. As the declaration emphasized, "We Japanese are members of the Pacific so the objective of a nuclear-free Pacific should be a task for us too. But now Japan, a country which experienced the nuclear destruction of Hiroshima and Nagasaki, operates thirty-two nuclear power stations, and it has become a nuclear aggressor country toward the people of the Pacific as evidenced in uranium mining and the plan to ocean dump nuclear waste material."[131]

Indeed, the antidumping movement among Pacific activists made two things patently clear to the Japanese antinuclear advocates involved. First, there could be no such thing as transnational solidarity until the Japanese antinuclear movement gave up its insular victim consciousness and faced the country's atomic aggression head on. As *No Nuke News Japan* concluded in an April 1981 article at the height of the dispute, "Nuclear power promotion for the Japanese means that Japan, the world's first victim of nuclear power, will become a nuclear assailant. At the front end of the nuclear fuel cycle, it will exploit and destroy the lives and environment of indigenous peoples, (e.g., the Black people of South Africa, Native Americans, and Australian Aborigines) while at the [back] end of the cycle, impose spent nuclear wastes on the Pacific Island people."[132] There could be no genuine solidarity with the people of the Pacific so long as the domestic movement was based solely on empathy toward national victims. On the contrary, the movement revealed that silently accepting the energy policy of Japanese elites—permitting them to construct power plants and nuclear fuel reprocessing facilities—inevitably and necessarily invited criticism from people at all stages of the nuclear fuel cycle who could rightly accuse ordinary Japanese of being perpetrators—

"atomic aggressors" in the destruction of their lives, their health, and their environment.[133]

Second, through this transnational movement the Japanese activists involved came to understand the perspective of Pacific protesters, who saw the antidumping movement in the context of a wider battle against injustice, discrimination, and neocolonialism. Yokoyama Masaki of the ILP astutely recognized this sentiment after attending the Nuclear-Free Pacific conference in Pohnpei in 1978. As he observed, all of the issues—antiwar, anti-bases, anti-A-bomb testing—all of these "necessarily lead to the problem of colonial domination by large countries." Hence, the antinuclear movement of Pacific island peoples was quite naturally unfolding within their "struggle for independence."[134] As he explained in an article written after Pohnpei, Pacific activists' "antinuclear struggles necessarily evolved into independence struggles because local residents said 'It is not us but *you* who should get out of here!' " According to Yokoyama, this was something "difficult to see" for people "sitting in Tokyo." "Debating the dangers of radioactive fallout and appealing for an end to atomic power because hydrogen bombs were the enemy of humanity [made] it difficult to comprehend the obviousness of 'antinuclear struggle=independence struggle' " for Pacific Islanders and other indigenous peoples.[135]

Transnational interactions in the 1970s and 1980s with Asian and Pacific activists forced the Japanese groups involved to tackle regional iterations of environmental injustice disturbingly at odds with both global notions of "Spaceship Earth" and "our common future," as well as national narratives of victimhood. On one level, the struggles of people in these regions resonated with the earlier struggles of Japanese localities subjected to environmental injustices in the name of economic growth and the national interest. But, on another level, involvement in these struggles also helped fashion a new reflexivity (i.e., we are also aggressors) and a stronger focus on the invisible spaces of environmental injustice in a globalizing world of extreme inequity. By the mid-1980s, some within the Japanese environmental movement, such as Yokoyama Masaki, were becoming more and more committed to this developing-nation perspective in their environmental outlook. They began to suspect that processes of globalization, rather than making the whole Earth "our backyard," in many ways seemed to be replicating the injustices of an earlier age of colonialism—if in a more sophisticated way. As I argue in the following chapter, one outcome of such thinking was to make some Japanese activists at the forefront of initiatives for the global environment more committed, not less, to the local as a critical site of environmental contention and action in an age of global-scale problems. A worldview shaped by local experiences and notions of environmental injustice deeply informed this perspective.

CHAPTER 6

# Globality through Local Eyes

In June 1988, Dr. James Hansen, an atmospheric physicist at the National Aeronautics and Space Administration (NASA) Goddard Institute for Space Studies, told a US congressional committee on energy and natural resources that he was 99 percent confident the temperature increases of the 1980s were not caused by natural variation. Hansen's analysis of weather data in the United States for the previous hundred years revealed that the highest four temperatures had occurred in the 1980s and that current average temperatures were the highest in recorded history. Significantly, Hansen attributed the warming to anthropogenic emissions of greenhouse gases such as carbon dioxide ($CO_2$), which he said were not only contributing to "extreme weather events" such as heat waves and droughts but also detrimentally transforming the global climate.[1]

Unusual and in some cases severe weather events at the time seemed to corroborate Hansen's hypothesis. In Canada, the Calgary Winter Olympics witnessed some of the warmest temperatures ever experienced in the city at that time of year. On February 26 the mercury hit a balmy 64.6 degrees Fahrenheit (18.1 degrees Celsius).[2] In the United States, a three-month drought affecting states from California to Georgia resulted in terrible harvests in the Midwest and the loss of thousands of head of livestock. According to *Time* magazine, temperatures in excess of 100 degrees Fahrenheit (37.8 degrees Celsius) raised fears that the "dreaded greenhouse effect . . . might already be underway."[3] "Killer" hurricanes in the Caribbean, devastating floods covering four-fifths of Bangladesh, and mysterious seal deaths in the North Sea only added to the sense that some dramatic process of climate change had begun.[4] Coupled with these unsettling events were growing anxieties about the negative human health effects of the so-called hole in the ozone layer caused by damaging chlorofluorocarbons (CFCs). Of such concern was the issue that in September 1987 countries worldwide rallied to sign the Montreal Protocol on Substances that Deplete the Ozone Layer, in a last-ditch attempt to protect stratospheric ozone.

Sensing the mood of the moment, *Time* magazine abandoned its usual "Man of the Year" edition in early 1989, naming the Earth as its "Planet of the Year" for 1988. In his cover story, journalist Thomas A. Sancton observed how "everyone suddenly sensed that this gyrating globe, this precious repository of all the life that we know of, was in danger. No single individual, no event, no movement captured imaginations or dominated headlines more than the clump of rock and soil and water and air that is our common home."[5] The Japanese media responded even earlier to concern about the global environment. Beginning in late 1987, NHK, the public broadcaster, aired a highly rated television series on worldwide environmental problems; in January 1988 the newspaper *Asahi Shinbun* devoted its New Year's special edition to the "global environment"; and in September 1988, journalists at the newspaper *Yomiuri Shinbun* voted to make the "global environment" 1989's topic of the year.[6] So intense was media, popular, and political attention throughout 1988 that some observers in Japan began to optimistically look toward 1989 as "Year One of the Global Environmental Age" (Chikyū kankyō gannen) in the country.[7]

The combination of extreme weather, ozone holes, and dire scientific predictions encouraged political leaders of all ideological persuasions— ranging from Margaret Thatcher to Fidel Castro—to join in the environmental discussion, if only as a form of lip service. In May 1988, US president George H. W. Bush and Soviet leader Mikhail Gorbachev exchanged opinions on environmental issues for the first time, paving the way for further debate among leaders of the advanced industrialized nations' Group of Seven (G7) during their Toronto summit the following month. After the G7 summit, Canadian prime minister Brian Mulroney hosted the landmark Toronto Conference on the Changing Atmosphere, at which scientists and policymakers from around the globe formulated rudimentary countermeasures to address global warming, stratospheric ozone depletion, and acid rain. The conference participants called for an ambitious 20 percent reduction in $CO_2$ emissions, compared with 1988 levels, by the year 2000; the creation of a dedicated United Nations agency; and the implementation of a "fossil fuel tax" in developed nations to underwrite a global "atmospheric conservation fund."[8] In a speech at the United Nations General Assembly in September, Soviet foreign minister Eduard Shevardnadze noted that "the biosphere recognizes no division into blocs, alliances, or systems. All share the same climatic system and no one is in a position to build his own isolated and independent line of environmental defense."[9] The culmination of this political attention to global environmental problems came in December 1989 when the UN General Assembly decided to hold the United Nations Conference on Environment and Development (UNCED)—the Rio Earth Summit—in summer 1992. Thereafter global environmental problems—mainly climate change—became the central focus of environmental debate and discourse worldwide.

Just as *The Limits to Growth* and *Only One Earth* had framed environmental debate at events such as UNCHE in the early 1970s, the 1987 report *Our Common Future* by the World Commission on Environment and Development (WCED, also known as the Brundtland Commission after its chairperson) brought the idea of "sustainable development" to the very center of thinking about global environmental problems.[10] As Clapp and Dauvergne explain, *Our Common Future* "went further than any official international document to provide a new definition of development with the environment at its core."[11] It defined the concept of sustainable development as "development that meets the needs of the present without compromising the ability of future generations to meet their own needs," stressing three essential elements: environmental protection, economic growth, and social equity.[12] In spirit, at least, *Our Common Future* tried to chart a midpoint between the "North" and the "South" and between "market-liberal and institutionalist views on growth" and "social green and bioenvironmentalist views."[13] Economic growth and industrialization were seen as not "necessarily harmful to the environment," and WCED members did not see any "limits" to these processes, as the MIT group had. On the contrary, similar to the *Founex Report* prepared by Tsuru Shigeto and others before UNCHE, *Our Common Future* pointed to poverty as a fundamental cause of environmental disruption, hence it recognized the necessity and right of developing countries to industrialize and grow.[14]

For critics, however, the problem was how sustainable development would find expression in a real world shot through with economic and political inequities. As Thiele explains, "While the commission spoke of 'our common future,' the rhetorical question that critics asked was, whose common future is really being secured? Who [was] being protected by centralized control over environmental affairs, the local dwellers of the land or the bureaucracies and corporations that rule[d] over them?"[15] Such worries about autonomy in the face of an emergent global environmental governance structure dovetailed with concerns about the sudden dominance of global problems over and above other more localized yet nevertheless threatening environmental issues for many, like clean water or soil erosion. Just as Third World advocates had done at UNCHE in 1972, activists committed to an emancipatory environmentalism and global justice argued that disproportionate attention to global-level problems created a false image of unity that obscured more fundamental resource and power inequities worldwide. They argued there could not, in fact, would not, be any "common future" until such inequities were addressed and resolved by the wealthy societies of the global North that were responsible for the current environmental predicament. To be sure, in its concept of sustainable development, *Our Common Future* pointed at a middle way, but as advocates of the developing world pointed out, the WECD's definition did little to address historical injustices that greatly disadvantaged the global poor. Although by no means of one voice, a number of prominent Japanese environmental activists and groups agreed with and strongly advocated this latter opinion because it resonated with their own worldviews on environmental injustice.

In this chapter I analyze the involvement of Japanese groups in this moment of heightened attention to global-scale environmental problems beginning in the late 1980s and marked by important events such as the Earth Summit (1992) and the Kyoto Protocol climate conference (1997). These groups continued the legacy of Japanese transnational activism from UNCHE in 1972 and subsequent movements opposing forms of pollution in East Asia and the Pacific, particularly in their focus on environmental injustices worldwide. First I trace the role of Japanese groups in influential meetings and forums before and during UNCED—especially the Japan People's Forum for the United Nations Conference on Environment and Development (hereafter the People's Forum). I then analyze the ideas of leading activists such as Iwasaki Shunsuke on global-scale environmental problems. My primary objective is to show how extant notions of environmental injustice continued to deeply inform and shape approaches to the new global environmental agenda. While many Japanese activists did indeed became vocal advocates of a global perspective and ideas like "global citizenship," there was a steadfast core who remained resolutely committed to a very localized or situated paradigm of environmental injustice. The globe was warming, the ozone layer thinning, and tropical rain forests disappearing, but these activists asserted that such problems needed to be anchored in lived experience if they were to be solved in an equitable way. They argued that particular consideration must be afforded to the lived experience of those most marginalized within nations and globally.

Japanese groups such as the People's Forum tended to resist globalizing discourses, much as their predecessors had rejected collectivist ideologies of the "national interest," because they believed such ideas obscured fundamental structures of discrimination and marginalization. Instead of global solutions they proposed processes of "endogenous development" that would put control of life spaces in the hands of local people as opposed to corporations, governments, or the institutions of "global environmental governance"— regardless of how benign or well-intended these might be.[16] The central assertion of prominent activists such as Iwasaki Shunsuke of the People's Forum was that local self-management and autonomy, whether in the developed or developing world, could form the basis of an authentic and grounded approach to global environmental problems from the bottom up.

Needless to say, in an age of resplendent globalism, this approach left itself open to criticisms of naïve and blinkered NIMBYism—the Old Maid mentality. But it was more nuanced and historically informed than that. Japanese groups' appeals for the rights of local communities, developing nations, and other marginalized groups in an age of global-scale problems drew on a paradigm of environmental injustice shaped by firsthand knowledge of suffering and struggle at Minamata, Grassy Narrows, Incheon, Belau, and other local spaces worldwide. Viewed from this bottom-up perspective, the problem was not so much in the concept of sustainable development, which in ways resonated with their outlook. Rather, it was how this concept would be defined and who or what would control and monitor its implementation— questions, of course, that involved fundamental issues of power, autonomy, rights, and justice.

## Japanese Activism in the Global Environmental Movement: From Asia to Rio

The late 1980s was a moment of frenzied organization and activity for Japanese environmental NGOs, reminiscent on a smaller scale of the wave of activism during the country's "long environmental 1960s."[17] Numerous veteran transnational organizations opened branches in Japan around this time. In 1989, for instance, both Greenpeace and Friends of the Earth (FoE) began operations in the country, joining their more moderate cousin the World Wide Fund for Nature (WWF), which had been in Japan since 1971. Greenpeace and FoE immediately took aim at the Japanese state, lobbying vigorously on climate change issues and the environmental effects of Japanese official development assistance (ODA) throughout Asia.[18] These established transnational NGOs were "instrumental in disseminating knowledge and environmental values" from abroad and helping to "insert" environmental groups "into Japan's policy-making process."[19] They also provided valuable logistical and financial support to domestic groups with a transnational and global focus.

But it was a new cadre of homegrown environmental NGOs that led the civic engagement with global environmental problems from around the late 1980s. Although these homegrown groups were directly responding to the new global environmental agenda of the late 1980s, many—including some of the most influential—continued to draw on an environmentalism attentive to human rights, justice, and equity. Atsuko Satō has usefully defined these organizations as "transnationalized domestic actors," by which she means groups that do not have solid transnational institutional structures, like Greenpeace or FoE, but instead, "use transnational networks when necessary" while maintaining their "autonomy within a country."[20] Early prominent examples include the Japan Tropical Forest Action Network (JATAN), formed in 1987 by the consumer activist Kuroda Yōichi, and the Citizens' Alliance for Saving Earth and Atmosphere (CASA), formed by antipollution groups, consumer associations, scientists, and lawyers in 1989. Both of these groups adopted a decidedly anthropocentric focus in their activism for the global environment. In its movement for rain forest protection, JATAN, for example, stressed the plight of forest peoples whose living spaces were being decimated by logging over and above the destruction of virgin rain forests. CASA, likewise, drew on notions of "aggressors" and "victims" in its emphasis on Japan's international culpability as a perpetrator of atmospheric pollution. Its leaders drew heavily on their earlier experience supporting victims in struggles against air pollution in Japan. In December 1996, an alliance of groups including CASA and the WWF established the influential Kiko Forum, which brought together some 225 groups committed to influencing proceedings at the Third Session of the Conference of the Parties (COP3) to the United Nations Framework Convention on Climate Change (UNFCCC) held in Kyoto City the following year. Similar to CASA, Kiko Forum leaders' backgrounds in pollution victim advocacy within Japan deeply shaped their network's attention to questions of equity and justice in responding to climate change. To invoke Sidney Tarrow's terminology again, the leaders of these groups were ideally positioned to act as the "connective tissue" in this critical phase of environmental globalism, not only between Japanese groups and the outside world but now also between marginalized groups and the advocates of an all-encompassing global agenda for the environment. In this sense they continued in the tradition of rooted cosmopolitism begun many decades earlier by Ui Jun, Harada Masazumi, Tsuru Shigeto, and others.

CASA's expanding agenda from local industrial pollution to global-scale environmental problems offers an excellent example of the way these transnationalized domestic actors embraced the new agendas while staying faithful to local perspectives and earlier paradigms of environmental injustice. Established in March 1989 by the lawyer Yamamura Tsunetoshi and fellow activists in western Honshū (the Kansai region), CASA was initially called the Citizens' Conference to Consider Atmospheric Problems. Similar to the People's Forum in Tokyo, it consisted of grassroots groups and professionals with track records in local, transnational, and global environmental issues. Founding members included scientists researching atmospheric pollution; the Osaka Alliance of Consumer Associations, which had a background in CFC and global warming issues; lawyers such as Yamamura, with experience in environmental litigation; and local residents groups that had been protesting air pollution in the Osaka region from as early as the 1970s.[21] As a lawyer involved in domestic environmental litigation for pollution victims, Yamamura was instrumental in formulating and advocating the notion of "environmental rights" in the early 1970s as a method of preemptive regulatory protection for ordinary citizens. Together with Ui Jun and Japanese pollution victims, he and fellow lawyers in the JFBA had traveled to UNCHE in Stockholm in 1972 to promote this idea by way of a Declaration on Environmental Rights. Although their main aim in Stockholm had been primarily to advocate for the rights of domestic pollution victims in Japan, meeting with foreign NGOs and discussing environmental problems in other countries proved to be a "decisive" moment for Yamamura and others. As Yamamura later explained, it was a first step toward linking their struggle with domestic pollution to a broader global environmental awareness.[22] Indeed, so "domestic" was his mind-set at the time that Yamamura recalled being surprised when a foreign NGO gave him a pamphlet on the problem of Japanese whaling.[23] Yamamura and CASA activists went on to be involved in the People's Forum in 1991 and 1992, and thereafter they participated in COP (Conference of the Parties) meetings for the UNFCCC and in the 1996–1997 Kiko Forum movement. So, on one level, international experience undoubtedly fostered a more global outlook and approach among CASA activists.

But Yamamura and his colleagues in the movement stayed committed to local problems, knowledge, and perspectives. CASA was instrumental, for instance, in promoting Japanese grassroots citizen science practices such as air pollution monitoring to foreign activists. In 1994, for example, the group sent atmospheric pollution monitoring equipment to thirty-four NGOs in seventeen developing countries worldwide. CASA also became a member of the Atmospheric Action Network of East Asia formed in Seoul, South Korea, in 1995 by civic groups from China, Japan, South Korea, Mongolia, and Russia. This initiative set out to become a grassroots network of citizens collaboratively monitoring air pollution in the Northeast Asian region. Thus, CASA's involvement in global events and processes such as UNCHE, UNCED, and the UNFCCC process grew out of a local and regional program to address air pollution and to pursue justice for pollution victims. Climate change and ozone depletion were understood less as new issues than as extensions of these more concrete problems.

Other Japanese NGOs concerned about global-scale environmental problems began to collectively organize and network in the late 1980s, primarily in response to what they perceived as attempts by Prime Minister Takeshita Noboru and environmental bureaucrats to monopolize leadership over the emergent global environmental agenda. The immediate stimulus was the Tokyo Conference on the Global Environment and Human Responses toward Sustainable Development, cosponsored by the United Nations Environment Program (UNEP) and the Japanese government and presided over by Takeshita from September 11 to 13, 1989.[24] In response, activists organized "counter conferences" in the Kansai region (Osaka and Kyoto) and Tokyo. From September 8 to 10, 1989, Kansai activists in CASA, FoE Japan, the Rachel Carson Association of Japan, and the National Pollution Victims Alliance convened the Symposium on the Global Environment and Atmospheric Pollution, which attracted around 1,400 participants (1,250 in Osaka, 150 in Kyoto) and included thirteen invitees from nine foreign countries.[25] The symposium was particularly significant in its bold attempt to fuse the local and the global: participating groups ranged from domestic victims' movements opposing localized air pollution all the way to newer groups focused on global-scale environmental issues like climate change. Important too was the focus on rights, symbolized most poignantly on the final day of the Osaka symposium when participants sang a rendition of the United States Civil Rights Movement anthem *We Shall Overcome*, including a verse for "No More Hiroshimas."[26] Predictably, discussion gravitated around the (dis)connection between the new global environmental problems and the lingering, unsolved North-South issue. Marginalized communities received pride of place at the symposium, including a slideshow on the victims of atmospheric pollution in Japan and presentations by representatives of indigenous peoples in the Amazonian rain forest.

In Tokyo, activists held a similar event titled the International Citizens' Conference to Consider the Global Environment and Japan's Role. The Tokyo conference attracted around 1,500 participants from within Japan and twenty invited guests from ten foreign countries, including progressive lawyers, specialists on global environmental problems, and representatives from indigenous groups such as the Kayapo People of the Amazon.[27] Like the official Takeshita event, participants addressed global warming, extreme weather, rain forest preservation, biodiversity, and the destructive effects of ODA, but they did so through the eyes of local victims. For instance, special attention was afforded to grassroots groups within Japan from Minamata, from communities affected by resort developments, and from urban neighborhoods suffering the effects of automobile emissions. The domestic groups were joined by representatives from the Amazonian Kayapo People, the Penan forest people of Sarawak, and activists from West Papua, Thailand, and the Philippines—all of whom repeated a common refrain about daily lives ravaged by capital and ODA from rich nations.[28]

The Tokyo Appeal promulgated on the final day of the Tokyo conference flatly rejected the notion of "sustainable development" and laid blame on "modern industrial society," which had "expanded from the 16th century" onward on the basis of "exploiting nature and plundering resources from colonies." It was this history that produced the system of "mass consumption of fossil fuels" and "the use of chemical substances" that could not be safely reincorporated into the "natural cycle." The appeal argued that, to the extent mass use of synthetic chemicals and fossil fuels persisted, "economic growth" and "development" could not be "harmonized" with "global environmental protection." "Technological contrivances" would not produce solutions, only more "contradictions" for future generations and for the Third

World. Necessary were genuine changes in the lifestyles of citizens in wealthy countries, in the logic of administrative organizations and corporations, and in the understanding of and support for NGOs.[29]

The culmination of these grassroots initiatives for global environmental problems came in May 1991, when three hundred activists from sixty civic groups throughout Japan gathered at Tokyo's Meiji University to establish the People's Forum, which would represent Japan at the NGO events at UNCED.[30] The People's Forum was a fascinating blend of the national and the transnational, the local and the global, and the old and the new, and, in this sense, was an organizational manifestation of organizers' strong belief that global-scale environmental problems should not—indeed, could not—be separated from questions of local rights, equity, and justice. Prominent figures in the People's Forum, such as Miyamoto Ken'ichi and Iwasaki Shunsuke, drew on years of activism for marginalized groups. Miyamoto, as we have seen, was a longtime advocate for industrial pollution victims, while Iwasaki Shunsuke, a young architecture professor and leader of the People's Forum, had experience working with disadvantaged communities throughout Asia as director of the Japan International Volunteer Center (JVC). Member organizations represented a broad spectrum, including groups in very local struggles such as the Association to Protect the Nagara River in Aichi Prefecture, nationwide affiliations like the Japan Federation of Bar Associations (JFBA), and internationally active NGOs such as CASA, JATAN, and FoE Japan.[31] Iwasaki Shunsuke stated emphatically that the People's Forum was committed to a *"Glocal* Action Plan," which ensured that global environmental initiatives did not lose sight of all-important local problems.[32]

We can see this perspective clearly in the activities of the People's Forum in the lead-up to UNCED. In December 1991, for instance, representatives of the forum traveled to France to take part in the Paris NGO conference on the environment sponsored by the French government and attended by close to nine hundred activists from 150 countries. As if to confirm their own perspective, the overwhelming conclusion of the conference was that developed countries were to blame for both global environmental problems and poverty in developing nations.[33] Back in Japan, for three days beginning on May 1, 1992, the group sponsored the Forum on Asian NGOs and the Global Environment in Yokohama City. Once again, the explicit objective of this event was "to make clear the connection between the problems experienced by people living in Japan and the environmental problems experienced by people in the Third World, particularly Asia."[34] Around 2,700 people participated over the three days of the event, which featured invited foreign participants from the Narmada Dam opposition movement in India, the Third World Network in Malaysia, the Environmental Restoration Project in Thailand, and representatives of indigenous Peruvian peoples.[35] For Iwasaki and other leaders of the People's Forum, this and other events leading up to UNCED represented concrete ways for their movement to "go to Brazil via Asia."[36] As Iwasaki later recounted, from the outset their explicit objective was to avoid participating in UNCED simply as activists from a rich country. Rather, because Japan was located in Asia, Iwasaki and others in the forum set out to "clarify" their "position" and to "find points in common" with people in Thailand, Indonesia, the Philippines, Malaysia, and elsewhere.[37] Japan's position as a wealthy non-Western country seems to have engendered the belief in forum members that they had a responsibility to support and advocate for the globally marginalized.

The People's Forum advocated three fundamental principles with respect to global environmental problems: first, that the notion of "development"—including "sustainable development"—needed radical redefinition; second, that the local perspective be a central element in any program to address global environmental problems; and, third, that developed nations and their citizens recognize and act on their responsibility to the developing world.[38] These principles put the forum somewhat at odds with mainstream discourses and approaches to global environmental problems yet, as I have noted, unmistakably within a domestic tradition of activism animated by notions of rights and justice.

Dissatisfied by what they saw as the elite-monopolized discourse on "sustainable development," Iwasaki and others in the People's Forum proposed a radical recalibration of "development"—reminiscent of Tsuru Shigeto's endeavors in the 1970s—by introducing notions of equity, interconnectivity, and especially endogeneity into its definitional parameters. The forum's Kanagawa Declaration of 1992, for example, argued that the concept of development must be about far more than the processing of "things," and must also include the fair division of resources and the active construction of interconnections between people. Borrowing from Ardhen Chatterjee of the Regional Center for Development Cooperation in India, the declaration proposed that development for human beings was about "enriching the division of things with other people and living things" as well as "helping to strengthen social connections with the very weakest part of society or the very weakest people."[39] Indeed, the development of social connections between the "materially wealthy and the very poorest people" would be vital in stimulating citizens in wealthy nations to adopt the "problems of people in developing countries" as "their own problems." Conversely, development proceeding through the established channels of ODA and foreign investment did nothing to "restrain" the "unlimited material desires" of the rich, nor did it assist the "people of Southern countries" in "realizing independent societies" free from the "overwhelming domination of northern countries."[40] By broadening the definition of development beyond material processes of economic growth to include notions of resource equity and social development, then, the Kanagawa Declaration proposed a more multifaceted conceptualization that balanced the material with the ethical. Herein the people of the South were not merely seen as passive subjects in need of development from without (or, more to the point, from above), but as humans with the innate right to live their lives independently with dignity.

In place of the expansionistic and evolutionistic development model dominant under Eurocentric modernity, the People's Forum proposed internal or endogenous development as a revolutionary modification to the modern concept of development that would supposedly "transcend the contradictions of 'environment' and 'development'" and serve as the central dynamic of a "sustainable society of the twenty-first century."[41] This notion of endogeneity called on people in both the global North and global South to satisfy living needs "not by bringing things from afar" but from within the "cycle of materials in one's locality."[42] The Kanagawa Declaration encouraged people to "source food and other materials necessary for daily life from places as close as possible" to where they were living and, moreover, "not to dispose of waste material in places far away but to solve the problem close to home."[43] Indeed, dealing with waste locally could help Japanese people rethink, for example, their "throw-away culture" and begin searching for ways to reuse and recycle that waste. To promote endogenous development the declaration proposed a rather blunt policy "stick" in the form of a "resource import tax" to be imposed on all new resource imports into developed countries, the revenues of which would be transferred back to developing nations "for the restoration of environments destroyed by resource theft."[44]

Of course, the argument about endogeneity was not that people return to a world of absolute self-sufficiency and dis-integration but, on the contrary, through an exploration of local alternatives, that they confront the human and environmental costs produced by a modernity underwritten by relentless expansionistic development radiating out from North to South. As a People's Forum publication for the Earth Summit noted, "It is necessary to gain a clear understanding of how and by what means the things surrounding us—food, paper, timber, fuel, energy, industrial raw materials and so on—have reached us, and who is affected and in what way."[45] For example, people needed to think about the connection between the "structure" of a "wasteful, throwaway society" like Japan and "the destruction of natural environments and local societies in developing countries."[46] Since local resources "fundamentally belong to the people in that area," the development and utilization of those resources had to be "based on the will of the people in those localities," especially the most rooted individuals like "women" and "indigenous people."[47]

Underlying the People's Forum's notion of endogenous development was an acute sensitivity to the Japanese experience with industrial pollution and environmental injustice. A common theme running through all of the People's Forum's statements at this time was that the Japanese people had much to teach the world about their traumatic struggle with industrial pollution. The forum's official publication for the Earth Summit, the *People's Voice of Japan,* for instance, identified three lessons Japan could teach the world. First, contrary to the implicit endorsement of economic growth in the concept of sustainable development, the Japanese experience of industrial modernization and pollution taught that there were clear and incontrovertible limits to growth that, if violated, would result in unconscionable human injustices. The victims in Minamata, in Yokkaichi, and in the decimated forests of the Philippines and Malaysia were proof of this. Second, even if development somehow proceeded without physiological and natural side effects, the Japanese experience suggested that affluence born of breakneck economic development did not necessarily equate to happiness. Since the dawn of the country's industrial modernization in the mid-nineteenth century, the Japanese had recklessly pursued wealth and power. In the mid-twentieth century this resulted in national decimation and millions of "meaningless deaths" at home and throughout Asia and the Pacific.[48] In the 1960s it resulted in the environmental and human tragedies of industrial pollution, and it created a society in which people worked themselves to death for the good of the corporation. As the *People's Voice of Japan* observed, it was "quite clear" that rapid economic growth in developed countries such as Japan had "most certainly not caused the advancement of a fulfilling life for citizens."[49] Moreover, the Japanese response to pollution—especially in terms of regulatory reform—offered a sobering warning about the vulnerability of apparent solutions such as "sustainable development." The *People's Voice of Japan* reminded readers about Japan's Kōgai Taisaku Kihonhō (Basic law for environmental pollution control) of 1967, which anticipated the idea of sustainable development in its infamous "harmonization" clause, stating that "preservation of the living environment should proceed in harmony with sound economic development." "But, in the context of a market economy, this meant that environmental conservation was limited to the extent necessary . . . for industry to maintain normal levels of profit, with weak environmental quality standards for pollution."[50] The cautionary tale from Japan, according to the *People's Voice of Japan*, was that "the notion of 'sustainable development' adopted by UNCED must not be based on a 'harmony' type concept which admits environmental conservation only for the purpose of development to sustain the economy."[51]

Lying beneath and, to a degree, predetermining their commitment to endogeneity and localism was the People's Forum's viewpoint that solutions to global environmental problems would hinge on the capacity of developed nations' to accept their responsibility toward the developing world. The Japanese Citizens' Earth Charter, promulgated by the People's Forum prior to UNCED, described the Earth Summit as a truly historic opportunity to "rethink the nationalism and evolutionary theory" beating at the heart of a modernity that knew no limits.[52] "Northern countries, including Japan," had to "accept responsibility for their significant role in the destruction of the global environment" and for dividing the world into "rich societies" and "poor societies" over the course of half a millennia.[53] The "first step toward stopping environmental destruction and realizing a sustainable global society" would be the "restoration of equality between the countries of the north and those of the south."[54] The developed countries, which had become wealthy through imperialistic expansion and plundering the resources of the weak, needed to partake in serious historical soul-searching. "Solving the North-South problem" was thus a central issue in the movement to "protect the global environment."[55]

From this perspective it became possible for activists in the People's Forum to position the Earth Summit on numerous historical vectors. The year 1992 did indeed represent the twentieth anniversary of UNCHE in Stockholm, where Japanese pollution victims had appealed to the human limits to growth and Tsuru Shigeto to human welfare-sensitive development.

But 1992 also arguably marked five hundred years since the beginning of Western aggression and exploitation of the world in 1492. It was with this profound sense of historical responsibility to the Third World, and especially Asia, that members of the People's Forum and other Japanese groups departed for Brazil in the summer of 1992.

## The Earth Summit as Transnational Contact Zone

Hosted by the Brazilian government, the United Nations Conference on Environment and Development (UNCED) took place from June 3 to June 14, 1992, at the Riocentro Exhibition and Convention Center about twenty-five miles (forty kilometers) from downtown Rio de Janeiro. Representatives from 172 governments and 108 heads of state attended the "Earth Summit," as it was informally named, during which they discussed the principal themes of the environment and sustainable development. Participating countries signed on to a number of agreements and declarations, including the Rio Declaration and its implementation strategy, Agenda 21; the Statement of Forest Principles; the United Nations Convention on Biological Diversity; and the United Nations Framework Convention on Climate Change (UNFCCC). The summit also established a number of follow-up mechanisms, such as the Commission on Sustainable Development, which was charged with reviewing the implementation of Agenda 21 in the ensuing years.[56] The Earth Summit was "one of the most publicized large-scale political events since the end of the Cold War" and the largest UN conference up to that point.[57] As Clapp and Dauvergne note, the Brundtland Commission's recommendations—especially the concept of sustainable development—"dominated discussions at Rio." It was "politically easy" for governments to support the summit's objective to promote "more growth with more environmental protection." Few nations needed convincing that more growth would actually produce a "better environment."[58] At the summit's end, Secretary-General Maurice Strong hailed the event as a "historic moment for humanity," adding that, although documents such as Agenda 21 and the UNFCCC were "weakened by compromise and negotiation," the summit still created "the most comprehensive and, if implemented, effective program of action ever sanctioned by the international community."[59]

The Earth Summit was not without its controversies and criticisms, however. In statements made before the summit, US president George H. W. Bush more or less eliminated any possibility of an agreement on numerical targets or dates for greenhouse gas emission reductions under the UNFCCC.[60]

Japanese prime minister Miyazawa Kiichi also raised eyebrows after announcing he would not be attending UNCED because of important Diet deliberations on Japan Self-Defense Force participation in UN peacekeeping operations. He instead delivered a video address and sent his chief cabinet secretary, Katō Kōichi.[61] Both Japanese and foreigners alike were appalled by this decision, which prompted NGOs to confer on Miyazawa and the Japanese government the "Golden Baby Award" for the summit. As Honda Masakazu of the newspaper *Asahi Shinbun* later confessed, after Miyazawa's decision there was "nothing more embarrassing" than being a Japanese citizen at the Earth Summit.[62]

But beyond such immediate controversies, there were deeper reservations about the meaning of a summit that appeared to so seamlessly combine environmental protection with economic development. Some worried about the influence of big business because of Maurice Strong's background in industry as well as the corporate money funding the event.[63] Others, such as Japanese activists in the People's Forum, feared that the managerial tone of discussion might undermine the legitimacy of local responses to global problems.[64] For the most cynical of Japanese critics, "global environmental protection" had been hijacked by the project of promoting economic growth and was now nothing more than a shrewd method to solidify North-South inequities.[65] In his acerbic essay " 'Chikyū Samitto' no giman" (The fraud of the Earth Summit), Yamamoto Kazuhiko, secretary-general of the Zenkoku Shizen Hogō Rengō (National Nature Conservation Alliance), argued that "sustainable development" meant no more than "maintaining the system." It was "crystal clear" he said, that the "provision of funding and technology" to developing nations was merely "for the benefit of advanced countries."[66] Many activists—not all from developing countries—felt uncomfortable with *Our Common Future*-type approaches to environmental issues because they believed that the environmental crisis was "precipitated almost exclusively by . . . wasteful and excessive consumption in the North"—in other words, by the 20 percent of the world's population consuming roughly 80 percent of its resources.[67] Rather than "commonalities," some, such as Anil Agarwal and Sunita Narain of the Centre for Science and Environment in India, called for a clear distinction between the necessary "survival emissions" of the South and the reducible "luxury emissions" of the North.[68] As the British environmental writer Fred Pearce perceptively wondered, "Why is it that Western environmentalists worry so much about population growth in poor countries when each new child born in North

America or Europe will consume 10 or 100 times as much of the world's resources and contribute many times as much pollution? A three-child American family is, in logic, many more times as dangerous to the planet than an eight- (or even an eighty-) child African family."[69]

Most of these criticisms of the Earth Summit emanated from the "Global Forum," a parallel conference for NGOs held in Flamengo Park in downtown Rio about one hour by car from the main summit at Riocentro. As many attendees noted, the geographical separation of the Global Forum from the Earth Summit was clearly a deliberate strategy on the part of the Brazilian authorities to contain popular energies within a demarcated area well away from the formal proceedings where they could potentially cause trouble. The Riocentro summit venue itself was also awash with security, ensuring against any "undesirable" events arising in the vicinity.[70] Yonemoto Shōhei, a historian and science commentator who participated with Japanese NGOs, even suggested that the Global Forum be understood as a separate meeting of NGOs, rather than as a launchpad for directly lobbying and pressuring official delegations to the main summit. This was certainly true for Japanese NGOs, although perhaps less so for US and European groups, with their stronger lobbying capacities.[71]

Nevertheless, the Global Forum was a landmark transnational event for environmental NGOs and, in fact, a landmark event in the broader development of global civil society in the contemporary world. Around 17,000 members of 7,500 NGOs from 165 countries participated in the events at Flamengo Park. A report by the Center for Applied Studies recorded the breakdown of participants by region as follows: Latin America, 41 percent; North America, 22 percent; Europe, 20 percent; Asia, 12 percent; and Africa, 4 percent.[72] The forum consisted of four elements: (1) seven hundred booths and tent exhibitions set up by NGOs for information exchange and networking; (2) public lectures, seminars, and fora held at a central venue called "The Structure"; (3) the preparation of around thirty alternative NGO treaties on climate change, forest destruction, species diversity, agriculture, food safety, racial discrimination, the military, women, children, education, and indigenous people; and (4) the dissemination of information on daily developments at the Earth Summit.[73]

The Global Forum was as much a festive and performative space as it was a venue for dispassionate discussion and debate on the environment— hence the various characterizations of it as a "circus," a "jungle," and an "NGO Expo."[74] Kikuchi Yumi, of the Japan Environmental Action Network, likened

Flamengo Park to "all the circuses in the world having come to Rio" at once.[75] Among the gaudier of the events at the Global Forum was the opening ceremony, attended by Maurice Strong, Gro Harlem Brundtland, and the star of the James Bond 007 films, Roger Moore, all of whom watched on as a replica Viking ship, the *Gaia,* arrived with six youths bearing a message on environmental protection for political leaders from the people of Planet Earth. Adding to the political theater of the moment, on the beach a group of Rio street children raised banners reading "*Gaia* Go Home!" and "Five million rich men show off! Give the money to the favelas [slums]."[76]

Visitors to the forum were uniformly intrigued and, in some cases, a little overwhelmed by the carnivalesque of it all. In a fascinating dispatch written for the *Women's Feature Service,* Sujata Madhok described a mishmash of ideas, images, colors, and performances: "An earnest young Japanese girl asks you to sign a petition against the proposed Nagara dam in Japan"; a poster at the women's tent asserts "How's God? She's black"; "dozens of trash cans around—different ones for wet and dry wastes. The toilets are eco too, the latest, non-flush, water saving device from the US"; "solar cooker stalls stand cheek by jowl with the 'fridge of the future'—a green refrigerator that does not emit CFCs . . . and thin the ozone layer"; "a close-up of India's Nirmala Mata stares you in the face with the promise of Sahaja Yoga and instant bliss"; and "as you walk away from this fiesta there comes a last message from the Hare Krishna cult: 'Consider the cows' it tells you cryptically."[77] Another popular exhibit at the forum was the "Lie-O-Meter," a device depicting a Pinocchio-like figure whose extendable nose was used to indicate the "sincerity" (or lack thereof) of governmental declarations and commitments on the environment ranging from zero to 100 percent. US president Bush's declarations on biodiversity, for instance, pushed the Lie-O-Meter up to 100 percent, while the Japanese government scored in the high ninetieth percentiles for its environmental declarations.[78]

Amid this flurry of activity, Japanese NGOs operated one of the largest tents, the Japan People's Center, which served as the base for Japanese civic activity at the Global Forum.[79] Around eighty Japanese groups comprising 360 activists traveled to Brazil to participate in the events at Flamengo Park. Among these, the People's Forum, the central organizing group for Japanese NGOs, sent thirty-five representatives.[80] During the forum the Japan People's Center hosted a range of seminars, dialogues, and debates, many of which featured activists from developing countries, especially throughout Asia. The connection between Asia and Japan was

Youth from the vessel *Gaia* arrive at the Global Forum.
Third from the right is Japanese passenger Shibata Hiroko.
(The Mainichi Newspapers)

also a dominant theme in the many booths and exhibits run by Japanese NGOs both inside and in the vicinity of their tent.[81] Ui Jun, who had led the small Japanese NGO delegation to UNCHE twenty years earlier, observed that the participation from Japan this time stood out both in scale and quality compared with Stockholm.[82] He was deeply impressed by the positive impact of Japanese groups at the Global Forum, which ranged all the way from natural farming movements to children's road safety initiatives, evidencing for him the sheer breadth of groups involved in global environmental problems in Japan. Ui himself participated in a symposium organized by the Association to Protect the Nagara River, during which activists, not surprisingly, drew connections between their local anti-dam movement in Japan and the struggle of Indian activists to stop the Narmada Dam project in Gujarat.[83]

Of course, not all was perfect. Ui pointed out that Japanese governmental attitudes toward civic groups had changed little in the two decades since Stockholm. Unlike other governments, Japanese officials did not conduct daily briefings for NGOs and, in fact, did their best to keep activists

Dancers at "Japan Night" at
the Global Forum, 1992
(The Mainichi Newspapers)

at arm's length. Ui recalled hearing one Japanese official scoff, "NGOs are the ones making a ruckus over in that park, aren't they?"[84] Some, such as Amano Reiko, an outdoor writer and member of the Nagara River movement, even pointed the finger at Japanese NGOs, saying that it was their lack of strategy leading into the Earth Summit that left NGOs without any official pipeline once the event began.[85] Blame aside, however, the Earth Summit proved to be a wake-up call for Japanese activists in many ways. Despite their impressive efforts at the Global Forum, they still lagged far behind Western NGOs in terms of influence, organization, financing, information-gathering skills, and policymaking capacities. Unlike Western NGOs, they were not integrated into the policymaking process, nor did they have any established lines of communication with officials. Language limitations also made it difficult for the Japanese to influence foreign government delegations and the global media. Through the Rio experience many activists recognized the urgent need for a stronger financial base, which NGOs could use to nurture a cadre of specialists capable of giving Japanese

Celebrating "Japan Night" at the
Global Forum, 1992
(The Mainichi Newspapers)

civic groups a stronger voice in politics and public opinion at home and abroad.[86] In this sense, the Earth Summit also served as a crucial learning experience for Japanese activists and an important stimulus for the professionalization of civil society in the country throughout the 1990s.

But Japanese NGOs' lack of integration into formal policymaking channels, while certainly a function of their organizational and financial weaknesses, also stemmed from the localism and situated ethics they brought to Rio. One of their basic viewpoints was that established institutions and top-down, managerial, bureaucratized approaches to global environmental problems—encapsulated in ideas like sustainable development—only threatened to replicate patterns of inequity that had been in place for many hundreds of years. In the face of this institutional domination, activists saw their task as one of shining a local, situated light on global problems in order to expose the injustices and inequities often obscured beneath the surface. The range of presentations and discussions at the Japan People's Center offers the clearest evidence of this "glocal" agenda.

Discussions on big issues like global warming, forest conservation, and sustainable development were balanced by many more specific discussions about mercury poisoning, pesticides, plutonium storage, toxic nuclear waste, and air pollution—all of which the Japanese had dealt with either within their country or in the regional contexts of Asia and the Pacific. Activists from Minamata, the JFBA, and the Air Pollution Measuring Center used the Japanese tent as a platform to promote tactics and methods they had found successful in concrete, grassroots struggles against industrial pollution at home. The underlying focus of discussions in the Japan tent was not so much on the big environmental problems per se, but on the human victims of environmental degradation, whether local, regional, or global in origin and scale. Moreover, the solutions presented and discussed were not only comprehensive global strategies but were also specific, realizable initiatives undertaken by individuals or small groups of like-minded people, for instance, making and consuming safe food, recycling milk containers, measuring air pollution with homemade devices, or monitoring the operations of pollutive industries abroad.

The presentations of activist-lawyers belonging to the JFBA typified Japanese groups' advocacy of a local, justice-based approach to the global environment—in the JFBA's case, by highlighting their domestic and regional initiatives for victims of environmental pollution. Lawyers in the association explained how their activism began locally in legal struggles for industrial pollution victims at Minamata Bay and Yokkaichi City in the 1960s, culminating in momentous victories in the Big Four pollution lawsuits in the 1970s. Thereafter, their activities expanded to include other forms of environmental litigation such as nuclear power plant siting, vibration from high-speed railways, and sunlight access rights.[87] They told audiences how, at UNCHE in 1972, the JFBA group was the first to suggest the principle of "environmental rights" as a new concept for environmental law worldwide—an idea born in the context of domestic Japanese struggles. Throughout the 1970s and 1980s some of their members became involved in cases of Japanese corporate pollution export to other East Asian nations, for example, in Malaysia during the 1980s, when a Mitsubishi Corporation joint venture was found to be dumping radioactive thorium waste near human communities. Japanese lawyers had joined with Malaysian counterparts to bring the affected communities' complaints to court, eventually contributing to the company's decision to abandon operations.[88] The lawyers explained how the JFBA began to seriously engage with global environmental problems after holding an international human rights symposium in Tokyo in November 1988 that brought together researchers and activists involved in environmental movements worldwide.[89] The lawyers had been shocked to learn of the extent of rain forest logging in the Philippines, Malaysia, and Indonesia, and the terrible results for local and indigenous populations in these countries. They also became more attuned to the detrimental environmental consequences of ODA, especially Japanese ODA in Asia.

To complement their human rights agenda at the Global Forum, the JFBA invited a Brazilian lawyer to speak about mercury contamination from gold mining in the Amazon basin and an Italian judge who gave an address on his idea for the creation of an "International Environmental Court" similar to the International Criminal Court.[90] The overall message of the JFBA and, in fact, of the bulk of Japanese groups in attendance, was that engagement in environmental problems of any scale proceeded from recognition of, and support for, the rights of human victims of environmental injustices on the ground. Although delegates at the main summit were trumpeting sustainable development as a realistic way forward, the JFBA clearly saw global environmental problems in the context of their earlier (and ongoing) struggles for human rights and justice in Japan and East Asia to which there had been no magic solutions, simply relentless grassroots resistance.[91]

On the final day of the Earth Summit, members of the Japan People's Forum issued a Japanese Citizens' Rio Declaration, which, in hindsight, endures as a rather bleak commentary on their experience in Rio. The declaration made four points: first, that the Earth Summit had failed because nations were not able to conclude treaties strong enough to protect the Earth from environmental destruction; second, that the continuing domination of financial institutions meant further destruction of the global environment; third, that Japanese NGOs had communicated to other citizens at the Global Forum that, despite Japanese governmental claims to the contrary, their country was still dealing with its own problems of pollution and environmental degradation; and, finally, that their aims from now on were to change people's lifestyles by transforming the system of mass production, mass consumption, and mass destruction, and moreover, to work for the reform of the UN into an organization for people not states.[92]

Yet, although many Japanese activists left Rio somewhat disheartened by what they perceived as a lack of concrete progress, the Global Forum proved to be an important international opportunity for them to advocate their approach to global-scale environmental problems firmly committed to and anchored in the lived experience and daily lives of ordinary people. As the newspaper *Asahi Shinbun* noted on the one-year anniversary of the Earth Summit, the "greatest change" for Japanese NGOs after UNCED was the emergence of a new urgency to "internationalize" their local, justice-based perspective.[93] The article described a Tokyo recycling group now thinking seriously about natural resource problems in Asia, a river pollution group involved with an anti-dam movement in India, and a Minamata disease support group investigating mercury contamination in the Amazon Basin caused by mining activity. Moves were also afoot to establish a new organization, the Japan Center for a Sustainable Environment and Society (JACSES), which would serve as a gateway for Japanese and foreign environmental NGOs to build substantive activist networks.[94] As the activities of the JFBA and other groups at the Global Forum evidence, the process of engaging with this global environmental agenda involved an intricate blending of extant ideas about environmental injustice with new global agendas and paradigms such as sustainable development and climate change. Rather than an epistemic transformation, the outcome was more of an epistemic adaptation, in which new spheres and scales of concern were incorporated into an existing worldview that remained resolutely situated in outlook and committed to the perspectives and rights of the marginalized.

## Globality in the Local, the Invisible, and Daily Life

Networks such as the People's Forum and rooted cosmopolitan activists at the forefront of initiatives addressing global-scale environmental problems played a particularly important role in advocating an approach based on rights and justice. They presented a picture of daily life as an entangled locus of both vulnerability and complicity. They questioned erstwhile models of exogenous development and relentless capitalistic expansion and, most of all, they wondered about the feasibility of global solutions to global problems. Moreover, they demanded that the voices and rights of "invisible" localities—in the Third World, in the "peripheries of the peripheries," and in "rural Asia"—be duly recognized in any countermeasures for the global environment. To better understand this perspective, in this section I examine three emblematic examples: Iwasaki Shunsuke of the People's Forum, Kuroda Yōichi of JATAN, and the climate change NGO, Kiko Forum. I believe each example points to the continuing salience of environmental injustice as a critical paradigm for leading Japanese activists and groups in their engagement with global-scale environmental problems.

Consider first the seminal role of Iwasaki Shunsuke, leader of the Japan People's Forum. After graduating from the Department of Architecture at Tokyo University of the Arts in 1963, Iwasaki spent two years teaching at Kwame Nkrumah University of Science and Technology in Ghana before going on to complete a master's in Urban Design at Harvard University in 1970. Thereafter Iwasaki worked in the Yokohama City Planning and Coordination Bureau for close to a decade until being appointed director of the Bureau of Human Settlements Planning in the United Nations Economic and Social Commission for Asia and the Pacific (ESCAP).[95] Iwasaki did not particularly enjoy his time in the UN, describing his travel from city to city to attend conference after conference like "being on top of the clouds."[96] But the experience was an important one, nevertheless, because it gave Iwasaki a firsthand insight into the logic and operations of the national and international institutions that he would later challenge. In 1980 Iwasaki left the UN to take up directorship of the Japan International Volunteer Center (JVC), an atypically large and well-funded Japanese NGO that sent volunteers to assist in developing countries worldwide.[97] Different from his earlier activities high up in the "clouds" of the UN, as JVC director Iwasaki connected with people on the ground in "rural Asia." This experience proved transformative because, to use Iwasaki's own words, it forced him to "look at reality from a different angle."[98] Iwasaki became convinced that Japanese NGOs needed to become more active internationally for the global poor—a conviction that he faithfully pursued throughout the 1980s as JVC director.

More significant for this discussion, in the late 1980s Iwasaki brought his Third World advocacy into the Japanese environmental movement when he assumed leadership of the Japan People's Forum prior to the Earth Summit. The significance of Iwasaki's leadership of this group cannot be underestimated. In effect, it elevated a staunch advocate for the rights of developing nations to the very apex of the Japanese environmental movement at a formative moment of its engagement with global environmental problems. Thereafter Iwasaki served as an influential mouthpiece for fellow Japanese activists worldwide and, more importantly, used this position of influence to advocate his own provocative viewpoints on the causes of and solutions to global environmental problems.

Iwasaki described his approach as one of "making visible a world which cannot be seen" and "joining hands with those who are invisible."[99] Organizations like the UN, he said, failed to hear the voices of the "2.8 billion people living in the countrysides of developing nations" because they were distracted by the noise emanating from officials and political elites in the cities.[100] Personal experience had taught him, however, that the best way to see reality (including the real Japan) was not from the capital cities of developing nations but from their countrysides; in other words, from the "peripheries of the peripheries," where one could "clearly see Japan's position and its form in relative terms."[101] Such ideas found expression in the People's Forum's explicit strategy of approaching "Brazil via Asia." Herein Japanese NGOs were understood, first and foremost, as advocates and partners of other Asian NGOs at the Earth Summit rather than civic groups voicing the concerns of "First World Japan."[102]

To fully realize this partnership with Asia and the Third World, Iwasaki believed that the Japanese people first needed to fundamentally transform their own consciousness. Above all, they had to recognize the profound and undeniable interconnectedness of their daily lives to the developing world and especially to the rest of Asia. As he wrote in a 1988 essay, "The insignificance of one banana eaten in Japan is connected to the significance of this [same banana] for the people who grow it in the Philippines."[103] We have "no choice," he argued, "but to recognize that we are connected to people in other countries. . . . The food we eat every day, what we wear, and the materials used in the houses we live in—all of these are brought in from abroad."[104] For example, "the buckwheat noodles you ate for lunch today are a traditional Japanese food so you probably imagine that they are made from white flowers which blossomed somewhere in the foothills around Nagano [Prefecture]. But, actually, 75 percent of buckwheat flour is imported from abroad."[105] So, physically, at least, the Japanese people were no longer "purely homemade": they were "international organisms" constituted by the many foreign-sourced materials they consumed daily.[106]

But unfortunately, or "tragically," as Iwasaki put it, despite the reality of their physical interconnectedness, Japanese people appeared to have no significant recognition of the fact. The most "tragic thing" was that "almost all Japanese" had "limited themselves to the spatial sphere of Japan" and were "unable to understand phenomena in other countries across the sea as their own problems."[107] Iwasaki spoke of "the tragedy of the Japanese who cannot transcend national borders in their consciousness" and the "disappointment" of a contemporary Japan in which the people cannot "mentally" and "emotionally" transcend the spatial unit of the nation, despite the fact that "materially" and "physically" they were internationalized.[108] As he explained, for Japanese people foreign issues were still "wrapped in a veil" and treated as "outside events" without any connection to themselves. Most Japanese were "afraid to go and look outside this veil, preferring to "merely remain in a state of tentativeness, sometimes poking their necks out but quickly pulling them back in," even though they realized that the veil itself was just a construct.[109] The cause of this malady, according to Iwasaki, was the "political unit of the state," which divided people and attempted to "crush" any initiative to bring people together by "lodging between humans" and "creating unwanted obstacles."[110] Yet the "future of the globe" depended now more than ever on the "success or failure" of attempts by NGOs and others to "transcend the state."[111] In a perceptive observation on the condition of globality, Iwasaki noted,

> The contradictions among people today are no longer between capitalists and workers or urban dwellers and country folk in developed countries. They have been transformed into contradictions between those in developed and developing countries. For this reason I feel that in order to realize a new set of values, more than anything else, we need an international solidarity which transcends the framework of the state. In other words, it is not about going to developing countries and raising the Hinomaru [the Japanese national flag] but working out how to transcend the framework of the state as friends working together with the people there.[112]

But the important point to keep in mind here is that Iwasaki was advocating not so much a global-scale program as a post-national one. For Iwasaki solutions to the problems of globality and the barrier of national states began at home with local people and their local knowledge. Turning the popular catchphrase of the environmental movement on its head, Iwasaki said, "It's not 'think globally, act locally' but think locally, act globally."[113] Instead of waiting for top-down solutions, local people had to take the initiative, by circumventing metropoles such as Tokyo and actively "building connections with the world" with the help of NGOs.[114] NGOs too had to stand at the same level as the people they were trying to help. They needed to produce solutions based on local conditions.[115] For instance, although NGOs might offer technical know-how, Iwasaki envisioned their primary role more as one of empowering local people to combine "traditional" practices such as forest farming with "new sustainable agricultural technologies" like mixed farming." In other words, the process was not one of "sending in technicians from developed countries but of providing opportunities for people in developing countries to build up experience through individual trial and error."[116] The ultimate aim, argued Iwasaki, was to create a "new civic movement" that united local and transnational energies without replicating imperialistic hierarchies.[117] He was convinced that only through a translocal network originating in, and firmly committed to, local knowledge and local perspectives could NGOs successfully address global-scale environmental problems.[118] The key was that such activism had to proceed *from* the local and be steadfastly against the state—this was the essence of thinking locally, acting globally.

Of course, Iwasaki was well aware that his localist agenda practically invited criticism. After all, respect for the independence and traditions of local people was all well and good, but without a network of roads and ports or large-scale infrastructure such as electricity grids and power plants constructed or overseen by the nation-state, the gap between the developed and developing nations would not narrow.[119] This was a central assumption of the sustainable development idea and, as we saw in the thought of Tsuru Shigeto and the *Founex Report,* it was an idea with deep and often progressive roots (recall Tsuru's admiration for the Tennessee Valley Authority).

But it was precisely in such assumptions that Iwasaki identified what he and other activists felt to be the fundamental flaw of "development" (sustainable or otherwise) controlled by First World governments and international organizations. Iwasaki understood development somewhat differently from groups such as the WCED. Development was not only about material advancement but also about the development of independence, dignity, and relations of respect—all of which were local "products" and, hence, profoundly endogenous in nature. Iwasaki, for example, emphasized that, since the gap between the developed and developing nations had evolved over a period of five hundred years, from around the time of Columbus's arrival in the Americas, it would not be solved overnight through quick technological fixes. To the utmost, people's "independence" must be respected and restored. Assistance focused only on development of the "material environment" would simply push recipient communities back into a "position of subservience," replicating the historical legacy of inequity between the First and Third Worlds.[120] But a new alliance of local people and nongovernmental organizations promised to sever the link between "1492" and "1992" by restoring the primacy of endogenous, locally initiated development.

Iwasaki was by no means an outlier here, and his call on Japanese people, particularly those involved in environmental activism, to focus on the development of Third World endogeneity found expression in many other influential Japanese movements addressing global environmental problems from the late 1980s onward. That many activists cut their teeth in very local activism or had experience in developing countries as Iwasaki did only further encouraged this tendency. Kuroda Yōichi of the prominent JATAN movement to save tropical rain forests is a case in point.[121]

A graduate in rural sociology, Kuroda worked during the early 1980s at the Seikatsu Club, a progressive consumer cooperative based on principles of collective purchasing and food safety in the Tokyo area. Kuroda's transnational interests appear to have intensified in 1985–1986, when he was affiliated with the People's Research Institute on Energy and Environment, a nongovernmental think tank focused on alternative energy development, antinuclear issues, and alternative agriculture.[122] While conducting surveys on pesticide use in Southeast Asia, Kuroda came into contact with NGOs involved in rain forest conservation movements.[123] In Malaysia in 1986, Kuroda and seven Japanese activists attended the Penang Conference on the Timber Resource Crisis in the Third World, organized by the progressive Penang Consumers Association, Sahabat Alam Malaysia (an affiliate of Friends of the Earth International), and the Asia-Pacific Environment Network.[124] During the conference the Japanese participants were shocked to learn of the extent of Japanese corporate involvement in rain forest destruction throughout Southeast Asia and the Pacific. Moreover, they were stung by criticisms that Japanese citizens were not doing enough to oppose such practices and mortified at not being able to report on any significant opposition movements back in Japan.[125]

With the logistical and financial assistance of Friends of the Earth International, in 1987 FoE Japan, the Asian Women's Association, the Consumers' Union of Japan, and the JVC established JATAN, with Kuroda Yōichi as its director.[126] Thereafter, under Kuroda's leadership, JATAN engaged in a series of highly creative and successful initiatives within Japan to raise awareness about the importance of rain forests for the global environment as well as the destructive role of logging operations by companies from rich nations such as Japan. In 1988, Kuroda and fellow author François Nectoux published *Timber from the South Seas: An Analysis of Japan's Tropical Timber Trade and Its Environmental Impact,* a study commissioned by the WWF that outlined in graphic detail Japan's environmentally destructive logging practices throughout Southeast Asia and the Pacific.[127] JATAN also confronted responsible corporations head-on. In April 1989, JATAN activists took part in the International Action Day to Support the Indigenous People of Sarawak, a coordinated transnational protest in cities worldwide in support of the Malaysian Penan people, who were struggling to stop logging operations in their forest home in Sarawak State on Borneo Island.

JATAN's Tokyo mobilization focused on the Marubeni Corporation, a Japanese trading company involved in logging operations in the region. Outside Marubeni's Tokyo headquarters, activists presented the corporation's bewildered public relations' officer with an award for rain forest destruction and a large plywood cutout of a chainsaw. In a meeting with JATAN activists, Marubeni executives later refused to accept this "award" and denied any wrongdoing in Malaysia. On the same day, JATAN members met with government officials to whom they delivered a copy of *Timber from the South Seas* along with sixty thousand signatures calling for a stop to logging in Sarawak and support for the affected Penan people. As Kuroda and JATAN members would later learn, these actions made news in Malaysia and even on the radio news in far off Nepal.[128] Japanese and Malaysian activists also developed transnational ties. Kuroda visited Sarawak for the first time in September 1987, and on numerous occasions thereafter, JATAN brought representatives of the Penan people, their local advocates, and Malaysian academics to Japan to speak at rallies on rain forest destruction.[129] Notably, in June 1991 a group of Penan women traveled to thirteen local government offices throughout Japan to lobby for ordinances banning the use of rain forest timber in public works projects.[130] JATAN's public advocacy and political lobbying proved extremely successful. In October 1991 the Tokyo municipal government became the first local administration nationwide to announce a trial period during which only non-rain forest-sourced timber would be used in public works projects. This decision was followed by similar initiatives in cities and prefectures such as Osaka, Kyoto, and Nagoya.[131] By mid-1995, sixty-six local administrations had stopped using rain forest timber in public works altogether.[132]

Fascinating in such initiatives is the way Kuroda and his colleagues garnered empathy for the Penan people and their forest life by framing the issue in terms of a familiar local experience of environmental injustice. As he explained, his impression and, indeed, that of "most Japanese" who visited the Penan was not one of a destitute community but, on the contrary, of people living in a kind of "heaven" on earth. Although they were monetarily "poor," the Penan had "never been in need of food or water, and their life-style based on living with the natural cycles and diligently working together on the basis of the mutual support of families and villagers" was a lifestyle the Japanese people had "lost."[133] Malaysian leaders, however, were attempting to portray the Penan as ignorant, backward savages in need of enlightenment and domestication, much in the same way Japanese political elites had promoted industrial development as a cure-all for "backward" regions in 1960s Japan. Prime Minister Mahathir bin Mohamad, for example, said his government did not "intend to turn the Penan into human zoological specimens to be gawked at by tourists and studied by anthropologists while the rest of the world passes them by." There was "nothing romantic" about a "helpless, half-starved and disease-ridden people," Mahathir declared.[134] The Malaysian government even took aim at the Penan's public advocates, writing in a publication for the Earth Summit that "the transition from cave and forest dwelling to village and urban living is a phenomenon that has marked the transformation of human societies from time immemorial. The environmental activists have no right to stand in the way of the Penans in this process of change and human development."[135] Such negative portrayals of the Penan fed into popular misconceptions of them as uncivilized enemies of the Malaysian nation and impediments to economic development. Even though the Penan (correctly) saw foreign corporations and logging companies as the villains, it was the Penan who were arrested as they attempted to stop the loggers' trucks.[136]

Needless to say, JATAN's emphasis on the plight of the victimized Penan people (as opposed to the preservation of tropical rain forest for its own sake) resonated with powerful and painful memories of industrial pollution, corporate misbehavior, state complicity, and injustice within Japan—especially in rural peripheries. Political scientist Anny Wong, who studied JATAN closely at the time, observed how the movement "redefined" the Sarawak logging "issue within the context of a domestic experience and sentiments." Wong explained how "emphasizing the destructive role played by Japanese development assistance and Japanese big business in the tropical timber trade, the Japanese anti–tropical timber campaign stirred public memory of Japan's own deforestation and their anger towards the Japanese government and big business for their poor handling of domestic industrial pollution."[137] Moreover, JATAN activists joined a chorus of Japanese activists like Iwasaki Shunsuke who were attempting to qualify the "novelty" of global environmental problems by situating them within longer histories of imperialism, colonialism, and exploitation of the Third World—the so-called invisible local.

In a 1992 publication, Kuroda repeated Japanese activists' mantra of "1492–1992," explaining that, during five hundred years of colonial invasion, the Western nations had for many years controlled the land and forests of other people for their selfish ends, and they had massacred indigenous peoples. Japan did the same thing over the short period of a few decades during its own imperialistic adventures.[138] Kuroda argued that this domination continued in the present "through multinational corporations and the World Bank," which symbolized the way those with "money" and "power" protected their "self-interests" and continued to "extend the gap between rich and poor" to the point of "despair."[139] In order to bring a stop to rain forest destruction, citizens of the North and South had to unite. Moreover, Japanese people needed to address the "local" from two angles: by changing their own lifestyles in their own backyards, and by helping those in the marginalized corners of the Third World like farmers and indigenous people to attain true autonomy through the advancement of endogenous development. This, argued Kuroda, "is our challenge as we face the next century."[140]

This attentiveness to marginalization and injustice is apparent even in leading Japanese movements dedicated to global-scale problems such as climate change, where we might intuitively expect such sentiment to be less prominent. The Kiko Forum, established in 1996 in the lead-up to intergovernmental deliberations on the Kyoto Protocol, is a prime example. Similar to the two examples above, the background of the forum's leader, Asaoka Emi, appears to have been an important factor here.[141] Prior to her involvement in the Kiko Forum, Asaoka practiced law after graduating from the prestigious law faculty at Kyoto University in 1972. Asaoka was an activist lawyer, with a strong background in litigation on behalf of consumers, women, and victims of pharmaceutical and chemical contamination.[142] The Kiko Forum, which Asaoka and others formed in December 1996, brought together an array of progressive environmental groups, consumer cooperatives, religious organizations, agricultural associations, and youth groups concerned with environmental pollution, food safety, and related issues.[143] On one level, the forum was the prototype of a transnationalized domestic actor—firmly rooted at home yet transnationally connected and globally sensitive. In terms of organization and strategy, for example, the Kiko Forum (*kikō* means "climate" in Japanese) drew liberally on the example of the Klima Forum (*klima* also means "climate" in German) established

by German activists at the First Conference of the Parties (COP1) to the
UNFCCC, held in Berlin in 1995. Asaoka and other Kiko Forum activists
who attended COP1 stayed in close contact with Klima Forum activists
after initially meeting in Berlin, even inviting Klima's leader, Sasha Mueller-
Kraenner, to Japan in 1996 to help with the establishment of the Kiko Forum.[144] Klima Forum activists appear to have provided very concrete and
valuable assistance to their Japanese counterparts, for instance with respect to
event planning and budgeting.[145] Adding to this transnational character, as
Kim Reimann notes, some 40 percent of the Kiko Forum's finances were
sourced abroad, in some cases from governments such as Germany, Denmark,
and Norway, which wanted significant greenhouse gas emissions reductions at
Kyoto and saw NGO lobbying as one way to achieve this.[146] International
organizations such as the UN also opened previously closed doors for groups
such as the Kiko Forum, giving them "access to policy makers and a new
channel for lobbying the government, enabling them to overcome problems
of access they faced in Japan."[147]

Yet for all its internationalization, the Kiko Forum remained acutely
sensitive to questions of equity and justice in global environmental problems,
particularly as these related to the developing world. A four-page pamphlet
on global warming released by the Kiko Forum in 1996, for example,
explicitly connected climate change to "the inequity of 'North' and 'South.'"
The pamphlet carefully explained that, although all countries worldwide
would be affected by global warming, it was important to recognize that
"only people living in wealthy countries during the twentieth century" had
actually "enjoyed the affluence" from the "economic activity" that had caused
that global warming. It was the "Northern developed nations" that had consumed countless quantities of natural resources and produced colossal
emissions of greenhouse gases. The pamphlet offered the example of island
nations such as the Maldives, Kiribati, and Mauritius, whose existence was
threatened by rising ocean levels caused by global warming. "We simply must
not forget that these nations are emitting almost no greenhouse gases," the
pamphlet reminded readers.[148]

A May 1997 pamphlet released by Kiko Forum just months before the
deliberations over the Kyoto Protocol began reiterated this responsibility of
the rich to the poor. The pamphlet noted that each Japanese person was, on
average, responsible for greenhouse gas emissions ten times greater than those
of a person in India and one hundred times greater than those of a person
in Nepal. Hence "we need to change our lifestyles of excessive consumption

and excessive waste" and, concretely, to reduce individual emissions of $CO_2$ by 4 percent annually." Referring to the "North-South Problem," the pamphlet argued that the "exceedingly blameworthy" countries of the North needed to immediately decrease their emissions but not do so by merely shifting their industrial operations to Southern countries. Echoing Iwasaki and other activists' calls for endogenous as opposed to sustainable modes of development, the pamphlet called for "restraint of excessive trade" that tended to exacerbate global inequities.[149] Like earlier industrial pollution in Japan, "the problem of global warming" was also a "problem of equity," which would have the greatest impacts on people in conditions of weakness in the global South and, moreover, on "future generations."[150] More than anything else, the rich needed to examine their own daily lives and open their eyes to the existential crisis climate change posed to developing nations, some of which might be swallowed up by the rising seas.

The common refrain in all of these articulations was that the new global-level problems still required people to think locally and, also, to carefully reconsider the local made invisible by its marginalization within societies and globally. Solutions were as much individual as they were global, since they involved a reexamination of "aggression" knit in to the very fabric of affluent daily lives. Indeed, only by looking somewhere in particular, these activists asserted, would solutions to the larger problems become possible. This attentiveness to complicity, responsibility, injustice, inequity, and rights had inspired some Japanese activists to look beyond the borders of their polluted archipelago many decades earlier, and it still deeply informed the perspectives of a new generation of activists facing the environmental complications of globality in the twenty-first century.

CONCLUSION

# Transnational Activism, the Local, and Japanese Civil Society

The only way to find a larger vision is to be somewhere in particular.

Donna Haraway[1]

In a fascinating reflection on the emergence of global environmental consciousness, science and technology studies expert Sheila Jasanoff poses a number of critical questions about the motivations for transnational activism.[2] "What," Jasanoff asks, "makes people from different societies and cultures believe that they should act to further common goals, even if these goals require them to sacrifice or postpone perceived economic and social interests?" How do activists "form commitments to collective action on a global scale, and from where do they derive notions of an international common good that are strong enough to override the intense but parochial pull of national self-interest?" And, given that politics in the contemporary world is usually practiced "through national institutions," why have we witnessed "the rise of transnational coalitions, such as the contemporary environmental movement, that seem to articulate their objectives in defiance of the positions of nation states?"[3]

In this study I have attempted to address these questions by showing how a powerful environmental injustice paradigm born of Japan's traumatic experience with industrial pollution informed and invigorated overseas involvements from the late 1960s onward. By providing a coherent vocabulary and concrete vision, this paradigm or "master frame" of environmental injustice offered an overarching worldview for groups involved in diverse transnational initiatives over many decades.[4] Initially in the 1960s and early 1970s, the paradigm served as a persuasive explanation and source of motivation for protestors in thousands of very local struggles across the archipelago. But, in the context of growing international attention to the environment, a small number of intellectuals, activists, and pollution victims began to realize that the country's pollution problems—which were of a scale and intensity unwitnessed in human history—had significance beyond Japan. Their transnational involvement and that of subsequent groups propelled the Japanese environmental injustice paradigm "beyond the constraints of spatial [and] cultural particularity" into a range of environmental issues including mercury contamination in Europe and North America, the relocation of pollutive industries to East Asia, the planned ocean dumping of radioactive waste material in the Pacific, and global-scale environmental problems such as climate change.[5] In all cases the activists involved drew on and referred back to the seminal national encounter with environmental pollution and injustice, which they put forward as Japan's distinctive—if horrific—contribution to environmental knowledge worldwide.

This process of recalibrating and repositioning the local experience of environmental injustice in struggles and issues beyond Japan resembles what Saskia Sassen has called a "multi-scalar politics of the local"—in other words, a process in which "local initiatives can become part of a global network of activism without losing the focus on specific local struggles."[6] Central in this multiscalar politics of the local were individuals like Ui Jun, who not only communicated but also, importantly, interpreted the story of Japanese environmental injustice so that it could speak to issues and activists separated by geography, political systems, and culture. Their facilitative role cannot be underestimated in any attempt to address Jasanoff's question about why transnational activism happens. Such rooted cosmopolitans served as the all-important "connective tissue," translating the Japanese environmental injustice paradigm for different groups and situations and convincing local pollution victims within Japan that their experience could be meaningful—indeed lifesaving—for others far away. To borrow from Sidney Tarrow, these activists did not become "rootless cosmopolitans" in the process of transnational action but retained their links to place, to the social networks of those places, "and to the resources, experiences, and opportunities that place provide[d] them with."[7] Shared emotions such as "anger at injustice or exclusion, feelings of solidarity, or hope for change" helped foster in such activists the conviction that transnational collaboration could "produce desired social transformation" and, on a personal level, satisfy their growing sense of responsibility as citizens of the world's "most advanced polluted nation."[8] The result was a dynamic, multiscalar spectrum of transnational interaction that greatly enriched local struggles and multiplied the contexts in which activists lived their lives, institutions functioned, and ideas evolved.[9]

Although activists' idea of environmental injustice underwent significant modification in its various iterations beyond the archipelago, its attention to the local, to inequity, to marginalization, and to fundamental human rights remained as common threads connecting movements and activists over time. Four enduring attributes stand out. First, the paradigm identified the root cause of environmental problems in discrimination and injustices against local communities and marginalized peoples, especially by powerful, centralized political and economic institutions. Industrial activity was certainly the immediate cause of environmental degradation, but it was the underlying structures of power and inequity that really mattered. Second, the paradigm identified a solution in local or endogenous empowerment. If marginalized communities or developing nations gained full autonomy and control of their living environments, then environmental injustices would arguably not occur. Third, in terms of strategy, although the paradigm was sensitive to the class implications of environmental injustice, it pointed to an alliance of the marginalized that might transcend orthodox class divisions and ideological divides. This implied a "chain of equivalence" that could even connect local industrial pollution victims in advanced economies to marginalized people in developing nations.[10] Fourth, the paradigm was deeply skeptical of globalized discourses on the environment such as "only one earth," "our common future," or "Spaceship Earth" because experience in Japan taught that collectivist ideologies like "GNP" or the "national interest" often obscured fundamental injustices and discrimination against the marginalized in society.

At the core of these four attributes was a decidedly anthropocentric and "situated" approach to environmental problems—a distinctive feature of contemporary Japanese environmentalism produced by the postwar industrial pollution experience.[11] Significantly, this attention to the local, inequity, rights, and marginalization closely resonated with environmental ideas and critiques emanating from the global South and burgeoning global discourses on human rights such that, by the time of the Earth Summit in 1992, Japanese environmental groups were proactively advocating for the rights of developing nations alongside their traditional constituency of industrial pollution victims.

In this concluding chapter I reconsider the iterations of the Japanese environmental injustice paradigm of the preceding chapters in connection to two issues at the core of this study: first, the implications of the injustice paradigm for debates about the global and the local in contemporary environmentalism and, second, the insights a transnational historical approach offers for our understanding of the ideational trajectory of Japanese civic activism after the massive wave of protest in the 1960s and early 1970s. Here I state my conclusions upfront: I think the Japanese environmental injustice paradigm offers a compelling historical example of the relevance of local knowledge in a global age. Through their transnational interactions, the Japanese activists involved came to richer understanding of the local—not only as a besieged subnational space but also as a potent resource to generate and cultivate knowledge useful beyond the local and the national and, moreover, as a counterweight to homogenizing global discourses. In terms of the historical trajectory of Japanese civic activism, I think a transnational historical approach opens fascinating interpretive possibilities. In the case of the Japanese environmental movement, transnational involvement contributed to important ideational transformations. It encouraged a fundamental reconsideration of the victim consciousness in many earlier Japanese social movements and, in turn, opened the way for more reflexive and multidimensional activist identities and agendas.

## The Local, the Global, and Japanese Environmental Injustice

There is lively debate among scholars of globalization studies over the role of the local and of place consciousness in a globalizing age. Some, such as the eco-critic Ursula Heise, are thoroughly committed to the "deterritorialization of local knowledge" and the formation of an "eco-cosmopolitanism" that envisions "individuals and groups as part of planetary 'imagined communities' of both human and nonhuman kinds."[12] Heise argues that the deterritorialization of knowledge need not "necessarily . . . be detrimental for an environmental perspective" and actually "opens up new avenues into ecological consciousness."[13] Others such as the social theorist Arif Dirlik, however, have championed "place consciousness" and "place-based imagination."[14] Dirlik is dissatisfied with what he sees as the "relegation of the local to subordinate status against the global, which is also associated with the universal."[15] Rather than viewing the local and place consciousness "as a legacy of history or geography," Dirlik envisages these as part of "a project that is devoted to the creation and construction of new contexts for thinking about politics and the production of knowledge."[16] Places, argues Dirlik, "offer not only vantage points for a fundamental critique of globalism, but also locations for new kinds of radical political activity that reaffirm the priorities of everyday life against the abstract developmentalism of capitalist modernity."[17] In this connection, Sheila Jasanoff and Marybeth Long Martello suggest that we should "resist the tendency to equate 'global' with progress or inevitability and 'local' with tradition or resistance," and instead "explore the complementarity between the local and the global"—for example, how "different conceptions of the local help to authorize the turn to the global, or vice versa."[18]

From its very origins, contemporary environmentalism has incorporated these global and local "modes"—and tensions—in ideas like "our common future" or "think globally, act locally."[19] Occasionally, of course, they have come into open conflict, as at UNCHE in 1972 when delegates from developing countries vehemently defended their right to development in the face of collectivist discourses such as "only one earth." Indira Gandhi was the most forceful advocate of this position, arguing that "if pollution was the price of progress, her people wanted more of it."[20] Similar criticisms arose almost two decades later with the publication of the Brundtland Commission's *Our Common Future* in 1987. Critics wondered just whose common future was "being protected": "the local dwellers of the land or the bureaucracies and corporations that rule over them?"[21] The core of the problem for Gandhi and other critics of this "Spaceship Earth" imagery was that putting everyone on the same "ship" implied the existence of a "universal equality" that was clearly not the case.[22] Arguments linking overpopulation to environmental degradation tended to underplay the fact that around 80 percent of the resources of the planet are being consumed by the 20 percent living in rich countries.[23]

Similar problems of inequity and historical injustice continue to confound the issue of climate change, for example. As Brian Doherty and Timothy Doyle put it, "The story of climate has become such a large metanarrative that it almost embraces all elements of environmental discourse."[24] Such narratives, they warn, "are the songlines of ecological conditionality, mapping out the coordinates that determine which groups shall be included in agenda-setting and decision making; determining those who will be funded; selecting those who shall be corporatized into the global governance state and relegating those who shall remain on the non-institutionalized outer."[25] From the perspective of the global South, of course, climate change is often perceived as receiving excessive attention. "It is seen as a matter endorsed by affluent-world, Western, science, and then utilized as an environmental security issue to control the less affluent from pursuing the very path of development that the minority world has pursued without restraint since the industrial revolution."[26] Indeed, renowned Indian activist Vandana Shiva provocatively argues that the focus on "global environmental problems, instead of expanding the perspective, has in fact narrowed the radius of activism."[27]

Leading voices from the global South—but not only the South—have articulated their own alternative vision of environmentalism that refuses to separate global environmental issues from more immediate local issues such as securing the human food supply or health.[28] Advocates of this perspective argue for attention to environmental issues, such as atmospheric pollution, that are directly affecting humans.[29] As I noted in the previous chapter, in the climate change debate, some such as Anil Agarwal and Sunita Narain of the Centre for Science and Environment in India even draw a distinction between what they call the "survival emissions of the poor" and the "luxury emissions of the rich."[30] Needless to say, common to all of these perspectives is the assertion that any measures to address global-scale environmental problems will have to genuinely address local viewpoints and prerogatives. In the language of emancipatory environmentalism: "Only by engaging with the subjective voices of the local, traditional and indigenous peoples" will "adequate ecological management strategies be assembled."[31] As the political theorist Leslie Paul Thiele argues, "Local activism must work in tandem with, not become subservient to, global thinking. To the extent that ecological care begins at home, relatively small, active, self-responsible communities of citizens are required. Cultivating such communities proves difficult within large nation-states and would be even more difficult within a global regime."[32] "A good rule of thumb for environmentalists," says Thiele, is not to "globalize a problem if it can possibly be dealt with locally."[33]

The seeming impasse between these global and local perspectives on environmental issues, of course, only serves to highlight how, to a great extent, "the global and the local are terms that derive their meanings from each other."[34] As Sheila Jasanoff and Marybeth Long Martello note, "What is interesting about the local in all these senses is how it comes into being, sustains itself, competes with other localisms, and sometimes . . . moves beyond the constraints of spatial or cultural particularity."[35] This is what the geographer Ash Amin means about places having the potential to become "more than what they contain."[36]

The Japanese environmental injustice paradigm—precisely because of its focus on rights, marginalization, and discrimination—has clearly inclined toward the localist perspective in these debates. This has facilitated alliances with both environmental victims in other advanced industrialized nations and advocates from developing countries asserting their developmental rights. It has also influenced Japanese activists' contribution to the critical globalism that emerged and evolved in the 1970s as a corrective to the extant internationalism in organizations such as the United Nations. This critical globalism certainly addressed the very big questions of planetary limits but, under the influence of Southern advocates and Japanese groups like the ILP, it also incorporated local perspectives sensitive to inequity and injustice. In 1972—a watershed year for environmental concern worldwide—the prominent UN official Philippe de Seynes was among the first to differentiate "internationalism" and "globalism" in a speech delivered at the University of California at Berkeley. For de Seynes, internationalism "derived from the dictates of political wisdom and a sense of human solidarity in a world of growing inter-dependence but of unlimited horizons opened up by technology." Globalism, conversely, de Seynes described as a standpoint sensitive to "the ambivalence of technology, its negative effects on the degradation of the environment, the destruction of ecological balances, the limited capacity of the biosphere, the possible depletion of natural resources, the population explosion, the finiteness of the planet, and perhaps even the finiteness of knowledge."[37] In other words, a core element of the globalism de Seynes described was that we live in a world of limits, not unlimited possibilities, hence the need for "care and maintenance," as René Dubos and Barbara Ward put it in their influential 1972 book *Only One Earth*. Of course, the burning question was, "care and maintenance" for what and for whom.

Japanese activists articulated their own distinctly anthropocentric and situated version of this critical globalism by invoking injustices toward environmental victims at Minamata, Yokkaichi, Toyama, and elsewhere throughout Japan. In key controversies over the environment and development stretching from the "limits to growth" to "sustainable development," they concentrated first and foremost on questions of discrimination, inequity, and injustice. The Japanese case, they argued, taught that environmental problems occurred when local communities were excluded from decisions about development in their own backyards. They pointed to state-endorsed and defended industrial development in Japan that proceeded—indeed flourished—on the basis of a litany of injustices toward marginalized local communities. What this taught, they argued, was not about the discord between the environment and development but, more fundamentally, about the injustices born of grossly distorted power relations between marginalized communities and powerful political and economic institutions whether within Japan or between the global North and South. This was a perspective Japanese groups articulated repeatedly at international gatherings, in person-to-person exchanges, and though influential English-language publications such as *Polluted Japan*.

Recall Ui Jun's presentations and interviews on mercury contamination in European countries from the late 1960s. As much as the scientific facts of industrial pollution, Ui stressed its political causes in center-periphery disparities in Japan, which for him preordained the tragic human injustices in communities at Minamata and elsewhere. Harada Masazumi and the World Environment Investigative Mission brought a similar message about marginalization and suffering to the Native American communities affected by mercury contamination in Canada. Along with thorough medical investigations, Japanese activists and mercury poisoning victims conveyed a story of injustices against the very weakest in society that resonated deeply with the discrimination their Canadian hosts were enduring. *Polluted Japan* and other material documenting environmental injustices in Japan also served as damning indictments of economic development built on local disempowerment and environmental degradation. In Thailand, *Polluted Japan's* message of human suffering fueled student mobilizations against Japanese industrial pollution in Bangkok in the 1970s. On the Pacific Island of Belau, activists such as Moses Weldon also used the pamphlet to convince residents that the human and environmental costs of a planned Japanese-US oil storage and nuclear reprocessing facility far outweighed any promised economic benefits.[38] Just as Hiroshima and Nagasaki became iconic symbols in contemporary antiwar and antinuclear movements worldwide, in the global environmental movement *Polluted Japan* and *Minamata: The Victims and Their World* and other material emanating from Japan served as damning indictments of modern industrial excess, as if confirming the dire warnings of works such as Carson's *Silent Spring*, Commoner's *The Closing Circle*, and Hardin's "tragedy of the commons."

In 1970s events such as UNCHE and in swirling debates over the "limits to growth," Japanese activists' mantra of environmental injustice found common cause with the ideas of those such as Barry Commoner who identified poverty, underdevelopment, and global inequity as key causes of environmental degradation worldwide. At the base of both positions was a conviction that environmental problems were inextricably linked to the violation of human rights—a position, needless to say, that differed markedly from the demographic approaches of Paul Ehrlich and others who singled out overpopulation among the world's poor as a major source of environmental degradation. The same was true decades later at the Earth Summit in 1992. Japanese activists such as Iwasaki Shunsuke found common voice with activists from developing nations who argued that solutions to global-scale environmental problems like climate change must take into account the developmental rights of local communities and developing nations—not to mention recognizing the structural inequities resulting from centuries of Western and, for a time, Japanese imperialism. Iwasaki and others notion of "endogenous development" drew directly on the experience of local disempowerment and marginalization informing notions of environmental injustice in Japan, but now they used it to advocate for the relevance and the rights of local communities in an age of global concern.

This commitment to human victims and to defending a human living space resistant to the toxicity of industrial modernity and the intrusion of exogenous political power is a common thread running through the messages many Japanese activists conveyed over decades of involvement in transnational environmental initiatives. Along with its intrinsic symbolism, part of the paradigm's appeal no doubt had to do with the historical juncture at which human rights were emerging as a central issue in international politics. As Samuel Moyn has provocatively put it, "Human rights . . . emerged in the 1970s seemingly from nowhere," gaining "an unprecedented new prominence in world affairs."[39] Japanese industrial pollution victims and their environmental injustice paradigm exemplified the themes of this new age of human rights, as too did their advocates, who epitomized the mentality and approach of human rights advocacy and discourse. As Jan Eckle explains, the "political uses of suffering were widespread in the period and not the exclusive domain of human rights groups. More and more groups started to refer to their own history of suffering to justify claims for political participation and nondiscrimination; victimhood formed an integral element of what came to be called 'identity politics.' This was notably true for Holocaust survivors but also for homosexuals and nativist groups, to name just a few."[40] The same might be said of the Japanese environmental injustice paradigm, which spoke directly and shockingly to these very questions of suffering and discrimination. Indeed, looked at in this way, we can see how Japan's traumatic experience with industrial pollution converged with, benefited from, and actually fed in to the development of two central issues in contemporary international politics: namely, the environment and human rights.

## Victimhood, Aggression, and the Insights of Transnational History

Of course, engagement with the outside world was hardly a one-way street, so along with tracing the effects of Japanese activists and their environmental injustice paradigm overseas, a second major objective of this study has been to inquire into the reverse effects. In other words, how can a transnational historical approach enrich our understanding of the historical trajectory of Japanese environmental activism, especially after the massive wave of domestic protest in the 1960s and early 1970s? How did transnational engagement influence or transform activists' mentality and the shape and content of their environmental injustice paradigm? And, what effect did such transformations have on political and economic institutions and civic activism in Japan more generally—Keck and Sikkink's so-called boomerang pattern of influence?

Before answering these questions, it is worth reconsidering both the advantages and limits of a transnational historical approach. As Iacobelli, Leary, and Takahashi note in a recent volume on this topic, "Transnational history . . . as a category in its own right . . . remains a relatively new field within historical studies."[41] The same could be said—perhaps in more pronounced terms—in relation to the study of modern Japanese history, which has most often been approached within the container of the nation. That being said, I have not adopted a transnational approach in this study, because I think earlier national- or subnational-focused histories of pollution and environmental activism were somehow flawed or that national history, even in its most critical forms, merely authenticates the ideology of the nation-state as the only legitimate theater of history. As Richard White has perceptively observed, "There are no absolutely right or wrong scales" of historical analysis since "each scale reveals some things while masking others."[42] Indeed, one of my aims in transnationalizing the historical narrative of pollution and environmentalism in Japan was to show just how deeply events within the country were interconnected to those in other countries and to environmental developments on a global scale.

As the morphemes "trans" and "national" imply, for me the idea encompasses both the nation and the phenomena that move across and beyond it or exist on the other side of it. As one of the pioneers of transnational history, Ian Tyrell, has noted, the original focus of the transnational concept was "the relationship between the nation and factors both beyond and below the level of the nation that shaped the nation and, equally important, that the nation's institutions shaped."[43] Although the subsequent development of transnational history has arguably moved away from this somewhat nation-focused conceptualization, most studies continue to accept—as I do—the ongoing importance of the nation-state and "its capacity to control and channel border-transcending movements."[44] We might say there has been a gradual deemphasis of the nation and the nation-state in transnational history, such that the national, although an essential scale of analysis, becomes but "one spatial dimension among others ranging from global history and international dynamics to (supra- or subnational) regional to local and individual levels."[45] Bender usefully describes this as a process of historicizing the nation by relating "its dominant narrative . . . to other narratives that refer to both smaller histories and larger ones" and recognizing the "historical production of the nation and locating it in a context larger than itself."[46] The task is thus not one of substituting "a history of the nation-state with a history without or against the nation-state" but, as French historian Pierre-Yves Saunier suggests, finding "a way to study how nation-states and flows of all sorts are entangled components of the modern age."[47] How, for instance, is the history of pollution and injustice in Japan entangled in the global history of science, technology, capitalism, and warfare throughout the twentieth century?

In broad terms, then, the concept of transnational history I subscribe to and have attempted to employ in this study corresponds closely to the definition offered by David Thelen, who characterizes it as an exploration of "how people and ideas and institutions and cultures moved above, below, through, and around, as well as within, the nation-state" coupled with an investigation of "how well national borders contained or explained how people experienced history."[48] I was particularly interested in the ways transnational activism and spaces became resources for activists to address and overcome national issues such as pollution and environmental degradation and, throughout the study, have attempted to use these transnational movements and moments as a way to "listen" to historical actors (many Japanese, some not) as they looked beyond and within Japan's borders "to place in larger context and find solutions for problems they first discovered within" their countries.[49] While I was certainly interested in the simultaneity of Japanese domestic movements with those in other countries and with the global movement, I devoted most attention to the concrete material and intellectual connections Japanese activists forged with non-Japanese activists because I feel that it is in these person-to-person exchanges and the translocal spaces or places that evolved that a transnational historical approach has most to offer.[50]

I believe that repositioning the contemporary history of Japanese pollution and environmental activism within such a transnational history can at once defamiliarize and enrich the national while continuing to accept its importance as a crucial historical perspective in itself. In fact, in terms of the critical project to address dominant methodological nationalism and the so-called complicity of modern historiography in empowering the nation-state to, as Prasenjit Duara puts it, "define the framework of its self-understanding," transnational historians become kindred spirits with those who would write the subnational, shadow narratives of nations such as the micro-histories of local industrial pollution and overdevelopment throughout the Japanese archipelago.[51] Both approaches interrogate what Bernhard Struck and his colleagues call the "normative macro-model of modernisation theory," based as it was on "the successful building of states and nation states with their bureaucracy and institutions as an integral part of the Western story of successful modernisation."[52] Shadow narratives chip away at this ideology from the inside while transnational histories attempt to pierce its rigid external shell by connecting the sub- with the supranational. By excavating previously obscured or invisible histories, I believe historians of transnationalisms and shadow narratives together help in the deconstruction and disruption of the powerful naturalization of national space implicit in modernization theory, undermining "modernity's strategies of containment" and opening up an "awareness of what was suppressed in a historiography of order."[53]

I think the various transnational involvements and movements discussed in this book open up a new vista on the development of Japanese environmental and civic activism after the high point of environmental protest in the early 1970s. While not undermining or negating (and in some ways actually substantiating) the quantitative waning in contentious protest—the social movement "ice age"—these and other movements challenge us to reconsider the scope of activism in this period stretching from the early 1970s through until around the late 1980s. As Daniel Aldrich, Jeffrey Broadbent, Hasegawa Kōichi, Peter Wynn Kirby, and others have shown, although smaller scale than the earlier cycle of protest, contentious domestic environmental activism continued throughout this period over issues as diverse as regional development, nuclear power plant siting, toxic urban waste, and bullet train vibration.[54] Other environmental movements focusing on safe food, organic agriculture, and the improvement of local living environments also proliferated throughout the country.[55] The transnational interactions and movements explored in this book were also unfolding during this period, but they have largely escaped the attention of historians and other social scientists who, for the most part, have been interested in national and subnational phenomena.[56] I believe that this comes at a cost to our understanding for two reasons. First, empirically, these transnational involvements evidence a broader scope of civic activism complementing and feeding into the domestic movements. Second, ideationally, transnational involvement contributed in important ways to the evolution of activist identity and civic movement ethos.

Empirically speaking, the movements explored in earlier chapters belonged to a small yet growing sphere of transnational engagement by Japanese civic groups from the late 1960s onward.[57] This is an aspect of Japanese social activism that deserves more intensive historical research. Their areas of involvement were diverse and included environment, gender, minorities, peace and antiwar, anti–nuclear power, human and indigenous rights, and grassroots development. Pioneering groups such as the Independent Lectures on Pollution (1969–1985) and the anti–Vietnam War movement Beheiren (1965–1974) led the way, serving as models for overseas engagement and stepping-stones for later groups. In 1973, for instance, Oda Makoto, Mutoh Ichiyo, and other former Beheiren leaders established the Pacific Asia Resource Center, or PARC.[58] One of the earliest advocacy-style nongovernmental groups in postwar Japan, PARC became a kind of quasi-national center for information about grassroots movements in the Asia-Pacific region, a hub for Japanese, Western, and Asian activists and intellectuals, and a launchpad for nongovernmental research on regional problems. As we have seen, the center's English-language publication *AMPO: Japan-Asia Quarterly Review* also served as a mouthpiece for Japanese and other Asia-Pacific activists to communicate instances of economic and political exploitation in their countries.[59] Two years later, in 1975, the nuclear chemist Takagi Jinzaburō joined with other antinuclear activists and groups to form the Citizens' Nuclear Information Center (CNIC) to disseminate information on nuclear power and serve as a hub for antinuclear experts and activists nationwide. Importantly, Takagi and the CNIC had extensive transnational contacts from the outset, which they used to obtain information about nuclear power and protest worldwide as well as to communicate news from Japan through the CNIC's English-language newsletter, *Nuke Info Tokyo.*[60]

Japanese women's groups also began to develop new transnational ties from the 1970s, especially in Asia. In 1970 the prominent women's liberation activist Iijima Aiko and others established the Shinryaku=Sabetsu to Tatakau Ajia Fujin Kaigi (Asian Women's Conference Opposing Invasion= Discrimination), which took direct aim at the "victim consciousness" in existing women's liberationism and called on women to recognize their complicity as the one's "giving birth" to a Japan deeply implicated in the Vietnam War.[61] Some women's groups began to scrutinize the behavior of Japanese men abroad, notably in connection to *kiseng* or sex tourism in South Korea and other countries throughout Asia. The *kiseng* tourism opposition movement traced its origins to a historic July 1973 meeting of the South Korean and Japanese Councils of Churches in Seoul, at which women participants issued a declaration lambasting Japanese sex tourism. Groups in Japan such as the Association of Anti-Prostitution Activity immediately took up the issue. Representatives traveled to South Korea to conduct field research and, together with other women's groups, in December 1973 they formed the Kīsen Kankō ni Hantai suru Onnatachi no Kai (Women's Association to Oppose Kiseng Tourism).[62] Among this association's immediate activities was a demonstration at Haneda Airport in Tokyo in support of students from Ewha Women's University who had protested *kiseng* tourism a week earlier at Gimpo International Airport in Seoul.[63] Led by Matsui Yayori, a prominent journalist at the newspaper *Asahi Shinbun,* in 1977 this group was renamed the Ajia no Onnatachi no Kai (Asian Women's Association) and thereafter became a hub for information and activism relating to Asian sex tourism, cultural exploitation, Japan's war responsibility, women's movements in Asia, and Japan-Asia relations.[64]

Japanese grassroots groups involved in development, education, and public health issues overseas also proliferated during the 1970s and 1980s. A few of these groups, such as the PHD Association, grew out of earlier organizations—especially religions—but most were new.[65] Among the earliest was Shalpa Neer (Bengali for "lotus house"), established in 1972 by Japanese youths who had participated in agricultural volunteering in the wake of the Bangladesh Liberation War of 1971. Initially the group focused on educational assistance by sending pencils and notebooks to Bangladeshi children. But this approach failed miserably, as locals simply exchanged these items for food. The group faced a further setback in 1977 when two Japanese volunteers were seriously injured in a robbery by a group of local bandits. After much internal debate and rethinking of the movement, in the 1980s Shalpa Neer discarded its self-confessed indulgent, ignorant, and patronizing approach of "saving helpless Asians" in favor of local empowerment and participatory development with Japanese serving in a backup role only—similar in many aspects to the endogenous development model advocated by Japanese environmental activists.[66] Other developmental groups appeared around the same time, such as the Asian Rural Institute established by Toshihiro Takami in 1973 to train leaders from developing countries in sustainable agriculture, organic farming, community building, and leadership, and the Institute for Himalayan Conservation (1974), which focused on providing infrastructure such as mountain rope-lines to aid in the transportation of firewood and livestock, and pipelines for the provision of clean water.[67]

Considered alongside the environmental groups traced throughout this study, the above activism points to an expanding engagement with the outside world among Japanese civic groups, especially from the late 1960s onward. As already noted, this is an underresearched aspect of postwar Japanese history that deserves more attention for what it tells us about the growing internationalization of civil society in Japan as well as for charting the palpable effects of transnational interaction on many civic activists and their groups. On this latter point, I believe that the transnational involvements and movements explored in this study offer a novel perspective on our understanding of the ideational transformation of civil society in contemporary Japan, especially in the crucial 1970s decade. Throughout the study I have alluded to Margaret E. Keck and Kathryn Sikkink's notion of the boomerang pattern of influence of transnational activism on domestic politics. We saw this, for example, in the response of the Japanese government to the ILP's publication *Polluted Japan* at UNCHE in 1972 and, later, to the protest against proposed radioactive waste dumping in the Pacific. But along with these political outcomes I have also tried to emphasize the boomerang effect at the grassroots level. In other words, the ways activists, their movements, and their ideas (about environmental injustice, for example) were changed through transnational involvement. Taking this grassroots boomerang effect of transnationalism into account, I believe, offers a new angle on our understanding of the evolution of civil society in Japan.

The apparent burgeoning of the country's civil society in the 1990s stimulated a veritable flood of scholarship that attempted to explain its historical contours and internal dynamics and the reason for its rise to prominence at that moment. In very broad strokes, this scholarship proposed three key causative factors to explain the nature and development of civil society in the country: political institutions and regulations, globalization and international norms, and the role of civil society actors.

Institutional explanations have pointed to the crucial role of the Japanese state—purposively and inadvertently—in "molding" or shaping civil society.[68] Susan Pharr, for instance, argues that the Japanese state "has taken an activist stance toward civic life, monitoring it, penetrating it, and seeking to steer it with a wide range of distinct policy tools targeted by group or sector."[69] More specifically, Robert Pekkanen persuasively shows how the legal framework, limited funding, indirect regulations, and the limited opportunities for influencing policy in Japan have determined the contours of Japan's "dual civil society."[70] In the case of nuclear power plant siting, Daniel Aldrich compellingly shows how authorities chose "rural communities, which were less coordinated and more fragmented, and, hence, less likely to successfully mount antinuclear campaigns. To overcome any remaining opposition . . . the government often offered jobs and assistance to fishermen to ensure that the nuclear power plant would not be seen as curtailing their livelihoods."[71] The impact of the Japanese state on civil society utilizing hard and soft techniques is undeniable and, as we have seen in this study, Japanese environmental activists expended a great deal of energy attempting to counter state initiatives through transnational bridge-building. Nevertheless, institutional analysis focusing on the role of the state in shaping Japanese civil society—precisely because of its focus on the state-society nexus—tends to underplay the influence of exogenous factors on civil society such as the border-crossing movements outlined in this book.

Working from an "outside-in" perspective, another stream of scholarship directly addresses this issue by highlighting the role of international norms in the development of Japanese civil society. Notably, Kim Reimann has cogently demonstrated how international norms supportive of state-

NGO cooperation from the 1980s effectively pressured (even "shamed") Japanese officials into recalibrating and strengthening their relationships with and support for NGOs.[72] This scholarship pointing to the effects of globalization and international norms on civil society resonates closely with my emphasis on the transformative aspects of transnational activism. The difference, however, is the level of analysis. Whereas Reimann highlights the impact of international (top-down) norms on the Japanese state and, in turn, civil society, I emphasize the role of ideational factors shaped by the transnational interactions of civil society actors from the bottom up.

Another stream of scholarship—including that of Wesley Sasaki-Uemura and my own earlier work—looks to ideational factors and civic actors themselves, arguing that grassroots activism and the ideas that emerged from this have shaped the development of civil society in contemporary Japan.[73] Koichi Hasegawa, Chika Shinohara, and Jeffrey Broadbent have pointed to "initiatives taken by NGO leaders, scholars, younger liberal politicians, and the media to encourage civil activism in Japan."[74] Historians trace the constructivist role of civil society actors back even further. For instance, I have explored the instrumental role of civic activists and their movements in shaping visions of nonstate or "*shimin*" citizenship in contemporary Japan.[75] The argument there is that civic activists' ideas and their movements have helped to shape the dynamics and development of civil society in contemporary Japan. While that approach also resonates with my ideational perspective in this book, for the most part, in that earlier work I limited analysis to the national level and below, arguing that transformations in activists' consciousness and modes of behavior were attributable to endogenous factors, whether of an institutional or ideational nature.[76]

Although occasionally implicit in the above scholarship, researchers have not carefully considered the role of grassroots transnational interactions on the evolution of Japanese civil society. Yet, as I have shown in this book, looking abroad and engaging in transnational grassroots initiatives encouraged some activists to resituate their environmental injustice paradigm in the context of broader movements (regional and even global in scale) and, moreover, to rethink their activist identity and agenda. Indeed, in ideational terms, I think that these transnational involvements were extremely important in stimulating a more reflexive and multidimensional—perhaps even post-national—mentality among the activists involved, which broke sharply with long-established notions of victimhood within much civic activism and discourse in postwar Japan. Engagement with issues and movements in Asia and the Pacific in the 1970s and 1980s was particularly important in this respect. In the case of the environmental injustice paradigm, in each of its iterations activists had no choice but to reimagine injustice beyond its origins in discrete local experiences of industrial pollution in Japan. What began as a somewhat insular account of local Japanese pollution victims by necessity expanded to incorporate environmental victims in other countries as well as the perspectives of marginalized communities at the wrong end of so-called global economic development. Engagement in environmental problems overseas brought the aspect of victimhood in the environmental injustice paradigm into question by exposing the complicity—albeit indirect—of all Japanese in the operations of Japanese political and economic institutions abroad. The more reflexive and multidimensional conceptualization of environmental injustice that resulted resonated with similar ideational transformations under way in the peace and antiwar movement, women's movements, and the development NGOs discussed above. Historically, I believe this enriched concept of environmental injustice marks an important ideational transformation in postwar civic consciousness.

We saw this transformation under way in the 1974 Conference of Asians, where Oda Makoto and others from the anti–Vietnam War movement encouraged their environmentalist colleagues to draw direct connections between Japanese imperialism and colonialism of the past and the country's contemporary military alliance with the United States and its economic expansion throughout Asia. As Oda explained, this was not merely an intellectual exercise but a frank admission of Japan's ongoing aggression toward the people of Asia. Activists opposing the planned radioactive waste dumping in the Pacific pushed this self-critique even further, provocatively questioning the narrative of "national victimhood" built around the atomic bombings of Hiroshima and Nagasaki. When viewed from the perspective of regional and global history, they realized, the notion of victimhood appeared very brittle and even contradictory. Japanese claims about being the only nation to have suffered from atomic bombing, for instance, became problematic when the misery of people in the Marshall Islands and French Polynesia subjected to US and French nuclear weapons testing was taken into account. It appeared self-contradictory to many that a nation that proclaimed to understand the side effects of radiation firsthand would so nonchalantly consider a policy to dump such material despite there being no scientific consensus on the safety of ocean disposal. Moreover, as much as nuclear power was conceived of as a phenomenon and problem of the postwar era for many Japanese activists, the arrival of Pacific activists in Japanese localities opened residents' eyes to the concrete links these visitors drew to earlier Japanese imperialism and colonialism. Thus, while on one level involvement in Asia and the Pacific helped make the regional "local" by drawing activists into regional communities of fate, on another level, it also laid bare their ambivalent position as citizens of a nation perpetrating environmental injustices against these very same regions. In turn, this realization opened the way for a reconsideration of the motivations and methods of civic action that broke sharply with earlier models based on victimhood and domestic struggle alone.[77]

The result, I argue, was an enriched comprehension of environmental injustice, which combined the earlier consciousness of victimhood with a more reflexive, proactive, and multidimensional outlook. Together with the ideas of Oda Makoto in the peace movement and women's groups involved in the *kiseng* problem, I believe that this conceptual enrichment of environmental injustice served as another fertile intellectual springboard for the imagination and development of Japanese civil society in later decades. It offered a powerful model of open, advocacy-focused civic activism. As the debate and movement for civil society unfolded in Japan throughout the 1990s, transnationally active groups such as the JVC, the Kiko Forum, JATAN, and CASA became prominent models for the kind of civil society many civic advocates hoped to construct in Japan. These groups exemplified the image of civil society as a progressive, open space with solid domestic roots yet deeply cognizant of and connected to the multiple contexts in which the local and national were enmeshed. Such groups contributed to this enhanced vision of civic activism and civil society by employing novel ideas, approaches, and perspectives garnered through their interactions with foreign groups (recall how Kiko Forum activists learned from Klima Forum activists). A key factor fueling the resurgence of civil society in 1990s Japan was the notion that the country's institutions—political, economic, and social—were far too insular and that, in a globalizing age, Japan needed to become more open. A strong and independent civil society was seen as one crucial method of achieving this more open society. Transnationally active groups, as we have seen, had been practicing such open, multidimensional activism for many decades. In particular, their rethinking of victimhood and their formulation of a more reflexive activist identity (i.e., that victims might also be aggressors) offered a powerful vision for civil society in the country.

As Janet Conway has observed, "People, communities, organizations and movements are being political in ways that are not intelligible in the conventional narratives of liberal citizenship contained in the national (welfare) state."[78] Rather than "looking for the new sovereign," Conway advises us to search for "new citizens, in social movements whose practices are calling into being new sovereignties and new citizenships."[79] As I have attempted to show throughout this book, transnational involvement has been an important method for some Japanese activists to negotiate the dynamics of these new sovereignties and citizenships of civil society, especially with regard to conceptualizations of environmental injustice and local struggle in a globalizing age. To the extent that transnational interaction encouraged these Japanese activists to reconsider environmental injustice beyond the locality and the nation, it undoubtedly made their injustice paradigm less insular and more thoroughly global, cosmopolitan, and inclusive in outlook. In turn, this perspective arguably flowed back into and influenced the development of Japanese civic activism more generally, undermining entrenched notions of victimhood.

But neither globalism nor cosmopolitanism offered the initial spark for the environmental injustice paradigm. This came from attention to, and involvement in, local, situated struggles involving victimized people and communities. As Joachim Radkau argues, "Today it is frequently implied that the global perspective is morally superior, and the focus on the protection of one's own immediate environment is ridiculed as a short-sighted NIMBY . . . syndrome." But, in the end, the real task is one of forging genuine connections—to issues, to people, and to principles—rather than one of choosing a "better" scale.[80] Extending this to the case of Japanese transnational involvement, it was the national trauma of industrial pollution and the suffering of people in localities across the archipelago that provided the initial emotional, intellectual, and ethical spark for the Japanese environmental injustice paradigm. Although the paradigm was recalibrated and repositioned in subsequent iterations abroad, its anthropocentric focus on victims and marginalization endured as common, connecting threads. Indeed, this attention to injustice and fundamental human rights arguably represents one of the key contributions of the Japanese environmental experience to the evolution of environmentalism in the contemporary world.

# Notes

Source abbreviations used throughout the text:

AMPO    *AMPO: Japan-Asia Quarterly Review*

FJK    *Ui Jun Shūshū Kōgai Mondai Shiryō 1 Fukkoku "Jishu Kōza,"* edited by Saitama Daigaku Kyōsei Shakai Kenkyū Sentā. Tokyo: Suirensha, 2005–2006.

FKG    *Ui Jun Shūshū Kōgai Mondai Shiryō 2 Fukkoku "Kōgai Genron,"* edited by Saitama Daigaku Kyōsei Shakai Kenkyū Sentā. Tokyo: Suirensha, 2007.

GKN    *Geppō Kōgai o Nogasu na!*

HGS    *"Hangenpatsu Shinbun" Shukusatsuban (0–100),* edited by Hangenpatsu Undō Zenkoku Renrakukai. Nara: Yasōsha, 1986.

KOGAI    *KOGAI: The Newsletter from Polluted Japan*

TKT    *Tsuchi no Koe, Tami no Koe*

TKTG    *Tsuchi no Koe, Tami no Koe Gōgai Kaku Haikibutsu Kaiyō Tōki Hantai Undō Tokushū*

NNJ    *No Nuke News Japan*

## Introduction

1    Ui Jun, "Interview with Ui Jun: Minamata Disease in Canada," *AMPO: Japan-Asia Quarterly Review* 26 (October–December 1975): 69.

2    Ui Jun, ed., *Polluted Japan: Reports by Members of the Jishu-Koza Citizens' Movement* (Tokyo: Jishu-Koza, 1972), 8, 9.

3    Ui Jun, "Kōgai Genron I," in *Kōgai Genron Gappon*, by Ui Jun (Tokyo: Aki Shobō, 1990), 22.

4    Richard Curtis and Dave Fisher, "The Seven Wonders of the Polluted World," *New York Times,* September 26, 1971, 21.

5    Paul Ehrlich, "Foreword," in *Island of Dreams: Environmental Crisis in Japan,* ed. Norie Huddle, Michael Reich, and Nahum Stiskin (Rochester, VT: Schenkman Books, 1987), xiv.

6    John R. McNeill, *Something New Under the Sun: An Environmental History of the Twentieth-Century World* (London: Penguin Books, 2000), 98.

7    Miyamoto Ken'ichi, *Kankyō to Jichi: Watashi no Sengo Nōto* (Tokyo: Iwanami Shoten, 1996), 134–138.

8   Ursula K. Heise, *Sense of Place and Sense of Planet: The Environmental Imagination of the Global* (Oxford: Oxford University Press, 2008), 4.

9   John McCormick, *Reclaiming Paradise: The Global Environmental Movement* (Bloomington: Indiana University Press, 1991), 127.

10  Miyamoto Ken'ichi, *Nihon no Kankyō Mondai: Sono Seiji Keizaigakuteki Kōsatsu* (Tokyo: Yūhikaku, 1981), 322.

11  Julia Adeney Thomas, "Using Japan to Think Globally: The Natural Subject of History and Its Hopes," in *Japan at Nature's Edge: The Environmental Context of a Global Power,* ed. Ian Jared Miller, Julia Adeney Thomas, Brett L. Walker (Honolulu: University Hawai'i Press, 2013), 293.

12  Ibid., 303.

13  See Samuel Moyn, "The Return of the Prodigal: The 1970s as a Turning Point in Human Rights History," in *The Breakthrough: Human Rights in the 1970s,* ed. Jan Eckel and Samuel Moyn (Philadelphia: University of Pennsylvania Press, 2014), 1–14; and Jan Eckel, "The Rebirth of Politics from the Spirit of Morality: Explaining the Human Rights Revolution of the 1970s," in *The Breakthrough,* ed. Eckel and Moyn, 226–259.

14  Donna Haraway, "Situated Knowledges: The Science Question in Feminism and the Privilege of Partial Perspective," *Feminist Studies* 14, no. 3 (1988): 590.

15  Heise, *Sense of Place,* 46.

16  Ibid., 21.

17  Arif Dirlik, "Globalism and the Politics of Place," in *Globalisation and the Asia-Pacific: Contested Territories,* ed. Kris Olds, Peter Dicken, Philip F. Kelly, Lily Kong, and Henry Wai-Chung Yeung (London: Routledge), 38.

18  Marybeth Long Martello and Sheila Jasanoff, "Introduction: Globalization and Environmental Governance," in *Earthly Politics: Local and Global in Environmental Governance,* ed. Sheila Jasanoff and Marybeth Long Martello (Cambridge, MA: MIT Press, 2004), 6.

19  Ibid., 7.

20  Ibid., 13–14.

21  Roland Robertson, "Glocalization: Time-Space and Homogeneity-Heterogeneity," in *Global Modernities,* ed. Mike Featherstone, Scott Lash, and Roland Robertson (London: SAGE, 1995), 26.

22  Haraway, "Situated," 590.

23  Seminal research on industrial pollution and protest in Japan includes (in chronological order): Shōji Hikaru and Miyamoto Ken'ichi, *Osorubeki Kōgai* (Tokyo: Iwanami Shoten, 1964); Shōji Hikaru and Miyamoto Ken'ichi, *Nihon no Kōgai* (Tokyo: Iwanami Shoten, 1975); Kenneth Strong, *Ox against the Storm: A Biography of Tanaka Shozo: Japan's Conservationist Pioneer*

(Folkestone, UK: Japan Library, 1977); Margaret McKean, *Environmental Protest and Citizen Politics in Japan* (Berkeley: University of California Press, 1981); Julian Gresser, Koichiro Fujikura, and Akio Morishima, *Environmental Law in Japan* (London: MIT Press, 1981); Norie Huddle, Michael Reich, and Nahum Stiskin, eds., *Island of Dreams: Environmental Crisis in Japan* (Rochester, VT: Schenkman Books, 1987); Kawana Hideyuki, *Dokyumento Nihon no Kōgai,* vols. 1–13 (Tokyo: Ryokufu, 1987–1996); Ui Jun, ed. *Industrial Pollution in Japan* (Tokyo: United Nations University Press, 1992); Jeffrey Broadbent, *Environmental Politics in Japan: Networks of Power and Protest* (Cambridge: Cambridge University Press, 1998); Iijima Nobuko, *Kankyō Mondai no Shakaishi* (Tokyo: Yūhikaku, 2000); Timothy S. George, *Minamata: Pollution and the Struggle for Democracy in Postwar Japan* (Cambridge, MA: Harvard University Press, 2001); Brett L. Walker, *Toxic Archipelago: A History of Industrial Disease in Japan* (Seattle: University of Washington Press, 2010); essays in Ian Jared Miller, Julia Adeney Thomas, and Brett Walker, eds., *Japan at Nature's Edge: The Environmental Context of a Global Power* (Honolulu: University of Hawai'i Press, 2013); Robert Stolz, *Bad Water: Nature, Pollution, and Politics in Japan, 1870–1950* (Durham, NC: Duke University Press, 2015).

24  Walker, *Toxic Archipelago*; George, *Minamata;* Iijima, *Kankyō Mondai no Shakaishi;* Iijima Nobuko, *Kaiteiban Kankyō Mondai to Higaisha Undō* (Tokyo: Gakubunsha, 1993); Ishimure Michiko, *Paradise in the Sea of Sorrow: Our Minamata Disease,* trans. Livia Monnet (Ann Arbor: Center for Japanese Studies, University of Michigan, 2003); Ui Jun, *Kōgai Genron Gappon* (Tokyo: Aki Shobō, 1990).

25  Walker, *Toxic Archipelago,* 9.

26  Kwame Anthony Appiah, *The Ethics of Identity* (Princeton, NJ: Princeton University Press, 2005), 257.

27  Ibid., 258.

28  Ibid., 256.

29  Sidney Tarrow, *The New Transnational Activism* (Cambridge: Cambridge University Press, 2005), 29.

30  Ibid., 42.

31  Ibid., 28.

32  Ibid., 206.

33  See text for further discussion of this "boomerang" idea.

34  See Simon Avenell, *Making Japanese Citizens: Civil Society and the Mythology of the Shimin in Postwar Japan* (Berkeley: University of California Press, 2010), 195; Robert Pekkanen, *Japan's Dual Civil Society: Members without Advocates* (Stanford, CA: Stanford University Press, 2006), 165–169.

35 On the latter see Kim D. Reimann, *The Rise of Japanese NGOs: Activism from Above* (Oxon, UK: Routledge, 2010).

36 Pekkanen, *Japan's Dual Civil Society*, 8.

37 Frank Upham, *Law and Social Change in Postwar Japan* (Cambridge, MA: Harvard University Press, 1987); Frank Upham, "Unplaced Persons and Movements for Place," in *Postwar Japan as History*, ed. Andrew Gordon (Berkeley: University of California Press, 1993), 325–346.

38 Avenell, *Making*, chapter 5.

39 Pekkanen, *Japan's Dual Civil Society*, 168.

40 Important research includes (in chronological order): Jeffrey Broadbent, *Environmental Politics in Japan*; Robin LeBlanc, *Bicycle Citizens: The Political World of the Housewife* (Berkeley: University of California Press, 1999); Patricia L. Maclachlan, *Consumer Politics in Postwar Japan: The Institutional Boundaries of Citizen Activism* (New York: Columbia University Press, 2002); Hasegawa Kōichi, *Constructing Civil Society in Japan: Voices of Environmental Movements* (Melbourne: Trans Pacific Press, 2004); Daniel Aldrich, *Site Fights: Divisive Facilities and Civil Society in Japan and the West* (Ithaca, NY: Cornell University Press, 2008); Pradyumna P. Karan and Unryu Suganuma, eds., *Local Environmental Movements: A Comparative Study of the United States and Japan* (Lexington: University Press of Kentucky, 2008); Peter Wynn Kirby, *Troubled Natures: Waste, Environment, Japan* (Honolulu: University of Hawai'i Press, 2010).

41 William Robinson, "Theories of Globalization," in *The Blackwell Companion to Globalization*, ed. George Ritzer (Oxford: Blackwell, 2007), 136.

42 Sheila Jasanoff, "NGOs and the Environment: From Knowledge to Action," *Third World Quarterly* 18, no. 3 (1997): 581; Peter Haas, "Introduction: Epistemic Communities and International Policy Coordination," *International Organization* 46, no. 1 (1992): 1–35.

43 Arif Dirlik, "Performing the World: Reality and Representation in the Making of World Histor(ies)," *Journal of World History* 16, no. 4 (2005): 407; Mathias Albert, Gesa Bluhm, Jan Helmig, Andreas Leutzsch, and Jochen Walter, "Introduction: The Communicative Construction of Transnational Political Spaces," in *Transnational Political Spaces: Agents— Structures—Encounters*, ed. Mathias Albert, Gesa Bluhm, Jan Helmig, Andreas Leutzsch, and Jochen Walter (Frankfurt: Campus Verlag, 2009), 18.

44 John Hoffman, *Citizenship beyond the State* (London: SAGE Publications, 2004).

45 See Margaret E. Keck and Kathryn Sikkink, "Transnational Advocacy Networks in International and Regional Politics," *International Social Science*

*Journal* 51, no. 159 (1999): 89–101; and Margaret E. Keck and Kathryn Sikkink, *Activists beyond Borders: Advocacy Networks in International Politics* (Ithaca, NY: Cornell University Press, 1998).

46  Keck and Sikkink, "Transnational Advocacy Networks," 93.

47  Nina Glick-Schiller, "Transnationality," in *A Companion to the Anthropology of Politics*, ed. David Nugent and Joan Vincent (Malden, MA: Blackwell Publishing, 2004), 449.

48  See Wesley Sasaki-Uemura, *Organizing the Spontaneous: Citizen Protest in Postwar Japan* (Hawai'i: University of Hawaii Press, 2001). Also see Avenell, *Making*.

49  See Simon Avenell, "Transnationalism and the Evolution of Post-national Citizenship in Japan," *Asian Studies Review* 39, no. 3 (2015): 375–394.

50  On victimhood in postwar Japan see James J. Orr, *The Victim as Hero: Ideologies of Peace and National Identity in Postwar Japan* (Honolulu: University of Hawai'i Press, 2001).

51  Oda Makoto, "Heiwa o Tsukuru: Sono Genri to Kōdō—Hitotsu no Sengen," in Oda Makoto, *Oda Makoto Zenshigoto* vol. 9 (Tokyo: Kawade Shobō Shinsha, 1970), 113–131; and Avenell, *Making*, chapter 4.

52  Women's Group of the Conference of Asians, "Resolution on Women," *AMPO: Japan-Asia Quarterly Review* 21–22 (1974): 15.

53  Aoyama Tadashi, "Nikkan Jōyaku 10-nen to Kōgai Yushutsu Hantai Undō," *Jishu Kōza* 58 (January 1976): 64, in *Ui Jun Shūshū Kōgai Mondai Shiryō 1 Fukkoku "Jishu Kōza"* (hereafter *FJK*), 3–2, ed. Saitama Daigaku Kyōsei Shakai Kenkyū Sentā (Tokyo: Suirensha, 2006), 70.

54  Ibid., 68.

55  Tarrow, *The New*, 43.

56  Officially "The Third Conference of the Parties (COP3) to the United Nations Framework Convention on Climate Change (UNFCCC)." See http://unfccc.int/cop3/.

57  This was the prime minister of Vanuatu. On "nuclearism," see chapter 6.

### Chapter 1: Japanese Industrial Pollution and Environmental Injustice

1  William Gamson, "Injustice Frames," in *The Wiley-Blackwell Encyclopedia of Social and Political Movements*, ed. David A. Snow, Donatella della Porta, Bert Klandermans, and Doug McAdam (Hoboken, NJ: John Wiley & Sons, 2014), 319.

2  See Tsuru Shigeto, *The Political Economy of the Environment: The Case of Japan* (London: Athlone Press, 1999), 27–47; McKean, *Environmental Protest*, 35–42; Ui. "Kōgai Genron I," 189–274; Ui Jun, "Kōgai Genron II," in Ui, *Kōgai Genron Gappon*, 3–65; Iijima, *Kankyō Mondai no Shakaishi*,

chapters 1–6; Miyamoto Ken'ichi, "Japan's Environmental Policy: Lessons from Experience and Remaining Problems," in *Japan at Nature's Edge,* ed. Miller, Thomas, and Walker (Honolulu: University of Hawaiʻi Press), 222–251; Stolz, *Bad Water;* Strong, *Ox.*

3   On Morinaga milk contamination see Miwako Dakeishi, Katsuyuki Murata, and Philippe Grandjean, "Long-Term Consequences of Arsenic Poisoning during Infancy due to Contaminated Milk Powder," *Environmental Health* 5, no. 31 (2006), http://www.ehjournal.net/content/5/1/31 (accessed April 28, 2014); and Ui, ed. *Polluted Japan,* 28–29.

4   On the Kanemi Incident see Huddle et al., *Island,* 133–160.

5   Seminal works in English on Minamata include George, *Minamata;* Walker, *Toxic Archipelago*; Ui, ed. *Industrial Pollution,* chapter 4; Harada Masazumi, *Minamata Disease,* trans. Timothy George and Tsushima Sachie (Kumamoto: Kumamoto Nichinichi Shinbun, 2004); Ishimure, *Paradise;* Upham, *Law and Social Change,* chapter 2; and Mishima Akio, *Bitter Sea: The Human Cost of Minamata Disease* (Tokyo: Kosei Publishing Company, 1992).

6   Ui, ed. *Polluted Japan,* 14.

7   W. Eugene Smith and Aileen M. Smith, *MINAMATA: Words and Photographs* (New York: Holt, Rinehart and Winston, 1975).

8   Shōji and Miyamoto, *Osorubeki,* caption to the first photographic image in the book (no page number).

9   Ui, ed. *Polluted Japan,* 4.

10  Ibid., 18.

11  On the Big Four pollution incidents and lawsuits see Ui, "Kōgai Genron I," 73–188; Ui, "Kōgai Genron II," 104–135; Kawana Hideyuki, *Dokyumento Nihon no Kōgai 1*; Tsuru, *Political Economy,* 48–107; Simon Avenell, "Japan's Long Environmental Sixties and the Birth of a Green Leviathan," *Japanese Studies* 32, no. 3 (2012): 423–444; and Gresser et al., *Environmental Law,* chapters 2 and 3.

12  Shimizu Makoto, ed. *Kainō Michitaka Chosakushū 8: Kōgai* (Tokyo: Nihon Hyōronsha, 1970), 63–64; Kawana, *Dokyumento 1,* 394–400.

13  Tokyo Metropolitan Government, *Tokyo Fights Pollution* (Tokyo: Tokyo Metropolitan Government, 1977), 75.

14  On the Shizuoka movements see Avenell, *Making,* 151–153; Kawana, *Dokyumento 1,* 368–370; Tsuru, *Political Economy,* 61–62; Gresser, et al., *Environmental Law,* 22; Jack G. Lewis, "Civic Protest in Mishima: Citizens' Movements and the Politics of the Environment in Contemporary Japan," in *Political Opposition and Local Politics in Japan,* ed. Kurt Steiner, Ellis S. Krauss, and Scott C. Flanagan (Princeton, NJ: Princeton University Press, 1980), 274–313.

15   See Jūmin Toshokan, ed., *Minikomi Sōmokuroku* (Tokyo: Heibonsha, 1992).

16   Miyazaki Shōgo, *Ima, Kōkyōsei o Utsu: "Dokyumento" Yokohama Shinkamotsusen Hantai Undō* (Tokyo: Shinsensha, 1975); Michiba Chikanobu, "Sen Kyūhyaku Rokujū Nendai ni okeru 'Chiki' no Hakken to 'Kōkyōsei' no Saiteigi: Miketsu no Aporia o megutte," *Gendai Shisō* 31, no. 6 (May, 2002): 97–130.

17   Yokoyama Keiji, "Kono Wakitatsu Teikō no Nami," *Asahi Jyānaru* (April 23, 1971): 41–62. For data on these movements see McKean, *Environmental Protest,* 8 (note 14); Asahi Jyānaru, "Tokushū Minikomi '71: Honryū suru Chikasui," *Asahi Jyānaru* (March 26, 1971): 4–60.

18   Michael Reich, "Crisis and Routine: Pollution Reporting by the Japanese Press," in *Institutions for Change in Japanese Society,* ed. George DeVos (Berkeley: Institute of East Asian Studies, University of California, 1984), 152.

19   Asahi Shinbun Keizaibu, ed., *Kutabare GNP: Kōdo Keizai Seichō no Uchimaku* (Tokyo: Asahi Shinbunsha, 1971), 125.

20   Shimokawa Kōshi, ed., *Kankyōshi Nenpyō 1926–2000 Shōwa-Heisei Hen* (Kawade Shobō Shinsha, 2004), 232; Kanda Fuhito and Kobayashi Hideo, eds., *Sengoshi Nenpyō* (Tokyo: Shogakkan, 2005), 55, 65, 71.

21   "Not All Is Serene in Cities of Japan," *New York Times* (January 19, 1968), 51; Donald Kirk, "Students in the Elementary Schools Grow Up Suffering from Asthma. Plants Wither and Die. The Birds around Mount Fuji Are Decreasing in Number. They No Longer Visit the Town," *New York Times* (March 26, 1972), 33.

22   Tanaka Kakuei, *Building A New Japan: A Plan for Remodeling the Japanese Archipelago* (Tokyo: Simul Press, 1973), 220.

23   Rachel Carson, *Silent Spring* (Boston, MA: Houghton Mifflin, 1962); André Gorz, *Ecologie et Politique* (Paris: Seuil, 1978) (Gorz's book comprised articles published in the 1960s and 1970s).

24   Ariyoshi Sawako, *Fukugō Osen* (Tokyo: Shinchōsha, 1979).

25   For discussion of pollution prevention agreements see Kawana, *Dokyumento 1,* 388; Kazuo Yamanouchi and Kiyoharu Otsubo, "Agreements on Pollution Prevention: Overview and One Example," in *Environmental Policy in Japan,* ed. Shigeto Tsuru and Helmut Weidner (Berlin: Sigma, 1989), 221–245.

26   Shimokawa, ed., *Kankyōshi,* 215.

27   Kanda and Kobayashi, eds., *Sengoshi,* 43; Shimokawa, ed., *Kankyōshi,* 220.

28   Ishii Kuniyoshi, ed., *20 Seiki no Nihon Kankyōshi* (Tokyo: Sangyō Kankyō Kanri Kyōkai, 2002), 37; Shimokawa, ed., *Kankyōshi,* 268.

29    Tsuru, *Political Economy,* 62.
30    Gresser et al., *Environmental Law,* 22; Ōtsuka Tadashi, *Kankyōhō* (Tokyo: Yūhikaku, 2010), 262–263.
31    Ishii, ed., *20 Seiki,* 50–51.
32    Gresser et al., *Environmental Law,* 22; Ōtsuka, *Kankyōhō,* 9–11.
33    See Upham, *Law and Social Change,* 16–27.
34    See Broadbent, "Japan's Environmental Politics: Recognition and Response Processes," in *Environmental Policy in Japan,* ed. Hidefumi Imura and Miranda A. Schreurs (Gloucestershire, U.K. and Northampton, MA: Edward Elgar Publishing Limited, 2005), 118.
35    The complete archive of minutes and other RCP materials is held at the Institute of Economic Research (IER) Library at Hitotsubashi University in Tokyo. See: "Hitotsubashi Daigaku Keizai Kenkyūjo Shiryōshitsu," Hitotsubashi Daigaku Keizai Kenkyūjo, accessed May 28, 2014, http://www.ier.hit-u.ac.jp/library/Japanese/index.html. The eight founding members were Tsuru Shigeto (economist), Kainō Michitaka (legal scholar), Komori Takeshi (political consultant), Shōji Hikaru (engineer), Shibata Tokue (economist), Shimizu Makoto (legal scholar), Noguchi Yūichirō (economist), and Miyamoto Kenichi (economist). Later members included Uzawa Hirofumi (economist), Ui Jun (engineer), Harada Masazumi (geneticist and epidemiologist), and Tajiri Muneaki (coastguard officer/political consultant).
36    Ui Jun, ed., *Kōgai Jishu Kōza 15-nen* (Tokyo: Aki Shobō, 1991), 8.
37    See Gresser et al., *Environmental Law,* 105–124 for details of the case.
38    Miyamoto, *Kankyō to Jichi,* 6.
39    Itai Masaru, Shinohara Yoshihito, Toyoda Makoto, Muramatsu Akio, Awaji Takehisa, Isono Yayoi, Miyamoto Ken'ichi, Teranishi Shunichi, "Zadankai: Nihon Kankyō Kaigi 30nen no Ayumi to Kōgai-Kankyō Soshō," *Kanykyō to Kōgai* 39, no. 1 (Summer 2009): 51.
40    See Kuroda Ryōichi, *Ōsaka ni Runessansu o* (Kyoto: Hōritsu Bunka Sha, 1974).
41    Tsuru Shigeto, ed., *Tōkyō e no Teigen* (Tokyo: Teikoku Chihō Gyōsei Gakkai, 1969); Tsuru Shigeto, ed., *Gendai Shihonshugi to Kōgai* (Tokyo: Iwanami Shoten, 1968), v; Hanayama Yuzuru, "Kaisetsu: Tsuru Kyōju no Seiji Keizaigaku," in *Tsuru Shigeto Chosakushū 6: Toshi Mondai to Kōgai,* Tsuru Shigeto (Tokyo: Kōdansha, 1975), 522.
42    Kainō appointed two other members of the RCP to this bureau: legal scholar Shimizu Makoto and economist Shibata Tokue. See Shibata Tokue, "Kōgai to Tatakau Kyosei: Kainō Michitaka," *Kankyō to Kōgai* 39, no. 1 (Summer 2009): 38.

43   Shimizu Makoto, ed., *Kainō*, 59, 132–136.
44   Tōkyōto Kōgai Kenkyūjo, ed. *Kōgai to Tōkyōto* (Tokyo: Tōkyōto Kōgai Kenkyūjo, 1970); Shimizu, ed., *Kainō*, 55.
45   Shibata, "Kōgai," 41.
46   Miyamoto, *Kankyō to Jichi*, 92.
47   Tokyo Metropolitan Government, *Tokyo Fights*, 43–8.
48   For the second term lectures see Ui Jun, ed., *Gendai Shakai to Kōgai* (Tokyo: Keisō Shobō, 1972); Ui Jun, ed., *Gendai Kagaku to Kōgai* (Tokyo: Keisō Shobō, 1972); Ui Jun, ed., *Gendai Kagaku to Kōgai Zoku* (Tokyo: Keisō Shobō, 1972); Ui Jun, ed., *Kōgai Higaisha no Ronri* (Tokyo: Keisō Shobō, 1973). Many postwar environmentalists such as Miyamoto Ken'ichi drew inspiration from Tanaka Shōzō. See Miyamoto, *Nihon no Kankyō Mondai*, 321. On Ashio and Tanaka see Timothy George, "Tanaka Shozo's Vision of an Alternative Constitutional Modernity for Japan," in *Public Spheres, Private Lives in Modern Japan, 1600–1950: Essays in Honor of Albert M. Craig*, ed. Gail Lee Bernstein, Andrew Gordon, and Kate Wildman Nakai (Cambridge, MA: Harvard University Asia Center, 2005), 89–116; Strong, *Ox*; Komatsu Hiroshi and Kim Techan, *Kōkyō suru Ningen 4: Tanaka Shōzō: Shōgai o Kōkyō ni sasageta Kōdō suru Shisōnin* (Tokyo: Tōkyō Daigaku Shuppan Kai, 2010); Tessa Morris-Suzuki, "Environmental Problems and Perceptions in Early Industrial Japan," in *Sediments of Time: Environment and Society in Chinese History*, ed. Mark Elvin and Liu Tsui-jung (Cambridge: Cambridge University Press, 1998), 756–780; and Stolz, *Bad Water*.
49   Ui, ed., *Kōgai Jishu*, 14.
50   Ui, *Kōgai Genron Gappon*, 36–38.
51   Ui, ed., *Kōgai Jishu*, 11.
52   Tessa Morris-Suzuki, *A History of Japanese Economic Thought* (London: Routledge and Nissan Institute for Japanese Studies, 1991), 151.
53   Miyamoto Ken'ichi, *Omoide no Hitobito to* (Tokyo: Fujiwara Shoten, 2001), 159. On Marxism in Japanese intellectual history see Andrew Barshay, *The Social Sciences in Modern Japan: The Marxian and Modernist Traditions* (Berkeley: University of California Press, 2007).
54   Miyamoto recounts his investigations in the following works: Miyamoto, *Kankyō to Jichi*, 69, 73; Miyamoto, *Omoide*, 209, and Miyamoto, *Nihon no Kankyō Mondai*, 81, 317.
55   Miyamoto coined the term "corporate castle town" after visiting Yokkaichi and Kyushu. See Miyamoto, *Nihon no Kankyō Mondai*, 70–71.
56   Tsuru Shigeto, "Jo," in *Tsuru Shigeto Chosakushū*, Tsuru, iv; Shimizu, ed., *Kainō*, 27. These site investigations are documented in great detail in the

RCP's monthly reports (*kaigi hōkoku*) held at the IER collection. See, for example, the following reports: April 30, 1964; May 30, 1964; July 27, 1964; January 30, 1965.

57  Miyamoto Ken'ichi, "Shinobiyoru Kōgai," *Sekai* 204 (December 1962): 199–200; Miyamoto, *Omoide,* 209.

58  Shōji and Miyamoto, *Osorubeki.*

59  Ui Jun, *Yanaka Mura kara Minamata e—Sanrizuka e: Ekorogī no Genryū (Tokyo: Shakai Hyōronsha, 1991),* 187. Activists in the Mishima-Numazu-Shimizu movements opposing construction of a petrochemical combine, for instance, used the book to enlighten locals on the risks of industrial development. See Miyamoto Ken'ichi, "Chiisana Hon no Ōkina Sekinin," *Tosho* 227 (July 1968): 10.

60  Shinmura Izuru, ed. *Kōjien Dainihan* (Tokyo: Iwanami Shoten: 1969), 729.

61  Ui, *Yanaka,* 187. Miyamoto was also interviewed on the national television broadcaster, NHK. Miyamoto, *Kankyō to Jichi,* 83.

62  Shōji and Miyamoto, *Osorubeki,* vii, 140.

63  Ibid., 168–169; Miyamoto, *Nihon no Kankyō Mondai,* 81, 130; Tsuru, ed., *Gendai Shihonshugi,* 24.

64  Shōji and Miyamoto, *Osorubeki,* 174–175; Miyamoto, *Nihon no Kankyō Mondai,* 81, 137.

65  Shōji and Miyamoto, *Osorubeki,* 175.

66  Ui, "Kōgai Genron I," 34.

67  Miyamoto, *Omoide,* 168.

68  Ibid., 172, 177.

69  Ibid., 177.

70  Ernesto LaClau and Chantal Mouffe, *Hegemony and Socialist Strategy: Toward a Radical Democratic Politics* (New York: Verso, 1985), xviii.

71  Shōji and Miyamoto, *Osorubeki,* 158.

72  Ibid., 204–205.

73  These details are drawn from Ui, "Kōgai Genron I," 12–13.

74  Ibid., 274.

75  Ibid., 33–34.

76  Ibid., 37.

77  Harada Masazumi, *Minamata ga Utsusu Sekai* (Tokyo: Nihon Hyōronsha, 1989), 1.

78  Ibid., 2.

79  Ibid., 4.

80  Ibid., iv.

81  Ibid., 2.

## Chapter 2: The Therapy of Translocal Community

1   Tarrow, *The New*, 206.
2   Dirlik, "Performing," 406.
3   Ash Amin, "Spatialities of Globalisation," *Environment and Planning A* 34 (2002): 395.
4   Sallie A. Marston, John Paul Jones III, and Keith Woodward, "Human Geography without Scale," *Transactions of the Institute of British Geographers* 30, no. 4 (2005): 422.
5   Ibid., 426.
6   Ui Jun, *Ui Jun Repōto: Ōshū no Kōgai o otte* (Tokyo: Aki Shobō, 1970), 76.
7   Ui Jun, "Sekai no Kōgai Hantai Shimin Undō," in *Sekai no Kōgai Chizu* 2, ed. Tsuru Shigeto (Tokyo: Iwanami Shoten, 1977), 149.
8   Miyamoto's observations after touring Eastern Europe are recorded in the committee's monthly report, dated December 16, 1967 held at the Institute of Economic Research (IER) Library at Hitotsubashi University in Tokyo.
9   Miyamoto, *Kankyō to Jichi*, 148–149.
10  Ibid., 121–122.
11  For details see Ui, *Ui Jun Repōto*, 13–25.
12  Ibid., 26, 45–46, 48.
13  Ibid., 112.
14  Ui Jun, "Mercury Pollution of Sea and Fresh Water: Its Accumulation into Water Biomass," *Kogai: The Newsletter from Polluted Japan* (hereafter *KOGAI*) 8 (Special Issue 1975): 22.
15  Ui, *Ui Jun Repōto*, 135.
16  "La 'morte chimica' da noi come in Giappone?"
17  Ibid., 217.
18  Ibid.
19  Ibid., 210.
20  Ibid., 254–256.
21  Ibid., 263, 274.
22  See Ui Jun, "Kōgai Genron III," in Ui Jun, *Kōgai Genron Gappon* (Tokyo: Aki Shobō, 1990), 127–202.
23  Ui, *Ui Jun Repōto*, 287.
24  Ui Jun, "Minamatabyō to Kanada Indian," in *Genchi ni Miru Sekai no Kōgai Sōkatsu: Sekai Kankyō Chōsadan Hōkoku*, ed. Tsuru Shigeto (Tokyo: Chūnichi Shinbun Tokyo Honsha, 1975), 139.
25  Ui, *Ui Jun Repōto*, 236.
26  Miyamoto, *Kankyō to Jichi*, 119.
27  Tsuru Shigeto, "Maegaki," in *Sekai no Kōgai Chizu* 1, ed. Tsuru Shigeto (Tokyo: Iwanami Shoten, 1977), i.

28    Hanada Masanori and Inoue Yukari, "Kanada Senjūmin no Minamatabyō to Junan no Shakaishi Dai-1-kai," *Gekkan "Shakai Undō"* 382 (January 2012): 21; and Ui, "Minamatabyō to Kanada," 147.

29    See Smith and Smith, *MINAMATA*.

30    Miyamoto, *Kankyō to Jichi*, 120.

31    See Tsuru Shigeto, ed., *Genchi ni Miru Sekai no Kōgai Sōkatsu: Sekai Kankyō Chōsadan Hōkoku* (Tokyo: Chūnichi Shinbun Tokyo Honsha, 1975), 2, 3, 354.

32    Miyamoto Ken'ichi and Harada Masazumi, "Kanada Indian Suigin Chūdoku Jiken," in *Sekai no Kōgai Chizu* 1, ed. Tsuru Shigeto (Tokyo: Iwanami Shoten), 88.

33    Tsuru Shigeto, "Sekai Kankyō Chōsadan no Shuppatsu ni atatte," in *Genchi ni Miru*, 14.

34    See Tsuru Shigeto, ed., *Genchi ni Miru*; and Tsuru Shigeto, ed., *Sekai no Kōgai Chizu* 1 and 2 (Tokyo: Iwanami Shoten, 1977).

35    CVCC=Compound Vortex Controlled Combustion. Hanayama Yuzuru, "Jidōsha o Kangaeru," in *Sekai no Kōgai Chizu* 1, ed. Tsuru, 149.

36    Ibid., 146.

37    For details see Miyamoto, *Kankyō to Jichi*, 134–137.

38    Nagai Susumu, "Ōbei no Genpatsu Hantai Tōsō," in *Genchi ni Miru*, ed. Tsuru, 112.

39    See Nagai Susumu, "Sekai Kankyō Chōsadan Hōkoku: Ōbei Senshinkoku ni okeru Genpatsu Hantai Undō," *Kōgai Kenkyū* 5, no. 2 (October 1975): 52–58; and Nagai Susumu, "Ōbei Senshinkoku ni okeru Genpatsu Hantai Undō," in *Genchi ni Miru*, ed. Tsuru, 177.

40    Karaki Kiyoshi, "Wareware Chikyū Kazoku," in *Genchi ni Miru*, ed. Tsuru, 91; Nagai, "Ōbei Senshinkoku," 178; Nagai, "Ōbei no Genpatsu," 113.

41    Nagai, "Ōbei no Genpatsu," 111.

42    Ibid., 112–113.

43    Karaki, "Wareware," 90–91.

44    Ibid., 93–94.

45    Nagai, "Ōbei no Genpatsu," 114.

46    The following details are drawn from Harada Masazumi, "Finrando no Suigin Jiken," in *Sekai no Kōgai Chizu* 1, ed. Tsuru, 127–133.

47    Ibid., 131.

48    Ibid., 132–133.

49    Harada, *Minamata ga Utsusu*, 212. The typical symptoms of Hunter-Russell syndrome are concentric constriction of the visual field, paresthesia (skin numbness and tingling), ataxia (loss of muscle coordination affecting movement), impaired hearing, and speech impairment.

50    Ui, "Minamatabyō to Kanada," 165.

51  Miyamoto, *Kankyō to Jichi*, 132.
52  Karaki, "Wareware," 77.
53  Ui Jun, "Minamatabyō to Kanada," 165.
54  Ui Jun, "Jinrui ga Ikinokoru tame no Kakutō," in *Genchi ni Miru*, ed. Tsuru, 109.
55  Harada, *Minamata ga Utsusu*, 213.
56  Ui, "Minamatabyō to Kanada," 166.
57  Ui, "Jinrui," 109.
58  Harada, "Finrando," 134–135.
59  Ibid., 135.
60  Miyamoto, *Kankyō to Jichi*, 123.
61  See First National Bank in Albuquerque, As Guardian for and On behalf of Dorothy Jean Huckleby, et al., plaintiffs-appellants, v. United States of America, Defendant-appellee. 552 F.2d 370. United States Court of Appeals, Tenth Circuit. 1977. *JUSTIA US Law*, https://bulk.resource.org/courts.gov/c/F2/552/552.F2d.370.75-1301.html accessed May 2, 2014.
62  Miyamoto, *Kankyō to Jichi*, 125–126. For more on the case see, Jack Vancoevering, "The Truth about Mercury," *Field and Stream* 76, no.1 (May 1971): 14–20, 137.
63  Miyamoto, *Kankyō to Jichi*, 126.
64  Ibid., 127.
65  Miyamoto Ken'ichi and Harada Masazumi, "Aramogorudo Kokujin Suigin Chūdoku Jiken," in *Sekai no Kōgai Chizu* 1, ed. Tsuru, 82.
66  Ibid., 83.
67  Ibid.
68  Ibid., 77.
69  See the "Grassy Narrows and Islington Bands Fonds Collection," Library and Archives Canada, http://collectionscanada.gc.ca/pam_archives/index.php?fuseaction=genitem.displayItem&lang=eng&rec_nbr=98381&rec_nbr_list=98381,3026162, accessed January 7, 2016. Also see the "Lamm, Marion, Mercury Collection," Harvard University Library, accessed January 7, 2016, http://oasis.lib.harvard.edu/oasis/deliver/~env00002.
70  Miyamoto Ken'ichi, "Fukamaru Kōgai: Shinaseru Toshi," in *Genchi ni Miru*, ed. Tsuru, 28.
71  Barney Lamm initiated these investigations. See Jane M. Hightower, *Diagnosis Mercury: Money, Politics, and Poison* (Washington, DC: Island Press, 2009), 117.
72  Karaki Kiyoshi, "'Minamata' no Suiseki," in *Genchi ni Miru*, ed. Tsuru, 55.
73  Hanada and Inoue, "Kanada," 21.
74  Miyamoto, *Kankyō to Jichi*, 129–130; Hanada and Inoue, "Kanada," 20.
75  Karaki, "'Minamata," 60.

76 Miyamoto and Harada, "Kanada," 109.

77 Ibid., 105.

78 Ibid., 106.

79 Miyamoto, "Fukamaru," 30.

80 Miyamoto and Harada, "Kanada," 95; Karaki, "'Minamata," 56.

81 Ui, "Minamatabyō to Kanada," 163.

82 Ibid., 164.

83 Ibid.

84 Karaki, "'Minamata," 57.

85 Ui, "Minamatabyō to Kanada," 164.

86 Miyamoto and Harada, "Kanada," 104.

87 Ui, "Minamatabyō to Kanada," 163.

88 Harada, *Minamata ga Utsusu,* 232.

89 Tsuru, ed., *Genchi ni Miru,* 268.

90 Ibid., 271.

91 Ui, "Interview," 69.

92 Tsuru, ed., *Genchi ni Miru,* 275.

93 On this visit see ibid., 276–278.

94 Ui, "Interview," 69.

95 Ui, "Sekai," 129.

96 Harada, *Minamata ga Utsusu,* 214.

97 Miyamoto Ken'ichi, "Naze Gaikoku no Tabi ni Derunoka," in *Genchi ni Miru,* ed. Tsuru, 19–20.

98 Ibid., 20, 22.

99 Ibid., 22.

100 Ibid., 23.

101 Canadian Indian Dryden Minamata Disease Group, "Final Statement," *Jishu Kōza* 54 (September 1975): 12, *FJK* 3–1, 202.

**Chapter 3: The Human Limits to Growth**

1 Leslie Paul Thiele, *Environmentalism for a New Millennium: The Challenge of Coevolution* (New York: Oxford University Press, 1999), 125–126.

2 Albert Roland, Richard Wilson, and Michael Rahill, *Adlai Stevenson of the United Nations* (Manila: Free Asia Press, 1965), 224.

3 On Kenneth Boulding see Edward de Steiguer, *The Origins of Modern Environmental Thought* (Tucson: The University of Arizona Press, 2011), chapter 8.

4 See John S. Dryzek, *The Politics of the Earth: Environmental Discourses* (Oxford: Oxford University Press, 2005), 50; McCormick, *Reclaiming,* 68.

5 Heise, *Sense of Place,* 4.

6 Clarke, quoted in McCormick, *Reclaiming,* 68.

7   See McCormick, *Reclaiming,* chapter 4.

8   Paul R. Ehrlich, *The Population Bomb* (New York: Ballantine Books, 1968). On Ehrlich see de Steiguer, *Origins,* chapter 10.

9   Barry Commoner, *The Closing Circle: Nature, Man, and Technology* (New York: Alfred A. Knopf, 1971). McCormick, *Reclaiming,* 70–71.

10  Donella H. Meadows, Dennis L. Meadows, Jørgen Randers, and William W. Behrens III, *The Limits to Growth: A Report for the Club of Rome's Project on The Predicament of Mankind* (New York: Universe Books, 1972), 154. McCormick, *Reclaiming,* 77–78; de Steiguer, *Origins,* chapter 14.

11  Albert et al, "Introduction," 7–31.

12  Saskia Sassen, "Globalization or Denationalization?" *Review of International Political Economy* 10, no.1 (2003): 12.

13  McCormick, *Reclaiming,* 88.

14  Jennifer Clapp and Peter Dauvergne, *Paths to a Green World: The Political Economy of the Global Environment* (Cambridge, MA: MIT Press, 2005), 54.

15  NGO Committee on Education of the Conference of NGOs, "UN Documents: Gathering a Body of Global Agreements: United Nations Conference on the Human Environment," http://www.un-documents.net /unche.htm, accessed May 28, 2014.

16  See Principle 1 of the Declaration on the Human Environment, available at ibid. Also see Tsuru Shigeto and Okamoto Masami, "Gendai Sekai to Kōgai Mondai," in *Sekai no Kōgai Chizu* 1, ed. Tsuru, 3; and Tsuru Shigeto, "Kokuren Kaigi Junbi Katei deno Mondaiten," in Tsuru, *Tsuru Shigeto Chosakushū,* 453–454.

17  Jacob Darwin Hamblin, "Gods and Devils in the Details: Marine Pollution, Radioactive Waste, and an Environmental Regime circa 1972," *Diplomatic History* 32 (2008): 553.

18  Norman J. Faramelli, "Toying with the Environment and the Poor: A Report on the Stockholm Environmental Conferences," *Boston College Environmental Affairs Law Review* 2, no. 3 (1972): 471.

19  Sally Jacobsen, "II: A Call to Environmental Order," *Bulletin of the Atomic Scientists* 28, no. 7 (1972): 23.

20  Matsui Yayori, "Kokuren Kankyō Kaigi Hōkoku II," *Kōgai Genron* 15 (November 1972): 7, in *Ui Jun Shūshū Kōgai Mondai Shiryō 2 Fukkoku "Kōgai Genron"* (hereafter *FKG*) *Dai 1-kai Haihon Dai 3-kan,* ed. Saitama Daigaku Kyōsei Shakai Kenkyū Sentā (Tokyo: Suirensha, 2007), 339.

21  Faramelli, "Toying," 472.

22  McCormick, *Reclaiming,* 99.

23  Faramelli, "Toying," 469; Frances Gendlin, "III: Voices from the Gallery," *Bulletin of the Atomic Scientists* 28, no. 7 (1972): 26.

24  McCormick, *Reclaiming,* 105.

25   Lars Emmelin, "The Stockholm Conferences," *Ambio* 1, no. 4 (1972): 139.
26   Emmelin, "Stockholm," 140.
27   For this discussion see Ui Jun and Barry Commoner, "Taidan: Nichibei no Kōgai Hantai Undō," *Asahi Shinbun* (morning edition, March 15, 1972): 23.
28   Gendlin, "III," 27.
29   Isomura Eiichi, " 'Kakegae no nai Jikoku' kara 'Kakegae no nai Chikyū e': Kokuren Ningen Kankyō Kaigi e no Kokumin Sanka o," *Kakushin* 24 (July 1972): 99.
30   Gaimushō Kokusai Rengōkyoku, *Nihon ni okeru Ningen Kankyō Mondai: Sono Genjō to Taisaku: 1972-nen no "Kokuren Ningen Kankyō Kaigi" no tame ni Kokuren ni Teishutsu shita Wagakuni no Hōkokusho* (Tokyo: Gaimushō Kokusai Rengōkyoku, 1971). The report is also reproduced in full with critical annotations by Ui Jun. See: Ui Jun, "Higaisha Fuzai no Kōgai Hōkoku: Kokuren Ningen Kankyō Kaigi e no Nihon Seifu Hōkoku Hihan," *Jishu Kōza* 10 (January 1972): 1–17, *FJK* 2, 221–251.
31   Ui, "Higaisha Fuzai," 223.
32   Ui, ed., *Kōgai Jishu*, 15; Ui Jun, "Shingikai no Yakuwari, Nashonaru Repōto Hihan," *Kōgai Genron* 3 (December 1971): 20, *FKG* 1–1, 120.
33   Ui Jun, "Ningen Kankyō ni kansuru Kokuren Sōkai e no Repōto," *Kōgai Genron* 6 (March 1972): 7, *FKG* 1–1, 271.
34   Ui, "Shingikai," 120.
35   Ibid., 123.
36   Ui, ed., *Kōgai Jishu*, 16; Ui, "Ningen," 297.
37   Ui, ed., *Kōgai Jishu*, 16.
38   Ibid.; Isomura, " 'Kakegae,' " 102.
39   "Kokuren Kankyō Kaigi e: Nō Moa Minamata: Kōgai Higaisha no Hōkoku wa Uttaeru," *Asahi Shinbun* (morning edition, February 18, 1972), 3.
40   Ui Jun, "Junrei no Tabi kara Kaette," *Jishu Kōza* 16 (July 1972): 1, *FJK* 3, 209.
41   Ui, ed., *Polluted Japan*.
42   Ibid., 9.
43   Other Japanese groups at UNCHE included the JFBA and the Kōgai Taisaku Zenkoku Renrakukai (the Pollution Countermeasures National Liaison Committee). See "Minamatabyō Kanja nado 2 Dantai ga Ketsudanshiki: Kokuren Kankyō Kaigi o Mae ni," *Asahi Shinbun* (morning edition, June 3, 1972), 18; "Itaibyō Soshō Kiroku Okuru: Nichibenren Suēden Bengoshikai ni," *Asahi Shinbun* (morning edition, June 8, 1972), 23; Zenkoku Kōgairen, "Kokuren Ningen Kankyō Kaigi ni taisuru Zenkoku Kōgairen no Repōto," *Gekkan Sōhyō* 180 (May 1972): 83–89.
44   Ui, ed., *Kōgai Jishu*, 16.
45   "Suēden e Shuppatsu: Minamata Kanjara Sannin," *Asahi Shinbun* (morning edition, June 1, 1972), 23.

46  Ui, ed., *Kōgai Jishu*, 21; Ui, "Ningen," 266; Kawana Hideyuki, *Dokyumento Nihon no Kōgai 2: Kankyōchō* (Tokyo: Ryokufu, 1988), 211.

47  Matsui Yayori, "Kaimaku Semaru Kokuren Ningen Kankyō Kaigi. Kakkizuku Sutokkuhorumu. 'Kōgai Nippon' ni Kanshin. Oshiyoseru Hōdō Kankeisha," *Asahi Shinbun* (evening edition, June 3, 1972): 8.

48  Kawana, *Dokyumento 2*, 212.

49  Ibid.

50  See Matsui Yayori, " 'Seifu wa Nani o Shite ita: Kōgai Kanja Tōchaku Umeku Kishadan," *Asahi Shinbun* (morning edition, June 5, 1972): 2; Honsha Kishadan, " 'Kōgai Nippon' Kō Uttaeru. Kokuren Ningen Kankyō Kaigi: Hatsugen o Matsu Higaishara. 'Teokure ni shita Seifu: Osoroshisa, Kono Mi de Shimesu'," *Asahi Shinbun* (morning edition, June 5, 1972): 23; Kawana, *Dokyumento 2*, 212.

51  Matsui Yayori, "Hisansa ni Ikinomu. Kiroku Eiga 'Minamata' o Jōei. Jinmin Hiroba de 'Nihon no Yūbe,' " *Asahi Shinbun* (June 6, 1972): 8.

52  Ibid.

53  Ui Jun, "Kokuren Kankyō Kaigi Hōkoku I," *Kōgai Genron* 13 (July 1972): 6, *FKG* 1–3, 210.

54  Ui, "Kokuren," 210.

55  "Kite Yokkata: Minamatabyō no Hamamoto san," *Asahi Shinbun* (evening edition, June 17, 1972): 3.

56  Ui, ed., *Kōgai Jishu*, 22.

57  Italics in original. Meadows et al., *Limits*, 126. McCormick, *Reclaiming*, 81.

58  Tsuru Shigeto, *Tsuru Shigeto Jiden: Ikutsumo no Kiro o Kaiko shite* (Tokyo: Iwanami Shoten, 2001), 340.

59  Ibid., 38.

60  Ibid., 45–46.

61  Ibid., 47.

62  Ibid., 48.

63  Ibid., 54.

64  Tsuru Shigeto, "Introduction," in Tsuru Shigeto, *Economic Theory and Capitalist Society: The Selected Essays of Shigeto Tsuru* 1 (Aldershot, UK: Edward Elgar, 1994), xxvi.

65  Tsuru, *Tsuru Shigeto Jiden*, 217.

66  Ibid., 221.

67  Ibid., 224, 226, 255.

68  Tsuru, "Jo," ii.

69  Ibid., iii.

70  Ibid.

71  Hanayama, "Kaisetsu," 522.

72   Tsuru Shigeto, "Foreword," in *Proceedings of International Symposium on Environmental Disruption: A Challenge to Social Scientists,* ed. Tsuru Shigeto (Paris: International Social Science Council, 1970), xiii.

73   K. William Kapp, "Environmental Disruption: General Issues and Methodological Problems," in *Proceedings,* ed. Tsuru, 3.

74   Tsuru, "Foreword," xix.

75   Tsuru, *Political Economy,* 67.

76   Tsuru Shigeto, *Kōgai no Seijikeizaigaku* (Tokyo: Iwanami Shoten, 1972), 17.

77   Tsuru Shigeto, "'North-South' Relations on Environment," in Tsuru, *Economic Theory,* 273.

78   Tsuru, "North-South," 276. On the idea of growth see Scott O'Bryan, *The Growth Idea: Purpose and Prosperity in Postwar Japan* (Honolulu: University of Hawai'i Press, 2009).

79   Tsuru Shigeto, "Shimin Jichi no Atarashii Dankai," in Tsuru, *Tsuru Shigeto Chosakushū,* 108.

80   Ibid.

81   Tsuru Shigeto, "In Place of GNP," in Tsuru, *Economic Theory,* 76.

82   Ibid., 68.

83   Ibid.

84   Italics in original. Tsuru, "'North-South,'" 272.

85   Tsuru, "Jo," iii.

86   Ibid., iv; Tsuru, *Tsuru Shigeto Jiden,* 340.

87   Tsuru Shigeto, "Jūmin no Tachiba kara mita Toshi Mondai," in Tsuru, *Tsuru Shigeto Chosakushū,* 29.

88   Tsuru, "'North-South,'" 278.

89   Tsuru, "In Place," 77.

90   Tsuru, "'North-South,'" 287.

91   Tsuru Shigeto, "Towards a New Political Economy," in Tsuru, *Economic Theory,* 103.

92   See "Summary of Discussion," in *Proceedings,* ed. Tsuru, 143.

93   Erik Dahmén, "Environmental Control and Economic Systems," in *Proceedings,* ed. Tsuru, 153.

94   Ibid., 157.

95   See "Summary of Discussion," in *Proceedings,* ed. Tsuru, 145.

96   Tsuru, "Towards," 101.

97   Indira Gandhi, "Address of Shrimati Indira Gandhi, Prime Minister of India," *Bulletin of the Atomic Scientists* 28, no. 7 (1972): 36.

98   Ibid., 37.

99   "Third World Ecology," *Stockholm Conference Eco* (June 7, 1972): 5.

100  Adebayo Adedeji, "Excerpts from the Statement of Adebayo Adedeji, Federal Commissioner for Economic Development and Reconstruction, Nigeria,

and Head of Nigerian Delegation: Deeds vs. Intentions," *Bulletin of the Atomic Scientists* 28, no. 7 (1972): 53.

101  Clapp and Dauvergne, *Paths,* 56.

102  Founex Conference, *The Founex Report on Environment and Development* (Washington, DC: Carnegie Endowment for International Peace, 1972), Manitou Foundation Homepage, accessed May 28, 2014, http://www .mauricestrong.net/index.php/the-founex-report.

103  McCormick, *Reclaiming,* 92.

104  Founex Conference, *Founex Report.*

105  Tsuru, " 'North-South,' " 283.

106  Tsuru Shigeto and Okamoto Masami, "Gendai Sekai to Kōgai Mondai," in *Sekai no Kōgai Chizu* 1, ed. Tsuru, 14.

107  Tsuru, " 'North-South,' " 284.

108  Ibid., 285.

109  Tsuru and Okamoto, "Gendai," 16.

110  Tsuru, " 'North-South,' " 287.

111  Tsuru and Okamoto, "Gendai," 15–16.

112  Ibid., 16.

113  Tsuru, " 'North-South,' " 288.

114  Founex Conference, *Founex Report.*

115  Tsuru, " 'North-South,' " 291.

116  Ibid.

117  Anthony Lewis, "One Confused Earth," *New York Times* (June 17, 1972), 29.

118  Ibid.

119  McCormick, *Reclaiming,* 104.

120  Ui, "Junrei," 210.

## Chapter 4: Pollution Export and Victimhood

1   Ui, "Kokuren," 221–222.

2   Ui Jun, " 'Kōgai Senshin Koku Nippon' no Sekinin: 'Kokuren Ningen Kankyō Kaigi' ni Sanka shite," *Kōmei* 119 (September 1972): 66.

3   Isomura, " 'Kakegae," 104.

4   T. J. Pempel, "Gulliver in Lilliput: Japan and Asian Economic Regionalism," *World Policy Journal* 13, no. 4 (winter 1996–1997): 17; Derek Hall, "Pollution Export as State and Corporate Strategy: Japan in the 1970s," *Review of International Political Economy* 16, no. 2 (2009): 262.

5   Pempel, "Gulliver," 18.

6   Hall, "Pollution," 262.

7   Oda Makoto, ed., *Ajia o Kangaeru: Ajiajin Kaigi no Zenkiroku* (Tokyo: Ushio Shuppansha, 1976), 151.

8   Hall, "Pollution," 260.

9   Derek Hall, "Environmental Change, Protest, and Havens of Environmental Degradation: Evidence from Asia," *Global Environmental Politics* 2, no. 2 (2002): 22.

10  Hall, "Environmental Change," 23.

11  Kaji Etsuko, "Kawasaki Steel: The Giant at Home," *AMPO: Japan-Asia Quarterly Review* (hereafter *AMPO*) 26 (October–December 1975): 38.

12  Ogawa Hiroshi, "Ajia no Mado: Nihon Kagaku no Kōgai Yushutsu o Kokuhatsu suru," *Jishu Kōza* 42 (September 1974): 57, *FJK* 2–3, 307.

13  Hall, "Pollution," 269. For the original see "Kōgai, Amari Shinkei o Tsukawanuyō," *Geppō Kōgai o Nogasu na!* (hereafter *GKN*) 1 (June 1974): 15–16.

14  Wilfredo Salvatierra, "Kawasaki Steel: The Giant Abroad," *AMPO* 26 (October–December 1975): 25.

15  Hall, "Pollution," 269.

16  Beheiren is the acronym for Betonamu ni Heiwa o! Shimin Rengō; in English, The Citizens' Federation for Peace in Vietnam. On Beheiren see Avenell, *Making;* Michiba Chikanobu, *Senryō to Heiwa: Sengo to iu Keiken* (Tokyo: Seidosha, 2005); and Thomas R. H. Havens, *Fire Across the Sea: The Vietnam War and Japan 1965–1975* (New Jersey: Princeton University Press, 1987).

17  "Conference of Asians," *AMPO* 21–22 (Summer-Autumn 1974): 2. For a discussion of the conference in the context of other early 1970s engagement between Japanese and Asian activists, see Michiba Chikanobu, "Posuto-Betonamu Sensōki ni okeru Ajia Rentai Undō: 'Uchi naru Ajia' to 'Ajia no naka no Nihon' no Aida de," in *Betonamu Sensō no Jidai 1960–1975-nen: Iwanami Kōza Higashi Ajia Kindai Tsūshi Dai 8-kan,* ed. Wada Haruki, Gotō Ken'ichi, Kibata Yōichi, Yamamuro Shin'ichi, Cho Kyeungdal, Nakano Satoshi, Kawashima Shin (Tokyo: Iwanami Shoten, 2011), 111–115.

18  Himeno Seiichirō and Yoshimatsu Sōichirō, "Nihon no Genchi o Otozurete," *Jishu Kōza* 40 (July 1974): 4, *FJK* 2–3, 128.

19  "Conference of Asians," 8.

20  Ibid., 12.

21  Hirayama Takasada, "Fujisawashi Yugyōji ni okeru Tīchiin," *Jishu Kōza* 40 (July 1974): 5–9, *FJK* 2–3, 129–133.

22  "Conference of Asians," 3–4.

23  Oda, ed., *Ajia o Kangaeru,* 56.

24  Ibid., 5–9; Matsuoka Nobuo, "Hachiōji no Honkaigi," *Jishu Kōza* 40 (July 1974): 10–13, *FJK* 2–3, 134–137.

25  See "Conference of Asians," 7, 9; Ajiajin Kaigi, "Komittomento (Yaruzo!)," *Jishu Kōza* 40 (July 1974): 18–19, *FJK* 2–3, 142–143.

26  Henshūbu, "'Ajiajin Kaigi' ni tsuite," in *Ajia o Kangaeru*, ed. Oda, 3.

27  Oda, ed., *Ajia o Kangaeru*, 133.

28  Ibid., 173.

29  Ibid., 17.

30  "Conference of Asians," 14.

31  Oda, ed., *Ajia o Kangaeru*, 171.

32  "Conference of Asians," 8, 11.

33  Oda, ed., *Ajia o Kangaeru*, 327.

34  Ibid., 328.

35  Inoue Sumio, "Babanuki no Riron o koete: Nihon Kagaku no Kuromu Tarenagashi to Kankoku e no Kōgai Yushutsu," *Tenbō* 204 (December 1977): 87.

36  Simon Avenell, "Regional Egoism as the Public Good: Residents' Movements in Japan during the 1960s and 1970s," *Japan Forum* 18, no. 1 (2006): 89–113.

37  Matsuoka Nobuo, "Tōnan Ajia no Tabi kara (Marēshia nite)," *Jishu Kōza* 18 (September 1972): 1–4, *FJK* 3, 345–348. On his Singapore visit see Matsuoka Nobuo, "Tōnan Ajia no Tabi kara (ni): Shingapōru nite," *Jishu Kōza* 19 (October 1972): 55–58, *FJK* 4, 59–62.

38  Matsuoka Nobuo, "Mō Hitotsu no Omoni o Seou Kakugo o: Higashi Ajia no Tabi kara (san)," *Jishu Kōza* 20 (November 1972): 38, *FJK* 4, 106.

39  Ibid., 104.

40  Ibid.

41  Matsuoka Nobuo, "Watashitachi ni Nani ga Dekirunoka," *Jishu Kōza* 24 (March 1973): 41, *FJK* 4, 379.

42  Inoue Sumio, "Exporting Pollution: Asahi Glass in Thailand," *AMPO* 18 (Autumn 1973): 39; Inoue Sumio, "Bokura wa Kōgai Yushtsu to Tatakai Hajimeta," *Tenbō* 191 (November 1974): 50.

43  Inoue, "Exporting," 39; Inoue, "Bokura," 50–51; Hirayama Takasada, "Exporting Pollution (The Export of 'KOGAI')," *KOGAI* 2 (Winter 1974): 4.

44  Hirayama, "Exporting," 3.

45  Jishu Kōza Ajia Gurūpu, "Tai Asahi Kasei Sōda no Kasen Osen," *Jishu Kōza* 31 (October 1973): 45–48, *FJK* 2–1, 375–378.

46  Inoue, "Bokura," 51.

47  Hirayama, "Exporting," 5.

48  Jishu Kōza Ajia Gurūpu, "Tai Asahi," 376.

49  Inoue, "Bokura," 52.

50  Inoue, "Exporting," 41.

51  Hirayama Takasada, "Tōnan Ajia Kōgai Saihakken no Tabi (1) Tai nite," *Jishu Kōza* 31 (October 1973): 51, *FJK* 2–1, 381.

52   Hirayama, "Tōnan," 382; Inoue, "Bokura," 50.
53   Hirayama, "Tōnan," 382.
54   Jishu Kōza Ajia Gurūpu, "Tai Asahi," 378; Inoue, "Bokura," 50; Hirayama, "Exporting," 2.
55   Inoue, "Bokura," 51.
56   Ibid.
57   Okuda Takaharu, "Nichitai o Musubu Kōgai Hantai Undō," *Jishu Kōza* 44 (November 1974): 53, *FJK* 2–4, 57.
58   Inoue, "Bokura," 52.
59   Ibid., 52–53.
60   Onodera Takuji, "9-gatsu 14-ka 'Asahi Garasu wa Tai kara Tettai seyo! Nichitai Dōji Kōdō' Hōkoku: Han-Keizai Shinryaku, Han-Kōgai Yushutsu no Kyōdō Sensen o," *GKN* 5 (October 1974): 8.
61   Inoue, "Bokura," 53.
62   Okuda, "Nichitai," 58.
63   Ibid., 53.
64   Ibid.; Okuda Takaharu, "Documents of the First Co-operation Between Japanese Citizens and Thai People Acting Simultaneously to Stop the Exporting Pollution," *KOGAI* 7 (Spring 1975): 10–11.
65   Okuda, "Nichitai," 52–53.
66   Ibid., 45.
67   Ibid., 51.
68   Ibid.
69   Ibid., 52.
70   Okuda, "Documents," 53.
71   Inoue, "Bokura," 53.
72   Okuda, "Nichitai," 57.
73   Okuda, "Nichitai," 54.
74   Ibid., 53.
75   Ibid., 45.
76   Hirayama, "Tōnan," 383.
77   Inoue, "Bokura," 54.
78   Inoue, "Bokura," 55; Hirayama Takasada, "Toyama Kagaku, Kōgai Yushutsu Chūshi!?" *Jishu Kōza* 39 (June 1974): 28, *FJK* 2–3, 94.
79   Inoue, "Bokura," 54.
80   Hirayama, "Toyama," 94.
81   Executive Committee to Stop the Toyama Chemical Co. from Exporting Pollution, "Cut Off the Path of Retreat for Pollution: The Beginning of Anti-'Pollution Exporting' Movements by Combined Forces of Japanese and Korean Citizens," *KOGAI* 7 (Spring 1975): 2.

82  Inoue, "Bokura," 55.
83  Executive Committee, "Cut Off," 4–5.
84  Hirayama, "Toyama," 93.
85  Inoue, "Bokura," 55.
86  Hirayama, "Toyama," 95.
87  Ibid., 94; Inoue, "Bokura," 55.
88  Executive Committee, "Cut Off," 7.
89  Inoue, "Babanuki," 89; Inoue, "Bokura," 56.
90  Executive Committee, "Cut Off," 3; Inoue, "Bokura," 56.
91  "Toyama Kagaku no Kōgai Yushutsu o Yamesaseru" Jikkō Iinkai, "Toyama Kagaku e no Tegami Zenbun," *GKN* 2 (July 1974): 4.
92  "Toyama Kagaku no Kōgai Yushutsu o Yamesaseru" Jikkō Iinkai, "Toyama Kagaku e no Tegami Zenbun," 4–5.
93  Inoue, "Bokura," 57; Ogawa Yoshio, "Dai 2 no Toyama Kagaku = Nihon Kagaku no Kankoku e no Kōgai Yushutsu o Yamesaseyo," *GKN* 3 (August 1974): 2.
94  Inoue, "Bokura," 58.
95  Action Committee to Stop Toyama Kagaku's Pollution Export, "The Development of the Chromium Pollution Struggle: The Voices of the People of Japan and South Korea Encircle Nihon Kagaku," *AMPO* 26 (October–December 1974): 84.
96  Inoue, "Bokura," 58.
97  Ibid., 59.
98  Ibid.
99  Ogawa, "Dai 2," 2; Hirayama Takasada, "Nihon Kagaku wa Kankoku kara Tettai seyo! Kuromu Kōgai Oshitsukeni Nikkan Ryōkoku Minshū no Ikari wa Takamaru," *Jishu Kōza* 54 (September 1975): 55, *FJK* 3–1, 245.
100 Inoue, "Babanuki," 89.
101 Masayoshi Hideo, "Nikkan no Genjō to Kōgai Yushutsu Soshi Undō," *GKN* 7 (December 1974): 1.
102 "Hokkaidō Tankōmura: Ikijigoku no naka no Chōsenjintachi," *GKN* 38 (July 1976): 41–45. Translation of 1975 article in the South Korean publication *Chukan Kyŏnghyang*. For more on Nippon Chemical's wartime misdemeanors, see Ushio Tetsuya, "Nihon Kagaku no Kankoku de no 5-gatsu Sōgyō Kaishi Soshi," *Jishu Kōza* 49 (April 1975): 54–62, *FJK* 2–4, 386–394.
103 Hirayama, "Nihon," 248.
104 Masayoshi, "Nikkan," 2.
105 Ōno Yoshio, "Yattaze 31-nichikan!" *Jishu Kōza* 55 (October 1975): 37–40, *FJK* 3–1, 291–294.

106 Hirayama, "Nihon," 231.

107 "Bokutō" refers to the three Tokyo wards of Edogawa, Kōtō, and Sumida.

108 Kawana Hideyuki, *Dokyumento Nihon no Kōgai 13: Ajia no Kankyō Hakai to Nihon* (Tokyo: Ryokufu, 1996): 101.

109 "Nihon Kagaku Dai 8-kai Kōgi Demo ni Sanka: 'Damatte irarenai' Jimoto Higaisha ga Dantai o Kessei," *Tōyō Keizai Nippō* (June 27, 1975), *GKN* 14 (July 1975): 31.

110 Ibid.

111 Ibid.

112 "'Kōgai Sangyō Kankoku Shinshutsu' Nihon de Hantai Undō," translation from original article in *Tong-A Ilbo* (August 13, 1975), *GKN* 16 (September 1975): 2.

113 "Kōgai Sangyō Dōnyū ni Shinchō o," *GKN* 16 (September 1975): 6–7. Translation from article in *Tong-A Ilbo* (August 13, 1975).

114 Okuda, "Documents," 11.

115 Yoshiwara Toshiyuki, "The Kawasaki Steel Corporation: A Case Study of Japanese Pollution Export," *KOGAI* 14 (Summer 1977): 12.

116 Kaji, "Kawasaki," 30.

117 Yoshiwara, "Kawasaki Steel Corporation,"12.

118 Kaji, "Kawasaki," 31.

119 Yoshiwara, "Kawasaki Steel Corporation," 12.

120 Kaji, "Kawasaki," 31.

121 Sakakibara Shirō, "'Shūdan no Hakken': Chiba Kōgai Juku," *Gendai no Me* 19, no. 2 (February 1978): 214.

122 Kaji, "Kawasaki," 32.

123 Ibid.

124 Kawana, *Dokyumento 13*, 102.

125 Sakakibara, "'Shūdan," 216; Akino Kaoru, "Genchi Repōto: Kawatetsu Mindanao Kōjō to Chikaku no Gyoson o Otozurete," *GKN* 149 (November–December 1985): 18; Kaji, "Kawasaki," 34.

126 Sakakibara, "'Shūdan,'" 216.

127 Kawana, *Dokyumento 13*, 102.

128 Salvatierra, "Kawasaki Steel," 25; Kaji, "Kawasaki," 35.

129 Tan Nobuhiro, "Firipin e no Kōgai Yushutsu—Kawasaki Seitetsu," *GKN* 26 (January 1976): 90.

130 Yoshiwara, "Kawasaki Steel Corporation," 18.

131 Kaji, "Kawasaki," 31.

132 Yoshiwara, "Kawasaki Steel Corporation," 17.

133 For one of the earliest reports from the sintering plant site, see Wilfredo Salvatierra, "Kawasaki Seitetsu to Firipin Kaihatsu: Nihon Kigyō Yūchi ni karamu Seiryoku Shinchō e no Omowaku kara Shinshutsu ni taisuru

Bimyō na Zure ga Umarehajimeteiru," *Gendai no Me* 16, no. 12 (December 1975): 219–225.

134 Salvatierra, "Kawasaki Steel," 23; Yoshiwara, "Kawasaki Steel Corporation," 17.

135 Salvatierra, "Kawasaki Steel," 23.

136 Ibid., 24.

137 Ibid., 25.

138 Ajia to Nihon o Kangae Kōdō suru Kai, "Ajia o Okasu Kawatetsu o Ute," *Jishu Kōza* 64 (July 1976): 11, *FJK* 3–2, 409.

139 Kawana, *Dokyumento 13*, 107.

140 Akino, "Genchi," 22.

141 Salvatierra, "Kawasaki Steel," 25.

142 Sakakibara, "'Shūdan,'" 214, 217.

143 Kawana, *Dokyumento 13*, 106.

144 Kaji, "Kawasaki," 38.

145 Kawana, *Dokyumento 13*, 106.

146 Tsukamoto Hiroki, "Kokonatsu no Mura wa Kieta," *Jishu Kōza* 69 (December 1976): 12 *FJK* 3–3, 268.

147 Ibid., 269.

148 "Tomo ni Rentai shite Tatakaō! Firipin Katoriku Shinpu wa Uttaeru," *GKN* 47 (March 1977): 6.

149 Ibid., 8.

150 Yamada Keizō, "Mindanao e no 'Kōgai Yushutsu,'" *Ushio* (December 1976): 194–203.

151 Tsukamoto, "Kokonatsu," 272.

152 Ajia to Nihon, "Ajia o Okasu," *FJK* 3–2, 410.

153 Ibid., 411.

154 Ibid.

155 "'Kōgai Yushutsu wa Yurusanu': Jūmin Dantai Tsūhō Sentā o Settchi," *Asahi Shinbun* (morning edition, April 9, 1976): 22; Yoneda Hideo, "Kōgai Yushutsu o Sasaeru Kōzō o Ute: Nihon Kagaku no Kankoku Urusan Kōjō Shigatsu Sōgyō Kaishi Soshi," *Jishu Kōza* 61 (April 1976): 24–25, *FJK* 3–2, 229–230.

156 Okuda Takaharu, "Anti-Pollution Movements Get Together to Oppose Japan's Overseas Aggression," *AMPO* 28 (April–September 1976): 10; Yamagishi Junko, "Tatakai wa Korekara da! Nihon Kagaku no Kankoku Urusan Kōjō no Sōgyō o Yamesaseyō!" *GKN* 35 (May 1976): 4; Ushio Tsunao, "4.8 Ajia e no Kōgai Yushutsu o Kokuhatsu suru Shimin Daishūkai: Hōkoku," *GKN* 35 (May 1976): 16–21.

157 "Anata no Jōshiki Watashi no Odoroki: Han Kōgai Yushutsu Tsūhō Sentā Setsuritsu," *GKN* 35 (May 1976): 24.

158 Ibid., 23–24.
159 Okuda, "Anti-Pollution," 11.
160 Tokyo Minamatabyō o Kokuhatsu suru kai, "4.25 Tokyo Minamatabyō o Kokuhatsu suru Kai no Apīru," *GKN* 35 (May 1976): 33.
161 Han-Kōgai Yushutsu Tsuhō Sentā, "Ajia no Gisei no Ue ni Naritatsu Bunmei o kyohi suru," *Jishu Kōza* 62 (May 1976): 7, *FJK* 3–2, 275.
162 Ibid.
163 4.8 "Ajia e no Kōgai Yushutsu o Kokuhatsu suru Shimin Daishūkai" Sankasha Ichidō, "Kyōdō Sengen," *GKN* 35 (May 1976): 21. Also see Michiba, "Posuto-Betonamu," 116–120.
164 Han-Kōgai, "Ajia," 271.
165 Two years later, in April 1978 (issue number 84) the Independent Lectures movement changed the title of its monthly from *Jishu Kōza* (*The Independent Lectures*) to *Tsuchi no Koe, Tami no Koe* (*Voices of the Earth, Voices of the People*), a title borrowed from the nineteenth-century Japanese antipollution activist Tanaka Shōzō, which resonated with the Third World sensitivity developing among some Japanese environmental groups.

## Chapter 5: Pacific Solidarity and Atomic Aggression

1 "2.28 Hangenpatsu-Hansaishori-Hankaiyō Tōki: Tokyo Shūkai o Seikō saseyō," *Tsuchi no Koe, Tami no Koe Gōgai Kaku Haikibutsu Kaiyō Tōki Hantai Undō Tokushū* (hereafter *TKTG*) 6 (February 1981): 2.
2 Bedor quoted in Nakamura Ryōji, "Sekine Hama no 'Mutsu' Shinbokōka o Yurusanai," *Tsuchi no Koe, Tami no Koe* (hereafter *TKT*) 123 (August 1981): 5.
3 For uses of this metaphor see Kume Sanshirō, "Genshiryoku Hatsuden no Anzensei to Jūmin Undō," *Kankyō to Kōgai* 4, no. 1 (1974): 46; Mizuguchi Ken'ya, "Hōshasei Haikibutsu no Kaiyō Tōki o Yurusuna (Jō): Tairyō no Hōshanō Tarenagashi no Kikensei," *Hangenpatsu Shinbun* 29 (September 1980): 4, in *"Hangenpatsu Shinbun" Shukusatsuban (0–100)* (hereafter *HGS*), ed. Hangenpatsu Undō Zenkoku Renrakukai (Nara: Yasōsha, 1986), 144.
4 William M. Alley and Rosemarie Alley, *Too Hot to Touch: The Problem of High-Level Nuclear Waste* (Cambridge: Cambridge University Press, 2012), 16.
5 Naikakufu Genshiryoku Seisaku Tantōshitsu, *Hōshasei Haikibutsu no Shori-Shobun o Meguru Torikumi no Genjō ni tsuite,* document no. 3–1 (March 8, 2001), 8.
6 On waste in Japan see Kirby, *Troubled Natures.*
7 Naikakufu, *Hōshasei,* 8.
8 Alley and Alley, *Too Hot,* 37.

9   See Aoyama Tadashi, "Kaku Haikibutsu no Taiheiyō Tōki o Yurusuna! Moriagaru Shomei Undō," *GKN* 93 (August 1980): 1.

10  David A. Snow and Robert D. Benford, "Master Frames and Cycles of Protest," in *Frontiers in Social Movement Theory,* ed. Aldon D. Morris and Carol McClurg Mueller (New Haven: Yale University Press, 1992), 141.

11  Robert D. Benford and David A. Snow, "Framing Processes and Social Movements: An Overview and Assessment," *Annual Review of Sociology* 26 (2000): 621.

12  Maeda Tetsuo, "Kaku to Taiheiyō: Ima, Watashitachi ni totte no Mondai," *TKT* 97 (April 1979): 22.

13  Yokoyama Masaki, "Hankaku-Dokuritsu Taiheiyō Kaigi '83 Banuatsu Kaigi: Shōten to natta Dokuritsu Tōsō," *GKN* 125 (August 1983): 7; David Robie, *Blood on Their Banner: Nationalist Struggles in the South Pacific* (London: Zed Books, 1989), 142.

14  On ocean dumping of radioactive waste see Jacob Darwin Hamblin, *Poison in the Well: Radioactive Waste in the Oceans at the Dawn of the Nuclear Age* (Piscataway, NJ: Rutgers University Press, 2008).

15  Alley and Alley, *Too Hot,* 34–35.

16  Ibid., 35.

17  Ibid., 36.

18  Aoyama, "Kaku," 2.

19  Kawana Hideyuki, *Dokyumento Nihon no Kōgai 12: Chikyū Kankyō no Kiki* (Tokyo: Ryokufu, 1995), 351–352.

20  Alley and Alley, *Too Hot,* 36.

21  Kawana, *Dokyumento 12,* 351–352. On the *Topaz* see Hamblin, "Gods," 539–560.

22  Alley and Alley, *Too Hot,* 39.

23  Kawana, *Dokyumento 12,* 352.

24  Ibid.

25  The geographic coordinates of the dumping sites (1955–1969) are available at "Wagakuni no Kaiyō Tōki Chūshi ni itaru Keii," contained in *Genshiryoku Hyakka Jiten ATOMICA,* Kōdo Jōhō Kagaku Gijutsu Kenkyū Kikō (RIST), accessed May 28, 2014, http://www.rist.or.jp/atomica/data/dat_detail.php ?Title_Key=05–01–03–11. See Chart 1 on this webpage.

26  Ishikawa Haruo, "Kaku Haikibutsu no Kaiyō Tōki Keikaku: 'Anzen' nante Tondemonai," *GKN* 94 (September 1980): 6.

27  Kawana, *Dokyumento 12,* 353.

28  Ibid., 354.

29  Saitō Tamotsu, "Hōshasei Haikibutsu no Kaiyō Tōki ni Hantai suru," *TKT* 112 (August 1980): 15; Kawana, *Dokyumento 12,* 354–355.

30 James B. Branch, "The Waste Bin: Nuclear Waste Dumping and Storage in the Pacific," *Ambio* 13, no. 5/6 (1984): 327; Saitō, "Hōshasei," 15; and "Wagakuni no Kaiyō Tōki," in *Genshiryoku Hyakka Jiten,* http://www.rist.or .jp/atomica/data/dat_detail.php?Title_Key=05–01–03–11, accessed May 28, 2014.

31 Kawana, *Dokyumento 12,* 354–355.

32 Ibid., 370; Genshiryoku Iinkai, "Hōshasei Haikibutsu Taisaku ni tsuite," *Genshiryoku Iinkai Geppō* 21, no. 10 (1976), Japan Atomic Energy Commission Homepage, accessed May 28, 2014, http://www.aec.go.jp/jicst /NC/about/ugoki/geppou/V21/N10/197600V21N10.html#menu_top.

33 Shimin no Te de Nikkan yuchaku o Tadasu Chōsa Undō—Jishu Kōza Jikkō Iinkai, "Kinkyū Apīru: Kaku Nenryō Saishori Kōjō o Kankoku ni Oshitsukeruna! Ajia-Taiheiyō Minshū ni Tekitai suru Nikkan no Kaku Busō—Kan-Taiheiyō Genshiryoku Kyōdōtai Kōsō Jitsugen e no Michi o Yurusuna!" *GKN* 97 (January 1981): 11; Tateno Kōichi and Saitō Tamotsu, "Saishori Kōjō Kensetsu o Yurusanai Amami—Okinawa Jūmin no Sensei Kōgeki," *TKT* 108 (April 1980): 28.

34 Yamaka Junko, "Pacific Islanders Oppose Japan's Nuclear Imperialism," *AMPO* 47 (April–September 1981), 33.

35 Zenkoku Genshiryoku Kagaku Gijutsusha Rengō, "Genshiryoku Kaihatsu to Kōgai Mondai," *Kankyō to Kōgai* 2, no. 1 (July 1972): 21.

36 *GKN* 92 (July 1980): 6 [No title or author given].

37 Alley and Alley, *Too Hot,* 37.

38 Roman Bedor and Jishu Kōza, "Roman's Tour of Europe: Pacific Problems Delivered to Their Source," *No Nuke News Japan* (hereafter NNJ) 16 (1983): 4.

39 Ibid.

40 Yamaka Junko, "N. Mariana Gov. Camacho Presents Anti-Dumping Petition to Diet," *NNJ* 2 (June 1981): 2.

41 Yokoyama Masaki, "Kaku Haikibutsu no Kaiyō Tōki Hantai Undō: Taiheiyō Shotō no Jūmin no Baai," *Kōgai Kenkyū* 10, no. 4 (April 1981): 22.

42 Ibid.

43 Ibid., 23.

44 Arakawa Shunji, "Genchi Repōto 1: Mikuroneshia kara no Chokugen: Nihon no Kaku Tōki Keikaku o Megutte," *GKN* 93 (August 1980): 5.

45 Yokoyama, "Kaku," 23.

46 Ibid.

47 Ibid.; Yamaka, "Pacific," 34.

48 Kaku Haikibutsu no Kaiyō Tōki ni Hantai suru Mariana Dōmei, "Nihon no Tomo e: Mariana Dōmei kara no Tegami," *TKT* 3 (October 1980): 3.

49 Yamaka, "Pacific," 34.

50 On the forum see Aki Yukio, "Hikaku Taiheiyō Fōramu demo Kaiyō Tōki o Hinan," *Hangenpatsu Shinbun* 31 (November 1980): 2, *HGS,* 152.

51 Aki, "'Hikaku Taiheiyō Fōramu demo," 25.

52 Yokoyama Masaki, "Kaku," 24.

53 "Minami Taiheiyō e Setsumeidan: Hōshasei Haikibutsu Tōki Keikaku Seifu Haken Kimeru," *Asahi Shinbun* (morning edition, August 6, 1980): 1.

54 "'Sakana' ka 'Kaku' ka: Hōshasei Haikibutsu no Tōki. 'Nemawashi' Okure no Kagichō ni Fushin o Kakusanu Suisanchō," *Mainichi Shinbun* (August 9, 1980), *GKN* 92 (July 1980): 3.

55 Kawana, *Dokyumento 12,* 373.

56 "Minami Taiheiyō," 4.

57 Kawana, *Dokyumento 12,* 378.

58 On this event see Arakawa Shunji, "Hantai Ketsugi o Tsukitsukerareta Nihon Seifu no 'Setsumeidan,'" *GKN* 94 (September 1980): 10–13.

59 Kawana, *Dokyumento 12,* 373–374.

60 Ibid., 375.

61 Ibid., 376.

62 Yokoyama, "Kaku," 24.

63 Kawana, *Dokyumento 12,* 378.

64 Yokoyama, "Kaku," 24; Kawana, *Dokyumento 12,* 379.

65 Ogasawara Umi o Mamoru Kai, "Kaku no Gomi o Sutesaseruna! Dasaseruna! Kaiyō Tōki Hantai ni Kakuji de Tachagaru. Ogasawara no Utsukushi Umi o Yogosuna!" *Hangenpatsu Shinbun* 31 (November 1980): 1, *HGS,* 151.

66 Matsumura Naoki, "Uran wa Iranai: Ōsutoraria Fukushushō e Yōsei," *Jishu Kōza* 60 (March 1976): 8, *FJK* 3–2, 148.

67 In Japanese: *Geppō Kōgai o Nogasuna! Daisan Sekai e no Kōgai Yushutsu o Kokuhatsu suru* 118 (November–December 1982).

68 In Japanese: *Geppō Hankaku Taiheiyō Pashifika: Nihon no Shinryaku ni Kōshite Ajia Taiheiyō Minshū to tomo ni* 153 (June 1986).

69 Yokoyama Masaki, "Taiheiyō kara Kaku o Nakusō! 3–1 Tokyo Shūkai," *TKT* 97 (April 1979): 18.

70 Ibid., 18.

71 See *TKTG* 1 (August 1980): 4.

72 "Hōshasei Haikibutsu no Taiheiyō Tōki: Shimin Dantai mo 'Hantai.' Kagichō ni Keikaku Tekkai Motomeru," *Mainichi Shinbun* (Aug 10, 1980), *GKN* 92 (July 1980): 2.

73 Ibid.

74 "Watashitachi ga Motomete iru no wa, Keikaku no Hakushi tekkai da: Dai-ikki Shomei Teishutsu—45,134-mei no Koe Seifu e," *TKTG* 6 (February 1981): 6.

75  Roman Bedor, "Sekai no Subete no Minshū e no Apīru: Taiheiyō ni Okeru Furansu no Kaku Jikken to Nihon no Kaku Haikibutsu Tōki Keikaku ni Hantai suru Sekai Kibo no Shomei Undō o Uttaeru," *TKT* 13 (September 1981): 3.

76  "Kirisutosha no Shomei: Kagakugijutsuchō e," *TKTG* 6 (February 1981): 7.

77  Ibid.

78  Gyomin Kenkyūkai, "Hirogaru Gyomin no Tatakai: 6–21 Umi o Yogosuna! Gyomin Shūkai to 6–22 Kaiyō Tōki Hantai Shomei Teishutsu Kōdō no Hōkoku," *TKT* 11 (July 1981): 4.

79  Arakawa Shunji and Ōkawa Hōsaku, "Amami-Okinawa-Sanrizuka to Parao-Guamu o Musubu Tabi kara," *TKTG* 6 (February 1981): 3.

80  See *TKT* 119 (March 1981): 2.

81  Arakawa and Ōkawa, "Amami," *TKTG* 6 (February 1981): 4.

82  *Kuroshio Tsūshin: Taiheiyō Shotō Rentai o Motomete!* 1 (Fall 1981), *GKN* 98 (February 1981): 18.

83  Taiheiyō o Kaku no Gomi Suteba ni suru na! 10.22 Tokyo Shūkai Sankasha Ichidō, "Nihon-Amami-Okinawa Minshū no Apīru," *TKT* 115 (November 1980): 11.

84  "'Kaku Kagaisha ni naru Osore': Gensuikin Taikai Bunkakai Tōgi Nihon no Haikibutsu Tōki," *Asahi Shinbun* (morning edition, August 3, 1980): 22; Yokoyama Masaki, "Suzuki Shinseiken no Genshiryoku Seisaku to Hōshanō Osen no Yushutsu," *TKT* 113 (September 1980): 17.

85  Yamaka, "Pacific," 34.

86  "Hōshasei Haikibutsu no Taiheiyō Tōki: Nihon wa Keikaku Chūshi seyo. Saipan Shichō Rainichi, Uttae," *Mainichi Shinbun* (August 1, 1980), *TKTG* 1 (August 1980): 4.

87  Yamaka, "Pacific," 35; Felipe Mendiola, "Nihon Seifu ni Naguraretemo Iimasu: Kaku no Gomi o Watashitachi no Umi ni Suteruna!" *TKT* 115 (November 1980): 2.

88  Aoyama, "Kaitōki," 1.

89  Felipe Mendiola, "Tenian kara no Uttae: Nihon Seifu wa Doko made Watashitachi o Fumitsubuseba Ki ga Sumunoka!" *GKN* 96 (November–December 1980): 2.

90  Ibid., 4.

91  Arakawa Shunji, "Kaku Haikibutsu no Taiheiyō Tōki Hantai o Uttaeru: F. Mendiora-san (Tenian)," *Hangenpatsu Shinbun* 31 (November 1980): 3, *HGS*, 153.

92  Ibid.; Mendiola, "Nihon," 2, 3.

93  Mendiola, "Nihon," 3.

94  Arakawa, "Kaku," 153.

95  "Kaku Haikibutsu Tōki, Shima Agete Soshi: Teniantō Shichō ga Tsuyoi Ketsui," *Asahi Shinbun* (morning edition, October 14, 1980): 22; Mendiola, "Tenian," 8.

96  Arakawa Shunji, "Ignatio Giin (Parao) Seiryokuteki ni Kyanpēn," *TKTG* 7 (March 1981): 4; Han-Genpatsu News Editorial Committee Jishu Kōza, "Unifying the Nuclear Struggle: Belauan Keynotes to Tokyo Rally," *NNJ* 0 (April 1981): 2; Ignatio Anastacio, "Utsukushii Shizen o Mamori, Tomo ni Ikiyō," *TKT* 120 (April 1981): 12.

97  Anastacio, "Utsukushii," 13.

98  Ibid., 12.

99  Han-Genpatsu News, "Unifying," 2.

100  Ibid.

101  Ibid; Anastacio, "Utsukushii," 14.

102  Anastacio, "Utsukushii," 14.

103  Ibid., 14–15.

104  For Meyer's schedule see *TKTG* 7 (March 1981): 8; and *TKTG* 8 (April 1981): 4–6.

105  Inose Kōhei, "Genshiryoku Teikoku e no Taikō Seiji ni Mukatte: Kubokawa Genpatsu Hantai Undō o Tegakari ni," *Puraimu* 35 (March 2012): 71–91.

106  Kōno Masayoshi, "Shiten," *TKT* 120 (April 1981): 1.

107  Nakajima Ryūji, "Amerika ni Tayoranakutemo Yatte ikeru," *TKTG* 9 (May 1981): 8.

108  Ichikawa Hiroshi, "Parao kara Meyer-san o Mukaete: Soko ga Muzukashii!" *TKTG* 9 (May 1981): 9.

109  Ibid.

110  Machi to Seikatsu o Kangaeru Shimin Sentā, "Taiheiyō wa 'Mijikana' Watashitachi no Umi da: Parao kara Meyer-shi o Mukaete," *TKTG* 8 (April 1981): 5.

111  Ibid.

112  Katō Takashi, "Meyer-shi Raisatsu o Ki ni Zenshin shita Hangenpatsu Tōsō," *TKTG* 8 (April 1981): 6.

113  Yamaka, "N. Mariana," 1.

114  Ibid., 2–3.

115  Ibid.

116  Ibid., 4.

117  "Zensekai Sūhyakuman-nin no Kōgi no Koe o Tazusae: Kita Mariana— Camacho-chijira Kokkai Seigan e," *TKTG* 10 (June 1981): 3; Yamaka, "N. Mariana," 2.

118  Yamaka, "N. Mariana," 2.

119 Roman Bedor, "Seizon no tame no Wareware no Tatakai," *TKT* 113 (September 1980): 13.

120 Ibid.

121 Yamate Noboru, "Aborijinī Hakugai ni Te o Kasu Nihon Shihon: Ōsutoraria no Uran Kaihatsu Hantai Undō ni Rentai suru," *GKN* 96 (Nov-Dec 1980): 28–29.

122 Roman Bedor, "Roman Bedor Speech at Anti-AMPO Rally in Tokyo, June 7, 1981," *NNJ* 3–4 (July–August 1981): 6.

123 Bedor, "Seizon," 13.

124 Bedor and Jishu Kōza, "Roman's Tour," 2–3.

125 Friends of the Earth, Berlin, "Message from Friends of the Earth, Berlin," *NNJ* 17 (1983): 8–9.

126 Ibid.

127 Yokoyama, "Kaku," 22.

128 Branch, "Waste Bin," 329.

129 "'Kaku Haikibutsu no Tōki o Tōketsu Bōeiryoku Zōkyō wa Senshu Tsuranuku': Setsumei o Ryōkoku Kangei," *Asahi Shinbun* (morning edition, January 15, 1985): 1; Kawana, *Dokyumento 12*," 379.

130 Hankaku Pashifiku Sentā Tokyo Ichidō, "Kaku no nai Taiheiyō o Mezashite Ganbarimasu! Hankaku Pashifiku Sentā Hossoku shimashita," *GKG* 151 (February 1986): 1.

131 "Kaku no nai Taiheiyō o Tsukuridasō 3.1 Tokyo Shūkai" Sankasha Ichidō, "Watashitachi no Hankaku Taiheiyō Sengen," *GKN* 151 (February 1986): 2.

132 Han-Genpatsu News Editorial Committee Jishu Kōza, "Editorial," *NNJ* 0 (April 1981): 1.

133 Hankaku-Hangenpatsu-Hansaishori o Tatakau 7-gatsu Kōdō Jikkō Iinkai, "7.3 Shūkai Mondai Teiki," *TKT* 112 (August 1980): 25.

134 Yokoyama, "Kaku," 26.

135 Yokoyama Masaki, "Taiheiyō Shominzoku no Hankaku-Dokuritsu Undō: Ponape Kaigi ni Sanka shite," *TKT* 93 (January 1979): 18.

## Chapter 6: Globality through Local Eyes

1   Kawana, *Dokyumento 12*, 65; Atsuko Sato, "Beyond Boundaries: Japan, Knowledge, and Transnational Networks in Global Atmospheric Politics" (PhD diss., University of Hawai'i, 2002), 233.

2   Historical temperature data obtained from http://climate.weather.gc.ca/.

3   Thomas A. Sancton, "Cover Stories: What on Earth Are We Doing?" *Time* 133, no. 1 (January 2, 1989): 24, available at Academic Search Complete, EBSCOhost (accessed May 14, 2014).

4   Katō Saburō, Takeuchi Ken, Awaji Kōji, Akiyama Noriko, Teranishi Shun'ichi, Kihara Keikichi, "1992 Kokuren Kankyō Kaihatsu Kaigi to Nihon no Kadai," *Kankyō to Kōgai* 20, no. 4 (April 1991): 31.

5   Sancton, "Cover," 24. *Time*'s break with tradition was noted in the Japanese press: " 'Kotoshi no Hito' wa 'Kiki ni sarasareta Chikyū': Kankyō Osen no Shinkokuka ni Keishō," *Asahi Shinbun* (morning edition, December 26, 1988): 7.

6   Ishi Hiroyuki, Okajima Shigeyuki, and Hara Takeshi, *Tettei Tōron: Chikyū Kankyō Jyānarisuto no "Genba" kara* (Tokyo: Fukutake Shoten, 1992), 78–79.

7   Kawana, *Dokyumento 12*, 71; Ishi et al., *Tettei*, 77; " 'Kankyō Gannen' Chikyūjin no Jikaku o," *Asahi Shinbun* (morning edition, November 20, 1989): 15.

8   Kawana, *Dokyumento 12*, 77.

9   See Carol White and Rogelio Maduro, " 'Greenhouse Effect' Hoaxsters Seek World Dictatorship," *EIR: Executive Intelligence Review* 16, no. 3 (January 13, 1989): 31–32.

10  On Japanese involvement in the WCED and the concept of "sustainable development," see Miranda Schreurs, "Shifting Priorities and the Internationalization of Environmental Risk Management in Japan," in *Learning to Manage Global Environmental Risks, Volume 2: A Functional Analysis of Social Responses to Climate Change, Ozone Depletion, and Acid Rain,* ed. Social Learning Group (Cambridge, MA: MIT Press, 2001), 191–212; Reimann, *Rise;* and Kawana, *Dokyumento 12*, 11–14.

11  Clapp and Dauvergne, *Paths*, 60.

12  Gary Haq and Alistair Paul, *Environmentalism since 1945* (London: 2012), 31.

13  Clapp and Dauvergne, *Paths*, 60–61. On sustainable development see Anne E. Egelston, *Sustainable Development: A History* (New York: Springer, 2006); and Dryzek, *Politics*, 145–161.

14  Clapp and Dauvergne, *Paths*, 60–61.

15  Thiele, *Environmentalism*, 128.

16  Miyamoto Ken'ichi discusses his idea of "endogenous development" in Miyamoto Ken'ichi, *Kankyō Keizaigaku* (Tokyo: Iwanami Shoten, 1989), 273–311. On "global environmental governance," see Rosaleen Duffy, "Non-governmental Organisations and Governance States: The Impact of Transnational Environmental Management Networks in Madagascar," *Environmental Politics* 15, no. 5 (2006): 731–749.

17  Avenell, "Japan's Long," 423–444.

18  Miranda Schreurs, "Assessing Japan's Role as a Global Environmental Leader," *Policy and Society* 23, no. 1 (2004): 99.

19  Sato, "Beyond," 253.

20  Ibid., 344–345.

21  For details on CASA see Chikyū Kankyō to Taiki Osen o Kangaeru Zenkoku Shimin Kaigi (CASA), "Chikyū Kankyō to Taiki Osen o

Kangaeru Zenkoku Shimin Kaigi—Citizens' Alliance for Saving the Atmosphere and the Earth," accessed May 16, 2014, http://www.bnet.jp /casa/.

22 Yamamura Tsunetoshi, *Kankyō NGO* (Tokyo: Shinzansha Shuppan, 1998), 22.

23 Ibid.

24 For the proceedings, see Kankyōchō Chikyū Kankyōbu Kikakuka, *Tokyo Conference on the Global Environment and Human Response toward Sustainable Development* (Tokyo: Gyōsei, 1990).

25 On these symposia see Kawana, *Dokyumento 12,* 148; Hayakawa Mitsutoshi, "Chikyū Kankyō to Taiki Osen o Kangaeru Kokusai Shimin Shinpojiumu no Hōkoku," *Kankyō to Kōgai* 19, no. 3 (January 1990): 63.

26 Ibid., 63.

27 On this event see Kawana, *Dokyumento 12,* 148; Reimann, *Rise,* 140; Ikeda Susumu, "Chikyū Kankyō Shimin Kaigi Hōkoku," *Kankyō to Kōgai* 19, no. 3 (January 1990): 64; Iwasaki Shunsuke, "Chikyū Junkan to Dai-3 Sekai o Utsu Seichō to Kaihatsu," *Kōmei* 334 (November 1989): 106.

28 Ibid.

29 Ikeda, "Chikyū," 64.

30 The group's Japanese name was "92 Kokuren Burajiru Kaigi Shimin Renraku Kai," which translates as "the '92 UN Brazil Conference Citizens' Liaison Association." See "Shimin Dantai ga Renraku Kessei, Teigen matome Daihyōdan: 92-nen 6-gatsu Chikyū Samitto," *Asahi Shinbun* (morning edition, May 26, 1991): 3.

31 Ichihara Akane, "Chikyū Samitto Hōkoku: '92 Gurōbaru Fōramu ni Sanka shite," *Cures Newsletter* 24 (August 1992): 5; Kawana, *Dokyumento 12,* 151; Iwasaki Shunsuke, "Kaihatsu to Kankyō: Chikyū Samitto o Shimin kara Tō," *Heiwa Keizai* 367 (June 1992): 15–16.

32 Iwasaki Shunsuke, "'Sekai Kankyō Kaigi' de Nihon wa Nani o Shuchō dekiruka: Posuto Reisen de sarani Jūyō ni natta Konseiki Saigo no Kankyō Samitto no Kadai," *Ushio* 394 (January 1992): 137.

33 "Kokunai no NGO, Senshinkoku no Sekinin Kyōchō shi Chikyū Samitto e Teigen (Osaka)," *Asahi Shinbun* (evening edition, December 12, 1991): 18.

34 92 Kokuren Burajiru Kaigi Shimin Renraku Kai, "92 Kokuren Burajiru Kaigi Shimin Renraku Kai kara no Teigen," *Kōgai Kenkyū* 21, no. 4 (April 1992): 59.

35 "Shinrin Hakai de Nihon ni Chūmon: NGO Fōramu Kaimaku Chikyū Samitto," *Asahi Shinbun* (morning edition, May 2, 1992): 26.

36 Iwasaki Shunsuke, *NGO wa Hito to Chikyū o Musubu: Ima Kokkyō o Koete, Dekiru Koto, Surubeki Koto* (Tokyo: Daisan Shokan, 1993), 61.

37 Ibid.

38   Important primary sources are the Kanagawa Declaration; "The People's
     Voice of Japan: I Have the Earth in Mind, the Earth Has Me in Hand";
     and The Japanese Citizens' Earth Charter. On the Kanagawa Declaration,
     see Kawana, *Dokyumento 12*, 152; " 'Jūmin Shuken' Kakuritsu Motome
     Sengen: NGO Fōramu Heimaku Yokohama," *Asahi Shinbun* (morning
     edition, May 4, 1992): 26; Iwasaki, *NGO wa*, 61–64. On "The People's
     Voice of Japan: I Have the Earth in Mind, the Earth Has Me in Hand,"
     see 92 Kokuren, "92 Kokuren," 57; Kawana, *Dokyumento 12*, 151; and for
     a full English version, 92 NGO Forum Japan, "People's Voice of Japan: I
     Have the Earth in Mind, The Earth Has Me in Hand," contained on
     *Earth Summit: The NGO Archives* (Hamilton, Canada: CCOHS, 1995),
     CD ROM. For the Japanese Citizens' Earth Charter, see 92 Kokuren
     Burajiru Kaigi Shimin Renraku Kai, *Shimin no Chikyū Kenshō* (Tokyo:
     Iwanami Shoten, 1992).
39   Iwasaki, *NGO wa*, 62, 72.
40   Ibid., 62.
41   92 Kokuren, *Shimin*, 9.
42   Ibid., 9–10.
43   Iwasaki, *NGO wa*, 64.
44   Ibid.
45   92 NGO, *People's Voice*, 133.
46   Ibid.
47   Iwasaki, *NGO wa*, 62.
48   See Oda Makoto, "Nanshi no Shisō," in Oda Makoto, *Oda Makoto
     Zenshigoto* 8 (Tokyo: Kawade Shobō Shinsha, 1970), 13–31.
49   92 NGO, *People's Voice*, 127–128.
50   Ibid., 129.
51   Ibid.
52   92 Kokuren, *Shimin*, 24.
53   92 NGO, *People's Voice*, 8; 92 Kokuren, *Shimin*, 5.
54   Iwasaki, *NGO wa*, 62.
55   " 'Jūmin Shuken,' " 26.
56   See United Nations Department of Information, "UN Conference on
     Environment and Development (1992)," accessed May 15, 2014, http://www
     .un.org/geninfo/bp/enviro.html.
57   Haq and Paul, *Environmentalism*, 31–32; Clapp and Dauvergne, *Paths*, 64.
58   Clapp and Dauvergne, *Paths*, 64–65.
59   See United Nations, "UN Conference." Also quoted in Haq and Paul,
     *Environmentalism*, 33.
60   Haq and Paul, *Environmentalism*, 32.
61   Kawana, *Dokyumento 12*, 133.

62 Honda Masakazu, "'Bideo Sanka' no Kokusai Onchido: Kyokushiteki 'Chikyū Samitto'ron," in *Chikyū Samitto Live in Rio,* ed. Yamazaki Kōichi (Tokyo: Asahi Shinbunsha, 1992), 120.

63 Clapp and Dauvergne, *Paths,* 66.

64 Ibid.

65 92 Kokuren, "92 Kokuren," 55.

66 Yamamoto Kazuhiko, "'Chikyū Samitto' no Giman," *Gijutsu to Ningen* 21, no. 6 (June 1992): 10.

67 Ramachandra Guha, *Environmentalism: A Global History* (New York: Longman, 2000), 143.

68 Ibid., 141–142.

69 Quoted ibid., 143.

70 Yonemoto Shōhei, *Chikyū Kankyō Mondai to wa Nanika* (Tokyo: Iwanami Shoten, 1994), 148; Amano Reiko, "Waga Nippon no 'Osamui' Genjitsu: Japan Day Jiken ga 'Nagaragawa' o Sekai ni Shiraseta," in *Chikyū Samitto,* ed. Yamazaki, 110.

71 Yonemoto, *Chikyū,* 148.

72 Centre for Applied Studies in International Negotiations Issues and Non-Governmental Organizations Programme, "Report on NGO Activities at the United Nations Conference on Environment and Development and the Global Forum, Rio de Janeiro, 1–14 June 1992," *Earth Summit* CD ROM.

73 Ichihara, "Chikyū," 5.

74 Yonemoto, *Chikyū,* 148; Centre for Applied Studies, "Report."

75 Kikuchi Yumi, "NGO Jōyaku-zukuri no Genba kara," *Kankyō to Kōgai* 22, no. 1 (September 1992): 39.

76 Centre for Applied Studies, "Report."

77 Sujata Madhok, "Graffiti Greens the Forum" (June 13, 1992), in *Women's Feature Service (WFS) coverage of UNCED,* contained in *Earth Summit* CD ROM.

78 Yamazaki, ed., *Chikyū Samitto,* 4; Centre for Applied Studies, "Report."

79 For a list of the Japanese and other Asian NGOs that attended the Global Forum, see Yamazaki, ed., *Chikyū Samitto,* 225–226.

80 Kawana, *Dokyumento 12,* 153.

81 Ichihara, "Chikyū," 5.

82 Ui Jun, "Kakumo Yutakana Shizen no naka no, Kakumo Shinkokuna Hinkon: '72 Sutokkuhorumu kara '92 Rio e," in *Chikyū Samitto,* ed. Yamazaki, 101.

83 Ibid., 102.

84 Ibid., 101.

85 Amano, "Waga," 110.

86  Kawana, *Dokyumento 12,* 154.

87  On sunlight rights see Osaka Bengoshikai, *Nisshōken no Tebiki* (Osaka: Osaka Bengoshikai, 1981). On environmental rights see Osaka Bengoshikai Kankyōken Kenkyūkai, *Kankyōken.* (Tokyo: Nihon Hyōronsha, 1973).

88  See Kawana, *Dokyumento 13,* 111–144.

89  Nichibenren, "'92 NGO Gurōbaru Fōramu Nichibenren Shusai Shinpojiumu—Exchanging the Ideas about International Environmental Law," *Jiyū to Seigi* 43, no. 11 (November 1992): 116.

90  Ibid., 115.

91  Nichibenren, *UN Earth Summit/Global Forum 1992: Japanese Lawyers' Environmental Struggle,* Conference Recordings RIO92–046, 1992, cassette tape; Nichibenren, "'92 NGO," 112–116.

92  Kawana, *Dokyumento 12,* 154.

93  "Kankyō NGO to no Nininsankyaku o," *Asahi Shinbun* (morning edition, June 3, 1993): 2.

94  The organization's Japanese name is Kankyō Jizoku Shakai Kenkyū Sentā. See JACSES, "Japan Center for a Sustainable Environment and Society (JACSES)," accessed May 16, 2014, http://www.jacses.org/en/index.html.

95  Iwasaki Shunsuke, "NGO (Hiseifu Soshiki) ga Mezasu mono: Kokkyō o Koeru Shimin Sanka," *Kōmei* 318 (July 1988): 56.

96  Iwasaki Shunsuke, Kobayashi Akira, Okajima Nariyuki, Takeuchi Yuzuru, Hara Takeshi, Teranishi Shun'ichi, and Awaji Kōji, "'92 Kokuren Burajiru Kaigi to Nihon no NGO," *Kōgai Kenkyū* 21, no. 2 (October 1991): 42.

97  See Japan International Volunteer Center, "Specified Non-Profit Organization: Japan International Volunteer Center," accessed May 16, 2014, http://www.ngo-jvc.net/en/.

98  Iwasaki et al., "'92 Kokuren," 42; Iwasaki, "Kaihatsu," 14.

99  Iwasaki Shunsuke, "Ajia no Inaka kara Nihon no Ciiki o Miru," *Gekkan Jichi Kenkyū* 30, no. 10 (October 1988): 24.

100 Iwasaki, "'Sekai,'" 133.

101 Iwasaki, "Ajia," 19.

102 Iwasaki, "'Sekai,'" 136; Iwasaki, *NGO wa,* 61.

103 Iwasaki, "Ajia," 24.

104 Iwasaki, "NGO (Hiseifu Soshiki)," 56.

105 Ibid., 56–57.

106 Iwasaki Shunsuke, "Shimin ni yoru Kokusai Kyōryoku (NGO)," *Tsukuba Fōramu* 28–32 (March 1990): 71.

107 Iwasaki, *NGO wa,* 1.

108 Ibid., 3, 77.

109 Ibid., 4.

110 Ibid., 74.

111 Ibid., 2.

112 Iwasaki, "NGO (Hiseifu Soshiki)," 60.

113 Asahi Shinbun "Chikyū Samitto" Shuzaihan, *"Chikyū Samitto" Handobukku* (Tokyo: Asahi Shinbunsha, 1992), 39.

114 Iwasaki, "Ajia," 24.

115 Iwasaki, *NGO wa,* 51.

116 Ibid., 52.

117 Iwasaki, "'Sekai,'" 137.

118 Iwasaki et al., "'92 Kokuren," 47.

119 Iwasaki, *NGO wa,* 52.

120 Ibid., 52–53.

121 On Japanese logging, see Peter Dauvergne, *Shadows in the Forest: Japan and the Politics of Timber in Southeast Asia* (Cambridge, MA: MIT Press, 1997); Anny Wong, "The Anti-Tropical Timber Campaign in Japan," in *Environmental Movements in Asia,* ed. Arne Kalland and Gerard Persoon (Surrey: Curzon Press, 1998), 131–150; Anny Wong, *The Roots of Japan's International Environmental Policies* (New York: Garland Publishing, 2001); Joshua Karliner, *The Corporate Planet: Ecology and Politics in the Age of Globalization* (San Francisco: Sierra Club Books, 1997), 123–128; François Nectoux and Yoichi Kuroda, *Timber from the South Seas: An Analysis of Japan's Tropical Timber Trade and Its Environmental Impact* (London: Banson, 1990); Nihon Bengoshi Rengōkai Kōgai Taisaku-Kankyō Hozen Iinkai, ed., *Nihon no Kōgai Yushutsu to Kankyō Hakai* (Tokyo: Nihon Hyōronsha, 1991); Kuroda Yōichi, *Nettairin Hakai to Tatakau: Mori ni Ikiru Hitobito to Nihon* (Tokyo: Iwanami Shoten, 1992).

122 On this organization, see Shimin Enerugī Kenkyūjo, "Shimin Enerugī Kenkyūjo—People's Research Institute on Energy and Environment," accessed May 16, 2014, http://www.priee.org/.

123 Kuroda, *Nettairin Hakai,* 64.

124 Kuroda, *Nettairin Hakai,* 12; Kuroda Yōichi, "Nettairin no Kiki to Nihon Shakai no Shinro," *Kankyō to Kōgai* 21, no. 1 (July 1991): 11; Wong, "The Anti-Tropical," 140.

125 Wong, "The Anti-Tropical," 140; Kuroda, *Nettairin Hakai,* 12.

126 Kuroda, "Nettairin no Kiki," 11.

127 Nectoux and Kuroda, *Timber.* The Japanese-language version: Kuroda Yōichi and François Nectoux, *Nettairin Hakai to Nihon no Mokuzai Bōeki: Sekai Shizen Hogo Kikin (WWF) Repōto* (Tokyo: Tsukiji Shokan, 1989).

128 Kuroda, *Nettairin Hakai,* 39–40.

129 Ibid., 13.

130 Ibid., 13, 50; Wong, "The Anti-Tropical," 141.

131 Kuroda, *Nettairin Hakai,* 50–51.

132 Wong, "The Anti-Tropical," 142.
133 Kuroda, *Nettairin Hakai,* 5.
134 Guha, *Environmentalism,* 124.
135 Ibid.
136 Kuroda, *Nettairin Hakai,* 3.
137 Wong, *Roots,* 189.
138 Kuroda, *Nettairin Hakai,* 60.
139 Ibid., 61.
140 Ibid., 62.
141 See Kim Reimann "Building Networks from the Outside In: Japanese NGOs and the Kyoto Climate Change Conference 2002," in *Globalization and Resistance: Transnational Dimensions of Social Movements,* ed. Jackie Smith and Hank Johnston (Lanham, MD: Rowman & Littlefield, 2002), 173–187.
142 Saitō Kiyoaki, "Kankyō Mondai to Borantia," in *Borantiagaku no Susume,* ed. Utsumi Seiji (Kyoto: Shōwadō, 2001), 24.
143 Matsuo Makoto, "Kikō Fōramu no Seika to Kankyō NGO no Imi: Kankyō Seijigaku Kōchiku ni mukete no Oboegaki (2)—The Consequences of KIKO Forum and Significance of Environment NGOs," *Kyoto Seika Daigaku Kiyō* 17 (1999): 213.
144 Saitō, "Kankyō," 7.
145 Reimann "Building Networks," 181.
146 Ibid., 179.
147 Ibid., 181.
148 Kikō Fōramu, "21-seiki no Kodomotachi, Magotachi ni, Seimei no Hoshi, Chikyū o tewatasu tame ni Chikyū Ondanka o kuitomeru Chie to Kōdō o ima suguni," reproduced in *Kikō Fōramu kara Kikō Nettowāku e: Kyoto Kaigi kara no Shuppatsu—Kikō Fōramu no Katsudō no Kiroku,* ed. Anzai Naoto, Suda Eriko, Taura Kenrō, Maruta Shōichi, and Yamaguchi Hironori (Kyoto: Kikō Fōramu—Kikō Hendō / Chikyū Ondanka o Fusegu Shimin Kaigi—Kikō Nettowāku, 1998), no page numbering.
149 Kikō Fōramu, "Kikō Fōramu 10 no Shuchō," reproduced *Kikō Fōramu* ed. Anzai et al., no page numbering.
150 Ibid.

## Conclusion: Transnational Activism, the Local, and Japanese Civil Society

1  Haraway, "Situated," 590.
2  Sheila Jasanoff, "Image and Imagination: The Formation of Global Environmental Consciousness," in *Changing the Atmosphere: Expert Knowledge and Environmental Governance,* ed. Clark A. Miller and Paul N. Edwards (Cambridge, MA: MIT Press, 2001), 312.

3   Ibid., 312.
4   On "master" conceptual frameworks see Snow and Benford, "Master Frames," 133–155.
5   Martello and Jasanoff, "Introduction," 13–14.
6   Sassen, "Globalization," 11, 12, 14.
7   Tarrow, *The New*, 139.
8   Sonja K. Pieck, "Transnational Activist Networks: Mobilization between Emotion and Bureaucracy," *Social Movement Studies: Journal of Social, Cultural and Political Protest*, 12:2 (2013): 123.
9   Thomas Bender, "Introduction: Historians, the Nation, and the Plenitude of Narratives," in *Rethinking American History in a Global Age*, ed. Thomas Bender (Berkeley: University of California Press, 2002), 8.
10  Laclau and Mouffe, *Hegemony*, xviii.
11  Also see Walker, *Toxic Archipelago*, 218; and Mike Danaher, "Whaling: A Conflict of Environmental and Human Rights," *Social Alternatives* 23, no. 3 (2004): 42–43.
12  Heise, *Sense of Place*, 61.
13  Ibid., 55.
14  Dirlik, "Globalism," 47.
15  Ibid., 41.
16  Ibid., 38.
17  Ibid.
18  Martello and Jasanoff, "Introduction," 17.
19  Lawrence Buell, Ursula K. Heise, and Karen Thornber, "Literature and the Environment," *Annual Review of Environment and Resources* 36 (2011): 421.
20  Guha, *Environmentalism*, 112.
21  Thiele, *Environmentalism*, 128.
22  Ibid., 126.
23  Guha, *Environmentalism*, 143.
24  Timothy Doyle and Brian Doherty, "Green Public Spheres and the Green Governance State: The Politics of Emancipation and Ecological Conditionality," *Environmental Politics* 15, no. 5 (2006): 889.
25  Ibid.
26  Ibid., 890.
27  Quoted in Joachim Radkau, *Nature and Power: A Global History of the Environment*, trans. Thomas Dunlap (New York: Cambridge University Press, 2008), 294.
28  Ibid., 4.
29  Doyle and Doherty, "Green," 890.
30  Guha, *Environmentalism*, 141.

31   Doyle and Doherty, "Green," 889. Robyn Eckersley, *Environmentalism and Political Theory: Toward an Ecocentric Approach* (New York: State University of New York Press, 1992), chapter 1.

32   Thiele, *Environmentalism,* 132.

33   Ibid., 132.

34   Dirlik, "Globalism," 38.

35   Martello and Jasanoff, "Introduction," 13–14.

36   Amin, "Spatialities," 395.

37   Philippe de Seynes, "Prospects for a Future Whole World," *International Organization* 26, no. 1 (1972): 1.

38   Yokoyama Masaki, "Genchi Hōkoku: Nichibei no Kan-Taiheiyō Senryaku vs Taiheiyō Shominzoku no Hankaku-Dokuritsu Undō—Ponape Kaigi ni Sanka shite," *GKN* 75 (Jan 1979): 11–12.

39   Samuel Moyn, *The Last Utopia: Human Rights in History* (Cambridge, MA: Belknap Press of Harvard University Press, 2010), 3; and Moyn, "Return," 2.

40   Jan Eckel, "Rebirth," 248.

41   Pedro Iacobelli, Danton Leary, and Shinnosuke Takahashi, *Transnational Japan as History: Empire, Migration, and Social Movements* (Basingstoke, UK: Palgrave Macmillan, 2015), 1–2.

42   Richard White, "The Nationalization of Nature," *Journal of American History* 86, no. 3 (December 1999): 978.

43   Ian Tyrell, "Reflections on the Transnational Turn in United States History: Theory and Practice," *Journal of Global History* 4 (2009): 460.

44   Matthias Middell and Katja Naumann, "Global History and the Spatial Turn: From the Impact of Area Studies to the Study of Critical Junctures of Globalization," *Journal of Global History* 5 (2010): 160.

45   Bernhard Struck, Kate Ferris, and Jacques Revel, "Introduction: Space and Scale in Transnational History," *International History Review* 33, no. 4 (2011): 576.

46   Thomas Bender, "Preface," in *Rethinking American History in a Global Age,* ed. Thomas Bender (Berkeley: University of California Press, 2002), vii.

47   Pierre-Yves Saunier, "Learning by Doing: Notes about the Making of the Palgrave Dictionary of Transnational History," *Journal of Modern European History* 6 (2008): 169.

48   David Thelen, "The Nation and Beyond: Transnational Perspectives on United States History," *Journal of American History* 86, no. 3 (December 1999): 967.

49   Ibid., 973–974.

50   Tyrell, "Reflections," 463.

51   Prasenjit Duara, "Historicizing National Identity, or, Who Images What, and When," in *Becoming National: A Reader*, ed. Geoff Eley and Ronald G. Suny (New York: Oxford University Press, 1996), 151.

52   Struck et al., "Introduction," 575.

53   Dirlik, "Performing," 404.

54   Aldrich, *Site Fights*; Jeffrey Broadbent, *Environmental Politics in Japan*; Hasegawa, *Constructing*; Kirby, *Troubled Natures*; Karan and Suganuma, eds., *Local Environmental*.

55   Maggie Kinser-Saiki, ed., *Japanese Working for a Better World: Grassroots Voices and Access Guide to Citizens' Groups in Japan* (San Francisco: Honnoki USA, 1992); André Sorensen and Carolin Funck, eds., *Living Cities in Japan: Citizens' Movements, Machizukuri, and Local Environments* (New York: Routledge, 2007); Karan and Suganuma, eds., *Local Environmental*.

56   There are some important exceptions, especially with respect to Japanese movements addressing more recent global environmental issues such as deforestation and climate change. See, for example, Wong, "The Anti-Tropical," 131–150; Reimann "Building Networks," 173–187; Sato, "Beyond."

57   See Michiba, "Posuto-Betonamu," 97–127.

58   See http://www.parc-jp.org/.

59   "AMPO" referred to the *Treaty of Mutual Cooperation and Security between the United States and Japan* (*Nippon-koku to Amerika-gasshūkoku to no Aida no Sōgo Kyōryoku oyobi Anzen Hoshō Jōyaku*).

60   On the CNIC and Takagi, see Simon Avenell, "Antinuclear Radicals: Scientific Experts and Antinuclear Activism in Japan," *Science, Technology, and Society: An International Journal* 21, no. 1 (2016): 88–109.

61   See Kanō Mikiyo, "Shiryaku=Sabetsu to Tatakau Ajia Fujin Kaigi to Dainiha Feminizumu," *Joseigaku Kenkyū* 18 (2011): 149–165.

62   Kīsen Kankō ni Hantai suru Onnatachi no Kai, *Sei Shinryaku o Kokuhatsu suru: Kīsen Kankō* (Tokyo: Kīsen Kankō ni Hantai suru Onnatachi no Kai, 1974).

63   Michiba, "Posuto-Betonamu," 118.

64   Ibid., 120.

65   PHD stands for Peace, Health, and Human Development. On this movement see http://www.phd-kobe.org/.

66   On Shalpa Neer, see http://www.shaplaneer.org/.

67   On ARI, see http://www.ari-edu.org/en/about-us/. On IHC, see http://ihc-japan.org/.

68   Seminal scholarship includes Pekkanen, *Japan's Dual Civil Society*; Sheldon Garon, *Molding Japanese Minds: The State in Everyday Life* (Princeton NJ:

Princeton University Press, 1997); Frank J. Schwartz and Susan J. Pharr, eds, *The State of Civil Society in Japan* (Cambridge: Cambridge University, 2003).

69 Susan Pharr, "Conclusion: Targeting by an Activist State: Japan as a Civil Society Model," in *The State*, ed. Schwartz and Pharr, 325.

70 Pekkanen, *Japan's Dual Civil Society*, 2–3.

71 Daniel Aldrich, "Post-Crisis Japanese Nuclear Policy: From Top-Down Directives to Bottom-Up Activism," *Asia Pacific Issues* 103 (2012): 3; and Aldrich, *Site Fights*.

72 Kim Reimann, "Building Global Civil Society from the Outside In? Japanese International Development NGOs, the State, and International Norms," in *The State*, ed. Schwartz and Pharr, 301–304. Also see Reimann, *Rise*, and Reimann, "Building Networks," 173–187.

73 Wesley Sasaki-Uemura, *Organizing the Spontaneous: Citizen Protest in Postwar Japan* (Honolulu: University of Hawai'I Press, 2003).

74 Koichi Hasegawa, Chika Shinohara, and Jeffrey P. Broadbent, "The Effects of 'Social Expectation' on the Development of Civil Society in Japan," *Journal of Civil Society* 3, no. 28 (2007): 183.

75 Avenell, *Making.*

76 But see my discussion of the Japanese anti–Vietnam War movement, Beheiren, which was a quintessentially transnational endeavor. Avenell, *Making*, chapter 4.

77 Interesting also is the fact that very few of the environmental activists explored in this study wholeheartedly adopted the cause of groups in Japan opposing nuclear power plant construction. As I have argued elsewhere, a major difference between industrial pollution disputes and anti–nuclear power plant movements was the somewhat more ambiguous nature of injustice in the latter. Whereas the victims were easy to identify in cases of industrial pollution, in the case of nuclear power plants the risk was always potential, at least until a major accident at the Fukushima Daiichi plant in March 2011. Even then, victimization was more about displacement (temporary in many cases) and the effects of radiation on humans, never as clear-cut as industrial toxins. After March 11, for instance, the media was not flooded with disturbing images of human disfiguration and illness like those from Minamata and Yokkaichi in the 1960s—images that put fire in the belly of Ui Jun, Tsuru Shigeto, and other leading environmental activists. Moreover, as Daniel Aldrich has shown, communities that accepted nuclear facilities were richly rewarded, muddying the issue of victimization and injustice from the outset. See Aldrich, *Site Fights,* and Simon Avenell, "From Fearsome Pollution to Fukushima: Environmental Activism and the Nuclear Blind Spot in Contemporary Japan," *Environmental*

*History* 17, no. 2 (2012): 244–276. Some, like the nuclear chemist Takagi Jinzaburō, warned of the dangers of nuclear power and plutonium (see Avenell, "Antinuclear").

78  Janet Conway, "Citizenship in a Time of Empire: The World Social Forum as a New Public Space," *Citizenship Studies* 8, no. 4 (2004): 370.

79  Ibid., 369.

80  Radkau, *Nature*, 294.

# Bibliography

"2.28 Hangenpatsu-Hansaishori-Hankaiyō Tōki: Tokyo Shūkai o Seikō saseyō." *Tsuchi no Koe, Tami no Koe Gōgai Kaku Haikibutsu Kaiyō Tōki Hantai Undō Tokushū* 6 (February 1981): 2.

4.8 "Ajia e no Kōgai Yushutsu o Kokuhatsu suru Shimin Daishūkai" Sankasha Ichidō. "Kyōdō Sengen." *Geppō Kōgai o Nogasuna! Kankoku e no Kōgai Yushutsu o Kokuhatsu suru* 35 (May 1976): 20–21.

92 Kokuren Burajiru Kaigi Shimin Renraku Kai. "92 Kokuren Burajiru Kaigi Shimin Renraku Kai kara no Teigen." *Kōgai Kenkyū* 21, no. 4 (April 1992): 54–59.

92 Kokuren Burajiru Kaigi Shimin Renraku Kai. *Shimin no Chikyū Kenshō.* Tokyo: Iwanami Shoten, 1992.

92 NGO Forum Japan. *People's Voice of Japan: I Have the Earth in Mind, The Earth Has Me in Hand.* Contained on *Earth Summit: The NGO Archives* CD ROM (Hamilton, Canada: CCOHS, 1995), CD ROM.

Action Committee to Stop Toyama Kagaku's Pollution Export. "The Development of the Chromium Pollution Struggle: The Voices of the People of Japan and South Korea Encircle Nihon Kagaku." *AMPO: Japan-Asia Quarterly Review* 26 (October–December 1974): 84–91.

Adedeji, Adebayo. "Excerpts from the Statement of Adebayo Adedeji, Federal Commissioner for Economic Development and Reconstruction, Nigeria, and Head of Nigerian Delegation: Deeds vs. Intentions." *Bulletin of the Atomic Scientists* 28, no. 7 (1972): 53.

Ajiajin Kaigi. "Komittomento (Yaruzo!)." *Jishu Kōza* 40 (July 1974): 18–19. Reproduced in *Ui Jun Shūshū Kōgai Mondai Shiryō 1 Fukkoku "Jishu Kōza" Dai 2-kai Haihon Dai 3-kan,* edited by Saitama Daigaku Kyōsei Shakai Kenkyū Sentā, 142–143. Tokyo: Suirensha, 2006.

Ajia to Nihon o Kangae Kōdō suru Kai. "Ajia o Okasu Kawatetsu o Ute," *Jishu Kōza* 64 (July 1976): 8–14. Reproduced in *Ui Jun Shūshū Kōgai Mondai Shiryō 1 Fukkoku "Jishu Kōza" Dai 3-kai Haihon Dai 2-kan,* edited by Saitama Daigaku Kyōsei Shakai Kenkyū Sentā, 406–412. Tokyo: Suirensha, 2006.

Aki, Yukio. "Hikaku Taiheiyō Fōramu demo Kaiyō Tōki o Hinan." *Hangenpatsu Shinbun* 31 (November 1980): 2. Reproduced in *"Hangenpatsu Shinbun" Shukusatsuban (0–100),* edited by Hangenpatsu Undō Zenkoku Renrakukai, 152. Nara: Yasōsha, 1986.

Akino, Kaoru. "Genchi Repōto: Kawatetsu Mindanao Kōjō to Chikaku no Gyoson o Otozurete." *Geppō Kōgai o Nogasuna! Nihon no Shinryaku ni Kōshite Ajia Taiheiyō Minshū to Tomoni* 149 (November—December 1985): 17–25.

Albert, Mathias, Gesa Bluhm, Jan Helmig, Andreas Leutzsch, and Jochen Walter. "Introduction: The Communicative Construction of Transnational Political Spaces." In *Transnational Political Spaces: Agents—Structures—Encounters,* edited by Mathias Albert, Gesa Bluhm, Jan Helmig, Andreas Leutzsch, and Jochen Walter, 7–31. Frankfurt: Campus Verlag, 2009.

Aldrich, Daniel. "Post-Crisis Japanese Nuclear Policy: From Top-Down Directives to Bottom-Up Activism." *Asia Pacific Issues* 103 (2012): 1–11.

———. *Site Fights: Divisive Facilities and Civil Society in Japan and the West.* Ithaca, NY: Cornell University Press, 2008.

Alley, William M., and Rosemarie Alley. *Too Hot to Touch: The Problem of High-Level Nuclear Waste.* Cambridge: Cambridge University Press, 2012.

Amano, Reiko. "Waga Nippon no 'Osamui' Genjitsu: Japan Day Jiken ga 'Nagaragawa' o Sekai ni Shiraseta." In *Chikyū Samitto Live in Rio,* edited by Yamazaki Kōichi, 108–112. Tokyo: Asahi Shimbunsha, 1992.

Amin, Ash. "Spatialities of Globalisation." *Environment and Planning A* 34 (2002): 385–399.

Anastacio, Ignatio. "Utsukushii Shizen o Mamori, Tomo ni Ikiyō." *Tsuchi no Koe, Tami no Koe* 120 (April 1981): 12–15.

"Anata no Jōshiki Watashi no Odoroki: Han Kōgai Yushutsu Tsūhō Sentā Setsuritsu." *Geppō Kōgai o Nogasuna! Kankoku e no Kōgai Yushutsu o Kokuhatsu suru* 35 (May 1976): 22–25.

Aoyama, Tadashi. "Kaitōki Hantai Shomei 11-gatsumatsu no Dai-1ji Shūyaku! Tomoni Ganbarō!" *Geppō Kōgai o Nogasuna! Daisan Sekai e no Kōgai Yushutsu o Kokuhatsu suru* 95 (October 1980): 1.

———. "Kaku Haikibutsu no Taiheiyō Tōki o Yurusuna! Moriagaru Shomei Undō." *Geppō Kōgai o Nogasuna! Daisan Sekai e no Kōgai Yushutsu o Kokuhatsu suru* 93 (August 1980): 1–2.

Appiah, Kwame Anthony. *The Ethics of Identity.* Princeton, NJ: Princeton University Press, 2005.

Arakawa, Shunji. "Genchi Repōto 1: Mikuroneshia kara no Chokugen: Nihon no Kaku Tōki Keikaku o Megutte." *Geppō Kōgai o Nogasuna! Daisan Sekai e no Kōgai Yushutsu o Kokuhatsu suru* 93 (August 1980): 4–9.

———. "Hantai Ketsugi o Tsukitsukerareta Nihon Seifu no 'Setsumeidan.'" *Geppō Kōgai o Nogasuna! Daisan Sekai e no Kōgai Yushutsu o Kokuhatsu suru* 94 (September 1980): 10–13.

———. "Ignatio Giin (Parao) Seiryokuteki ni Kyanpēn." *Tsuchi no Koe, Tami no Koe Gōgai Kaku Haikibutsu Kaiyō Tōki Hantai Undō Tokushū* 7 (March 1981): 4.

———. "Kaku Haikibutsu no Taiheiyō Tōki Hantai o Uttaeru: F. Mendiora-san (Tenian)." *Hangenpatsu Shinbun* 31 (November 1980): 3. Reproduced in *"Hangenpatsu Shinbun" Shukusatsuban (0–100)*, edited by Hangenpatsu Undō Zenkoku Renrakukai, 153. Nara: Yasōsha, 1986.

Arakawa, Shunji, and Ōkawa Hōsaku. "Amami-Okinawa-Sanrizuka to Parao-Guamu o Musubu Tabi kara." *Tsuchi no Koe, Tami no Koe Gōgai* 6 (February 1981): 3–4.

Ariyoshi, Sawako. *Fukugō Osen.* Tokyo: Shinchōsha, 1979.

Asahi Jyānaru. "Tokushū Minikomi '71: Honryū suru Chikasui." *Asahi Jyānaru* (March 26, 1971): 4–60.

Asahi Shinbun "Chikyū Samitto" Shuzaihan. *"Chikyū Samitto" Handobukku.* Tokyo: Asahi Shimbunsha, 1992.

Asahi Shinbun Keizaibu, ed. *Kutabare GNP: Kōdo Keizai Seichō no Uchimaku.* Tokyo: Asahi Shimbunsha, 1971.

Avenell, Simon. "Antinuclear Radicals: Scientific Experts and Antinuclear Activism in Japan." *Science, Technology, and Society: An International Journal* (forthcoming 2016).

———. "Civil Society and the New Civic Movements in Contemporary Japan: Convergence, Collaboration, and Transformation." *Journal of Japanese Studies* 35, no. 2 (Summer, 2009): 247–283.

———. "From Fearsome Pollution to Fukushima: Environmental Activism and the Nuclear Blind Spot in Contemporary Japan." *Environmental History* 17, no. 2 (2012): 244–276.

———. "Japan's Long Environmental Sixties and the Birth of a Green Leviathan." *Japanese Studies* 32, no. 3 (2012): 423–444.

———. *Making Japanese Citizens: Civil Society and the Mythology of the Shimin in Postwar Japan.* Berkeley: University of California Press, 2010.

———. "Regional Egoism as the Public Good: Residents' Movements in Japan during the 1960s and 1970s." *Japan Forum* 18, no. 1 (2006): 89–113.

———. "Transnationalism and the Evolution of Post-National Citizenship in Japan." *Asian Studies Review* 39, no. 3 (2015): 375–394.

Barshay, Andrew. *The Social Sciences in Modern Japan: The Marxian and Modernist Traditions.* Berkeley: University of California Press, 2007.

Bedor, Roman. "Roman Bedor Speech at Anti-AMPO Rally in Tokyo, June 7, 1981." *No Nuke News Japan* 3–4 (July–August 1981): 6.

———. "Seizon no tame no Wareware no Tatakai." *Tsuchi no Koe, Tami no Koe* 113 (September 1980): 11–13.

————. "Sekai no Subete no Minshū e no Apīru: Taiheiyō ni Okeru Furansu no Kaku Jikken to Nihon no Kaku Haikibutsu Tōki Keikaku ni Hantai suru Sekai Kibo no Shomei Undō o Uttaeru." *Tsuchi no Koe, Tami no Koe Gōgai Kaku Haikibutsu Kaiyō Tōki Hantai Undō Tokushū* 13 (September 1981): 3.

————. "Yōroppa Shomei Teishutsu no Tabi kara." *Tsuchi no Koe, Tami no Koe* 143 (February–March 1983): 39–43.

Bedor, Roman, and Jishu Kōza. "Roman's Tour of Europe: Pacific Problems Delivered to Their Source." *No Nuke News Japan* 16 (1983): 2–4.

Bender, Thomas. "Introduction: Historians, the Nation, and the Plenitude of Narratives." In *Rethinking American History in a Global Age,* edited by Thomas Bender, 1–21. Berkeley: University of California Press, 2002.

————. "Preface." In *Rethinking American History in a Global Age,* edited by Thomas Bender, vii–ix. Berkeley: University of California Press, 2002.

Benford, Robert D., and David A. Snow. "Framing Processes and Social Movements: An Overview and Assessment." *Annual Review of Sociology* 26 (2000): 611–639.

Branch, James B. "The Waste Bin: Nuclear Waste Dumping and Storage in the Pacific." *Ambio* 13, no. 5/6 (1984): 327–330.

Broadbent, Jeffrey. *Environmental Politics in Japan: Networks of Power and Protest.* Cambridge: Cambridge University Press, 1998.

————. "Japan's Environmental Politics: Recognition and Response Processes." In *Environmental Policy in Japan,* edited by Hidefumi Imura and Miranda A. Schreurs, 102–134. Gloucestershire, UK: Edward Elgar, 2005.

Buell, Lawrence, Ursula K. Heise, and Karen Thornber. "Literature and the Environment." *Annual Review of Environment and Resources* 36 (2011): 417–440.

Canadian Indian Dryden Minamata Disease Group. "Final Statement." *Jishu Kōza* 54 (September 1975): 12. Reproduced in *Ui Jun Shūshū Kōgai Mondai Shiryō 1 Fukkoku "Jishu Kōza" Dai 3-kai Haihon Dai 1-kan,* edited by Saitama Daigaku Kyōsei Shakai Kenkyū Sentā. Tokyo: Suirensha, 2006.

Carson, Rachel. *Silent Spring.* Boston, MA: Houghton Mifflin, 1962.

Centre for Applied Studies in International Negotiations Issues and Non-Governmental Organizations Programme. "Report on NGO Activities at the United Nations Conference on Environment and Development and the Global Forum, Rio de Janeiro, 1–14 June 1992." *Earth Summit: The NGO Archives CD ROM.* Hamilton, Canada: CCOHS, 1995. CD ROM.

Chikyū Kankyō to Taiki Osen o Kangaeru Zenkoku Shimin Kaigi (CASA). "Chikyū Kankyō to Taiki Osen o Kangaeru Zenkoku Shimin Kaigi— Citizens' Alliance for Saving the Atmosphere and the Earth." Accessed May 16, 2014. http://www.bnet.jp/casa/.

Clapp, Jennifer, and Peter Dauvergne. *Paths to a Green World: The Political Economy of the Global Environment.* Cambridge, MA: MIT Press, 2005.

Commoner, Barry. *The Closing Circle: Nature, Man, and Technology.* New York: Alfred A. Knopf, 1971.

"Conference of Asians." *AMPO: Japan-Asia Quarterly Review* 21–22 (Summer–Autumn 1974): 1–15.

Conway, Janet. "Citizenship in a Time of Empire: The World Social Forum as a New Public Space." *Citizenship Studies* 8, no. 4 (2004): 367–381.

Curtis, Richard, and Dave Fisher. "The Seven Wonders of the Polluted World." *New York Times,* September 26, 1971: 21.

Dahmén, Erik. "Environmental Control and Economic Systems." In *Proceedings of International Symposium on Environmental Disruption: A Challenge to Social Scientists,* edited by Tsuru Shigeto, 149–159. Paris: International Social Science Council, 1970.

Dakeishi, Miwako, Katsuyuki Murata, and Philippe Grandjean. "Long-Term Consequences of Arsenic Poisoning during Infancy due to Contaminated Milk Powder." *Environmental Health* 5, no. 31 (2006). Accessed April 28, 2014. http://www.ehjournal.net/content/5/1/31.

Danaher, Mike. "Whaling: A Conflict of Environmental and Human Rights." *Social Alternatives* 23, no. 3 (2004): 42–43.

Dauvergne, Peter. *Shadows in the Forest: Japan and the Politics of Timber in Southeast Asia.* Cambridge, MA: MIT Press, 1997.

de Seynes, Philippe. "Prospects for a Future Whole World." *International Organization* 26, no. 1 (1972): 1–17.

de Steiguer, Edward. *The Origins of Modern Environmental Thought.* Tucson, AZ: University of Arizona Press, 2011.

Dirlik, Arif. "Globalism and the Politics of Place." In *Globalisation and the Asia-Pacific: Contested Territories,* edited by Kris Olds, Peter Dicken, Philip F. Kelly, Lily Kong, and Henry Wai-Chung Yeung, 37–54. London: Routledge.

———. "Performing the World: Reality and Representation in the Making of World Histor(ies)." *Journal of World History* 16, no. 4 (2005): 391–410.

Doyle, Timothy, and Brian Doherty. "Green Public Spheres and the Green Governance State: The Politics of Emancipation and Ecological Conditionality." *Environmental Politics* 15, no. 5 (2006): 881–892.

Dryzek, John S. *The Politics of the Earth: Environmental Discourses.* Oxford: Oxford University Press, 2005.

Duara, Prasenjit. "Historicizing National Identity, or, Who Images What, and When." In *Becoming National: A Reader,* edited by Geoff Eley and Ronald G. Suny, 151–177. New York: Oxford University Press, 1996.

Duffy, Rosaleen. "Non-Governmental Organisations and Governance States: The Impact of Transnational Environmental Management Networks in Madagascar." *Environmental Politics* 15, no. 5 (2006): 731–749.

Eckel, Jan. "The Rebirth of Politics from the Spirit of Morality: Explaining the Human Rights Revolution of the 1970s." In *The Breakthrough: Human Rights in the 1970s,* edited by Jan Eckel and Samuel Moyn, 226–259. Philadelphia: University of Pennsylvania Press, 2014.

Eckersley, Robyn. *Environmentalism and Political Theory: Toward an Ecocentric Approach.* New York: State University of New York Press, 1992.

Egelston, Anne E. *Sustainable Development: A History.* New York: Springer, 2006.

Ehrlich, Paul. "Foreword." In Norie Huddle, Michael Reich, and Nahum Stiskin, *Island of Dreams: Environmental Crisis in Japan,* ix–xiv. Rochester, VT: Schenkman Books, 1987.

———. *The Population Bomb.* New York: Ballantine Books, 1968.

Emmelin, Lars. "The Stockholm Conferences." *Ambio* 1, no. 4 (1972): 135–140.

Executive Committee to Stop the Toyama Chemical Co. from Exporting Pollution. "Cut Off the Path of Retreat for Pollution: The Beginning of Anti-'Pollution Exporting' Movements by Combined Forces of Japanese and Korean Citizens." *KOGAI: The Newsletter from Polluted Japan* 7 (Spring 1975): 2–7.

Faramelli, Norman J. "Toying with the Environment and the Poor: A Report on the Stockholm Environmental Conferences." *Boston College Environmental Affairs Law Review* 2, no. 3 (1972): 469–486.

First National Bank in Albuquerque, As Guardian for and On Behalf of Dorothy Jean Huckleby, et al., plaintiffs-appellants, v. United States of America, Defendant-appellee. 552 F.2d 370. United States Court of Appeals, Tenth Circuit. 1977. *Justia US Law.* Web. May 2, 2014.

Founex Conference, *The Founex Report on Environment and Development* (Washington, DC: Carnegie Endowment for International Peace, 1972). Manitou Foundation Homepage. Accessed May 28, 2014. http://www.mauricestrong.net/index.php/the-founex-report.

*The Founex Report on Environment and Development.* Washington, DC: Carnegie Endowment for International Peace, 1972. Accessed May 5, 2014. http://www.mauricestrong.net/index.php/the-founex-report.

Friends of the Earth, Berlin. "Message from Friends of the Earth, Berlin." *No Nuke News Japan* 17 (1983): 8–9.

Gaimushō Kokusai Rengōkyoku. *Nihon ni okeru Ningen Kankyō Mondai: Sono Genjō to Taisaku: 1972-nen no "Kokuren Ningen Kankyō Kaigi" no tame ni Kokuren ni Teishutsu shita Wagakuni no Hōkokusho.* Tokyo: Gaimushō Kokusai Rengōkyoku, 1971.

Gamson, William. "Injustice Frames." In The *Wiley-Blackwell Encyclopedia of Social and Political Movements*, edited by David A. Snow, Donatella della Porta, Bert Klandermans, and Doug McAdam, 319–320. Hoboken, NJ: John Wiley & Sons, 2014.

Gandhi, Indira. "Address of Shrimati Indira Gandhi, Prime Minister of India." *Bulletin of the Atomic Scientists* 28, no. 7 (1972): 35–38.

Garon, Sheldon. *Molding Japanese Minds: The State in Everyday Life*. Princeton, NJ: Princeton University Press, 1997.

Gendlin, Frances. "III: Voices from the Gallery." *Bulletin of the Atomic Scientists* 28, no. 7 (1972): 26–29.

Genshiryoku Iinkai. "Hōshasei Haikibutsu Taisaku ni tsuite." *Genshiryoku Iinkai Geppō* 21, no. 10 (1976). Accessed May 13, 2014. http://www.aec.go.jp/jicst /NC/about/ugoki/geppou/V21/N10/197600V21N10.htm.

George, Timothy S. *Minamata: Pollution and the Struggle for Democracy in Postwar Japan*. Cambridge, MA: Harvard University Press, 2001.

————. "Tanaka Shozo's Vision of an Alternative Constitutional Modernity for Japan." In *Public Spheres, Private Lives in Modern Japan, 1600–1950: Essays in Honor of Albert M. Craig*, edited by Gail Lee Bernstein, Andrew Gordon, and Kate Wildman Nakai, 89–116. Cambridge, MA: Harvard University Asia Center, 2005.

Glick-Schiller, Nina. "Transnationality." In *A Companion to the Anthropology of Politics*, edited by David Nugent and Joan Vincent, 448–467. Malden, MA: Blackwell, 2004.

Gorz, André Gorz. *Ecologie et Politique*. Paris: Seuil, 1978.

Gresser, Julian, Koichiro Fujikura, and Akio Morishima. *Environmental Law in Japan*. London: MIT Press, 1981.

Guha, Ramachandra. *Environmentalism: A Global History*. New York: Longman, 2000.

Gyomin Kenkyūkai. "Hirogaru Gyomin no Tatakai: 6–21 Umi o Yogosuna! Gyomin Shūkai to 6–22 Kaiyō Tōki Hantai Shomei Teishutsu Kōdō no Hōkoku." *Tsuchi no Koe, Tami no Koe Gōgai Kaku Haikibutsu Kaiyō Tōki Hantai Undō Tokushū* 11 (July 1981): 4–5.

Haas, Peter. "Introduction: Epistemic Communities and International Policy Coordination." *International Organization* 46, no. 1 (1992): 1–35.

Hall, Derek. "Environmental Change, Protest, and Havens of Environmental Degradation: Evidence from Asia." *Global Environmental Politics* 2, no. 2 (2002): 20–28.

————. "Pollution Export as State and Corporate Strategy: Japan in the 1970s." *Review of International Political Economy* 16, no. 2 (2009): 260–283.

Hamblin, Jacob Darwin. "Gods and Devils in the Details: Marine Pollution, Radioactive Waste, and an Environmental Regime circa 1972." *Diplomatic History* 32 (2008): 539–560.

———. *Poison in the Well: Radioactive Waste in the Oceans at the Dawn of the Nuclear Age.* Piscataway, NJ: Rutgers University Press, 2008.

Hanada, Masanori, and Inoue Yukari. "Kanada Senjūmin no Minamatabyō to Junan no Shakaishi Dai-1-kai." *Gekkan "Shakai Undō"* 382 (January 2012): 19–24.

Hanayama, Yuzuru. "Jidōsha o Kangaeru." In *Sekai no Kōgai Chizu* 1, edited by Tsuru Shigeto, 138–152. Tokyo: Iwanami Shoten, 1977.

———. "Kaisetsu: Tsuru Kyōju no Seiji Keizaigaku." In Tsuru Shigeto, *Tsuru Shigeto Chosakushū 6: Toshi Mondai to Kōgai*, 519–531. Tokyo: Kōdansha, 1975.

Han-Genpatsu News Editorial Committee Jishu Kōza. "Editorial." *No Nuke News Japan* 0 (April 1981): 1.

———. "Unifying the Nuclear Struggle: Belauan Keynotes to Tokyo Rally." *No Nuke News Japan* 0 (April 1981): 2–3.

Hankaku-Hangenpatsu-Hansaishori o Tatakau 7-gatsu Kōdō Jikkō Iinkai. "7.3 Shūkai Mondai Teiki." *Tsuchi no Koe, Tami no Koe* 112 (August 1980): 21–26.

Hankaku Pashifiku Sentā Tokyo Ichidō. "Kaku no nai Taiheiyō o Mezashite Ganbarimasu! Hankaku Pashifiku Sentā Hossoku shimashita." *Geppō Kōgai o Nogasuna! Nihon no Shinryaku no Kōshite Ajia Taiheiyō Minshū to tomo ni* 151 (February 1986): 1.

Han-Kōgai Yushutsu Tsuhō Sentā. "Ajia no Gisei no Ue ni Naritatsu Bunmei o kyohi suru." *Jishu Kōza* 62 (May 1976): 1–8. Reproduced in *Ui Jun Shūshū Kōgai Mondai Shiryō 1 Fukkoku "Jishu Kōza" Dai 3-kai Haihon Dai 2-kan*, edited by Saitama Daigaku Kyōsei Shakai Kenkyū Sentā, 269–276. Tokyo: Suirensha, 2006.

Haq, Gary, and Alistair Paul. *Environmentalism since 1945.* London: Routledge, 2012.

Harada, Masazumi. "Finrando no Suigin Jiken." In *Sekai no Kōgai Chizu* 1, edited by Tsuru Shigeto, 126–136. Tokyo: Iwanami Shoten, 1977.

———. *Minamata Disease*, translated by Timothy George and Tsushima Sachie. Kumamoto: Kumamoto Nichinichi Shinbun, 2004.

———. *Minamata ga Utsusu Sekai.* Tokyo: Nihon Hyōronsha, 1989.

Haraway, Donna. "Situated Knowledges: The Science Question in Feminism and the Privilege of Partial Perspective." *Feminist Studies* 14, no. 3 (Autumn 1988): 575–599.

Hasegawa, Koichi, Chika Shinohara, and Jeffrey P. Broadbent. "The Effects of 'Social Expectation' on the Development of Civil Society in Japan." *Journal of Civil Society* 3, no. 28 (2007): 179–203.

Hasegawa, Koichi. *Constructing Civil Society in Japan: Voices of Environmental Movements.* Melbourne: Trans Pacific Press, 2004.

Havens, Thomas R. H. *Fire across the Sea: The Vietnam War and Japan 1965–1975.* Princeton, NJ: Princeton University Press, 1987.

Hayakawa, Mitsutoshi. "Chikyū Kankyō to Taiki Osen o Kangaeru Kokusai Shimin Shinpojiumu no Hōkoku." *Kankyō to Kōgai* 19, no. 3 (January 1990): 63.

Heise, Ursula K. *Sense of Place and Sense of Planet: The Environmental Imagination of the Global.* Oxford: Oxford University Press, 2008.

Henshūbu. "'Ajiajin Kaigi' ni tsuite." In *Ajia o Kangaeru: Ajiajin Kaigi no Zenkiroku,* edited by Oda Makoto, 3–4. Tokyo: Ushio Shuppansha, 1976.

Hightower, Jane M. *Diagnosis Mercury: Money, Politics, and Poison.* Washington, DC: Island Press, 2009.

Himeno, Seiichirō, and Yoshimatsu Sōichirō. "Nihon no Genchi o Otozurete." *Jishu Kōza* 40 (July 1974): 2–5. Reproduced in *Ui Jun Shūshū Kōgai Mondai Shiryō 1 Fukkoku "Jishu Kōza" Dai 2-kai Haihon Dai 3-kan,* edited by Saitama Daigaku Kyōsei Shakai Kenkyū Sentā, 126–129. Tokyo: Suirensha, 2006.

Hirayama, Takasada. "Exporting Pollution (The Export of 'KOGAI')." *KOGAI: The Newsletter from Polluted Japan* 2 (Winter 1974): 2–10.

————. "Fujisawashi Yugyōji ni okeru Tīchiin." *Jishu Kōza* 40 (July 1974): 5–9. Reproduced in *Ui Jun Shūshū Kōgai Mondai Shiryō 1 Fukkoku "Jishu Kōza" Dai 2-kai Haihon Dai 3-kan,* edited by Saitama Daigaku Kyōsei Shakai Kenkyū Sentā, 129–133. Tokyo: Suirensha, 2006.

————. "Nihon Kagaku wa Kankoku kara Tettai seyo! Kuromu Kōgai Oshitsukeni Nikkan Ryōkoku Minshū no Ikari wa Takamaru." *Jishu Kōza* 54 (September 1975): 41–58. Reproduced in *Ui Jun Shūshū Kōgai Mondai Shiryō 1 Fukkoku "Jishu Kōza" Dai 3-kai Haihon Dai 1-kan,* edited by Saitama Daigaku Kyōsei Shakai Kenkyū Sentā, 231–248. Tokyo: Suirensha, 2006.

————. "Tōnan Ajia Kōgai Saihakken no Tabi (1) Tai nite." *Jishu Kōza* 31 (October 1973): 49–53. Reproduced in *Ui Jun Shūshū Kōgai Mondai Shiryō 1 Fukkoku "Jishu Kōza" Dai 2-kai Haihon Dai 1-kan,* edited by Saitama Daigaku Kyōsei Shakai Kenkyū Sentā, 379–383. Tokyo: Suirensha, 2006.

————. "Toyama Kagaku, Kōgai Yushutsu Chūshi!?" *Jishu Kōza* 39 (June 1974): 26–29. Reproduced in *Ui Jun Shūshū Kōgai Mondai Shiryō 1 Fukkoku "Jishu Kōza" Dai 2-kai Haihon Dai 3-kan,* edited by Saitama Daigaku Kyōsei Shakai Kenkyū Sentā, 92–95. Tokyo: Suirensha, 2006.

Hoffman, John. *Citizenship beyond the State.* London: SAGE, 2004.

"Hokkaidō Tankōmura: Ikijigoku no naka no Chōsenjintachi." *Geppō Kōgai o Nogasuna! Kankoku e no Kōgai Yushutsu o Kokuhatsu suru* 38 (July 1976): 41–45.

Honda, Masakazu. "'Bideo Sanka' no Kokusai Onchido: Kyokushiteki 'Chikyū Samitto'ron." *Chikyū Samitto Live in Rio,* edited by Yamazaki Kōichi, 120–123. Tokyo: Asahi Shimbunsha, 1992.

Honsha Kishadan. "'Kōgai Nippon' Kō Uttaeru. Kokuren Ningen Kankyō Kaigi: Hatsugen o Matsu Higaishara. 'Teokure ni shita Seifu: Osoroshisa, Kono Mi de Shimesu'." *Asahi Shinbun* (morning edition, June 5, 1972): 23.

"Hōshasei Haikibutsu no Taiheiyō Tōki: Nihon wa Keikaku Chūshi seyo. Saipan Shichō Rainichi, Uttae." *Mainichi Shinbun* (Aug 1, 1980). Reproduced in *Tsuchi no Koe, Tami no Koe Gōgai* (August 1980): 4.

"Hōshasei Haikibutsu no Taiheiyō Tōki: Shimin Dantai mo 'Hantai.' Kagichō ni Keikaku Tekkai Motomeru." *Mainichi Shinbun* (Aug 10, 1980). Reproduced in *Geppō Kōgai o Nogasuna! Daisan Sekai e no Kōgai Yushutsu o Kokuhatsu suru* 92 (July 1980): 2.

Huddle, Norie, Michael Reich, and Nahum Stiskin. *Island of Dreams: Environmental Crisis in Japan.* Rochester, VT: Schenkman Books, 1987.

Iacobelli, Pedro, Danton Leary, and Shinnosuke Takahashi. *Transnational Japan as History: Empire, Migration, and Social Movements.* Basingstoke, UK: Palgrave Macmillan, 2015.

Ichihara, Akane. "Chikyū Samitto Hōkoku: '92 Gurōbaru Fōramu ni Sanka shite." *Cures Newsletter* 24 (August 1992): 4–6.

Ichikawa, Hiroshi. "Parao kara Meyer-sa o Mukaete: Soko ga Muzukashii!" *Tsuchi no Koe, Tami no Koe Gōgai Kaku Haikibutsu Kaiyō Tōki Hantai Undō Tokushū* 9 (May 1981): 9.

Iijima, Nobuko. *Kaiteiban Kankyō Mondai to Higaisha Undō.* Tokyo: Gakubunsha, 1993.

———. *Kankyō Mondai no Shakaishi.* Tokyo: Yūhikaku, 2000.

Ikeda, Susumu. "Chikyū Kankyō Shimin Kaigi Hōkoku." *Kankyō to Kōgai* 19, no. 3 (January 1990): 64.

Inose, Kōhei. "Genshiryoku Teikoku e no Taikō Seiji ni Mukatte: Kubokawa Genpatsu Hantai Undō o Tegakari ni." *Puraimu* 35 (March 2012): 71–91.

Inoue, Sumio. "Babanuki no Riron o koete: Nihon Kagaku no Kuromu Tarenagashi to Kankoku e no Kōgai Yushutsu." *Tenbō* 204 (December 1977): 87–102.

———. "Bokura wa Kōgai Yushtsu to Tatakai Hajimeta." *Tenbō* 191 (November 1974): 48–62.

———. "Exporting Pollution: Asahi Glass in Thailand." *AMPO: Japan-Asia Quarterly Review* 18 (Autumn 1973): 39–44.

Ishi, Hiroyuki, Okajima Shigeyuki, and Hara Takeshi. *Tettei Tōron: Chikyuū Kankyō Jyānarisuto no "Genba"kara.* Tokyo: Fukutake Shoten, 1992.

Ishii, Kuniyoshi, ed. *20 Seiki no Nihon Kankyōshi*. Tokyo: Sangyō Kankyō Kanri Kyōkai, 2002.

Ishikawa, Haruo. "Kaku Haikibutsu no Kaiyō Tōki Keikaku: 'Anzen' nante Tondemonai.'" *Geppō Kōgai o Nogasuna! Daisan Sekai e no Kōgai Yushutsu o Kokuhatsu suru* 94 (September 1980): 6–9.

Ishimure, Michiko. *Paradise in the Sea of Sorrow: Our Minamata Disease.* Translated by Livia Monnet. Ann Arbor: Center for Japanese Studies, University of Michigan, 2003.

Isomura, Eiichi. "'Kakegae no nai Jikoku' kara 'Kakegae no nai Chikyū e': Kokuren Ningen Kankyō Kaigi e no Kokumin Sanka o." *Kakushin* 24 (July 1972): 98–104.

Itai, Masaru, Shinohara Yoshihito, Toyoda Makoto, Muramatsu Akio, Awaji Takehisa, Isono Yayoi, Miyamoto Ken'ichi, Teranishi Shunichi. "Zadankai: Nihon Kankyō Kaigi 30nen no Ayumi to Kōgai-Kankyō Soshō." *Kanykyō to Kōgai* 39, no. 1 (Summer 2009): 50–58.

"Itaibyō Soshō Kiroku Okuru: Nichibenren Suēden Bengoshikai ni." *Asahi Shinbun* (morning edition, June 8, 1972): 23.

Iwasaki, Shunsuke. "Ajia no Inaka kara Nihon no Ciiki o Miru." *Gekkan Jichi Kenkyū* 30, no. 10 (October 1988): 18–24.

———. "Chikyū Junkan to Dai-3 Sekai o Utsu Seichō to Kaihatsu." *Kōmei* 334 (November 1989): 106–110.

———. "Kaihatsu to Kankyō: Chikyū Samitto o Shimin kara Tō." *Heiwa Keizai* 367 (June 1992): 13–28.

———. "NGO (Hiseifu Soshiki) ga Mezasu mono: Kokkyō o Koeru Shimin Sanka." *Kōmei* 318 (July 1988): 56–60.

———. *NGO wa Hito to Chikyū o Musubu: Ima Kokkyō o Koete, Dekiru Koto, Surubeki Koto.* Tokyo: Daisan Shokan, 1993.

———. "'Sekai Kankyō Kaigi' de Nihon wa Nani o Shuchō dekiruka: Posuto Reisen de sarani Jūyō ni natta Konseiki Saigo no Kankyō Samitto no Kadai." *Ushio* 394 (January 1992): 132–137.

———. "Shimin ni yoru Kokusai Kyōryoku (NGO)." *Tsukuba Fōramu* 28–32 (March 1990): 70–74.

Iwasaki, Shunsuke, Kobayashi Akira, Okajima Nariyuki, Takeuchi Yuzuru, Hara Takeshi, Teranishi Shun'ichi, and Awaji Kōji. "'92 Kokuren Burajiru Kaigi to Nihon no NGO." *Kōgai Kenkyū* 21, no. 2 (October 1991): 41–51.

Jacobsen, Sally. "II: A Call to Environmental Order." *Bulletin of the Atomic Scientists* 28, no. 7 (1972): 21–25.

JACSES. "Japan Center for a Sustainable Environment and Society (JACSES)." Accessed May 16, 2014. http://www.jacses.org/en/index.html.

Japan International Volunteer Center. "Specified Non-Profit Organization: Japan International Volunteer Center." Accessed May 16, 2014. http://www.ngo -jvc.net/en/.

Jasanoff, Sheila. "Image and Imagination: The Formation of Global Environmental Consciousness." In *Changing the Atmosphere: Expert Knowledge and Environmental Governance*, edited by Clark A. Miller, Paul N. Edwards, 309–338. Cambridge, MA: MIT Press, 2001.

————. "NGOs and the Environment: From Knowledge to Action." *Third World Quarterly* 18, no. 3 (1997): 579–594.

Jishu Kōza Ajia Gurūpu. "Tai Asahi Kasei Sōda no Kasen Osen." *Jishu Kōza* 31 (October 1973), 45–48. Reproduced in *Ui Jun Shūshū Kōgai Mondai Shiryō 1 Fukkoku "Jishu Kōza" Dai 2-kai Haihon Dai 1-kan*, edited by Saitama Daigaku Kyōsei Shakai Kenkyū Sentā, 375–378. Tokyo: Suirensha, 2006.

"'Jūmin Shuken' Kakuritsu Motome Sengen: NGO Fōramu Heimaku Yokohama." *Asahi Shinbun* (morning edition, May 4, 1992): 26.

Jūmin Toshokan, ed. *Minikomi Sōmokuroku*. Tokyo: Heibonsha, 1992.

Kaji, Etsuko. "Kawasaki Steel: The Giant at Home." *AMPO: Japan-Asia Quarterly Review* 26 (October–December 1975): 28–38.

Kaku Haikibutsu no Kaiyō Tōki ni Hantai suru Mariana Dōmei. "Nihon no Tomo e: Mariana Dōmei kara no Tegami." *Tsuchi no Koe, Tami no Koe: Gōgai Kaku Haikibutsu Kaiyō Tōki Hantai Shomei Undō Tokushū* 3 (October 1980): 3.

"'Kaku Haikibutsu no Tōki o Tōketsu Bōeiryoku Zōkyō wa Senshu Tsuranuku': Setsumei o Ryōkoku Kangei." *Asahi Shinbun* (morning edition, January 15, 1985): 1.

"Kaku Haikibutsu Tōki, Shima Agete Soshi: Teniantō Shichō ga Tsuyoi Ketsui." *Asahi Shinbun* (morning edition, October 14, 1980): 22.

"'Kaku Kagaisha ni naru Osore': Gensuikin Taikai Bunkakai Tōgi Nihon no Haikibutsu Tōki." *Asahi Shinbun* (morning edition, August 3, 1980): 22.

"Kaku no nai Taiheiyō o Tsukuridasō 3.1 Tokyo Shūkai" Sankasha Ichidō. "Watashitachi no Hankaku Taiheiyō Sengen." *Geppō Kōgai o Nogasuna! Nihon no Shinryaku no Kōshite Ajia Taiheiyō Minshū to tomo ni* 151 (February 1986): 2.

Kanda, Fuhito, and Kobayashi Hideo, eds. *Sengoshi Nenpyō*. Tokyo: Shogakkan, 2005.

Kankyōchō Chikyū Kankyōbu Kikakuka. *Tokyo Conference on the Global Environment and Human Response toward Sustainable Development*. Tokyo: Gyōsei, 1990.

"'Kankyō Gannen' Chikyūjin no Jikaku o." *Asahi Shinbun* (morning edition, November 20, 1989): 15.

"Kankyō NGO to no Nininsankyaku o." *Asahi Shinbun* (morning edition, June 3, 1993): 2.

Kanō Mikiyo. "Shiryaku=Sabetsu to Tatakau Ajia Fujin Kaigi to Dainiha Feminizumu." *Joseigaku Kenkyū* 18 (2011): 149–165.

Kapp, K. William. "Environmental Disruption: General Issues and Methodological Problems." In *Proceedings of International Symposium on Environmental Disruption: A Challenge to Social Scientists,* edited by Tsuru Shigeto, 3–22. Paris: International Social Science Council, 1970.

Karaki, Kiyoshi. "'Minamata' no Suiseki." In *Genchi ni Miru Sekai no Kōgai Sōkatsu: Sekai Kankyō Chōsadan Hōkoku,* edited by Tsuru Shigeto, 53–63. Tokyo: Chūnichi Shinbun Tokyo Honsha, 1975.

———. "Wareware Chikyū Kazoku." In *Genchi ni Miru Sekai no Kōgai Sōkatsu: Sekai Kankyō Chōsadan Hōkoku,* edited by Tsuru Shigeto, 69–98. Tokyo: Chūnichi Shinbun Tokyo Honsha, 1975.

Karan, Pradyumna P., and Unryu Suganuma, eds. *Local Environmental Movements: A Comparative Study of the United States and Japan.* Lexington: University Press of Kentucky, 2008.

Karliner, Joshua. *The Corporate Planet: Ecology and Politics in the Age of Globalization.* San Francisco: Sierra Club Books, 1997.

Katō, Saburō, Takeuchi Ken, Awaji Kōji, Akiyama Noriko, Teranishi Shun'ichi, and Kihara Keikichi. "1992 Kokuren Kankyō Kaihatsu Kaigi to Nihon no Kadai." *Kankyō to Kōgai* 20, no. 4 (April 1991): 30–40.

Katō, Takashi. "Meyer-shi Raisatsu o Ki ni Zenshin shita Hangenpatsu Tōsō." *Tsuchi no Koe, Tami no Koe Gōgai Kaku Haikibutsu Kaiyō Tōki Hantai Undō Tokushū* 8 (April 1981): 6.

Kawana, Hideyuki. *Dokyumento Nihon no Kōgai 1: Kōgai no Gekika.* Tokyo: Ryokufu, 1987.

———. *Dokyumento Nihon no Kōgai 2: Kankyōchō.* Tokyo: Ryokufu, 1988.

———. *Dokyumento Nihon no Kōgai 12: Chikyū Kankyō no Kiki.* Tokyo: Ryokufu, 1995.

———. *Dokyumento Nihon no Kōgai 13: Ajia no Kankyō Hakai to Nihon.* Tokyo: Ryokufu, 1996.

Keck, Margaret E., and Kathryn Sikkink. *Activists beyond Borders: Advocacy Networks in International Politics.* Ithaca, NY: Cornell University Press, 1998.

———. "Transnational Advocacy Networks in International and Regional Politics." *International Social Science Journal* 51, no. 159 (1999): 89–101.

Kikō Fōramu. "21-seiki no Kodomotachi, Magotachi ni, Seimei no Hoshi, Chikyū o tewatasu tame ni Chikyū Ondanka o kuitomeru Chie to Kōdō o ima suguni." Reproduced in *Kikō Fōramu kara Kikō Nettowāku e: Kyoto*

*Kaigi kara no Shuppatsu—Kikō Fōramu no Katsudō no Kiroku,* edited by Anzai Naoto, Suda Eriko, Taura Kenrō, Maruta Shōichi, and Yamaguchi Hironori. Kyoto: Kikō Fōramu—Kikō Hendō / Chikyū Ondanka o Fusegu Shimin Kaigi—Kikō Nettowāku, 1998.

————. "Kikō Fōramu 10 no Shuchō." Reproduced in *Kikō Fōramu kara Kikō Nettowāku e: Kyoto Kaigi kara no Shuppatsu—Kikō Fōramu no Katsudō no Kiroku,* edited by Anzai Naoto, Suda Eriko, Taura Kenrō, Maruta Shōichi, and Yamaguchi Hironori. Kyoto: Kikō Fōramu—Kikō Hendō / Chikyū Ondanka o Fusegu Shimin Kaigi—Kikō Nettowāku, 1998.

Kikuchi Yumi. "NGO Jōyaku-zukuri no Genba kara." *Kankyō to Kōgai* 22, no. 1 (September 1992): 39–41.

Kinser-Saiki, Maggie, ed. *Japanese Working for a Better World: Grassroots Voices and Access Guide to Citizens' Groups in Japan.* San Francisco: Honnoki USA, 1992.

Kirby, Peter Wynn. *Troubled Natures: Waste, Environment, Japan.* Honolulu: University of Hawai'i Press, 2010.

"Kirisutosha no Shomei: Kagakugijutsuchō e." *Tsuchi no Koe, Tami no Koe Gōgai* (February 1981): 7.

Kirk, Donald. "Students in the Elementary Schools Grow Up Suffering from Asthma. Plants Wither and Die. The Birds around Mount Fuji Are Decreasing in Number. They No Longer Visit the Town." *New York Times* (March 26, 1972): 33.

Kīsen Kankō ni Hantai suru Onnatachi no Kai. *Sei Shinryaku o Kokuhatsu suru: Kīsen Kankō.* Tokyo: Kīsen Kankō ni Hantai suru Onnatachi no Kai, 1974.

"Kite Yokkata: Minamatabyō no Hamamoto san." *Asahi Shinbun* (evening edition, June 17, 1972): 3.

"Kōgai, Amari Shinkei o Tsukawanuyō." *Geppō Kōgai o Nogasu na!* 1 (June 1974): 15–16.

"Kōgai Sangyō Dōnyū ni Shinchō o." Translation from original article in *Tong-A Ilbo* (August 13, 1975). Reproduced in *Geppō Kōgai o Nogasuna! Kankoku e no Kōgai Yushutsu o Kokuhatsu suru* 16 (September 1975): 6–7.

"'Kōgai Sangyō Kankoku Shinshutsu' Nihon de Hantai Undō." Translation from original article in *Tong-A Ilbo* (August 11, 1975). Reproduced in *Geppō Kōgai o Nogasuna! Kankoku e no Kōgai Yushutsu o Kokuhatsu suru* 16 (September 1975): 2.

"'Kōgai Yushutsu wa Yurusanu': Jūmin Dantai Tsūhō Sentā o Settchi." *Asahi Shinbun* (morning edition, April 9, 1976): 22.

"Kokunai no NGO, Senshinkoku no Sekinin Kyōchō shi Chikyū Samitto e Teigen (Osaka)." *Asahi Shinbun* (evening edition, December 12, 1991): 18.

"Kokuren Kankyō Kaigi e: Nō Moa Minamata: Kōgai Higaisha no Hōkoku wa Uttaeru." *Asahi Shinbun* (morning edition, February 18, 1972): 3.

Komatsu, Hiroshi, and Kim Techan. *Kōkyō suru Ningen 4:Tanaka Shōzō: Shōgai o Kōkyō ni sasageta Kōdō suru Shisōnin.* Tokyo: Tōkyō Daigaku Shuppan Kai, 2010.

Kōno Masayoshi. "Shiten." *Tsuchi no Koe, Tami no Koe* 120 (April 1981): 1.

"'Kotoshi no Hito' wa 'Kiki ni sarasareta Chikyū': Kankyō Osen no Shinkokuka ni Keishō." *Asahi Shinbun* (morning edition, December 26, 1988): 7.

Kume Sanshirō. "Genshiryoku Hatsuden no Anzensei to Jūmin Undō." *Kankyō to Kōgai* 4, no. 1 (1974): 37–47.

Kuroda, Ryōichi. *Ōsaka ni Runessansu o.* Kyoto: Hōritsu Bunka Sha, 1974.

Kuroda, Yōichi. *Nettairin Hakai to Tatakau: Mori ni Ikiru Hitobito to Nihon.* Tokyo: Iwanami Shoten, 1992.

———. "Nettairin no Kiki to Nihon Shakai no Shinro." *Kankyō to Kōgai* 21, no. 1 (July 1991): 8–14.

Kuroda, Yōichi, and François Nectoux. *Nettairin Hakai to Nihon no Mokuzai Bōeki: Sekai Shizen Hogo Kikin (WWF) Repōto.* Tokyo: Tsukiji Shokan, 1989.

*Kuroshio Tsūshin: Taiheiyō Shotō Rentai o Motomete!* 1 (Fall 1981). Contained in *Geppō Kōgai o Nogasuna! Daisan Sekai e no Kōgai Yushutsu o Kokuhatsu suru* 98 (February 1981): 17–25.

Laclau, Ernesto, and Chantal Mouffe. *Hegemony and Socialist Strategy: Toward a Radical Democratic Politics.* New York: Verso, 1985.

LeBlanc, Robin. *Bicycle Citizens: The Political World of the Housewife.* Berkeley: University of California Press, 1999.

Lewis, Anthony. "One Confused Earth." *New York Times* (June 17, 1972): 29.

Lewis, Jack G. "Civic Protest in Mishima: Citizens' Movements and the Politics of the Environment in Contemporary Japan." In *Political Opposition and Local Politics in Japan,* edited by Kurt Steiner, Ellis S. Krauss, and Scott C. Flanagan, 274–313. Princeton, NJ: Princeton University Press, 1980.

Machi to Seikatsu o Kangaeru Shimin Sentā. "Taiheiyō wa 'Mijikana' Watashitachi no Umi da: Parao kara Meyer-shi o Mukaete." *Tsuchi no Koe, Tami no Koe Gōgai Kaku Haikibutsu Kaiyō Tōki Hantai Undō Tokushū* 8 (April 1981): 5.

Maclachlan, Patricia L. *Consumer Politics in Postwar Japan: The Institutional Boundaries of Citizen Activism.* New York: Columbia University Press, 2002.

Madhok, Sujata. "Graffiti Greens the Forum." June 13, 1992. In *Women's Feature Service (WFS) coverage of UNCED.* Contained in *Earth Summit: The NGO Archives CD ROM.* Hamilton, Canada: CCOHS, 1995. CD ROM.

Maeda, Tetsuo. "Kaku to Taiheiyō: Ima, Watashitachi ni totte no Mondai." *Tsuchi no Koe, Tami no Koe* 97 (April 1979): 20–23.

Marston, Sallie A., John Paul Jones III, and Keith Woodward. "Human Geography without Scale." *Transactions of the Institute of British Geographers* 30, no. 4 (2005): 416–432.

Martello, Marybeth Long, and Sheila Jasanoff. "Introduction: Globalization and Environmental Governance." In *Earthly Politics: Local and Global in Environmental Governance,* edited by Sheila Jasanoff and Marybeth Long Martello, 1–29. Cambridge, MA: MIT Press, 2004.

Masayoshi, Hideo. "Nikkan no Genjō to Kōgai Yushutsu Soshi Undō." *Geppō Kōgai o Nogasuna! Kankoku e no Kōgai Yushutsu o Kokuhatsu suru* 7 (December 1974): 1–3.

Matsui, Yayori. "Hisansa ni Ikinomu. Kiroku Eiga 'Minamata' o Jōei. Jinmin Hiroba de 'Nihon no Yūbe.'" *Asahi Shinbun* (June 6, 1972): 8.

———. "Kaimaku Semaru Kokuren Ningen Kankyō Kaigi. Kakkizuku Sutokkuhorumu. 'Kōgai Nippon' ni Kanshin. Oshiyoseru Hōdō Kankeisha." *Asahi Shinbun* (evening edition, June 3, 1972): 8.

———. "Kokuren Kankyō Kaigi Hōkoku II." *Kōgai Genron* 15 (November 1972): 1–34. Reproduced in *Ui Jun Shūshū Kōgai Mondai Shiryō 2 Fukkoku "Kōgai Genron" Dai 1-kai Haihon Dai 3-kan,* edited by Saitama Daigaku Kyōsei Shakai Kenkyū Sentā, 333–366. Tokyo: Suirensha, 2007.

———. "'Seifu wa Nani o Shite ita: Kōgai Kanja Tōchaku Umeku Kishadan." *Asahi Shinbun* (morning edition, June 5, 1972): 2.

Matsumura, Naoki. "Uran wa Iranai: Ōsutoraria Fukushushō e Yōsei." *Jishu Kōza* 60 (March 1976): 6–8. Reproduced in *Ui Jun Shūshū Kōgai Mondai Shiryō 1 Fukkoku "Jishu Kōza" Dai 3-kai Haihon Dai 2-kan,* edited by Saitama Daigaku Kyōsei Shakai Kenkyū Sentā, 146–148. Tokyo: Suirensha, 2006.

Matsuo, Makoto. "Kikō Fōramu no Seika to Kankyō NGO no Imi: Kankyō Seijigaku Kōchiku ni mukete no Oboegaki (2)—The Consequences of KIKO Forum and Significance of Environment NGOs." *Kyoto Seika Daigaku Kiyō* 17 (1999): 212–228.

———. "Hachiōji no Honkaigi." *Jishu Kōza* 40 (July 1974): 10–13. Reproduced in *Ui Jun Shūshū Kōgai Mondai Shiryō 1 Fukkoku "Jishu Kōza" Dai 2-kai Haihon Dai 3-kan,* edited by Saitama Daigaku Kyōsei Shakai Kenkyū Sentā, 134–137. Tokyo: Suirensha, 2006.

———. "Mō Hitotsu no Omoni o Seou Kakugo o: Higashi Ajia no Tabi kara (3)." *Jishu Kōza* 20 (November 1972): 35–38. Reproduced in *Ui Jun Shūshū Kōgai Mondai Shiryō 1 Fukkoku "Jishu Kōza" Dai 4-kan,* edited by Saitama Daigaku Kyōsei Shakai Kenkyū Sentā, 103–106. Tokyo: Suirensha, 2005.

———. "Tōnan Ajia no Tabi kara (Marēshia nite)." *Jishu Kōza* 18 (September 1972): 1–4. Reproduced in *Ui Jun Shūshū Kōgai Mondai Shiryō 1 Fukkoku "Jishu Kōza" Dai 3-kan,* edited by Saitama Daigaku Kyōsei Shakai Kenkyū Sentā, 345–348. Tokyo: Suirensha, 2005.

———. "Tōnan Ajia no Tabi kara (ni): Shingapōru nite." *Jishu Kōza* 19 (October 1972): 555–558. Reproduced in *Ui Jun Shūshū Kōgai Mondai Shiryō 1*

*Fukkoku "Jishu Kōza" Dai 4-kan*, edited by Saitama Daigaku Kyōsei Shakai Kenkyū Sentā, 59–62. Tokyo: Suirensha, 2005.

———. "Watashitachi ni Nani ga Dekirunoka." *Jishu Kōza* 24 (March 1973): 41. Reproduced in *Ui Jun Shūshū Kōgai Mondai Shiryō 1 Fukkoku "Jishu Kōza" Dai 4-kan*, edited by Saitama Daigaku Kyōsei Shakai Kenkyū Sentā, 379. Tokyo: Suirensha, 2005.

McCormick, John. *Reclaiming Paradise: The Global Environmental Movement*. Bloomington: Indiana University Press, 1991.

McKean, Margaret. *Environmental Protest and Citizen Politics in Japan*. Berkeley: University of California Press, 1981.

McNeill, John R. *Something New Under the Sun: An Environmental History of the Twentieth-Century World*. London: Penguin Books, 2000.

Meadows, Donella H., Dennis L. Meadows, Jørgen Randers, and William W. Behrens III. *The Limits to Growth: A Report for the Club of Rome's Project on The Predicament of Mankind*. New York: Universe Books, 1972.

Mendiola, Felipe. "Nihon Seifu ni Naguraretemo Iimasu: Kaku no Gomi o Watashitachi no Umi ni Suteruna!" *Tsuchi no Koe, Tami no Koe* 115 (November 1980): 2–7.

———. "Tenian kara no Uttae: Nihon Seifu wa Doko made Watashitachi o Fumitsubuseba Ki ga Sumunoka!" *Geppō Kōgai o Nogasuna! Daisan Sekai e no Kōgai Yushutsu o Kokuhatsu suru* 96 (November–December 1980): 1–8.

Michiba Chikanobu. "Posuto-Betonamu Sensōki ni okeru Ajia Rentai Undō: 'Uchinaru Ajia' to 'Ajia no naka no Nihon' no aida de." In *Iwanami Kōza Higashi Ajia Kingendai Tsūshi Dai8kan: Betonamu Sensō no Jidai 1960–1975nen*, edited by Wada Haruki, Gotō Ken'ichi, Kibata Yōichi, Yamamuro Shin'ichi, Cho Kyeungdal, Nakano Satoshi, and Kawashima Shin, 97–127. Tokyo: Iwanami Shoten, 2011.

———. "Sen Kyūhyaku Rokujū Nendai ni okeru 'Chiki' no Hakken to 'Kōkyōsei' no Saiteigi: Miketsu no Aporia o megutte." *Gendai Shisō* 31, no.6 (May 2002): 97–130.

———. *Senryō to Heiwa: Sengo to iu Keiken*. Tokyo: Seidosha, 2005.

Middell, Matthias, and Katja Naumann. "Global History and the Spatial Turn: From the Impact of Area Studies to the Study of Critical Junctures of Globalization." *Journal of Global History* 5 (2010): 149–170.

Miller, Ian Jared, Julia Adeney Thomas, and Brett Walker, eds. *Japan at Nature's Edge: The Environmental Context of a Global Power*. Honolulu: University of Hawai'i Press, 2013.

"Minamatabyō Kanja nado 2 Dantai ga Ketsudanshiki: Kokuren Kankyō Kaigi o Mae ni." *Asahi Shinbun* (morning edition, June 3, 1972): 18.

"Minami Taiheiyō e Setsumeidan: Hōshasei Haikibutsu Tōki Keikaku Seifu Haken Kimeru." *Asahi Shinbun* (morning edition, August 6, 1980): 1.

Mishima, Akio. *Bitter Sea: The Human Cost of Minamata Disease.* Tokyo: Kosei, 1992.

Miyamoto, Ken'ichi. "Chiisana Hon no Ōkina Sekinin." *Tosho* 227 (July 1968): 10.

———. "Fukamaru Kōgai: Shinaseru Toshi." In *Genchi ni Miru Sekai no Kōgai Sōkatsu: Sekai Kankyō Chōsadan Hōkoku,* edited by Tsuru Shigeto, 24–45. Tokyo: Chūnichi Shinbun Tokyo Honsha, 1975.

———. "Japan's Environmental Policy: Lessons from Experience and Remaining Problems." In *Japan at Nature's Edge: The Environmental Context of a Global Power,* edited by Ian Jared Miller, Julia Adeney Thomas, and Brett Walker, 222–251. Honolulu: University of Hawai'i Press, 2013.

———. *Kankyō Keizaigaku.* Tokyo: Iwanami Shoten, 1989.

———. *Kankyō to Jichi: Watashi no Sengo Nōto.* Tokyo: Iwanami Shoten, 1996.

———. "Naze Gaikoku no Tabi ni Derunoka." In *Genchi ni Miru Sekai no Kōgai Sōkatsu: Sekai Kankyō Chōsadan Hōkoku,* edited by Tsuru Shigeto, 19–23. Tokyo: Chūnichi Shinbun Tokyo Honsha, 1975.

———. *Nihon no Kankyō Mondai: Sono Seiji Keizaigakuteki Kōsatsu.* Tokyo: Yūhikaku, 1981.

———. *Omoide no Hitobito to.* Tokyo: Fujiwara Shoten, 2001.

———. "Shinobiyoru Kōgai." *Sekai* 204 (December 1962): 199–214.

Miyamoto, Ken'ichi, and Harada Masazumi. "Aramogorudo Kokujin Suigin Chūdoku Jiken." In *Sekai no Kōgai Chizu* 1, edited by Tsuru Shigeto, 70–83. Tokyo: Iwanami Shoten, 1977.

———. "Kanada Indian Suigin Chūdoku Jiken." In *Sekai no Kōgai Chizu* 1, edited by Tsuru Shigeto, 84–125. Tokyo: Iwanami Shoten, 1977.

Miyazaki, Shōgo. *Ima, Kōkyōsei o Utsu: "Dokyumento" Yokohama Shinkamotsusen Hantai Undō.* Tokyo: Shinsensha, 1975.

Mizuguchi, Ken'ya. "Hōshasei Haikibutsu no Kaiyō Tōki o Yurusuna (Jō): Tairyō no Hōshanō Tarenagashi no Kikensei." *Hangenpatsu Shinbun* 29 (September 1980): 4. Reproduced in *"Hangenpatsu Shinbun" Shukusatsuban (0–100),* edited by Hangenpatsu Undō Zenkoku Renrakukai, 144. Nara: Yasōsha, 1986.

Morris-Suzuki, Tessa. *A History of Japanese Economic Thought.* London: Routledge and Nissan Institute for Japanese Studies, 1991.

———. "Environmental Problems and Perceptions in Early Industrial Japan." In *Sediments of Time: Environment and Society in Chinese History,* edited by Mark Elvin and Liu Tsui-jung, 756–780. Cambridge: Cambridge University Press, 1998.

Moyn, Samuel Moyn. *The Last Utopia: Human Rights in History.* Cambridge, MA: Belknap Press of Harvard University Press, 2010.

———. "The Return of the Prodigal: The 1970s as a Turning Point in Human Rights History." In *The Breakthrough: Human Rights in the 1970s,* edited by Jan Eckel and Samuel Moyn, 1–14. Philadelphia: University of Pennsylvania Press, 2014.

Nagai, Susumu. "Ōbei no Genpatsu Hantai Tōsō." In *Genchi ni Miru Sekai no Kōgai Sōkatsu: Sekai Kankyō Chōsadan Hōkoku,* edited by Tsuru Shigeto, 111–114. Tokyo: Chūnichi Shinbun Tokyo Honsha, 1975.

———. "Ōbei Senshinkoku ni okeru Genpatsu Hantai Undō." In *Genchi ni Miru Sekai no Kōgai Sōkatsu: Sekai Kankyō Chōsadan Hōkoku,* edited by Tsuru Shigeto, 168–184. Tokyo: Chūnichi Shinbun Tokyo Honsha, 1975.

———. "Sekai Kankyō Chōsadan Hōkoku: Ōbei Senshinkoku ni okeru Genpatsu Hantai Undō." *Kōgai Kenkyū* 5, no. 2 (October 1975): 52–58.

Naikakufu Genshiryoku Seisaku Tantōshitsu. *Hōshasei Haikibutsu no Shori-Shobun o Meguru Torikumi no Genjō ni tsuite.* Document no. 3–1. March 8, 2001.

Nakajima, Ryūji. "Amerika ni Tayoranakutemo Yatte ikeru." *Tsuchi no Koe, Tami no Koe Gōgai Kaku Haikibutsu Kaiyō Tōki Hantai Undō Tokushū* 9 (May 1981): 8.

Nakamura, Ryōji. "Sekine Hama no 'Mutsu' Shinbokōka o Yurusanai." *Tsuchi no Koe, Tami no Koe* 123 (August 1981): 2–5.

Nectoux, François, and Yoichi Kuroda. *Timber from the South Seas: An Analysis of Japan's Tropical Timber Trade and Its Environmental Impact.* London: Banson, 1990.

NGO Committee on Education. "UN Documents: Gathering a Body of Global Agreements: United Nations Conference on the Human Environment." Accessed May 5, 2014. http://www.un-documents.net/unche.htm.

Nichibenren. "'92 NGO Gurōbaru Fōramu Nichibenren Shusai Shinpojiumu— Exchanging the Ideas about International Environmental Law." *Jiyū to Seigi* 43, no. 11 (November 1992): 103–116.

———. *UN Earth Summit/Global Forum 1992: Japanese Lawyers' Environmental Struggle.* Conference Recordings RIO92–046, 1992, cassette tape.

Nihon Bengoshi Rengōkai Kōgai Taisaku-Kankyō Hozen Iinkai, ed. *Nihon no Kōgai Yushutsu to Kankyō Hakai.* Tokyo: Nihon Hyōronsha, 1991.

"Nihon Kagaku Dai 8-kai Kōgi Demo ni Sanka: 'Damatte irarenai' Jimoto Higaisha ga Dantai o Kessei." *Tōyō Keizai Nippō* (June 27, 1975). Reproduced in *Geppō Kōgai o Nogasuna! Kankoku e no Kōgai Yushutsu o Kokuhatsu suru* 14 (July 1975): 31.

"Not All Is Serene in Cities of Japan." *New York Times* (19 January 19, 1968): 51.

O'Bryan, Scott. *The Growth Idea: Purpose and Prosperity in Postwar Japan.* Honolulu: University of Hawai'i Press, 2009.

Oda, Makoto, ed. *Ajia o Kangaeru: Ajiajin Kaigi no Zenkiroku*. Tokyo: Ushio Shuppansha, 1976.

Oda, Makoto. "Heiwa o Tsukuru: Sono Genri to Kōdō—Hitotsu no Sengen." In Oda Makoto, *Oda Makoto Zenshigoto* 9, 113–131. Tokyo: Kawade Shobō Shinsha, 1970.

———. "Nanshi no Shisō." In Oda Makoto, *Oda Makoto Zenshigoto* 8, 13–31. Tokyo: Kawade Shobō Shinsha, 1970.

Ogasawara Umi o Mamoru Kai. "Kaku no Gomi o Sutesaseruna! Dasaseruna! Kaiyō Tōki Hantai ni Kakuji de Tachagaru. Ogasawara no Utsukushi Umi o Yogosuna!" *Hangenpatsu Shinbun* 31 (November 1980): 1. Reproduced in *"Hangenpatsu Shinbun" Shukusatsuban (0–100)*, edited by Hangenpatsu Undō Zenkoku Renrakukai, 151. Nara: Yasōsha, 1986.

Ogawa, Hiroshi. "Ajia no Mado: Nihon Kagaku no Kōgai Yushutsu o Kokuhatsu suru." *Jishu Kōza* 42 (September 1974): 46–62. Reproduced in *Ui Jun Shūshū Kōgai Mondai Shiryō 1 Fukkoku "Jishu Kōza" Dai 2-kai Haihon Dai 3-kan*, edited by Saitama Daigaku Kyōsei Shakai Kenkyū Sentā, 298–314. Tokyo: Suirensha, 2006.

Ogawa, Yoshio. "Dai 2 no Toyama Kagaku=Nihon Kagaku no Kankoku e no Kōgai Yushutsu o Yamesaseyo." *Geppō Kōgai o Nogasuna! Kankoku e no Kōgai Yushutsu o Kokuhatsu suru* 3 (August 1974): 2–3.

Okakura, Kakuzo. *The Ideals of the East with Special Reference to the Arts of Japan*. New York: E. P. Dutton and Company, 1920.

Okuda, Takaharu. "Anti-Pollution Movements Get Together to Oppose Japan's Overseas Aggression." *AMPO: Japan-Asia Quarterly Review* 28 (April–September 1976): 10–11, 26.

Okuda, Takahara. "Documents of the First Co-operation between Japanese Citizens and Thai People Acting Simultaneously to Stop the Exporting Pollution." *KOGAI: The Newsletter from Polluted Japan* 7 (Spring 1975): 8–11.

———. "Nichitai o Musubu Kōgai Hantai Undō." *Jishu Kōza* 44 (November 1974): 41–54. Reproduced in *Ui Jun Shūshū Kōgai Mondai Shiryō 1 Fukkoku "Jishu Kōza" Dai 2-kai Haihon Dai 4-kan*, edited by Saitama Daigaku Kyōsei Shakai Kenkyū Sentā, 45–58. Tokyo: Suirensha, 2006.

Ōno, Yoshio. "Yattaze 31-nichikan!" *Jishu Kōza* 55 (October 1975): 37–40. Reproduced in *Ui Jun Shūshū Kōgai Mondai Shiryō 1 Fukkoku "Jishu Kōza" Dai 3-kai Haihon Dai 1-kan*, edited by Saitama Daigaku Kyōsei Shakai Kenkyū Sentā, 291–294. Tokyo: Suirensha, 2006.

Onodera, Takuji. "9-gatsu 14-ka 'Asahi Garasu wa Tai kara Tettai seyo! Nichitai Dōji Kōdō' Hōkoku: Han-Keizai Shinryaku, Han-Kōgai Yushutsu no Kyōdō Sensen o." *Geppō Kōgai o Nogasuna! Kankoku e no Kōgai Yushutsu o Kokuhatsu suru* 5 (October 1974): 7–9.

Orr, James J. *The Victim as Hero: Ideologies of Peace and National Identity in Postwar Japan.* Honolulu: University of Hawai'i Press, 2001.

Osaka Bengoshikai. *Nisshōken no Tebiki.* Osaka: Osaka Bengoshikai, 1981.

Osaka Bengoshikai Kankyōken Kenkyūkai. *Kankyōken.* Tokyo: Nihon Hyōronsha, 1973.

Ōtsuka, Tadashi. *Kankyōhō.* Tokyo: Yūhikaku, 2010.

Pekkanen, Robert. "After the Developmental State: Civil Society in Japan." *Journal of East Asian Studies* 4 (2004): 363–388.

———. *Japan's Dual Civil Society: Members without Advocates.* Stanford, CA: Stanford University Press, 2006.

Pempel, T. J. "Gulliver in Lilliput: Japan and Asian Economic Regionalism." *World Policy Journal* 13, no. 4 (Winter 1996–1997): 13–26.

Pharr, Susan J. "Conclusion: Targeting by an Activist State: Japan as a Civil Society Model." In *The State of Civil Society in Japan,* edited by Frank J. Schwartz and Susan J. Pharr, 316–336. Cambridge: Cambridge University Press, 2003.

Pieck, Sonja K. "Transnational Activist Networks: Mobilization between Emotion and Bureaucracy." *Social Movement Studies: Journal of Social, Cultural and Political Protest* 12, no. 2 (2013): 121–137.

Radkau, Joachim. *Nature and Power: A Global History of the Environment.* Translated by Thomas Dunlap. New York: Cambridge University Press, 2008.

Reich, Michael. "Crisis and Routine: Pollution Reporting by the Japanese Press." In *Institutions for Change in Japanese Society,* edited by George DeVos, 114–147. Berkeley: Institute of East Asian Studies, University of California at Berkeley, 1984.

Reimann, Kim D. "Building Global Civil Society from the Outside In? Japanese International Development NGOs, the State, and International Norms." In *The State of Civil Society in Japan,* edited by Frank J. Schwartz and Susan J. Pharr, 298–315. Cambridge: Cambridge University Press, 2003.

———. "Building Networks from the outside in: Japanese NGOs and the Kyoto Climate Change Conference 2002." In *Globalization and Resistance: Transnational Dimensions of Social Movements,* edited by Jackie Smith and Hank Johnston, 173–187. Lanham, MD: Rowman & Littlefield, 2002.

———. *The Rise of Japanese NGOs: Activism from Above.* Oxon, UK: Routledge, 2010.

Robertson, Roland. "Glocalization: Time-Space and Homogeneity-Heterogeneity." In *Global Modernities,* edited by Mike Featherstone, Scott Lash, and Roland Robertson, 25–44. London: SAGE, 1995.

Robie, David. *Blood on Their Banner: Nationalist Struggles in the South Pacific.* London: Zed Books, 1989.

Robinson, William. "Theories of Globalization." In *The Blackwell Companion to Globalization*, edited by George Ritzer, 125–143. Oxford: Blackwell, 2007.

Roland, Albert, Richard Wilson, and Michael Rahill. *Adlai Stevenson of the United Nations*. Manila: Free Asia Press, 1965.

Saitama Daigaku Kyōsei Shakai Kenkyū Sentā, ed. *Ui Jun Shūshū Kōgai Mondai Shiryō 1 Fukkoku "Jishu Kōza" Dai 3-kai Haihon Dai 1-kan*. Tokyo: Suirensha, 2006.

Saitō, Kiyoaki. "Kankyō Mondai to Borantia." In *Borantiagaku no Susume*, edited by Utsumi Seiji, 2–23. Kyoto: Shōwadō, 2001.

Saitō, Tamotsu. "Hōshasei Haikibutsu no Kaiyō Tōki ni Hantai suru." *Tsuchi no Koe, Tami no Koe* 112 (August 1980): 14–17, 46.

Sakakibara, Shirō. " 'Shūdan no Hakken': Chiba Kōgai Juku." *Gendai no Me* 19, no. 2 (February 1978): 212–217.

"'Sakana' ka 'Kaku' ka: Hōshasei Haikibutsu no Tōki. 'Nemawashi' Okure no Kagichō ni Fushin o Kakusanu Suisanchō." *Mainichi Shinbun* (August 9, 1980). Reproduced in *Geppō Kōgai o Nogasuna! Daisan Sekai e no Kōgai Yushutsu o Kokuhatsu suru* 92 (July 1980): 3.

Salvatierra, Wilfredo. "Kawasaki Seitetsu to Firipin Kaihatsu: Nihon Kigyō Yūchi ni karamu Seiryoku Shinchō e no Omowaku kara Shinshutsu ni taisuru Bimyō na Zure ga Umarehajimeteiru." *Gendai no Me* 16, no. 12 (December 1975): 219–225.

———. "Kawasaki Steel: The Giant Abroad." *AMPO: Japan-Asia Quarterly Review* 26 (October–December 1975): 3–27.

Sancton, Thomas A. "Cover Stories: What on EARTH Are We Doing?" *Time* 133, no. 1 (January 2, 1989): 24. Accessed May 14, 2014. Available at Academic Search Complete, EBSCOhost.

Sasaki-Uemura, Wesley. *Organizing the Spontaneous: Citizen Protest in Postwar Japan*. Honolulu: University of Hawai'i Press, 2001.

Sassen, Saskia. Globalization or Denationalization? *Review of International Political Economy* 10, no.1 (2003): 1–22.

Sato, Atsuko. "Beyond Boundaries: Japan, Knowledge, and Transnational Networks in Global Atmospheric Politics." PhD diss., University of Hawai'i, 2002.

Saunier, Pierre-Yves. "Learning by Doing: Notes about the Making of the Palgrave Dictionary of Transnational History." *Journal of Modern European History* 6 (2008): 159–180.

Schreurs, Miranda. "Assessing Japan's Role as a Global Environmental Leader." *Policy and Society* 23, no. 1 (2004): 88–110.

———. "Shifting Priorities and the Internationalization of Environmental Risk Management in Japan." In *Learning to Manage Global Environmental Risks, Volume 2: A Functional Analysis of Social Responses to Climate Change, Ozone*

*Depletion, and Acid Rain*, edited by Social Learning Group, 191–212. Cambridge, MA: MIT Press, 2001.

Schwartz, Frank J., and Susan J. Pharr, ed. *The State of Civil Society in Japan.* Cambridge: Cambridge University Press, 2003.

Shibata, Tokue. "Kōgai to Tatakau Kyosei: Kainō Michitaka." *Kankyō to Kōgai* 39, no. 1 (Summer 2009): 38–43.

"Shimin Dantai ga Renraku Kessei, Teigen matome Daihyōdan: 92-nen 6-gatsu Chikyū Samitto." *Asahi Shinbun* (morning edition, May 26, 1991): 3.

Shimin Enerugī Kenkyūjo. "Shimin Enerugī Kenkyūjo—People's Research Institute on Energy and Environment." Accessed May 16, 2014. http://www.priee.org/.

Shimin no Te de Nikkan yuchaku o Tadasu Chōsa Undō—Jishu Kōza Jikkō Iinkai. "Kinkyū Apīru: Kaku Nenryō Saishori Kōjō o Kankoku ni Oshitsukeruna! Ajia-Taiheiyō Minshū ni Tekitai suru Nikkan no Kaku Busō—Kan-Taiheiyō Genshiryoku Kyōdōtai Kōsō Jitsugen e no Michi o Yurusuna!" *Geppō Kōgai o Nogasuna! Daisan Sekai e no Kōgai Yushutsu o Kokuhatsu suru* 97 (January 1981): 10–13.

Shimizu, Makoto, ed. *Kainō Michitaka Chosakushū 8: Kōgai.* Tokyo: Nihon Hyōronsha, 1970.

Shimokawa, Kōshi, ed. *Kankyōshi Nenpyō 1926–2000 Shōwa-Heisei Hen.* Kawade Shobō Shinsha, 2004.

Shinmura, Izuru, ed. *Kōjien Dainihan.* Tokyo: Iwanami Shoten, 1969.

"Shinrin Hakai de Nihon ni Chūmon: NGO Fōramu Kaimaku Chikyū Samitto." *Asahi Shinbun* (morning edition, May 2, 1992): 26.

Shōji, Hikaru, and Miyamoto Ken'ichi. *Nihon no Kōgai.* Tokyo: Iwanami Shoten, 1975.

———. *Osorubeki Kōgai.* Tokyo: Iwanami Shoten, 1964.

Smith, W. Eugene, and Aileen M. Smith. *Minamata: Words and Photographs.* New York: Holt, Rinehart and Winston, 1975.

Snow, David A., and Robert D. Benford. "Framing Processes and Social Movements: An Overview and Assessment." *Annual Review of Sociology* 26 (2000): 611–639.

———. "Master Frames and Cycles of Protest." In *Frontiers in Social Movement Theory,* edited by Aldon D. Morris and Carol McClurg Mueller, 133–155. New Haven, CT: Yale University Press, 1992.

Sorensen, André and Carolin Funck, eds. *Living Cities in Japan: Citizens' Movements, Machizukuri, and Local Environments.* New York: Routledge, 2007.

Stolz, Robert. *Bad Water: Nature, Pollution, and Politics in Japan, 1870–1950.* Durham, NC: Duke University Press, 2015.

Strong, Kenneth. *Ox against the Storm: A Biography of Tanaka Shozo: Japan's Conservationist Pioneer.* Folkestone, UK: Japan Library, 1977.

Struck, Bernhard, Kate Ferris, and Jacques Revel. "Introduction: Space and Scale in Transnational History." *The International History Review* 33, no. 4 (2011): 573–584.

"Suēden e Shuppatsu: Minamata Kanjara Sannin." *Asahi Shinbun* (morning edition, June 1, 1972): 23.

Taiheiyō o Kaku no Gomi Suteba ni suru na! 10.22 Tokyo Shūkai Sankasha Ichidō. "Nihon-Amami-Okinawa Minshū no Apīru." *Tsuchi no Koe, Tami no Koe* 115 (November 1980): 11.

Tanaka, Kakuei. *Building a New Japan: A Plan for Remodelling the Japanese Archipelago.* Tokyo: Simul Press, 1973.

Tan, Nobuhiro. "Firipin e no Kōgai Yushutsu—Kawasaki Seitetsu." *Geppō Kōgai o Nogasuna! Kankoku e no Kōgai Yushutsu o Kokuhatsu suru* 26 (January 1976): 90–91.

Tarrow, Sidney. *The New Transnational Activism.* Cambridge: Cambridge University Press, 2005.

Tateno, Kōichi, and Saitō Tamotsu. "Saishori Kōjō Kensetsu o Yurusanai Amami—Okinawa Jūmin no Sensei Kōgeki." *Tsuchi no Koe, Tami no Koe* 108 (April 1980): 25–28.

Thelen, David. "The Nation and Beyond: Transnational Perspectives on United States History." *The Journal of American History* 86, no. 3 (December 1999): 965–975.

Thiele, Leslie Paul. *Environmentalism for a New Millennium: The Challenge of Coevolution.* New York: Oxford University Press, 1999.

"Third World Ecology." *Stockholm Conference Eco* (June 7, 1972): 5.

Thomas, Julia Adeney. "Using Japan to Think Globally: The Natural Subject of History and Its Hopes." In *Japan at Nature's Edge: The Environmental Context of a Global Power,* edited by Ian Jared Miller, Julia Adeney Thomas, Brett L. Walker, 293–310. Honolulu: University Hawai'i Press, 2013.

Tokyo Metropolitan Government. *Tokyo Fights Pollution.* Tokyo: Tokyo Metropolitan Government, 1977.

Tokyo Minamatabyō o Kokuhatsu suru Kai. "4.25 Tokyo Minamatabyō o Kokuhatsu suru Kai no Apīru." *Geppō Kōgai o Nogasuna! Kankoku e no Kōgai Yushutsu o Kokuhatsu suru* 35 (May 1976): 32–33.

Tokyoto Kōgai Kenkyūjo, ed. *Kōgai to Tōkyōto.* Tokyo: Tōkyōto Kōgai Kenkyūjo, 1970.

"Tomo ni Rentai shite Tatakaō! Firipin Katoriku Shinpu wa Uttaeru." *Geppō Kōgai o Nogasuna! Dai San Sekai e no Kōgai Yushutsu o Kokuhatsu suru* 47 (March 1977): 6–8.

"Toyama Kagaku no Kōgai Yushutsu o Yamesaseru" Jikkō Iinkai. "Toyama Kagaku e no Tegami Zenbun." *Geppō Kōgai o Nogasuna! Kankoku e no Kōgai Yushutsu o Kokuhatsu suru* 2 (July 1974): 4–5.

Tsukamoto Hiroki. "Kokonatsu no Mura wa Kieta." *Jishu Kōza* 69 (December 1976): 12. Reproduced in *Ui Jun Shūshū Kōgai Mondai Shiryō 1 Fukkoku "Jishu Kōza" Dai 3-kai Haihon Dai 3-kan,* edited by Saitama Daigaku Kyōsei Shakai Kenkyū Sentā, 268–272. Tokyo: Suirensha, 2006.

Tsuru, Shigeto. "Foreword." In *Proceedings of International Symposium on Environmental Disruption: A Challenge to Social Scientists,* edited by Tsuru Shigeto, xiii–xiv. Paris: International Social Science Council, 1970.

———, ed. *Genchi ni Miru Sekai no Kōgai Sōkatsu: Sekai Kankyō Chōsadan Hōkoku.* Tokyo: Chūnichi Shinbun Tokyo Honsha, 1975.

———, ed. *Gendai Shihonshugi to Kōgai.* Tokyo: Iwanami Shoten, 1968.

———. "In Place of GNP." In Tsuru Shigeto, *Economic Theory and Capitalist Society: The Selected Essays of Shigeto Tsuru* 1, 64–84. Aldershot, UK: Edward Elgar, 1994.

———. "Introduction." In Tsuru Shigeto, *Economic Theory and Capitalist Society: The Selected Essays of Shigeto Tsuru* 1, ix–xxviii. Aldershot, UK: Edward Elgar, 1994.

———. "Jo." In Tsuru Shigeto, *Tsuru Shigeto Chosakushū 6: Toshi Mondai to Kōgai,* i–vii. Tokyo: Kōdansha, 1975.

———. "Jūmin no Tachiba kara mita Toshi Mondai." In Tsuru Shigeto, *Tsuru Shigeto Chosakushū 6: Toshi Mondai to Kōgai,* 21–42. Tokyo: Kōdansha, 1975.

———. *Kōgai no Seijikeizaigaku.* Tokyo: Iwanami Shoten, 1972.

———. "Kokuren Kaigi Junbi Katei deno Mondaiten." In Tsuru Shigeto, *Tsuru Shigeto Chosakushū 6: Toshi Mondai to Kōgai,* 450–461. Tokyo: Kōdansha, 1975.

———. "Maegaki." In *Sekai no Kōgai Chizu* 1, edited by Tsuru Shigeto, i–iii. Tokyo: Iwanami Shoten, 1977.

———. " 'North-South' Relations on Environment." In Tsuru Shigeto, *Economic Theory and Capitalist Society: The Selected Essays of Shigeto Tsuru* 1, 268–295. Aldershot, UK: Edward Elgar, 1994.

———. *The Political Economy of the Environment: The Case of Japan.* London: Athlone Press, 1999.

———, ed. *Proceedings of International Symposium on Environmental Disruption: A Challenge to Social Scientists.* Paris: International Social Science Council, 1970.

———. "Sekai Kankyō Chōsadan no Shuppatsu ni atatte." In *Genchi ni Miru Sekai no Kōgai Sōkatsu: Sekai Kankyō Chōsadan Hōkoku,* edited by Tsuru Shigeto, 12–14. Tokyo: Chūnichi Shinbun Tokyo Honsha, 1975.

———, ed. *Sekai no Kōgai Chizu* 1 and 2. Tokyo: Iwanami Shoten, 1977.

———. "Shimin Jichi no Atarashii Dankai." In Tsuru Shigeto, *Tsuru Shigeto Chosakushū 6: Toshi Mondai to Kōgai,* 105–125. Tokyo: Kōdansha, 1975.

———, ed. *Tōkyō e no Teigen*. Tokyo: Teikoku Chihō Gyōsei Gakkai, 1969.

———. "Towards a New Political Economy." In Tsuru Shigeto, *Economic Theory and Capitalist Society: The Selected Essays of Shigeto Tsuru* 1, 99–112. Aldershot, UK: Edward Elgar, 1994.

———. *Tsuru Shigeto Chosakushū 6: Toshi Mondai to Kōgai*. Tokyo: Kōdansha, 1975.

———. *Tsuru Shigeto Jiden: Ikutsumo no Kiro o Kaiko shite*. Tokyo: Iwanami Shoten, 2001.

Tsuru, Shigeto, and Okamoto Masami. "Gendai Sekai to Kōgai Mondai." In *Sekai no Kōgai Chizu* 1, edited by Tsuru Shigeto, 1–48. Tokyo: Iwanami Shoten, 1977.

Tyrell, Ian. "Reflections on the Transnational Turn in United States History: Theory and Practice." *Journal of Global History* 4 (2009): 453–474.

Ui, Jun, ed. *Gendai Kagaku to Kōgai*. Tokyo: Keisō Shobō, 1972.

———, ed. *Gendai Kagaku to Kōgai Zoku*. Tokyo: Keisō Shobō, 1972.

———, ed. *Gendai Shakai to Kōgai*. Tokyo: Keisō Shobō, 1972.

———. "Higaisha Fuzai no Kōgai Hōkoku: Kokuren Ningen Kankyō Kaigi e no Nihon Seifu Hōkoku Hihan." *Jishu Kōza* 10 (January 1972): 1–17. Reproduced in *Ui Jun Shūshū Kōgai Mondai Shiryō 1 Fukkoku "Jishu Kōza" Dai 2-kan*, edited by Saitama Daigaku Kyōsei Shakai Kenkyū Sentā, 221–251. Tokyo: Suirensha, 2005.

———, ed. *Industrial Pollution in Japan*. Tokyo: United Nations University Press, 1992.

———. "Interview with Ui Jun: Minamata Disease in Canada." *AMPO: Japan-Asia Quarterly Review* 26 (October–December 1975): 65–69.

———. "Jinrui ga Ikinokoru tame no Kakutō." In *Genchi ni Miru Sekai no Kōgai Sōkatsu: Sekai Kankyō Chōsadan Hōkoku*, edited by Tsuru Shigeto, 107–110. Tokyo: Chūnichi Shinbun Tokyo Honsha, 1975.

———. "Junrei no Tabi kara Kaette." *Jishu Kōza* 16 (July 1972): 1–2. Reproduced in *Ui Jun Shūshū Kōgai Mondai Shiryō 1 Fukkoku "Jishu Kōza" Dai 3-kan*, edited by Saitama Daigaku Kyōsei Shakai Kenkyū Sentā, 209–210. Tokyo: Suirensha, 2005.

———. "Kakumo Yutakana Shizen no naka no, Kakumo Shinkokuna Hinkon: '72 Sutokkuhorumu kara '92 Rio e." In *Chikyū Samitto Live in Rio*, edited by Yamazaki Kōichi, 100–107. Tokyo: Asahi Shimbunsha, 1992.

———. "Kōgai Genron I." In Ui Jun, *Kōgai Genron Gappon*, chapters 1–3. Tokyo: Aki Shobō, 1990.

———. "Kōgai Genron II." In Ui Jun, *Kōgai Genron Gappon*, chapters 4–9. Tokyo: Aki Shobō, 1990.

———. "Kōgai Genron III." In Ui Jun, *Kōgai Genron Gappon*, chapters 7–9. Tokyo: Aki Shobō, 1990.

————. *Kōgai Genron Gappon*. Tokyo: Aki Shobō, 1990.

————, ed. *Kōgai Higaisha no Ronri*. Tokyo: Keisō Shobō, 1973.

————, ed. *Kōgai Jishu Kōza 15-nen*. Tokyo: Aki Shobō, 1991.

————. " 'Kōgai Senshin Koku Nippon' no Sekinin: 'Kokuren Ningen Kankyō Kaigi' ni Sanka shite." *Kōmei* 119 (September 1972): 56–70.

————. "Kokuren Kankyō Kaigi Hōkoku I." *Kōgai Genron* 13 (July 1972): 1–19. Reproduced in *Ui Jun Shūshū Kōgai Mondai Shiryō 2 Fukkoku "Kōgai Genron" Dai 1-kai Haihon Dai 3-kan*, edited by Saitama Daigaku Kyōsei Shakai Kenkyū Sentā, 205–223. Tokyo: Suirensha, 2007.

————. "Mercury Pollution of Sea and Fresh Water: Its Accumulation into Water Biomass." *KOGAI: The Newsletter from Polluted Japan* 8 (Special Issue 1975): 6–30.

————. "Minamatabyō to Kanada Indian." In *Genchi ni Miru Sekai no Kōgai Sōkatsu: Sekai Kankyō Chōsadan Hōkoku*, edited by Tsuru Shigeto, 139–167. Tokyo: Chūnichi Shinbun Tokyo Honsha, 1975.

————. "Ningen Kankyō ni kansuru Kokuren Sōkai e no Repōto." *Kōgai Genron* 6 (March 1972): 1–37. Reproduced in *Ui Jun Shūshū Kōgai Mondai Shiryō 2 Fukkoku "Kōgai Genron" Dai 1-kai Haihon Dai 1-kan*, edited by Saitama Daigaku Kyōsei Shakai Kenkyū Sentā, 265–301. Tokyo: Suirensha, 2007.

————, ed. *Polluted Japan: Reports by Members of the Jishu-Koza Citizens' Movement*. Tokyo: Jishu-Koza, 1972.

————. "Sekai no Kōgai Hantai Shimin Undō." In *Sekai no Kōgai Chizu 2*, edited by Tsuru Shigeto, 127–164. Tokyo: Iwanami Shoten, 1977.

————. "Shingikai no Yakuwari, Nashonaru Repōto Hihan." *Kōgai Genron* 3 (December 1971): 20. Reproduced in *Ui Jun Shūshū Kōgai Mondai Shiryō 2 Fukkoku "Kōgai Genron" Dai 1-kai Haihon Dai 1-kan*, edited by Saitama Daigaku Kyōsei Shakai Kenkyū Sentā, 1–25. Tokyo: Suirensha, 2007.

Ui, Jun. *Yanaka Mura kara Minamata e—Sanrizuka e: Ekorogī no Genryū*. Tokyo: Shakai Hyōronsha, 1991.

————. *Ui Jun Repōto: Ōshū no Kōgai o otte*. Tokyo: Aki Shobō, 1970.

Ui, Jun, and Barry Commoner. "Taidan: Nichibei no Kōgai Hantai Undō." *Asahi Shinbun* (morning edition, March 15, 1972): 23.

United Nations Department of Information. "UN Conference on Environment and Development (1992)." Accessed May 15, 2014. http://www.un.org /geninfo/bp/enviro.html.

United Nations Educational, Scientific, and Cultural Organization (UNESCO). *Conferences Parallel to the United Nations Conference on the Human Environment* (June 5, 1973). UN Doc ED/WS/397.

Upham, Frank. *Law and Social Change in Postwar Japan*. Cambridge, MA: Harvard University Press, 1987.

———. "Unplaced Persons and Movements for Place." In *Postwar Japan as History,* edited by Andrew Gordon, 325–346. Berkeley: University of California Press, 1993.

Ushio, Tetsuya. "Nihon Kagaku no Kankoku de no 5-gatsu Sōgyō Kaishi Soshi." *Jishu Kōza* 49 (April 1975): 54–62. Reproduced in *Ui Jun Shūshū Kōgai Mondai Shiryō 1 Fukkoku "Jishu Kōza" Dai 2-kai Haihon Dai 4-kan,* edited by Saitama Daigaku Kyōsei Shakai Kenkyū Sentā, 386–394. Tokyo: Suirensha, 2006.

Ushio, Tsunao. "4.8 Ajia e no Kōgai Yushutsu o Kokuhatsu suru Shimin Daishūkai: Hōkoku." *Geppō Kōgai o Nogasuna! Kankoku e no Kōgai Yushutsu o Kokuhatsu suru* 35 (May 1976): 16–21.

Vancoevering, Jack. "The Truth about Mercury." *Field and Stream* 76, no. 1 (May 1971): 14–20, 137.

Walker, Brett L. *Toxic Archipelago: A History of Industrial Disease in Japan.* Seattle: University of Washington Press, 2010.

Ward, Barbara, and Rene Dubos. *Only One Earth: The Care and Maintenance of a Small Planet.* New York: Norton, 1972.

"Watashitachi ga Motomete iru no wa, Keikaku no Hakushi tekkai da: Dai-ikki Shomei Teishutsu—45,134-mei no Koe Seifu e." *Tsuchi no Koe, Tami no Koe Gōgai* 6 (February 1981): 6.

White, Carol, and Rogelio Maduro. " 'Greenhouse Effect' Hoaxsters Seek World Dictatorship." *EIR: Executive Intelligence Review* 16, no. 3 (January 13, 1989): 24–33.

White, Richard. "The Nationalization of Nature." *Journal of American History* 86, no. 3 (December 1999): 976–986.

Women's Group of the Conference of Asians. "Resolution on Women." *AMPO: Japan-Asia Quarterly Review* 21–22 (1974): 15.

Wong, Anny. "The Anti-Tropical Timber Campaign in Japan." In *Environmental Movements in Asia,* edited by Arne Kalland and Gerard Persoon, 131–150. Surrey, UK: Curzon Press, 1998.

———. *The Roots of Japan's International Environmental Policies.* New York: Garland Publishing, 2001.

Yamada, Keizō. "Mindanao e no 'Kōgai Yushutsu.' " *Ushio* (December 1976): 194–203.

Yamagishi, Junko. "Tatakai wa Korekarada! Nihon Kagaku no Kankoku Urusan Kōjō no Sōgyō o Yamesaseyō!" *Geppō Kōgai o Nogasuna! Kankoku e no Kōgai Yushutsu o Kokuhatsu suru* 35 (May 1976): 2–11.

Yamaka, Junko. "N. Mariana Gov. Camacho Presents Anti-Dumping Petition to Diet." *No Nuke News Japan* 2 (June 1981): 1–4.

———. "Pacific Islanders Oppose Japan's Nuclear Imperialism." *AMPO: Japan-Asia Quarterly* 47 (April–September 1981): 32–36.

————. "Results and Conclusions of the Campaign: Secretariat." *No Nuke News Japan* 16 (1983): 1.

Yamamoto, Kazuhiko. "'Chikyū Samitto' no Giman." *Gijutsu to Ningen* 21, no. 6 (June 1992): 8–15.

Yamamura, Tsunetoshi. *Kankyō NGO*. Tokyo: Shinzansha Shuppan, 1998.

Yamanouchi, Kazuo, and Kiyoharu Otsubo. "Agreements on Pollution Prevention: Overview and One Example." In *Environmental Policy in Japan*, edited by Shigeto Tsuru and Helmut Weidner, 221–245. Berlin: Sigma, 1989.

Yamate, Noboru. "Aborijinī Hakugai ni Te o Kasu Nihon Shihon: Ōsutoraria no Uran Kaihatsu Hantai Undō ni Rentai suru." *Geppō Kōgai o Nogasuna! Daisan Sekai e no Kōgai Yushutsu o Kokuhatsu suru* 96 (November-December 1980): 25–29.

Yamazaki, Kōichi, ed. *Chikyū Samitto Live in Rio*. Tokyo: Asahi Shimbunsha, 1992.

Yokoyama, Keiji. "Kono Wakitatsu Teikō no Nami." *Asahi Jyānaru* (April 23, 1971): 41–62.

Yokoyama, Masaki. "Genchi Hōkoku: Nichibei no Kan-Taiheiyō Senryaku vs Taiheiyō Shominzoku no Hankaku-Dokuritsu Undō—Ponape Kaigi ni Sanka shite." *Geppō Kōgai o Nogasuna! Daisan Sekai e no Kōgai Yushutsu o Kokuhatsu suru* 75 (January 1979): 11–17.

————. "Hankaku-Dokuritsu Taiheiyō Kaigi '83 Banuatsu Kaigi: Shōten to natta Dokuritsu Tōsō." *Geppō Kōgai o Nogasuna! Nihon no Shinryaku no Kōshite Ajia Taiheiyō Minshū to tomo ni* 125 (August 1983): 7–14.

————. "Kaku Haikibutsu no Kaiyō Tōki Hantai Undō: Taiheiyō Shotō no Jūmin no Baai." *Kōgai Kenkyū* 10, no. 4 (April 1981): 22–29.

————. "Suzuki Shinseiken no Genshiryoku Seisaku to Hōshanō Osen no Yushutsu." *Tsuchi no Koe, Tami no Koe* 113 (September 1980): 15–18, 31.

————. "Taiheiyō kara Kaku o Nakusō! 3–1 Tokyo Shūkai." *Tsuchi no Koe, Tami no Koe* 97 (April 1979): 18–19.

————. "Taiheiyō Shominzoku no Hankaku-Dokuritsu Undō: Ponape Kaigi ni Sanka shite." *Tsuchi no Koe, Tami no Koe* 93 (January 1979): 13–20.

Yoneda, Hideo. "Kōgai Yushutsu o Sasaeru Kōzō o Ute: Nihon Kagaku no Kankoku Urusan Kōjō Shigatsu Sōgyō Kaishi Soshi." *Jishu Kōza* 61 (April 1976): 24–31. Reproduced in *Ui Jun Shūshū Kōgai Mondai Shiryō 1 Fukkoku "Jishu Kōza" Dai 3-kai Haihon Dai 2-kan*, edited by Saitama Daigaku Kyōsei Shakai Kenkyū Sentā, 228–235. Tokyo: Suirensha, 2006.

Yonemoto, Shōhei. *Chikyū Kankyō Mondai to wa Nanika*. Tokyo: Iwanami Shoten, 1994.

Yoshiwara, Toshiyuki. "The Kawasaki Steel Corporation: A Case Study of Japanese Pollution Export." *KOGAI: The Newsletter from Polluted Japan* 14 (Summer 1977): 12–24.

Zenkoku Genshiryoku Kagaku Gijutsusha Rengō. "Genshiryoku Kaihatsu to Kōgai Mondai." *Kankyō to Kōgai* 2, no. 1 (July 1972): 13–23.

Zenkoku Kōgairen. "Kokuren Ningen Kankyō Kaigi ni taisuru Zenkoku Kōgairen no Repōto." *Gekkan Sōhyō* 180 (May 1972): 83–89.

"Zensekai Sūhyakuman-nin no Kōgi no Koe o Tazusae: Kita Mariana— Camacho-chijira Kokkai Seigan e." *Tsuchi no Koe, Tami no Koe Gōgai Kaku Haikibutsu Kaiyō Tōki Hantai Undō Tokushū* 10 (June 1981): 3.

# Index

*Photographs indicated by page numbers in italics*

## ABOUT THE AUTHOR

Simon Avenell is associate professor of history at the College of Asia and the Pacific, the Australian National University. His research interests include social movements, environmentalism, transnational activism, and political thought with a focus on contemporary Japan. His work has been published in journals such as *Environment and History, Journal of Japanese Studies, Environmental History, Modern Asian Studies,* and *positions: east asia cultures critique.* His previous publications include the monograph *Making Japanese Citizens: Civil Society and the Mythology of the Shimin in Postwar Japan,* which traces the emergence and evolution of civic activism and thought in postwar Japan.